STUDIES IN BRITISH ART

English Vernacular Furniture

1750–1900

Christopher Gilbert

Published for the
Paul Mellon Centre for Studies in British Art by
Yale University Press
New Haven and London
1991

Copyright © 1991 by Christopher Gilbert

Designed by Hubert Brissonneau
Filmset in Linotron Bembo by Excel Typesetters Company, Hong Kong
Printed in Hong Kong by Kwong Fat Offset Printing Co. Ltd

Library of Congress Cataloging-in-Publication Data

Gilbert, Christopher.
    English vernacular furniture 1750–1900 / Christopher Gilbert.
      p.   cm.
    Includes bibliographical references (p. 277) and index.
    ISBN 0-300-04762-2
    1. Country furniture — England — History.   I. Title.
NK2528.G45   1991
749.22′09′033 — dc20   90-12754
                                          CIP

Contents

Preface

Museum curators of my generation were trained to admire and study fashionable eighteenth-century decorative art. As a consequence twelve supremely happy years were spent cataloguing the fine collection of furniture at Temple Newsam House, Leeds, and researching the career of Thomas Chippendale in precise detail. I have been a very lucky fellow. While keenly interested in exciting discoveries being made by scholars exploring Victorian furniture or pursuing the work of continental craftsmen my own enthusiasms lay in other directions. Spanish and Dutch colonial furniture have always intrigued me, especially the way in which European designs cross-fertilized with native aboriginal traditions to create strange new idioms; however, the chances of making a useful contribution to this fascinating subject seemed remote.

As the years passed I became slightly wearied by the methodology of mainstream English country-house furniture research with its emphasis on provenance, authorship, date, designer, stylistic analysis and context. Investigating the commissions of provincial cabinet makers as opposed to leading London firms suggested itself as an alternative line of attack; how did furniture made in Edinburgh, Wakefield or Doncaster differ from metropolitan pieces? This switch of emphasis proved refreshing and later on I was uncommonly fortunate to be associated as co-editor with Geoffrey Beard in the ambitious *Dictionary of English Furniture Makers* project. Gathering material for the *Dictionary* was certainly rewarding, but, inevitably, involved dealing with the familiar themes of patronage, documentation and evidence for authorship. Thus, following publication in 1986, I was eager for a new challenge.

The foundation of the Regional Furniture Society, also in 1986, served to revive a longstanding but, until then, rather desultory interest in vernacular furniture, nurtured by a series of pioneering exhibitions held at Temple Newsam, starting in 1971 with a show which attempted to illuminate the regional personality of seventeenth-century oak furniture from Yorkshire churches. This became very much the special subject of my colleague, Anthony Wells-Cole, who has achieved so much in mapping local decorative preferences and design types. The opening up of this broad field of study served to emphasize how little was known about native Georgian and Victorian vernacular traditions, which had for too long been regarded by professional furniture historians as beneath the threshold of serious interest.

This neglected area was explored in a rambling exhibition organized at Temple Newsam in 1972 titled 'Town and Country Furniture' and followed up by two rather more systematic catalogues devoted to *Back-stairs Furniture* (1977) and *School Furniture* (1978). The last in this short series, *Common Furniture* (1982), brought together an anthology of ordinary pieces made for workhouses, prisons, asylums, nonconformist chapels, alehouses, railway premises, factories, Sunday Schools, offices, etc, supported by a range of provenanced domestic items. Staging these exhibitions proved so enjoyable that I kept my files open, in time identifying other coherent sub-groups and, with the encouragement of many friends, was induced to embark upon this book-length study.

Throughout I have been greatly inspired by the broad perspectives and dynamic quality of American furniture research, notably the work of Bob Trent, Brock Jobe, Wallace Gusler and the late Charles Montgomery. Books, articles and field-trips investigating vernacular buildings introduced me to an absorbing new branch of study which enriched my appreciation of rural furniture, while Bill Cotton's flow of publications on regional chairs offered heartening evidence of what can be achieved by combining energetic fieldwork with archival research. The activities of the Regional Furniture Society point to a burgeoning awareness that common furniture, as it was often known at the time, possesses much the same interest as the glamorous products of London workshops and that furniture from all places, and not just country-houses, is worthy of study. So, this book became something of a personal Odyssey although, as my debts of gratitude plainly show, it certainly has not been accomplished single-handed.

It is impossible to mention and adequately to thank all the owners, curators, archivists, librarians, dealers, auctioneers and well-wishers who have allowed me to examine their collections, contributed information or helped over photography. Amongst the individuals to whom I am particularly grateful for support and the generous sharing of information are Geoffrey Beard, John Boram, Susan Bourne, Peter Brears, David Butler, Bill Connor, Bill and Gerry Cotton, Tom Crispin, Sandy Fenton, the late Benno Forman, Ian Gow, Stephen Green, Simon Jervis, David Jones, Tony Lewery, Sarah Medlam, Tessa Murdoch, Ross Noble, Evelyn Newby, Gabriel Olive, Malcolm Seaborne, Ivan Sparkes, Susan Stuart, Roger Warner, Anthony Wells-Cole and Bridget Yates. Many other scholars and institutions to whom I am indebted are named either in Chapter Notes, the Select Bibliography or photographic acknowledgements given in the captions.

The British Academy provided a most welcome travel grant while the Paul Mellon Centre for Studies in British Art helped with photographic costs. Illustrations are a vital ingredient of any book about furniture and I gladly acknowledge the skill and patience of John Berry, Bill Cotton, John Freeman, Gabriel Olive, Douglas Smith and Ron Turner who, between them, took most of the photographs reproduced in this volume. John Nicoll of Yale University Press and Professor Michael Kitson of the Paul Mellon Centre both gave invaluable assistance at the publication stage. Angela Evans undertook with speed and efficiency the laborious task of typing my manuscript and also helped with illustrations research while Denise Lawson cheerfully typed the untold letters which are inseparable from a project of this nature. Lastly, I am supremely grateful to Rosemary Amos for copy-editing and seeing my manuscript through the press.

Temple Newsam House
February 1990

Introduction

English furniture studies have until recently concentrated on the elegant products of London firms and, to a lesser extent, on provincial work that reflects fashionable styles. The vernacular tradition has either been neglected or left to amateur collectors, country antique dealers and a few eccentrics.[1] Happily, research is now far more broadly based than it was even a few years ago, largely to due the inspired example of American furniture historians[2] and active members of the Regional Furniture Society founded in 1986. Nonetheless, 'common' furniture – a generic term coined in the eighteenth century to describe plain domestic pieces made of native timber – is still an excitingly fresh topic and the present volume attempts to establish sound bearings in this field.

Common furniture is essentially anonymous; it is rarely possible to build bridges between documents and surviving pieces, while few tradesmen employed a maker's mark. Establishing a firm provenance counts as success in this project. One way of tackling the subject is to identify coherent sub-groups and treat each one separately. This approach has been adopted to cover furniture made for shops, alehouses, prisons, schools, urban working-class homes, Quaker Meeting Houses, wicker and straw furniture — to take a few examples at random. In all, thirty groups are defined and investigated with varying degrees of success. An equally viable method involves examining types of furniture and this course has been chosen for dealing with beds and chairs — both major branches which seemed to invite separate treatment. Categories such as dressers and clock cases would also benefit from regional surveys, but are in fact discussed in the omnibus chapter on cottage and farmhouse furniture: many themes await fuller exploration. There is, too, a need for studies of the Welsh, Scottish, Irish and Manx traditions which are glanced at from time to time, but not focused on.

Vernacular furniture offers abundant scope for fieldwork rather than digesting the results of previous research and every effort has been made to trace and illustrate soundly provenanced examples. The most energetic search is, however, unlikely to discover much in the way of accredited furniture from eighteenth-century hospitals, asylums, army barracks, Victorian soup kitchens or the first generation of back-to-back houses. In such cases facts must be sought elsewhere and valuable evidence has been gleaned from collections of inventories, old joiners' account books, travel journals, newspapers and contemporary pictorial sources. In addition, a chapter is devoted to examining the fund of precise information in various provincial cabinet makers' and chairmakers' *Books of Prices* which contain specifications for a wide range of furniture in common production. A capital source, not hitherto exploited, are the Minutes of Evidence appended to Victorian Parliamentary Reports on Sanitation, the Poor Law, the Employment of Women and Children in Agriculture, Mines, Factories, Prisons, Mad Houses, etc, which often quote splendidly detailed first-hand accounts of living conditions. J.C. Loudon's *Encyclopaedia of Cottage, Farm, and Villa Architecture and Furniture* (1833) and Henry Mayhew's *London Labour and the London Poor* (1861) provide bedrock material on rural and urban households.

1. Dug-out chair made from the shell of a hollow elm, branded on the back H^{S}E, for Humphrey and Eleanor Senhouse of Netherhall, Cumbria, who married in 1696. *Leeds Art Galleries*

2. Double-weighted cheese-press, ash, elm and oak, nineteenth century. Such objects mark the point where furniture merges with traditional farm woodwork. *Bolton Metropolitan Borough*

The multi-layered tradition which, by the end of the eighteenth century, was producing many grades of ordinary domestic furniture, needs to be brought into sharper focus. At one level furniture merges with country crafts such as the hewing of husbandry gear, making field gates, hay rakes and wheelwrights' work. The sheep-shearing stool (see Plate 30), dug-out chair (Plate 1) and Highland chairs made from naturally bent scrub wood (see Plate 203) illustrate this point. Farm equipment like cheese-presses, pig benches and milking stools (Plate 2) occupy the same twilight area where basic furniture merges with 'hedge carpentry'. This association has a long history, for in 1649 Randle Holme remarked that in the country, chairs and stools were 'made by the Turner or wheele wright'.[3] The surviving account books of rural joiners reveal just how versatile they were in serving their neighbours' needs. It is, however, as well to remember that beside the really great feats of traditional woodcrafts, such as the construction of waggons, windmills and boat building, making a 'Windsor' chair, while skilled, was a relatively humble occupation.

The functional tradition of furniture design, vividly represented by kneading troughs (see Plate 73), go-gins (see Plate 399), turned chairs and lip-work (see Plate 231), owes nothing to personal preferences or fashionable taste. It is a profoundly anonymous tradition – disciplined, unselfconscious and inspired by simple inherited characteristics – and the forms are in harmony with the settled values of rural communities[4] (Plate 3). Village joiners could rarely afford to specialize on furniture because their livelihood was chiefly earned by making hog troughs, mangers and plows or setting up stiles, cattle stalls and fencing. Other activities usually included tree-felling, sawing, wheelwrighting and frequently farming on a small scale, so it is hardly surprising that vernacular furniture shares many of the robust qualities of farm woodwork. A ledger kept by the Hayward family of Selling in Kent between 1732 and 1754 vividly records how country joiners used their time and skills to best advantage to muster a living.

As the eighteenth century advanced, cumbersome joiner-made carved oak furniture in the 'Jacobean' style such as panel-back armchairs, backstools, hall cupboards, settles and framed chests were gradually phased out, although in remote areas like the Lake District archaic chairs bearing dates in the 1740s and 1750s (Plate 4) show that the tradition expired slowly.[5] It was succeeded by a generation of oak and elm furniture conforming to new designs and devoid of carved enrichment, although in choice of materials, pegged construction and responsiveness to regional variations in form, it continued the earlier oak tradition. Kitchen dressers with a shelved rear structure, long panel-back settles (known in the north as couch chairs), corner cupboards with fielded panels and plain chests of drawers typify this new repertoire. Following the creation of a canal network, improvements to roads and finally the coming of railways, this range was itself replaced during the early nineteenth century by cheap painted pine furniture made from imported deal and a tide of showy consumer pieces manufactured in towns. Flora Thompson's *Lark Rise to Candleford* (1945) chronicles this transition as it occurred in an Oxfordshire hamlet.

Some of the lighter and more handsome common furniture that evolved during the eighteenth century assimilated elements from mainstream 'period' styles. Simple versions of 'Queen Anne', 'Chippendale' and 'Hepplewhite' chair patterns and cabinet furniture were translated into homely idioms (Plate 5), but while many grades of sophistication existed it would be very misleading to suggest that vernacular furniture had a complex interrelationship with London taste. It is possible to propose certain criteria that identify pieces which belong unambiguously to the native vernacular tradition. The term does not apply to professionally designed furniture made from mahogany or other imported woods; neither does it include pieces which display specialist decorative techniques such as veneering, marquetry work, carving,[6] gilding and japanning or which sport luxurious upholstery. Its essential character is expressed through a profound understanding of native timbers

3. Wayside seat by a toll-bridge over the Wye near Whitney, Herefordshire. It is as much a product of the anonymous tradition of country woodcrafts as the fence stakes behind.

4. Armchair initialled DB and dated 1742, made for the Browne family of Townend, Troutbeck. A very late expression of a Lake District tradition of carving. *The National Trust*

5. Chair, elm frame united by pegs, *c.* 1760–80, illustrating a bold simplification of fashionable designs. Probably from an urban workshop in the Leeds area. *C.G. Gilbert*

used in the solid, traditional construction, a marked preference for rush or plank seats, painted finishes and a persistence of archaic features. Although boldly simplified elements derived from fashionable designs may be present, innovative impulses are rare. Other, more subtle indications include the existence of 'setting-out' lines on visible surfaces made by the workman before shaping components (Plate 6), rough marks suggesting the limitations of the maker's formal training or tool-chest, the use of wrought-iron hardware and nails instead of screws. The presence of inlaid shells (Plate 7), fan medallions, stringing lines, etc, on otherwise plain oak furniture (see Plate 99) is explained by their availability ready-made from many hardware shops.[7]

Painting became a cheap and popular way of embellishing pine furniture during the nineteenth century.[8] Surfaces could be painted a single colour (see Plate 26), grained to imitate a finer wood (Plates 8 and 27) or ornamented with fanciful patterns. This treatment never became as widespread in England as it was abroad, but many items of kitchen furniture, lodging boxes and cradles were finished in a manner indicative of showy woods. However, pieces which exactly copied highly decorative veneers, such as rosewood or bird's-eye maple were, on the whole, restricted to inferior rooms in large houses (Plate 9). The only really flamboyant pictorial compositions occur on fitted furniture in gypsy caravans and canal narrowboats (see Plates 393–397) or on the lids of sea-chests (see Plate 390). This tradition, which only emerged about 1850, is treated separately.

6. 'Setting-out' marks on an elm chair frame of *c.* 1740. *Leeds Art Galleries*

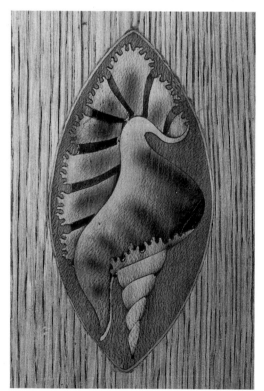

7. Shell inlay on the door of an oak long-case clock by J. Barraclough, Haworth, Yorkshire, *c.* 1815. These elements could be bought ready-made. *Leeds Art Galleries*

8. Painted pine chest on stand built in one body with simulated fielded panels. The interior lined with the *York Herald* for 27 June 1795. Descended in the Penrose family of Redhouse Farm, Maunby, near Thirsk, Yorkshire. *Leeds Art Galleries*

9. Chest with drawers, pine painted to simulate bird's-eye maple, rosewood and ebony strings. From a Victorian town house at Blythe Bridge, near Stoke-on-Trent, Staffordshire. *Leeds Art Galleries*

Much honest furniture popularly believed to have been made by rural craftsmen for country people actually originated in urban workshops. Many Lancashire ladder- and spindle-back chairs were, for example, produced in large towns, while the various Books of Prices published by masters and journeymen in a dozen regional centres between about 1790 and 1810 contain specifications for common elm chairs and routine oak and pine furniture, in addition to a repertoire of more up-market pieces. There were of course significant differences in the furnishing requirements of, on the one hand, cottages and farmhouses, and on the other, homes of factory workers, miners and handloom weavers – these are analysed in relevant chapters – but it is clear from contemporary sources that a measure of overlap existed. By the early nineteenth century, urban working-class families were more likely to own pieces of inexpensive fashion-conscious furniture than their country cousins. The wives of miners, who regularly earned higher wages than other industrial workers, took a special pride in buying ostentatiously splendid beds with carved mahogany posts (see Plate 83), handsome chests of drawers (see Plate 82) and other showy status symbols. Social pressures played a major part in the disintegration of the vernacular tradition.

5

10. *The Undergraduate's Room*, watercolour by Thomas Rowlandson (1756–1827). *Yale Center for British Art*

It is impossible to divorce furniture from social history: conditions in offices and factories document attitudes to the drudgery of work; the amenities provided in workhouses, bridewells and almshouses reflect views about the welfare of their inmates, while simply styled Friends Meeting House furniture evolved in harmony with their sincere religious beliefs and way of life (see Plate 322). The confidence and vigour of the Victorian tradition of functional design is demonstrated by corn factors' desks which were required to fulfil practical needs for lockable desk accommodation, a display unit to hold samples of corn, space for a nameboard and a standing platform or perching seat (see Plate 352). The versatile ways in which simple solutions were found to combine these features is a tribute to the functional tradition. Since corn exchanges were usually buildings of considerable pretension, it is likely that these large sets of desks were sometimes architect-designed.

A high proportion of the furniture researched in this survey is institutional rather than domestic; although straightforward and practical, it can hardly be described as vernacular. Prisons, workhouses and army barracks were often equipped with furniture made under contract, while the needs of Board Schools, offices and ships were frequently met by large specialist suppliers. It is the sections dealing with institutional and similarly neglected sub-groups that make perhaps the most original contribution to furniture history. The choice of themes to some extent reflects personal preferences, and their treatment is unavoidably uneven. Sports pavilions and ducking stools are in, but theatres or college furniture are not, although fine original seating survives at the Theatre Royal Bristol[9] and at the Georgian Theatre, Richmond, North Yorkshire; and Thomas Rowlandson's drawing of an undergraduate in his room (Plate 10) suggests this subject might offer an interesting field for research. Despite obvious shortcomings, the following chapters attempt to stake out a new area for serious study which others hopefully will refine and expand.

1 Traditional Crafts and Native Timbers

Today Britain has less forest than any other country in Europe, but in the past timber was our most important industrial raw material; and over the centuries craftsmen acquired a deep knowledge of the versatile properties of different native woods.[1] The felling and conversion of trees, cleaving timber, bark stripping, charcoal burning, chair bodging, hurdle making and the coppice crafts are just a few ancient woodland skills. Each craftworker had his own special tools, equipment and chosen timbers to suit his purpose; some tasks could only be performed at certain seasons of the year and there were, of course, many local customs and regional variations. Although, at first sight, coopering, clog making, wheelwrights' work, willow weaving or the construction of field gates may appear to bear scant relevance to furniture making, certain branches merge almost imperceptibly with hedge carpentry and woodland crafts. All are timber-using trades which combine traditional skills with a sound practical knowledge of wood, and every furniture historian has much of value to learn from studying their techniques and materials. It was not until the Industrial Revolution that cheap imported deal became readily available to country joiners and led them to foresake native hardwood for many types of work.

A classic example of how, until fairly recently, furniture making interacted with woodland crafts, is the chair-bodging tradition. In the beechwoods of Buckinghamshire and elsewhere in the Chilterns, 'bodgers' lived and worked during the summer in thatched huts, fashioning legs and stretchers for chair manufacturers in the towns[2] (Plate 11). The woods were managed by the selection system whereby, instead of clearing a stretch of forest, trees were thinned out over a wide area and the gaps left to be filled by natural regeneration. The bodgers felled trees in the winter when the sap was down and then set up their workshops nearby in the open to save the labour of transporting the material. Logs were cross-sawn into sections of the required length, barked and split into segments which were then cleft with a froe and mallet into billets and trimmed with a side hatchet. Each billet was set in the jaws of a shaving horse and rounded with a drawknife into roughly the shape of a chair leg or stretcher with tapered ends. The round was finally turned while still green on a primitive pole lathe with a reciprocal action driven by a foot treadle. This operation was normally performed in one of the thatched shelters. Finished legs were stacked in the open to season before being carted to the town for sale (Plate 12). Windsor chairs made from this straight-grained cleft beech were stronger than those turned from sawn wood. Until 1922 the War Office, which ordered large numbers of ordinary Windsors for army barracks, stipulated that the frames be made from cleft timber.[3] Some bodgers also produced beech tent-pegs, clothes-pegs and last blocks. Other workmen who lived out in the woods (in distinctive wigwam-shaped cabins) were charcoal burners who needed large quantities of branch and coppice wood to form stacks, which were covered with turf to exclude the air before being fired and allowed to burn slowly for several days.

11. Bodgers working in a Buckinghamshire beechwood. The man and boy are preparing billets for the pole-lathe turner in the thatched shelter. *Museum of English Rural Life*

12. Turned beech chair legs and stretchers stacked in the open awaiting delivery to Wycombe. *Wycombe Chair Museum*

The willow crafts, practiced in fertile river valleys, contributed to the furniture trade. Willow is our lightest native timber so, besides being used in the solid for cricket bats, cart bottoms and artificial limbs, the light, elastic and quick growing osier wands were ideal for weaving baskets, bassinets, fish-traps, invalid carriages (see Plate 365) and seat furniture. Willow was sometimes woven on a framework of cleft oak, ash or hazel rods, it was usually peeled and worked in the round, but could be split into skeins for fine work. Wicker was occasionally used as an alternative to rush for the seats of common turned chairs (Plate 13).

Woodland known as coppice was formerly of great economic value, although many are now sadly neglected. Hazel, which never grows into a large tree, is a fine coppice species, but alder, ash and oak also yield good crops. Coppices are cut in regular cycles, seven years being customary for hazel, while oak coppice is normally worked over every twenty-four years. Long straight stakes, poles and thin springy rods were felled in winter with a billhook and used for making fencing hurdles (Plate 14), wattles for building, pea- or bean-sticks, hop poles, hedge stakes, thatching spars and small turnery such as bobbins, cotton-reels, etc. When split and steamed, hazel proved ideal for barrel hoops, while J.C. Loudon recommended that 'Hazel rods form an admirable material for constructing rustic garden seats and flower baskets'; he even illustrated several picturesque examples[4] (Plate 15). Curiously, veined hazel roots were sometimes used by cabinet makers for veneering tea-chests and also, either peeled or unpeeled, for constructing furniture. The 1775 inventory of a house on Jersey lists in the drawing-room 'Six new chairs of white hazel'.[5] It is intriguing that in 1820, J. & R. Prior, Windsor chairmakers and turners of Uxbridge, invoiced Samuel Hall for: '2 bundles Espallier stakes / 7 Harbor Poles / 30 Small Do / 7 bundles pea stick / 11 Harbor Poles 14s. 8d.'.[6] Obviously a successful maker of turned chairs maintained close contact with traditional coppice crafts. A similar scrap of evidence is a bill from James Todd of Caistor, Lincolnshire, recording that in 1825 he was supplying chairs and hay rakes, probably of coppiced ash.[7] The history of William Brear & Sons, Addingham, Yorkshire, considered in the next chapter, illustrates how even in the early years of this century, a small country firm combined the trades of sawyer, timber merchant, wheelwright, general turner, rake maker and supplier of fence posts, rails and field gates to the farming community with the production of a range of common chairs (Plate 16).

13. In some districts wicker was used as an alternative to rush for chair seats. *Leeds Art Galleries*

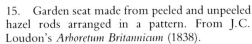

14. (*left*) A hurdle-maker's yard, Uxbridge, 1910. The pile of sixteen cleft willow hurdles represents a day's work. *The Country Home*

15. Garden seat made from peeled and unpeeled hazel rods arranged in a pattern. From J.C. Loudon's *Arboretum Britannicum* (1838).

16. Catalogue of William Brear & Sons, saw-yers, timber merchants, chair manufacturers and general turners of Addingham, Yorkshire, c. 1900. *Private collection*

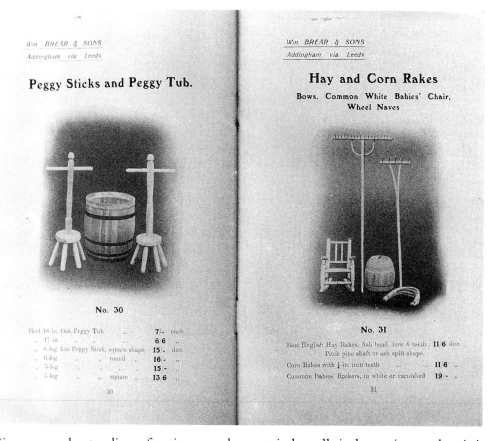

Wm. BREAR & SONS
Addingham via Leeds

Peggy Sticks and Peggy Tub.

No. 30

Best 18-in. Oak Peggy Tub	...	**7/-**	each
„ 17-in. „	...	**6 6**	„
„ 6-leg Ash Peggy Stick, square shape	**15/-**	doz.
„ 6-leg „ „ round „	**16/-**	„
„ 5-leg „ „ „	**15/-**	„
„ 5-leg „ „ square „	**13 6**	„

30

Wm. BREAR & SONS
Addingham via Leeds

Hay and Corn Rakes

Bows, Common White Babies' Chair, Wheel Naves

No. 31

Best English Hay Rakes, Ash head, bow & teeth	**11 6**	doz.
Pitch pine shaft or ash split shape.		
Corn Rakes with ½-in. iron teeth	...	**11 6**	„
Common Babies' Rockers, in white or varnished	**19/-**	„

31

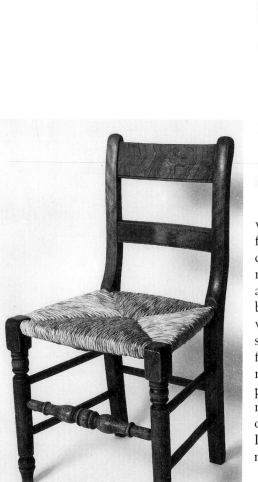

17. Alder chair, Lancashire, mid-nineteenth century. *Courtesy B.D. Cotton*

Since an understanding of native woods was vital to all timber-using trades, it is well-worth describing the various properties of those most often employed by local furniture makers. Alder is compact, fine grained, easy to cut when green and very durable in damp conditions; it is highly esteemed for piles in water courses and for making clog soles. In the past, itinerant workers camped out in alder woodlands and, with swivel-fixed knives, roughed out clog blocks which were then stacked in beehive piles to season before being sold to clog makers for the final shaping. The wood was also in demand for turning purposes; it acquires a fine polish, does not splinter and will take stain to imitate mahogany or walnut. In the Highlands, where few other trees thrive, clumps of alders are found scattered over the lower parts of mountain slopes and, according to H.L. Edlin, 'logs were sometimes immersed in peat bogs after felling, when they assumed an attractive reddish stain. This Scots mahogany was then used for furniture making'.[8] An inventory of the stock-in-trade of Mark Chippindale, bobbin turner and chairmaker of Aighton Bailey in Lancashire,[9] compiled in 1815, included 'Crab and Alder Boards £4. 10s.' and it is now realized that many regional turned chairs are in fact made from alder (Plate 17).

Ash is a highly-regarded close and long-grained wood, very tough and elastic, well able to withstand rough usage and sudden strains. T. Sheraton remarked that it was 'reckoned in strength next to the oak and is much used amongst wheelers, plow makers and country wrights'. Its resilient qualities made it valuable for scythe and spade handles, carriage work, husbandry gear, oars, ladder poles, etc. The frames of many spindle- (see Plate 161), ladder-back and Windsor chairs are made from cleft coppice-grown ash because it is light, strong, pliant and also easily bent on setting benches. On account of its whitish hue and clean appearance, ash was also employed for table-tops and kitchen dressers. The kitchen at Temple Newsam House, furnished in 1796, contained 'A very large ash dresser with 3 drawers with divisions and a very strong frame, a Ditto with 2 Drawers'.[10]

Elm was by no means as valuable as ash in traditional timberwork, realizing less than half the price; nevertheless, its resistance to damp and unsplittable characteristics gave this timber a wide range of applications. The fact that it was cheap and plentiful meant that it could be used in large quantities for wharves, watermills, weather-boarding, partitions in stables, the keels of ships, coffins and many other purposes where toughness and durability in water were essential. Its cross-grained growth, which rendered it unsplittable, made it ideal when used by wheelwrights for heavy felloes and hubs which needed to be drilled, and likewise for the seats of Windsor chairs. Sheraton commented 'in the country, this wood is used for chairs instead of beech', an observation that is confirmed by the survival of many joiner-made elm chairs in simple Chippendale or Hepplewhite styles. Although elm works well, it is rather inclined to warp; however, because large boards were plentiful, this material was often used by rural furniture makers for kitchen tables, kneading troughs (see Plate 73) and chests. Most of the references to elm in provincial Price Books occur in costings for 'common' chairs or stools.

Oak is the principal timber of Britain, prized for its robust qualities and, until recently, the bark was an important source of tannin for treating leather. Hewn or cleft oak was used for constructing timber-framed houses and boats, gate bars, fence posts, shingles and countless other purposes where a strong material is required. Because the wood was split, no weak points were left that might lead to decay. However, since at least Tudor times, furniture makers and their customers preferred oak shipped from the Baltic ports because it was of a higher class in every way, being more uniform in colour, straighter and easier to work. An account book entry, dated 1709, from the Farnley Hall papers is typical of many which mention the foreign origin of oak: 'A new close stool of Norway oak 9s. 6d.'.[11] Sheraton stated 'The oak used by our cabinet makers is imported from Russia, Norway, Sweden and Holland, some in logs and some cut into various thickness'. Baltic oak was known as 'wainscot', a rather vague term derived from 'wandt', a wall, and 'schot', a defense, but generally taken to refer to quarter-sawn oak which reveals the attractive figure called silver grain.[12] (See Plate 36.)

Despite its inferior character and working qualities, British oak was certainly used in very considerable amounts by provincial joiners for making furniture. It is significant that *The Preston Book of Prices* (1802), specifies the labour cost of making 'a Dantzic oak clock case, with square head, door and pedestal banded £1. If made of English oak extra per £. 2s. 6d.'. A Chester specification book also contains many references to 'Dantzic oak' dressers, tables, etc[13] (Plate 18). The supremacy of oak was only seriously challenged when the canal network brought cheap imported sawn deal-boards to many previously isolated districts. The fact that soft wood was labour-saving is indicated by a note in *The Nottingham Book of Prices* (1791): 'All deal work not inserted in this book to deduct 2s. 6d. per £1'. The rapidity of this transition is emphasized by the speed with which traditional oak dressers and cupboards were supplanted by deal examples in many areas during the early nineteenth century (see Plate 59). In 1833 Loudon wrote that dressers 'are generally made of deal by joiners' but 'in old farmhouses, the dressers are generally of oak rubbed bright . . .'.[14]

Beech has always been commercially important. Sheraton remarked that 'it is brought to London in great quantities and is now the cheapest wood in use'; elsewhere it has been described as 'the bread and cheese of the chair-trade'. This timber is hard, close grained, uniform and of a whitish brown hue; although it takes stain admirably it does not polish well and is sadly prone to attack by worms. When softened by steaming, beech is an excellent bending timber and most imported bentwood furniture was made of this material. Because beech is liable to twist and warp, its use by furniture makers is largely confined to the production of squared or turned frames for chairs (Plates 12 and 273), sofas, stools, easy chairs, etc; it was also extensively used for making bedsteads and certain other articles which were normally stained or painted. Sheraton advised 'particularly it should be noticed, that the frame of a compting-house desk be of beech stained, and put together with bed-

18. Diminutive sketch for a 'Dantzic Oak Dresser' from the Chester specification book, *c. 1830. Cheshire Record Office*

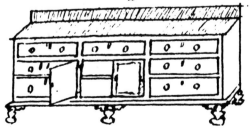

Dantzick Oak Dresser

11

screws'.[15] The Gillow Estimate Sketch Books contain a drawing and detailed cost analysis for making a beech bedstead in 1797[16] (see Plate 111); examples are often recorded in servants' rooms in country-house inventories.

According to Loudon, 'In the Highlands of Scotland birch may be said to be the universal wood. The Highlander makes everything of it; they build their houses of it; make their beds, chairs, tables, dishes and spoons of it; construct their mills of it; make their plows, harrows, gates and fences of it . . .'.[17] This timber was the most easily available hardwood in the upland regions of Scotland, but in England native birch has never been much esteemed by furniture makers, although in the Victorian period large quantities of imported Quebec and American birch were employed in the chair trade and for smart bedroom suites. Some evidence exists that birch was more favoured in the North West, for example *The Whitehaven Book of Prices* (1810), is unique in including a costing for a birch chair 'with plain bannister and pedestal' and a 'Birch Stand Table'; the Chester specification book gives a costing for a 'Birch snap table pillar and three claws', while William Chippindale's inventory records that in 1815 he stocked '133¼ feet of Birch Boards' in addition to supplies of ash, willow, alder, crab-apple and deal.

Walnut was the first wood to supercede oak as the material for fashionable furniture: it has the merits of being close textured, soft and taking a high polish (see Plate 131). However, English sources of this wood were soon exhausted and the native timber came to be regarded as a material only suitable for gun stocks. Sheraton stated 'The common English walnut tree cannot be used but for the most common purposes'. It appears, however, to have been employed by country chairmakers: many descriptions of kitchen chairs and other ordinary types in *The Norwich Book of Prices* (1801), start 'For framing a . . . Chair, elm, ash, beech or walnut-tree . . .'. This prime evidence suggests that East Anglian chairs made of an unfamiliar wood may well be indifferent cuts of walnut (see Plate 194). It is also interesting that the York manuscript list of prices for cabinet and chair work, compiled as late as 1764, quotes costs for executing pieces in walnut as well as wainscot and mahogany.[18]

The timber produced from sycamore works well; the grain is close, even and fine, and the surface a lustrous creamy colour. It is excellent for mangle rollers, dairy utensils and general turnery, while the smooth white texture is also ideal for kitchen table-tops, chopping blocks and stool seats (see Plates 92 and 130). Sheraton, who was trained as a furniture maker, as usual has something of value to say: 'sycamore is in many places in the country, used by cabinet makers instead of beech, for painted chairs or the fly joint rails of card and pembroke tables'.

Cherry is a handsome, delicately shaded, reddish-brown wood in durability second only to oak. When stained with lime, oiled and varnished, it resembles mahogany and, since mature trees have a diameter of up to two feet, it was used by furniture makers for general purposes, being particularly suitable for chairs (see Plates 171 and 198). In 1750 Thomas Hayward, a village joiner in Kent, supplied a customer with '½ doz Cherry tree chairs / ½ Doz Ash Chairs / two Round Tables one Cherry tree';[19] the Chester specification book gives costings for a night chair and a lounging chair in cherry while *The Norwich Book of Prices* (1801), contains a rider 'If these chairs are made of cherry-tree charge extra from other common wood in each shilling 1½d.' — which shows that more labour was involved in working this timber than ash, elm, beech or walnut. The other orchard woods are also dense grained and possess some fine qualities (see Plate 189). Apple was used for high-class general turnery and when available, country joiners employed it for articles such as tripod tables and other small furniture. Pear works 'sweet and clean' in all directions and is a capital timber for carving; it is an excellent turnery wood and also absorbs stain admirably, being used for dyed veneers and small wares such as ebonized coffee or teapot handles.

Yew is famous for its dense grain, toughness and flexibility which renders it capable of taking heavy strains: in the past it was employed for the best long-bows. These qualities, combined with beautiful orange, red and deep brown veining, made it the aristocrat of woods for Windsor chairs (see Plate 167). In a late Victorian price-list issued by Isaac Allsop & Son of Worksop (see Plate 169) their 'Roman Windsors' cost 10s. in yew, 7s. 6d. in cherry and 7s. in elm.[20] This timber makes the strongest gate posts, it being said that a post of yew will outlast one of iron. The Revd. Francis Kilvert of Clyro, noted in his diary under 16 March 1870: 'One of the twin yews was lately blown down and cut up into gate posts which will last twice as long as oak. The wood was so hard that Morgan said it turned many of the axes as if they were made of lead'.[21]

Although supplies of holly were limited, this wood deserves a mention because it is very white, hard, uniform and clean and was widely used in its natural state and when dyed black for stringing lines, especially corner strings in cabinet work. One often wonders from what tree these pale lines are cut (see Plate 7), and it is clear from evidence in Books of Prices that holly was generally favoured. For instance, the Nottingham edition of 1795 lists: 'Cutting white hollin string, per yard ½d.'.

There are native woods that made no contribution to the vernacular furniture tradition, but were of value to certain tradesmen. Lime, for example, was ideal for delicately-carved, japanned or gilded chair, table and looking-glass frames. Sweet-chestnut was once largely used for building construction and for cleaving shingles, laths and fencing poles. Poplar, which is light and unsplittable, makes good floorboards and packing-cases. Hornbeam was favoured by millwrights for wheel cogs, while many of the minor hardwoods were regularly employed for small turnery. As a caution against over-simplifying traditional codes of practice observed by provincial furniture makers, everyone should mark well the following passage in *The Preston Book of Prices* of 1801: 'Making drawer sides, of English oak, American oak, maple, beech, ash or elm, &c. extra from Dantzic oak each side 1d.'.

2 Country Joiners

Manuscript account books kept by village joiners show how, at its humblest level, furniture making merges almost imperceptibly with a versatile tradition of rural craftsmanship, embracing the hewing of husbandry gear, wheelwrighting, the making of field gates, hay rakes, pig troughs, cattle cribs, carts, ladders, coffins and all branches of carpentry work connected with the farm. A wonderfully vivid account of how, during the last century, a family of rural joiners served the needs of their local community, is given in Walter Rose's *The Village Carpenter* (1937), where he describes the 'old country business' run by his grandfather who died in 1893.[1] He was concerned mainly with hedge carpentry, being expected only to repair, not make his neighbours' furniture, apart from simple articles such as yellow pine washing-trays and lodging boxes. The author's memories of tree-felling, the sawpit, timber yard, workshop practices, house carpentry, outwork on the farm, undertaking and millwright's work succeed in bringing one into living contact with the woodwork of the Victorian countryside.

A classic illustration of how one branch of furniture making developed as an offshoot of traditional woodcrafts is afforded by Windsor chairs which, from an early date, were often fashioned by wheelwrights[2] (see Plate 185). Both products depended on native timbers having the same technical properties – unsplittable elm and springy ash – and involved similar methods of assembly. The example of William Brear & Son, a firm of sawyers, timber merchants and general turners in Addingham, shows how a strong vernacular woodworking tradition survived in the Yorkshire Dales until well into the present century. In addition to supplying timber to local builders, they produced larch and oak field gates, fencing posts and rails, mallets, oak-framed wheelbarrows, hay and corn rakes, shafts, felloes and naves for wheels and a range of domestic turnery including baby walkers, peggy sticks, rolling-pins, clothes-pegs, breadboards, towel-rollers, potato-mashers and wash-tubs. This repertoire, together with a stock of plain turned chairs (Plate 20), is illustrated in two small catalogues issued in about 1900 and 1920[3] (see Plates 16 and 193). Their shop tradition confirms that country craftsmen could rarely afford to specialize, but earned a livelihood by applying their skills to a diversity of work in which furniture making was frequently a low priority.[4]

One way of learning about the activities of country joiners is through old account books. A dozen or so ledgers have been investigated, mostly dating from the nineteenth century, but a richly informative early manuscript volume now at Winterthur records work carried out between 1732 and 1754 by Thomas and Ambrose Hayward of Selling, a village near Faversham in Kent.[5] They combined their trade with farming and many entries refer to the sale of pigs, beef, mutton, cheese, etc, while they sometimes accepted payment in kind — a sack of wheat, bushels of apples or malt, a pair of shoes, 2 oz. of tobacco, a pig and so forth. Many jobs were charged by the day or half-day: 'a Days work for one man' cost 2s.; the time of an apprentice half this rate. By way of comparison Thomas Chippendale paid his senior workmen a guinea a week. About 60 per cent of entries are in this form, the nature of the work seldom being specified, but it is clear that tree-felling

20. Second size girl's rocking-chair, ash with a beech yoke and sticks, elm seat. Made by William Brear & Sons, Addingham, Yorkshire, early twentieth century. *Kate Mason*

19. (*Opposite*) Oak book cupboard and dado made by Joseph Peacock, joiner, in 1771, for the village school at Burnt Yates, Yorkshire.

15

and jobbing on neighbouring farms was reckoned thus. The sawpit was well used, a typical item being 3 July 1739 'for Sawing 950 foot at 3s. 4d. the hundred £1. 11s. 8d.'; elm boards were sold at 2d. a foot.

Before moving on to the Haywards' furniture output, which formed an interesting but fairly modest part of their trade, it is instructive to glance at other branches of the business. Local pig owners regularly ordered hog troughs, hog yokes, hog forms, hog styes and hog blocks (Plate 21); other customers required hen coops, mangers, bullock cribs, wheelbarrows (Plate 22), hopping stools, 'rowls, handles, lidds & curbs for wells' and, on one occasion, a weathercock. The hewing of husbandry gear such as harrows, plows and hay rakes came within their province, as did the making of wheels and millwrighting. Living in a hop-growing district, the Haywards also supplied cleft and sharpened hop poles by the hundred and in season they often assisted with the hop harvest. The hedge carpentry side of the business involved setting up stiles, field gates (Plate 23) and fencing; many wattle gates of chestnut were fabricated and there was a constant demand for ladders — a tall one with 29 slats cost 7s. 6d. In 1744 Ambrose Hayward contracted to build for Goodman Sprat a barn measuring 18 by 20 feet 'providing Lats, Nails, Elm boards and Workmanship as far as Carpenter's work goes £9.'.

Timbers mentioned in the ledger are all native: willow for thatching spars and spokes, oaken pins at 1s. per hundred for building, elm and deal for shelving, cherry or ash for chairs; references also occur to witch elm, perry (pear), birch and beech. Oak butts cost between £1. 12s. and £2. per ton and beech was purchased at £1. 6s. a ton. The splendidly detailed picture that emerges is of a traditional workshop run by a father and his son with the help of three or four journeymen and an apprentice. They were proficient in almost every woodworking skill demanded by their neighbours, except for certain specialized trades like waggon building, coopering and the production of elm water pumps. Most local villagers were buried in coffins from the Hayward workshops.

In contrast to Walter Rose's grandfather, these country joiners were also making to order a repertoire of common household furniture and utensils. A century later improved transport, combined with the vast quantities of cheap furniture manufactured in industrial towns, meant that it was no longer necessary or economic for rural joiners to supply ordinary domestic furniture. Many entries in the account book are for humble articles verging on treen: trenchers; milking stools; pipe, candle, knife, salt or tinder-boxes; butter-scales; clothes-horses and corn chests. Higher up the furniture scale come boarded kists; kneading troughs; cupboards;

21.   Ash stand from the West Country, probably late eighteenth century. The notched ends are a common regional feature. *Courtesy Gabriel Olive*

22.   Pig trough, wheelbarrow and stool, from W.H. Pyne's *Microcosm; or, Picturesque Views of Rural Occupations* (1808).

23. The making of an old English field gate from heart oak was considered a day's work for a qualified carpenter. From W. Rose, *The Village Carpenter* (1937)

kitchen tables for working; oval tables for dining; tripod tea tables and fixtures such as 'a mantleshelf, fireboard and spit rack'. Amongst the most interesting items are bed settles, dressers and chairs. The former, which cost on average 13s. to 18s., sound like a genuine regional design type, perhaps akin to the settle beds found in Ireland, but so far no examples have been traced. References also occur to side beds and couch beds besides familiar tester beds. A structure usually recorded simply as 'a Dresser Board and shelves' was much in demand, either open or with a cupboard in the lower stage.

A loose letter in the ledger, from Wm Bennett of Faversham (a town ten miles distant from Selling), shows that the Haywards enjoyed a reputation for turned chairs:

27 Jan. 1754

Send me Next waggon from your town 6 of the same pattarn and Mad in Ash Chears as I had of you Last. Pt ass foot mold and dont fail to send the desk as soon as possibel. No great Chear no Lo Chear.

Another valuable order was fulfilled in November 1750:

two large Ovel tables	2	10	0
a Dressing table	–	15	–
two Round tables one Cherry tree table	1	2	0
half a Dousand of Cherry tree Cheyers	–	18	–
half a Dousand of Ash Cheyers	–	18	–
half a Dousand of Common Ash Cheyers	–	12	–
a payer of Weels	2	8	0

This old account book illustrates how an average family of country joiners who, typically, were also engaged in farming, employed their time and craft skills to earn a livelihood within an agricultural community. They could not afford to concentrate on furniture making — plain joinery and turned chairs accounted for a relatively minor part of their income; farming activities, house carpentry, sawing, hewing husbandry gear and jobbing were equally important branches of the business. The custom of craftsmen working for local farmers at haymaking and harvest time was taken for granted in the old rural economy. Because the Haywards were farmer–joiners, work followed a seasonal pattern; also it was possible for them to settle transactions by barter rather than in hard cash.[6]

William Parkinson, joiner, of Gretford, Lincolnshire, kept two account books spanning the years 1770–94 and 1795–1820.[7] He was aided by two men and an apprentice and his business followed a similar pattern to that of the Haywards a generation earlier. Much time was spent tree-felling, sawing, making plows, cow cribs, wheels, fencing, erecting barns, hovels and on general joinery about the farm. In 1788 he made and hung two new Town gates for the Constable of Barholm and in 1801 was paid £1. 3s. 0d. by the Gretford churchwardens for a 'new wheel for the Bell'. In the late summer Parkinson usually helped with the harvest. A seasonal cycle of work geared to the needs of the farming community they served is typical of country joiners. Scattered references occur to furniture – cupboards, bedsteads, tables, dressers, chests and the occasional chair – amid the constant payments for domestic jobbing, repairs and agricultural work.

Eight ledgers and estimate books kept by John and William Myers of Wheldrake, near York, between 1778 and the mid-nineteenth century, provide an excellent record of their activities.[8] They at first combined the trades of general joiner and house carpenter with making traditional furniture, but by the 1840s the business was concerned mainly with farmwork and undertaking. In 1788 John Myers made benefaction and commandment boards for Wheldrake Church which still adorn the nave and in 1790 the firm pewed Bubwith Church. The earlier ledger preserves many detailed estimates for making wheelbarrows, chests, bureaux, press beds, etc.

Various memoranda, including how to remove stains from tea-tables, a recipe for staining beech a mahogany colour and directions for polishing mahogany doors, provide rewarding insights into current trade practices: 'To Polish Mahogany Doors Oyle it over with linseed Oyle over Night then in the Morning take sum Brick Dust put it into a silk stocking or anything that is fine then dash it over door and take a piece of new Carpitt or any Woolon cloth and Rub it. Oyle Coat After Another with Brick Dust and Oyle till you Make a glow till you can see your self in it'.

24. Oak deed-chest with three locks, made by William Chippindale of Farnley in 1770 for the Trustees of the village school at Burnt Yates, Yorkshire.

James Pratt, joiner, of Bubwith, near Howden in Yorkshire, has left four account books spanning the years 1823–44.[9] The population of Bubwith in 1822 was 540 and the entries in his ledgers breathe the life of the countryside. He made cartwheels, axles and nameboards for waggons; shafted axes, forks and hay knives for his neighbours; produced drag harrows, plows, sheep and swine troughs, churn dashes and winnowing machines for local farmers; repaired village pumps, beehives and mills; provided shoemakers' seats and shop counters; worked in the fields at fencing, making and hanging new gates or building stiles and often joined the reapers at harvest time. He accepted orders from the doctor for a pair of crutches and from others for boat paddles, privy seats, ladders, fishing rods and, of course, coffins. James Pratt and his four or five men obviously made a vital contribution to Bubwith village life. About once a year he supplied '½ Dozen Chares' which cost in the region of two pounds and, from time to time, made bedsteads, cupboards, tables, chests of drawers and cradles. It is unlikely that any of James Pratt's work will ever be identified and remarkable that documentation survives to preserve the memory of this sturdy representative of an anonymous tradition of country craftsmanship.

Normally the only hope of proving the authorship of pieces produced in the country by country-trained joiners for local clients is through the rare discovery of an inscription recording the maker's name, or by finding relevant references amongst family or institutional papers. An example of the former is a chair signed under the seat rail 'William John / Carpenter fecit / October 28 1778' (see Plate 197).[10] The school at Burnt Yates, ·a village near Harrogate, was founded by Admiral Long in 1761 and administered by six Trustees whose minute and cash books record that William Chippindale of Farnley, carpenter, was commissioned to make 'a strong wooden chest, well secured with iron clamps and three locks . . . wherein to reposit the Deeds and other writings relating to the Trust'; an entry in their cash book under 19 September 1770 notes that Wm Chippindale was paid £1. 11s. 6d. 'for one Oak Chest &c'.[11] This chest still serves, in the room for which it was made, as a repository for the Trustees's deeds (Plate 24). William Chippindale was a cousin to the famous London cabinet maker Thomas Chippendale, born nearby in Otley, so this sturdy chest is a moving reminder of the kind of furniture he would have made had he stayed in Wharfedale. In 1771 Joseph Peacock, a joiner and tenant farmer living at Burnt Yates, was paid £15. 12s. by the Trustees for panelling the upper room to dado height and making a large bookcase in two stages enclosed by double doors. The cupboard is a fine example of conservatively-styled raised-panel furniture with pegged joints (Plate 20). The school at Burnt Yates therefore provides a remarkable provenance group of documented vernacular furniture.[12] Another built-in cupboard in a cottage near Bristol is helpfully inscribed by a village joiner: 'Mr John Howard / this Woorke was done in ye year of our / Lord 1739 by Joseph Hurdacre / Joyner of ye parish of Huntspill / Somersett-Shire'[13] (Plate 25).

An inspiring account book which belonged to William Dawson of Otley (1844–57) illustrates the pattern of work of a joiner in a small market town before the railway came.[14] Dawson made a blackboard, pointing rod, benches and a large table for Mr Kerr, the schoolmaster, furniture for offices and inns, provided coffins for the Overseer at Otley workhouse, supplied timber to local cabinet makers and fitted out shops. His repertoire is fairly predictable, apart from some smart mahogany pieces and an interesting range of painted furniture: 'To 1 Round Deal Table, painting Do 7s. / To a New Clothes Box & painting & Graining oak 13s. / New Desk for Office & painting Do / To a New Cradle & Frame to Rock on & painting Mahogany outside & Blue in 12s. 6d.'. Every girl or youth leaving home to enter domestic service or seek employment on the land was provided with a strongly-made travelling or 'lodging' box to hold clothes and personal articles (Plate 26). The one itemized by William Dawson in 1850 must have been closely similar to a mid-nineteenth-century example from Holwick in Teesdale made of

25. Recessed cupboard, formerly one of a pair, in a cottage on the Ashton Court estate, near Bristol; one drawer is signed and dated by Joseph Hurdacre, joyner of Huntspill, Somerset, 1739. *Courtesy K.M. Walton*

pine with the original grained oak finish (Plate 27). According to Walter Rose, the making of such a box with dovetailed corners was reckoned a day's work. A painted pine cradle of traditional form mounted on rockers now at Gainsborough Old Hall is virtually identical to the cradle for which Dawson charged 12s. 6d. The outside is vividly decorated with fancy zigzag scumbling in black on an orange red ground, while the interior is painted blue. It is inscribed underneath 'Lilla Eliza Milner 1864 Gunthorpe' – a hamlet in the parish of Owston Ferry, Lincolnshire (see Plates 402 and 403). The choice of blue perpetuated an earlier custom of lining cradles with blue paper. John Milner, a master wheelwright, and his wife, lived at Gunthorpe, but the birth of Lilla Eliza has not been traced, which suggests this little cradle was made for one of their daughters' favourite dolls.[15]

The Tomlinson family of joiners and wheelwrights of Appleton-le-Moors, a village on the North York Moors, were in business from the early nineteenth century until the eve of the Second World War. Their workshop in two buildings behind the house has 'slept' for the past fifty years and still contains the benches, tools and scores of wooden patterns for making carts, plow beams, sledges and all manner of agricultural implements. The lathe was in a loft, reached for many years by a ladder, and driven by a large handcranked wheel situated in the yard (Plate 28). Two account books covering the years 1844–97 and 1900–24 chronicle the Tomlinsons's business.[16] In addition to carrying out traditional country work they also built carts and painted signboards. The art of decorative lettering was highly regarded at this time (Plate 29). Their premier commission was providing the woodwork for a new church built for the village by J.L. Pearson in 1863–5, which must have been a change from fitting out post offices, schools and Wesleyan chapels, endless jobbing repairs, wheelwrighting and making basic furniture. They occasionally dressed millstones or re-cogged mill wheels with crab-tree wood and even supplied local farms with expensive equipment such as straw cutters costing £6. 10s. and threshing machines at £11. Much of their timber was cut from neighbouring woods, but George and Henry Tomlinson sometimes visited Whitby or York to buy Baltic deal which was consigned by rail to Pickering, and then carted eight miles

28. Workshop of Henry Tomlinson, joiner, Appleton-le-Moors, Yorkshire, last used about 1940. The manual wheel turned a lathe in the upstairs room. *V. Tomlinson*

29. Victorian pine chest, grained light oak with fine sign lettering, from West Tanfield, Yorkshire.

26. (*Opposite, above*) Painted pine lodging box with dove-tailed corners from the Yorkshire Wolds. Every girl of youth leaving home to enter domestic service or work on the land was provided with a strongly-made travelling box. *Trustees of the Ryedale Folk Museum*

27. (*Opposite, below*) Lodging box, probably mid-nineteenth century, pine with the original grained oak finish, fitted with an internal till. From Holwick in Teesdale, Yorkshire. *Trustees of the Ryedale Folk Museum*

to their yard. Baltic softwoods first started to replace native hardwoods for everyday constructional uses when river navigation improved in the eighteenth century, and this trend accelerated with the expanding railway network.

A series of ledgers have survived in the Brumfitt family of Skipton, a firm of cabinet makers and upholsterers founded in 1790.[17] The earliest (1849–61) records many fashionable pieces, but they also sold ordinary deal tables and dressers, tool handles, ash crutches, oak clock cases, butter prints, etc, so it would be wrong to suppose that all common furniture was produced by joiners. Manby's, an ironmonger in the same market town, also have some early Victorian account books which show they were supplying furniture hardware — hinges, handles, castors, screws, locks, bolts, nails clock movements (charged by the pound) and sets of 'clock case tire' to joiners over a wide area. This is a branch of the furniture trade seldom illuminated by documentation.

A few other Victorian business records deserve a glance. William Pease, joiner, of Pontefract (1860–80) was producing 'spell back Windsor chairs' in the 1860s — a term that implies they were of 'Grecian' pattern, since spell was the local name for the horizontal bars of the field gate.[18] John Wainwright of Skelmanthorpe in Yorkshire, although described in trade directories as a joiner, supplied miners with ostentatiously splendid chiffonier bedsteads, made either of solid mahogany with carved panels (see Plate 228) or pine, grained to simulate oak, mahogany or maple.[19] A feature of his account book is a prefatory note headed 'Prisces of Town's Coffins 1896':

for Still Born	2s. 6d.
Under 1 year	7s.
1 year to 5 years	8s.
5 years to 10 years	10s.
10 years to 15 years	12s. 6d.
15 years to 18 years	15s. 6d.
18 years and upwards	17s.

Lastly, the workshop books kept by Owen Fitzpatrick of Birkenhead admirably record a Victorian urban bespoke cabinet-making business. Of particular interest and relevance are the descriptions of ship furniture, pieces commissioned by Railway Companies and for pubs, hospitals, workhouses and similar institutions.[20] This material is quoted in appropriate chapters.

A common feature of these old account books is that, without exception, the

30. A Yorkshire sheep-shearing cratch, oak and pine. The shearer sat astride the narrow end with the sheep resting on the bars in front of him. Such stools mark a point where basic furniture merges with husbandry gear. *Castle Museum, York*

business was confined to woodcrafts. There are no references to bricklaying, since this was the province of the village mason, while plumbing, glazing and decorating were likewise separate trades. This system started to change in late Victorian days when the small master craftsman was replaced by firms of general house builders, decorators and furnishers able to undertake contract work.

The furniture made by these town and country tradesmen was strictly functional, displayed a profound understanding of the technical properties of native woods and emphasized underlying form. Farm woodwork – carts, ladders, rakes, wheels, field gates, cheese-presses, sheep-shearing stools (Plate 30), etc, acquired unselfconsciously inherited characteristics that express the continuity of rural life; the same skills were applied to furniture. Regional traditions were reinforced by conservative design attitudes; furniture expressed few personal preferences and reflected local, rather than national, styles. Decorative treatment such as carving, veneers or inlay

31. Housekeeper's cupboard bearing the trade label of Edward Andrew, High Street, Welshpool, Montgomery, the clock movement by Richard Pugh, Llanbister. Oak, *c.* 1820. *Courtesy McCartney's Sale-rooms, Ludlow*

were unknown on the vernacular level, but well-cut mouldings, chamfers, turnings and carefully studied proportions bestowed a comeliness (Plate 31); ornament was generally confined to painted finishes, particularly after Baltic deal became widely available. Turned ash or cherry chairs displayed the same disciplined qualities as waggon wheels.

The transition from vernacular to 'period' styles occurred on the level represented by the Brumfitts of Skipton who owned *The Preston Cabinet and Chair-Makers Book of Prices* (1802) and the *Bolton Supplement to the London Book of Cabinet Piece Prices* (1802), and later acquired fashionable Victorian furniture-trade catalogues,[21] employed exotic woods, used a trade label and numbered the Tempests of Broughton Hall amongst their customers.[22] The Myers of Wheldrake successfully combined 'the old country business' with the production of a wider than average repertoire of routine household furniture, while with John Wainwright of Skelmanthorpe, who served a fairly affluent mining community, we see the full change from functionalism to innovative artistic design. His gleaming mahogany chiffonier beds, although traditional in form, reflect the showy styles of commercial Victorian furniture (see Plate 228). The transformation of England from an agricultural to an urban society seems finally to have extinguished the native vernacular tradition; the sincere qualities of say a cheese-press or a sheep-shearing stool[23] were no longer acceptable to the general public, who came to prefer elaborate derivative furniture designs. A nostalgic protest was made by the Arts and Crafts Movement, but their work can now be seen as yet another Victorian revival of historic styles.

3 Provincial Price Books

The various cabinet makers' and chairmakers' Books of Prices, sponsored by masters and journeymen in London and provincial centres from 1788 onwards, contain a fund of precise information, the value of which furniture historians have only just begun to appreciate.[1] These at first sight rather arid volumes, the result of Trade Union activity during a period of rapid inflation, were an attempt to fix standard piece-work rates for making a wide range of furniture in common production; in short, the agreed scales allowed both masters and journeymen to reckon labour costs and so avoid damaging disputes. The preface to *The Edinburgh Book of Prices*, 'as mutually agreed upon by the masters and journeymen' in September 1805, explains cogently why that price guide was issued and how it was intended to be applied:

> Many inconveniences having arisen from the want of an approved standard, by which to regulate the Prices of Piece Work in the Cabinet Business in Edinburgh and neighbourhood; and it being found that, owing to various local circumstances, none of the books on that subject published in other places applied properly to this, made it highly expedient to bring forward the present publication.
>
> The constant change of Fashion in the style of Cabinet Work, renders it difficult, if not impracticable, in a work of this kind, to embrace particularly the price of every article; but although this book is limited in point of extent, it is hoped it will be found to contain the general principles for ascertaining the value of work, so exemplified as to render it easy to make up the price of any piece of work by it. . . .

The printed price books were preceded by manuscript agreements, the earliest being struck between Robert Gillow of Lancaster and his workmen in about 1746.[2] Another price list, drawn up in 1764, apparently under the auspices of the York Carpenters' and Joiners' Guild,[3] is headed 'Prices of Cabinet and Chair Work' and laid down the labour cost of making fourteen routine articles ranging from 'Mahogany Double Chests Plain £1. 11s. 6d.' to 'Matted Bottom Chairs 3 flutes 2s. 3d.'. Thus, it is clear that a tradition of collective activity leading to local agreements existed well before *The Cabinet-Maker's London Book of Prices* first appeared in 1788. The original edition was revised in 1793, again in 1803, and was followed by volumes catering for chairmakers and carvers (1802), portable-desk makers and cabinet small workers (1806), and other branches of the trade. Its success inspired masters and workmen in the provinces to settle their differences by publishing comparable lists. Following a series of wage disputes, *The Leeds Cabinet and Chair-Makers Book of Prices* appeared, confirming an agreement reached in March 1791; *The Nottingham Book of Prices* was issued six weeks later, and over the next twenty years price books were published in Belfast, Birmingham, Bolton, Edinburgh, Glasgow, Liverpool, Manchester, Norwich, Preston and Whitehaven.[4] The dog-eared condition of most surviving copies testifies to their constant use in workshops.

Collectively, this source material is of inestimable value for the study of provincial furniture: besides offering rare insights into contemporary terminology trade practices and costs, an examination of the schedules helps to illuminate regional design preferences. Each book provides a basic specification for items of furniture in regular production, followed by a detailed table of optional refinements. In some towns tradesmen negotiated agreements based on the latest London edition, but published a supplement to cater for special local needs. For example, a sixteen-page *Bolton Supplement to the London Book of Cabinet Piece Prices* (1802), is entirely devoted to describing and costing a repertoire of furniture omitted from the London edition, but for which a brisk demand obviously existed in the neighbourhood. In the same year, the journeymen cabinet and chairmakers of Preston revised their own more comprehensive 'statement' which was endorsed by nine leading masters in the town. Accordingly, a careful analysis and collation of these now often very scarce publications yields significant clues about the regional character of common furniture.

The *Bolton Supplement*, a possibly unique copy of which descended in the old established Brumfitt family of cabinet makers active in Skipton, provides an instructive case study;[5] the entire text is reproduced as Appendix Two. To start with a fairly obvious point, clock cases are omitted from the London book because in the capital they were normally made in specialist workshops; but in Lancashire, clock cases were produced by many general cabinet makers,[6] thus detailed descriptions are included listing various decorative permutations for enriching 'square head' and 'arch head' clock cases. It would be salutary to investigate how closely long-case clocks with Bolton movements of *c.* 1800 conform to the published specifications. Again, due to subdivisions within the cabinet trade, the London book contains no reference to seat furniture (other than chamber horses) or beds (except for the fold-away variety); however, in the provinces practices were more flexible, so the compilers featured a selection of the more popular patterns of bedsteads, sofas, chairs and stools. Turned chairs were, however, traditionally regarded as forming a separate branch and are excluded.[7]

Of even keener interest to students of vernacular furniture are those pieces which express an obviously regional character. For instance, the *Bolton Supplement* describes a typically Lancashire form of dresser (Plate 32), designed as a chest faced by dummy drawers with true drawers below, the basic specification being for: 'a Dresser, with four drawers and four sham ditto, 5 feet 6 inches long and 3 feet 6 inches high, with quarter columns, all plain and solid £2. 1. 0'. There follows a cost analysis of various optional extras including:

32. A typically Lancashire form of oak dresser with three sham above four true drawers and quarter corner columns, *c.* 1800. From the Rochdale area. *Courtesy Phillips Sale-rooms, Leeds*

Each inch more or less in length or height	0	0	6
Each extra sham	0	0	9
Each sham made into a real drawer	0	2	0
Veneering drawer fronts, each	0	0	6
Ditto front framing long way	0	2	6
Frieze and astragal in front	0	2	0
Ditto on the ends	0	0	8
A framed top	0	2	6
Moulding brackets	0	1	2
Scollopping back board or fixing ends to a plain one	0	0	6
Polishing	0	1	0
For all other extras, see London Book			

The above figures of course relate only to the cost of labour; materials and the master's profit would have been charged extra to his customers.

The specifications for making 'straight-front' and 'round-front' hanging corner cupboards and a tall standing corner cupboard, termed a 'buffet', are of equal value in defining local design types and popular decorative treatments. It is significant that *The Whitehaven Book of Prices*[8] (1810) records that 'scroll pediments' were standard features on hanging corner cupboards and buffets made at this centre in the neighbouring county of Cumberland (Plate 33). The *Bolton Supplement* also reveals that the familiar North Country panel-back settle (Plate 34) was, rather surprisingly, known at the time as a 'couch chair' and 'dog leg' was the local term for a cabriole support:

33. 'Straight-front' hanging corner cupboard with scroll pediment and reeded cants, all solid oak, c. 1800. Probably from the Whitehaven area. *Courtesy Sotheby's Sale-rooms, Chester*

For a plain Couch Chair, 6 feet long and under, with 4 square pannels and plain Marlbro' legs	0	13	0
Each inch longer	0	0	2
Raising each pannel	0	0	4
Each extra pannel	0	1	0
A top rail with hollow corners, each corner	0	0	4
Ditto with ogee or three hollows, each	0	0	6
Raising each pannel to toprail, with hollow corners	0	0	7
Dog legs, each	0	1	3
Nailing in bottom	0	0	6
Tapering, sawing out and moulding feet see Chairs			
For banding, see London Book			
Sawing out seat rails	0	0	6
If a moulding in front under the capping	0	0	6
Polishing	0	0	9

If the tenon joints were secured by pegs, each dowel cost ½d. We also learn that in Lancashire an upholstered single-headed couch or day-bed (see Plate 45) was called a 'squab' — a word quite often encountered in Dales inventories. There also appears to be a very welcome costing for a type of chair commonly found in the Lancashire Dales which generally goes under the colourful modern name of a 'shepherd's' or 'lambing' chair:

An easy chair with lower rails and stretcher	0	10	0
Saddle tree wings	0	1	6
Hollow back	0	1	0
Close stool in ditto	0	4	0

The Preston Book of Prices indicates that for an extra 3s. 6d. this chair could be made with an adjustable reclining back. Many examples were boxed-in and fitted with a drawer beneath the seat (Plate 35). Other random points of interest to emerge are that corner chairs (often incorporating a commode) were known in these parts as

34. Oak couch chair with four raised panels and 'dog legs' corresponding to a specification in the Bolton *Book of Prices* (1802). Rufford Old Hall, Lancashire. *The National Trust*

35. An oak easy chair 'with saddle tree wings', early nineteenth century. From the Bay Horse, Clough Bottom, Lancashire. *Towneley Hall, Burnley*

'smoking' chairs[9] and, not unexpectedly for a county with a reputation for dairying, cheese-waggons were batch-produced.

The Preston Book contains several details worthy of passing mention. There is a reference to 'papering each drawer' of a lobby chest (Plates 36 and 37); 'making patterns' (e.g. templates) was paid for according to time rather than on a piece-work rate basis,[10] and it is clear that 'a stand', which occurs in farmhouse inventories, was a small tripod table (see Plates 49 and 123); putting a triangular metal plate 'on a pillar and claw table' to strengthen the base joint cost 1½d. Lastly, under 'Deal Work', there is a particularly lucid description of a plain gate-leg dining-table present in many cottage kitchens (see Plate 41): 'For do 4 feet long, with four fast and two fly-feet 7s. 6d.', while the specification for a 'round drinking table with a triangular frame' exactly describes many surviving examples (see Plate 124). Different points of interest will strike each reader while looking through these amazing factual compendiums.

Most price books concentrate on elegant mahogany furniture and devote comparatively little space to oak or deal work. However, the Edinburgh and Glasgow books include a few smart pieces which reflect distinctive Scottish design features – stage top sideboards and card tables with a frieze drawer partitioned for tea canisters – so other volumes may yield evidence of upmarket local styles.[11] While it is not feasible to comment here on all provincial publications, *The Norwich Chair Makers' Price Book* (1801) must be acclaimed as outstandingly good on East Anglian patterns;[12] excerpts from this and the Leeds book are provided, along with relevant illustrations in the section on regional joined chairs (see Plates 196 and 201). The chapter on timber also culls impeccable information from these, until recently, little-appreciated sources.

36. Lobby chest, oak with mahogany corner columns, bearing the label of John Mitchel, Kendal, inscribed 'December 25th 1779'. The design closely follows descriptions in Lancashire price books. *Private collection*

37. Trade label on lobby chest. The border design looks later than the ink inscription.

4 Farmhouses and Cottages

Although the study of smaller rural houses has been placed on a secure footing by the Vernacular Architecture Society, furniture historians have hardly begun seriously to investigate how such buildings were furnished. This survey attempts little more than to outline the range of available source material and, by sampling, suggest how it can be interpreted. The way forward is through local research and comparison of the results from one period and region with another. A good start has been made elsewhere on analysing and defining the stylistic character of seventeenth-century provincial oak furniture,[1] but our concern is to discover how, within the period c. 1740–1880, ordinary rural dwellings were furnished at various times and in different parts of the country.

THE EVIDENCE OF INVENTORIES

Any programme of research on cottage and farmhouse furniture must take into account the abundant information contained in probate inventories and wills. An Act of 1529 required an inventory and valuation of the movable goods of a deceased person to be made if these amounted to over £5., for the purpose of proving their will in the ecclesiastical courts. This system technically lasted until 1858, although the amount of detail tends to diminish during the early Georgian period and few inventories were made after about 1750. They were compiled under oath by 'honest and skilful persons' – usually neighbours – and provide a record of immense historical value. Several local collections have been published since F.W. Steer's *Farm and Cottage Inventories of Mid-Essex* appeared in 1950, notably volumes covering parts of Gloucestershire, Dorset, Shropshire and Yorkshire,[2] but they focus on the sixteenth and seventeenth centuries and the commentaries on furniture tend to be rather superficial. Probate inventories are, of course, always appended to wills, which may themselves contain interesting details.

The wills held at Leeds Record Office for the Eastern Deaneries of the Archdeaconry of Richmond Consistory Court (Richmond, Catterick and Boroughbridge) span the years 1541 to 1858 and number in all some 50,000 documents. Obviously not everyone made a will and by no means all are accompanied by probate inventories; nevertheless this still represents an impressive body of material and statistical methods would be needed to fully analyse the data. However, since the period 1750–73 yields (excluding gentry families) only 160 inventories, the furniture content can be studied in an orthodox way. The majority relate to yeoman farmers or widows, with a scattering of miners, labourers, innkeepers and tradesmen including one 'wand weaver', William Corner of Richmond,[3] who perhaps made some of the 'wanded' chairs recorded in local homes. Not all the inventories are of equal value, because the amount of detail varies, but about thirty compilers inserted room names as they progressed round the house listing furniture and utensils. Taken together, and interpreted with care, these records reveal much about the interplay of tradition and innovation, living standards and social customs in this largely rural community.

Detail from *Cottage Interior with an Old Woman Preparing Tea* by W.R. Bigg, oil-painting dated 1793 (see Plate 49). The tea things are set out on a typical tripod stand, the chair is draped with a rug; notice also the traditional warming-pan and clock. *Trustees of the Victoria and Albert Museum*

The area dealt with comprises the whole of Swaledale and Wensleydale extending as far as the lowland parishes of Whixley and Green Hammerton. It was thus, predominantly, a hill-farming district, Richmond being the only important urban centre. The commonest building form in the mid-eighteenth century was the two-unit house, having two ground-floor rooms, usually chambered over and possibly with an outshut extension serving as a dairy or back-kitchen. Many houses in the region were of cruck construction and thatched with heather.[4] The central entrance led directly into the living-kitchen, known as the 'firehouse', 'forehouse' or 'housestead'. The second downstairs room still functioned almost universally as the main sleeping apartment, although many families were starting to furnish it as a parlour where the family could also take meals and sit. The upstairs rooms generally contained beds and were widely used for storing farm gear, boxes, meal chests, wool, corn, cheese, malt and bulky objects not in daily use. The only single-purpose room was likely to be a milkhouse or dairy. Families tended to operate on a wave pattern: every thirty years or so they would become an extended family with old parents, their children and grandchildren sharing the same house. At such times, the attic chambers functioned as bedrooms rather than for storage.

The inventory of Matthew Heslop, yeoman, of Langton upon Swale (1751), reveals how a typical farmhouse was furnished:[5]

In the Fore house a Dresser and Pewter, a Table, Clock, Chairs and Long Settle	6	0	0
In the Parlour and Closets thereunto adjoining Beds and Bedding, Chests of Drawers, a Little Table, Chairs and Corner Cupboard	8	0	0
In the Kitching a Kettle, Pans, Bowls and Milk vessells and some other small Implements	2	0	0
In the Chambers 2 Chaff Bedds, a Chest, 2 Tables, a Churn, 4 Chairs and some other Implements	3	10	0
Bed and Table Linnen	1	10	0

He bequeathed to his youngest daughter, Hannah, 'the Great Drawers and Dresser standing in the Kitchen' which gives us a little more information about this important piece of furniture. Heslop's livestock, hay and crops were valued at £88. – in this community, wealth seems generally to have been translated into farming stock rather than luxurious living. Clearly, no man was judged by the quality of his furniture.

On reading through the inventories, one soon becomes aware that social custom governed not only the way in which houses were planned and rooms used, but also dictated, to a marked degree, how they should be furnished. There existed, for example, throughout the region, a clear concept of what comprised the standard 'kit' in a forehouse; consequently, there was no very obvious distinction between the furniture of a labourer or tradesman and a well-to-do farmer. Not every household mustered the full repertoire, but the community as a whole certainly subscribed to some such stereotyped idea, because the essential elements are encountered again and again. Take for instance Thomas Morland, mason, of Spennithorne, whose effects were valued in 1761 at only £4. 17s. 6d.[6] He inhabited a two-roomed dwelling, one up one down, yet the furniture in his living-room falls into exactly the same pattern as that owned by Matthew Heslop who, as we have seen, ten years earlier left an estate worth £109:

His purse and Apparel	1	0	0
In the low Room being but one. A Clock,	1	0	0
A Delph Rack with the Delph and a Warming Pan		5	0
A Dresser very little and Pewter	1	0	0
An Old Longsettle, a Table & Four Chairs		5	0

38. Oak dresser crossbanded in walnut, incorporating a clock, the movement by John Walls & Co., Coventry, c. 1800–1810. Descended in the Lee family, The Farm, Ashow, Kenilworth, Warwickshire. *Courtesy Gabriel Olive*

A Spinning Wheel, Knack Reel & a dressing Glass	2	0
A Smoothing iron, two Candlesticks three tinnes	2	0
An Iron Pott, a pan and Washing Tub, a pair of Balence	2	0
Tongs, Pocr & Fire Shovell	1	0
Upstairs 2 Chairs, a Form and a Table	7	6
One Bed of Chaf	6	0
The Working Tools	5	0

A long-case clock was a treasured possession and, like silver objects or bibles, they are quite often mentioned in wills, and sometimes inscribed with initials and dates (Plate 39). In 1763 Henry Sayer of Romaldkirk rather touchingly bequeathed to his namesake 'my Clock & Case to my Grandson Henry Sayer'.[7] John Johnson of Well also made arrangements to ensure that his clock should descend in the family, giving his wife 'the choice of so much of my Household furniture as will necessarily furnish a Room with needful things my Clock excepted, nevertheless she is left at liberty to take the free Loan of the sd Clock during her natural life, after her Deceas I give it to my son Richard . . . all the rest of my household furniture undisposed of I give to my Daughter Ann . . .'.[8] Brass-faced clocks, like gleaming warming-pans and a parade of pewter on the dresser, are a sign that farming families, their basic needs satisfied, were starting to become house-proud; although this process had not yet reached the stage of a craving for novelty, about which William Cobbett complained so bitterly in the early nineteenth century. Within two generations, clocks were being built into dressers (Plate 38), thus uniting two of the essential showpieces found in every decent Yorkshire farmhouse kitchen.

39. Clock by Jonas Barber, Winster, Cumbria, the hood dated 1760 and initialled J^{G}M for a member of the Gaskell family. The inscription serves to underline the high regard in which long-case clocks were held. *Julia M. Carter*

40. A late eighteenth-century oak dresser at Nunnington Hall, typical of a group featuring fluted pilasters from the Pickering area of the North York Moors. *The National Trust*

The most impressive piece of furniture in the forehouse was the oak dresser which, like its ancestor, the medieval tiered sideboard, combined utility and display (Plate 40). The inventory references are mostly very brief, but there appear to have been three shadowy design types, almost always with a shelved rear structure for pewter. Many entries refer simply to 'dresser and rails' or 'one dresser and shelves with the pewter standing thereon'; sometimes the lower stage is described as a 'table dresser' or a 'cupboard dresser'. It can be advanced that the lower part was either of open-framed construction (with a row of drawers under the top and a pot-board) enclosed by cupboards, and/or fitted with drawers. This does not get us very far, but available documentary evidence hardly merits firmer conclusions. Many households also owned a separate 'delf rack' or 'pewter rail' — that is a set of framed shelves fixed to the kitchen wall to hold additional plates and dishes. Corner cupboards were very popular. These, according to a passage in Thomas Webster's *Encyclopaedia of Domestic Economy* (1844), 'were much used in days of old, but now are seen only in the cottage, or old farm-house. They were used for holding the punch bowls, glasses and china . . .'.[9] His text is accompanied by a small illustration of a bow-fronted hanging corner cupboard containing such articles and a similar example is featured in one of Thomas Rowlandson's 'Dr Syntax' prints (see Plate 136).

Well over half the inventories sampled record a 'lang settle' in the forehouse. This was a seat with a low panelled back having either a corded or a wood bottom, open arms at each end and often raised on cabriole front legs; they were widely popular and many survive (see Plate 34). The majority are quite plain, although early

41. Interior from a series of mainly Yorkshire sketches by C.W. Cope, *c.* 1840. This watercolour showing part of a castle or abbey is interesting because it portrays a bed in a downstairs room. *Trustees of the Victoria and Albert Museum*

42. *Home Spun Thoughts* by J.H. Mole (1814–1886) showing a 'couch chair' or long settle against the wall to one side of the hearth. *Courtesy Apollo Galleries*

eighteenth-century examples may exhibit carved decoration on the top rail. A striking feature of these northern homes was immensely wide gable-end chimneys with, at one side, a fixed wooden partition supporting a plank-seat called the 'heck' or 'speer', which screened the ingle-nook from draughts (see Plates 54 and 133). The opposite wall typically contained a small 'fire window' to illuminate the hearth. According to verses in Robert Hird's (1768–1841) *Annals of Bedale*, the long settle stood against the wall (Plate 42):[10]

> The open chimneys in the town,
> I think, are done away,
> And now here's greater comfort known,
> All near the fire may stay.
>
> They then at a great distance sit,
> And quite against the wall,
> Both form and settle, some had fit,
> Sofa, they'd none at all.

During the nineteenth century, perhaps to compensate for the gradual disappearance of heck seats, painted pine settles with high, often curved, screen backs solid to the ground and profiled slab ends became popular in Yorkshire farmhouses (Plate 43).

Other furnishings usually present in the forehouse were a corner cupboard, either a long table (sometimes with forms) or a gate-leg table, little round tables and a few chairs commonly described as panel, elbow, bass-bottom, wood-bottom, wanded or covered in leather. Stools and forms are fairly rare and upholstered seat furniture was virtually unknown. Items such as a milk spence, cradle, kneading trough, ark, knife-and-fork box, cheese shelves, spinning-wheel occur, but we are here chiefly concerned with broad patterns; and the evidence strongly suggests that the basic repertoire, like the houses themselves, was a direct response to community needs rather than fashion.

Wills can provide welcome additional information. In 1769 George Cloughton of Butterset bequeathed all his household goods to his wife 'excepting . . . the cupboard that makes Part of the Partition between the Forehouse and Parlour';[11] it is interesting to find a built-in cupboard used as a room-divider in the parish of Aysgarth, since this arrangement is normally associated with Lake District farm-houses. The will made by Anne Metcalfe of Hawes in 1770 mentions 'the little oak Stand which I usually dine upon, a Firr Deal Chest with a Drawer in the Bottom . . . and the Elbow Chair in which my late Husband usually sat'.[12] A final example is taken from the will of Richard Willson, fellmonger, of Richmond who, in 1766, bequeathed to his father 'a dozen new Chairs, one Dresser, one Corner Cupboard, one Tea table, one little Square Table . . . which I bought with my own money'. His wife was left 'three Bedsteads . . . together with the household Goods of every kind which she brought with her after our marriage'.[13] Bed hangings are rarely specified, which makes a reference in the will of John Sheppard of Cowfold (1758), to 'one Bedstead and hangings being checkt linen' noteworthy.[14]

Nearly every family in the region still used their unheated parlour as the main bedroom, although in many households it was also beginning to satisfy new needs (Plate 41). Most parlours contained, besides one or two bedsteads, a panelled chest or chest of drawers for storing clothes and linen, a cupboard, at least one table and frequently a set of chairs. If the owner possessed a bureau, 'seeing glass' or pictures, they would be here. Typical ensembles can be quoted from the inventories of Henry Lodge of Stainton (1752): 'A Bed and Chest of Drawers, a Table, a Cudboard and six Chairs & a spinning Wheel'[15] and John Bucktrout of Whixley (1761): 'A Bed & Bedding, Bedstead, Ovel Table & Six Chairs & Corner Cupboard, a Square Table, Two Brass Candlesticks, a Shelf'.[16] The infiltration into the sleeping apartment of tables and chairs shows that by 1750, it had become a dual-purpose room; by the end of the century all the bedroom furniture had been moved upstairs and the status of

43. Pine settle from Uckerby Grange Farm, Scorton, North Yorkshire, originally painted buff. High screen-back settles superceded the 'lang settles' recorded in many eighteenth-century inventories of North Country farmhouse kitchens. *Private collection*

the parlour as a place where the family could take meals and entertain was fully accepted. These North Yorkshire inventories record the parlour on the threshold of change when social pressures were creating new furnishing schemes.

Because fresh milk soured quickly, butter and cheese making was a traditional part of the rural economy. The dairy or milkhouse, which needed to be cool, was often situated in a separate outshut or back-kitchen, the main requirements being stone slabs, a cheese-press, churns, racks, shelves (Plate 44), stands, firkins and wooden utensils. Some farms also had a cheese loft provided with racks for storing hardened cheese away from new moist cheeses. In 1756 Thomas Smith of Ripley kept in his Out Kitchen: '2 Iron Kettles; 2 Cheese Presses & 2 Cheese Troughs; one Barrill Churn & Frame; 2 Cream Stands; 6 Skeels, 2 Swiles, One Mash Tub & Four Barrels & other Householdments'.[17] This room clearly also functioned as a brewhouse. Washing-tubs and a 'winter hedge', the northern name for a clothes-horse, were also often recorded in the back-kitchen.

Robert Hird, in his *Annals of Bedale* (a village not far from Richmond), remembered a time in the late eighteenth century when the local houses were all of one storey with attics:[18]

> I think I here may safely say,
> All houses near as one
> One storey high Roof windows they
> Into the Chambers shone.

The low attic chambers in these cottages made very poor bedrooms which is why the upstairs was generally used for storage and inferior sleeping accommodation. John Bucktrout used his chamber for: '12 Bushell of Rye, 5 Bushell of Meslin, 3 Bushell of Barley, A Bed & Bedstead & Bedding & Hangings, A Half Bushell, a Kneading Trough, Two Churns'.[19] By the early 1800s, two-storied brick and stone buildings had largely replaced cruck-framed dwellings, and in the Dales thatch was just giving way to slate — a conversion that involved flattening the roof pitch by raising the walls, thus creating loftier upper rooms. These architectural improvements (which happened earlier in Richmond than the surrounding villages), soon led to the abandonment of the parlour bedroom and ushered in new standards of material comfort. The Great Rebuilding, as this comprehensive upgrading of the housing stock is known,[20] occurred two centuries earlier in parts of southern England; while at Arnol, a village of blackhouses on the west side of Lewis in the Hebrides, it did not happen until the 1920s, which serves as a warning that the study of vernacular architecture and furniture is an intensely local matter.

The traditional blackhouses at Arnol, built about 1875, were mostly vacated when modern two-storey brick houses were built for the community during the inter-war years. One has been preserved as an historic monument, but the others are now roofless ruins, abandoned with their original ensembles of furniture left *in situ* (Plates 46–8). It is apparent that until the end, each fire-room had a standard 'kit', dictated by custom consisting of a dresser, pair of box beds and long settle, just as in the eighteenth century, farmhouse kitchens in the Richmond area of North Yorkshire contained a distinctive repertoire of furniture. The pine pieces at Arnol, all strikingly uniform in design, were often constructed of driftwood; the drawer of the dresser illustrated actually being made from an Aberdeen fish-box.

The fact that the Archdeaconry of Richmond inventories tail off after 1770 is disappointing, because for our purposes the later ones are the most interesting. However, by rare good fortune, twenty-seven inventories have been traced amongst the Poor Law papers of Arkengarthdale,[21] a remote parish in upper Swaledale with a population of miners and sheep farmers. They list the possessions of paupers receiving out-relief, most of whom were, by definition, old or infirm and living in reduced circumstances; a splendidly detailed picture emerges of how their homes were furnished. The documents are sadly undated, but can be assigned

44. An early nineteenth-century Welsh (Carmarthen) dairy dresser in oak, the platform base was for milk churns, the shelves for cheeses. *Courtesy Gabriel Olive*

45. Interior of a cottage in Dent on the Yorkshire–Lancashire border by C.W. Cope, *c.* 1840, detail showing a squab under the window and a Lancashire pattern ladder-back chair. *Trustees of the Victoria and Albert Museum*

46–48. Three views showing driftwood furniture in a roofless blackhouse built at Arnol on the west side of Lewis, in the Hebrides about 1875. One of the modern houses built *c.* 1930 is just visible in the background. The drawer lining of the dresser is made from an Aberdeen fish-box. Every house had a long settle and twin box beds fronted by curtains.

49. (*Opposite*) *Cottage Interior with an Old Woman Preparing Tea* by W.R. Bigg, oil-painting dated 1793. The tea things are set out on a typical tripod stand, the chair is draped with a rug; notice also the traditional warming-pan and clock. *Trustees of the Victoria and Albert Museum*

to the 1820–30 period. Compared with the earlier probate inventories we have analysed from this region, it is significant that while long-case clocks, dressers and rails, delf racks, corner cupboards, kitchen tables and of course chairs still abound, very few chests are recorded and long settles have been generally replaced by the 'squab' — a couch with an upholstered seat (Plate 45). Twice, the compiler has crossed out the word 'long settle' and inserted 'squab'. Also, most of the living-kitchens now contained 'a round stand' and 'a tea-table'. The former was a common

type of circular table supported on three stick legs (see Plates 41 and 49); the latter, at which light meals were taken, was of ordinary tripod base design with a turned pillar and round, usually tip-up top, also named a 'snap' table (see Plate 55). Many kitchens had a 'fleak', that is a rack suspended from the ceiling on which soft oatcakes – the traditional diet of Dalesmen – were placed after being cooked on the bakestone (Plate 50). Other statistically noteworthy items are greatly increased numbers of spinning-wheels, seeing-glasses, pictures, tea-trays and, curiously, stools when compared with the 1750–70 probate inventories. Upholstered seat furniture when it occurs, was generally covered with leather (Plates 51 and 52).

William Marshall, author of *The Rural Economy of Yorkshire* (1788), referred to an interesting north-east Yorkshire custom known as the 'bride-wain'. This was the name given to a waggon loaded with household furniture and utensils which travelled from the bride's father's house to the bridegroom's house. 'Formerly, a great parade and ceremony were observed on this occasion. The wains were drawn by oxen, whose horns and heads were ornamented with ribbons, a young

50. In the north of England, flakes or creels were suspended under the kitchen ceiling and used for keeping loaves, bacon, soft oatcakes and the like safe from mice. This stained-pine Victorian example is from the Colne Valley, Yorkshire. *Colne Valley Museum, Golcar*

51. A late eighteenth-century elm settle with original basic upholstery and leather cover secured by brass-headed nails. Probably from Yorkshire. *Calderdale Museums Service*

52. Underside of the settle stuffed with hay, curled hair and sheeps' wool supported by canvas, scrim, ticken and a corded bottom.

53. Small wall cupboard, typical of many found in North Country farmhouses. They often bear initials and dates between *c.* 1670 and 1720. Hutton Buscel, Mole End, North York Moors. *Royal Commission on Historical Monuments, England*

woman at her spinning-wheel is seated on the centre of the load. In passing through towns and villages, the bride's friends and acquaintance throw up articles of furniture, until the "draught" is at last feigned to be overloaded; and at length set fast'.[22] The Revd. J.C. Atkinson, vicar of the moorland parish of Danby, near Whitby, who was also aware of the tradition, related that when he first came to the district in 1847: 'There were few farmhouses in which there was not one of those fine old black oak cabinets with carved panels, folding doors and knobby feet ... many times I have heard the name "bride-wain" attributed to them ... a handsome press stored with linen and provisions was one of the customary wedding gifts and so by an easy transition of idea the piece itself came to be called a bride-wain'.[23] Indeed, many surviving cupboards are carved with a date and the initials of a married couple. Interesting additional evidence about this time-honoured wedding gift is to be found in the writings of Robert Hird: 'Humphrey Davis, my great maternal grandfather, (or my grandmother's father) was by trade a joiner, and we yet have an Oak Dresser that he made for his daughter after that she had got married and after her death that my aunt Mary had left Westmorland, it was brought from Brough to Bedale, and by us is held in great esteem'.[24]

The Revd. Atkinson's *Forty Years in a Moorland Parish* largely inspired the foundation of the Ryedale Folk Museum which collects local furniture to place in re-erected cottages. The hearth wall in many of these buildings contains two recesses enclosed by small wooden doors; the upper one was a spice cupboard (Plate 53), while the lower served as a salt-box and, to avoid corrosion, had either leather or pin hinges.[25] Similar fireside 'keeping holes', often with carved, initialled and dated doors, survive from an earlier time in Lake District farmhouses.[26] Adjacent to the fireplace was a wooden partition or 'speer' supporting a fixed seat and having a robust square post at the end — this screen formed one side of the ingle-nook. In some of the seventeenth and early eighteenth-century houses on the North York Moors, the square upright functioned as a 'witch post'. To give protection against witches it had to be made of rowan tree and was boldly incised with a St Andrew's cross (Plate 54). About a dozen witch posts from this part of Yorkshire have been recorded: they are possibly a unique instance of the interplay of (built-in) furniture and superstition.[27]

PUBLIC REPORTS AND PRIVATE MEMOIRS

Parliamentary reports contain welcome information about rural housing during the Industrial Revolution period. Some *Local Reports on the Sanitary Conditions of the Labouring Population of England* (1842) even give details of how the homes of agricultural workers were furnished: the contributions of E.C. Tuffnell, an Assistant Poor Law Commissioner who collected evidence in Kent and Sussex, are particularly rewarding in this respect:[28]

> I will first describe the cottage and mode of living of a Sussex labourer, whose family is such as to make him one of the most distressed of his class. He has a wife and seven children. On entering, the cottage displays a room about 20 feet long by 15, paved with brick, and nearly divided into two by a partition; the fire-place is here, and it forms the sitting-room of the family. The furniture consists of one common looking deal table, a rather elegant round oak one, with moveable flaps, mahogany cupboard, and six chairs; there are curtains to the window. Adjoining is a pantry, which seems filled with all sorts of cooking utensils, and a bakehouse. Up stairs there are two bedrooms, in one of which the man, his wife, and the baby sleep, and in the other, which contains three beds, the rest of the children.

A second cottage that he visited was inhabited by a widower with four children:

> The first room on entering is the kitchen, about 18 feet square, and which contains five neat cushioned chairs, two rush-bottomed ones, a deal table, a

mahogany one, a mahogany commode, a shelf neatly adorned with crockery. There are curtains to the windows, and a handsome clock *case*, the works of which are gone, I suppose to pay a debt. A wash-house opens from this room. There are two bed-rooms up stairs, which I did not enter.

The Commissioner then reported on two labourers' cottages in Tunbridge Wells. The first, rented by a couple with six children, was 'a very old building of wood' with two ground-floor rooms and two bedrooms in the roof. 'The furniture of the sitting room of the family is very old and shabby, and consists of a painted chest of drawers, a very rickety old oaken table, six old chairs, a bit of old calico by way of a window curtain and a swinging shelf containing one or two religious books.' A similar wooden cottage tenanted by a man, his wife and four children had 'a neat, cleanly and orderly appearance'. The sitting room, ten feet square, contained 'two plain deal tables and a very small stained one, a neat corner cupboard, three shelves with earthenware; a few small ornaments are on the chimney-piece, and above it hang some small prints in black frames. There is a calico window curtain, two small bits of carpet on the floor, a cradle, four chairs, and an arm-chair. Some swinging book-shelves, with religious books'. An illustration published in 1846 records the interior of a Dorsetshire labourer's cottage (Plate 55).

It is clear from Tuffnell's analysis of these families' weekly incomes, expenditure and diet, that they were living on the poverty threshold; yet their homes were better furnished than those of many factory workers (see Plate 77). The oval gate-leg table was presumably ancient, but the presence of mahogany, deal and painted softwood pieces (probably grained to simulate expensive timbers), implies that the rural tradition of plain joiner-made oak furniture had expired in these counties, although it continued to flourish in Wales and parts of the North. The record reveals an interesting mixture of functional and elegant furniture such as deal and mahogany tables or rush-bottomed and upholstered chairs. The chimney ornaments, swinging bookshelves,[29] framed prints, displays of china and fragments of carpet in one of the rooms betrays a desire for a smart front parlour which, before the end of the century, was to come within the reach of many farm-labourer's wives.

Christopher Holdenby, a man of education who deliberately set out to share the life of farm labourers in the Kent/Sussex district, described his experiences in *Folk of the Furrow* (1913). He gives a remarkable account of the inconvenient, uncom-

54. Oak witch post in its traditional position at the end of the heck forming the back of an ingle-seat. Quarry Farm, Glaisdale, North York Moors. *Royal Commission on Historical Monuments, England*

55. Interior of a Dorsetshire labourer's cottage, the dresser reflects a regional design while a 'screen table' with circular tip-up top stands against the rear wall. *Illustrated London News* (1846)

fortable and cramped living conditions in the cottages where he lodged.[30] The small living-rooms generally contained one table, a bench, four chairs, a cupboard, range and copper which, on washing days, made the room unbearably oppressive and steamy. Because family life centred round the kitchen fire, there was room for what he calls a 'stuffed bird parlour' for the mother to keep her best things in such as wedding gifts: it often contained the only carpet and was a keen source of pride. Although seldom used except for receiving visitors, the front parlour was an important room psychologically. Holdenby also remarked on the very small bedrooms which usually only allowed space for a bed, chair and wash-stand. In one cottage he had to stand in half his portmanteau to unpack the other half, and often dressed standing on the bed.

The want of sufficient bedroom accommodation in Wiltshire, Dorset, Devon and Somerset was commented on in the Poor Law Commissioners' *Report on the Employment of Women and Children in Agriculture* (1843). The investigator recorded: 'cottages generally have only two bed-rooms (with very rare exceptions); a great many have only one'. He deplored 'the general want of new cottages, notwithstanding the universal increase of population' and provided a diagram showing the position of three beds in a two-roomed cottage at Stourpain, near Blandford[31] (Plate 56). 'Bed A was occupied by the father and moher, a little boy, Jeremiah, aged 1½ year and an infant aged 4 months.' The three daughters slept in bed B and the four sons shared bed C. The room was only ten feet square and there was no curtain, or any kind of separation between the beds. Sleeping conditions were no better in Leeds back-to-back houses or on the North York Moors, where the sleeping loft on a farm at Kilton Castle was 'one long low room, partitioned off into four compartments . . . such as those between stalls in a stable . . . the general gangway for all the occupants was along the open back'. The first bed space was allotted to the couple and their two youngest children, the next to their older children, the third to the farm-girls and the fourth to the man and farm-lad.[32]

In Northumberland, where most labourers lived in one-roomed, single-storey buildings the common apartment was normally partitioned by box beds with sliding doors. In 1833 J.C. Loudon published a plan showing the disposition of furniture in a farm-worker's cottage on the Beaufront Castle estate, near Hexham (Plate 57), with the following explanation: '*a* is the porch inside the house. *b* a small bedroom. *d* is a small closet or dairy. *ee* shows one mode of placing the beds, by which one bed opening to the fireplace, and the other behind, some privacy is obtained for the occupiers of both; *f* is the situation of the dresser; *g* of the bride's chest of drawers and *h* of the press or cupboard'.[33] In 1842 Mr Grey of Dilston in the same neighbourhood told the inspecting Poor Law Commissioner that labourers' cottages were now built 'with a loft for the younger members of the family to sleep in, the access to it being by step-ladder'.[34] A splendid account of a shepherd's cottage in the Cheviots built on this pattern is to be found in William Howitt's *The Rural Life of England* (1838):

The part of the house on your left as you entered was divided into two rooms. The one was a sort of entrance lobby, where stood the cheese press, and the pails, and were hung up various shepherds plaids, great coats and strong shoes. The other little room was the dairy. Over these rooms, a step-ladder led to an open attic in the roof, which formed at once the sleeping apartment of the shepherds, and a store room. Here were three or four beds, some of them woollen mattresses on rude stump bedsteads; others, pieces of wicker-work, like the lower half of a pot-crate cut off, about half a yard high, filled with straw, and a few blankets laid upon it. There were lots of fleeces of wool stowed away. The half of the house on the right on entering, was at all points such as I have before described, with its coved and matted ceiling, its chintz cornice, and its two beds with sliding doors.[35]

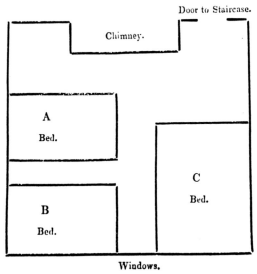

56. The bedroom (ten-feet square) of a cottage at Stourpain, Dorset, 1843. Bed A was shared by the parents and two youngest children; B was for their three daughters; C was for the four sons.

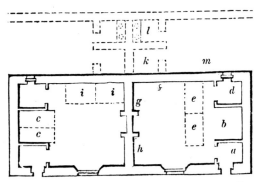

57. Plan showing interior arrangement of a day-labourer's cottage on the Beaufront estate, Northumberland, as recorded by J.C. Loudon in 1833.

Obviously Northumbrian cottages were very different from those in the South.

William Cobbett was aroused to anger by the social changes he observed in farmhouse life when attending a sale in Surrey in 1825:

> Here I had a view of what has long been going on all over the country. Everything about this farmhouse was formerly the scene of *plain manners* and *plentiful living*. Oak clothes-chests, oak bedsteads, oak chests of drawers, and oak tables to eat on, long, strong, and well supplied with joint stools. Some of the things were many hundreds of years old. But all appeared to be in a state of decay and nearly of *disuse*. There appeared to have been hardly any *family* in that house, where formerly there were, in all probability, from ten to fifteen men, boys, and maids; and, which was worst of all, there was a *parlour*. Aye, and a carpet and *bell-pull* too! One end of this house had been moulded into a 'parlour'; and there was the mahogany table, and the fine chairs, and the fine glass . . . This 'Squire' Charrington's father used, I daresay, to sit at the head of the oak table along with his men, say grace to them, and cut up the meat and pudding.[36]

He went on to deplore the trend towards 'painted shells of farmhouses, with a mistress within, who is stuck up in a place she calls a *parlour* . . . with some showy chairs and a sofa; half a dozen prints in gilt frames hanging up, some swinging bookshelves with novels and tracts upon them . . .'. The Revd. J.C. Atkinson of Danby on the North York Moors observed similar changes, noting that on his arrival in 1847 there was only one piano in the parish but 'it became supplemented in less than a score of years by some fifty or sixty other pianos and harmoniums'.[37]

The improvements in living standards which Cobbett ridiculed were made possible by the agricultural boom during the Napoleonic Wars but, as usual, his comments, while containing elements of truth, were exaggerated, for other evidence shows that if traditional farmhouse life was dying out, it was doing so slowly in many parts of the country. Gertrude Jekyll made exactly the same complaints in *Old West Surrey* (1904): 'Now alas, this fine old furniture is rare in these country dwellings. It has been replaced by wretched stuff, shoddy and pretentious. It is even more noticeable in the farmhouses, where even if a good piece or two remains, it is swamped by a quantity of things that are very flimsy and meretricious'.[38] Fortunately Miss Jekyll illustrated an anthology of traditional Surrey farmhouse furniture which now provides an important record of what both she and Cobbett regretted was fast disappearing from the countryside.

That it was the wives who insisted on having respectable furniture is borne out by the Minutes of Evidence given by Robert Merry of Luckton in North Yorkshire, to the Select Committee on Agriculture (1833), who were enquiring into the decline of living standards amongst agricultural labourers following the end of the Napoleonic Wars:

> Q. Do your perceive any difference in the furniture of their cottages?
> A. I cannot say there is much difference in that; I believe the cottagers' wives would rather suffer any hardship as not have useful, and what they call decent furniture; they pride themselves upon having a nice little furniture.[39]

An old Derbyshire farmer told S.O. Addy, author of *The Evolution of the English House* (1898), that in his youth: 'The master of the house and his servants had dinner in one and the same room – the kitchen – a large apartment. The master and his family sat at a table near the fire, and the servants at a long table on the opposite side of the room. First the master carved for his family and himself, and then the joint was passed on to the servants' table'.[40] Addy published a photograph and plan of a cruck house at Upper Midhope, near Penistone, Yorkshire, which still had a heavy carved oak servants' table standing at one end of the forehouse in front of a fixed oak bench, with forms on the other side and a round gate-leg table near the fire for the use of the farmer and his family; the illustration also shows a dresser and hanging corner cupboard. This house, like nearly all those recorded by Addy before 1898, had been destroyed or drastically altered when revisited by John Summerson about 1932.

In some parts of the country, instead of eating off wooden trenchers, the table at which the farm workers sat contained dished hollows.[41] Examples from Hertfordshire and Devon have been briefly recorded, but the best description comes from M.C.F. Morris's *Yorkshire Reminiscences* (1922): 'I was told of a resident of Tibthorpe who remembered, early last century, seeing a table the thick wooden top of which had round holes two inches deep and about the size of a dinner plate cut in it. Into these the broth and meat were poured and eaten with wooden spoons. The table had to be washed after every meal with hot water and soda'.[42] Tom Crispin, who in the 1940s saw one with a sycamore top at a farm near Ashridge, Hertfordshire, tells me they were known as 'harvest' tables.

George Plack, who farmed near Exeter, told the Commissioners collecting evidence for their *Report on the Employment of Women and Children in Agriculture* (1843): 'My father never made two tables in his house: that is still the case in many parts of Devonshire. My father is an old-fashioned man: he always sits in the kitchen, if there are no strangers there. All our family sit together. You may depend upon it that where farmers sit in parlours, apprentices are not so well looked after. Girls see boys only at dinner, and at night, when they all sit down in the kitchen together, the girls are there at needlework'.[43] It is important, when studying farmhouse furniture, not to lose sight of the fact that the partriarchal practice of unmarried servants eating and sitting with the family continued in parts of England well into the Victorian period. However, in those parts of Scotland where the bothy system prevailed, single labourers lived and slept well away from the farmhouse and, as Cobbett reported: 'never dream of being allowed to set foot within the farmhouse' (see Plate 375).

The evidence from Devon has a bearing on the pattern of furniture revealed in C.H. Laycock's memorable article 'The Devon Farmhouse its Interior Arrangements and Domestic Economy', published in 1922.[44] He wrote at a time when some

58. Oak kitchen table of *c.* 1800 with turn-over top from a North Devon farmhouse. *Courtesy Gabriel Olive*

60. (*Opposite, right*) Shropshire dresser, the matching frieze and apron prove that the two stages have always been together. Oak, *c.* 1800. *Courtesy McCartney's Salerooms, Ludlow*

61. (*Opposite, far right*) Elm dresser of a regional type common in the Bridgwater area of Somerset, late eighteenth century. Pine cornice and feet not original. *Courtesy Gabriel Olive*

remote Devon farmhouses were unmodernized and thus drew on personal observation which can no longer be readily gained from field-work. Traditional farmhouses had a best front-kitchen – the living-room – and a smaller rear-kitchen. Along the window wall was a fixed wooden bench, extending the full length of a long table placed before it with forms on the opposite side. A deep recess next to the fireplace contained a large built-in cupboard; the lower stage enclosed by double doors, was used for storing groceries, while the upper part often had open shelves for displaying china (see Plate 25). A large oak corner cupboard for keeping preserves, cordials, et cetera, stood in the corner on the right-hand side of the hearth; it, too, was a fixture. The bacon-rack, a square framework with a slatted bottom, was suspended from the ceiling in the left-hand corner near the fire. The principal item of movable furniture was a long framed elm or oak table standing in front of the windows, around which the whole household could sit at meal times — the farmer and his family at one end, dining off pewter plates; the servants at the other, using wooden trenchers. Knives and forks were kept in a box hung on the wall, the front sliding up in a groove; pewter spoons might be displayed on a rack. The table generally had a loose reversible top, one side being scrubbed for kitchen use, the polished surface turned over for meals (Plate 58).

Every Devon farmhouse kitchen boasted a dresser, the lower stage often containing two cupboards and three drawers with a shelved pewter-rack above. Laycock was unaware of any local design types, although dealers and collectors are now able to recognize various regional patterns (Plates 59, 60 and 61). In addition to open dressers, the closed or cupboard dresser for keeping china was also found in the

59. Penzance dresser, pine originally painted, *c.* 1830, with a typical arrangement of drawers and bow-fronted upper stage. *Courtesy Gabriel Olive*

62. Curved settle made of wide painted elm boards with a shelf below the seat, West Country, probably Dorset, late eighteenth century. *Courtesy Gabriel Olive*

West Country (Plate 64). Grandfather clocks – known in Devon as 'long-sleeve clocks' – always stood in the best kitchen. On the side of the fireplace, away from the window, stood a curved settle with a high back reaching almost to the ceiling (Plate 62). Many had box seats and often incorporated a full-height bacon cupboard in the back (Plate 65), which opened to reveal strong iron hooks from which large sides of bacon hung to be kept dry and away from flies. Occasionally these settles were fronted by two long cupboards across the top for groceries. Devon farmhouse settles, commonly of oak or elm, varied in length but were generally curved and movable — not fixtures. Very rarely, a kitchen might have two settles which could be hooked together to form a semicircle around the fire. On the opposite side of the hearth the 'maister's' chair – often a venerable oak armchair – was found. Other forms of seating were Windsor chairs and low 'cricket' stools for children. Small stools, immortalized in Dickens's story *The Cricket on the Hearth* (1846), were present in most houses (see Plates 63, 234 and 241).

The Revd. Francis Kilvert, in his diary under 14 October 1870, recorded how eighty or ninety years ago in Clyro: 'The old people would sit around the fire talking on the long winter evenings, and Hannah, then a child of 8 or 10 would sit on a little stool by her grandfather's chair in the chimney corner listening while they told their old world stories and tales of the "fairies" in whom they fully believed'.[45] The only other routine articles of furniture mentioned by Laycock was the salt-box which hung on the wall by the fireplace and the flour hutch.

Recessed cupboards, with open shelves headed by a shell-niche in the upper stage and enclosed by a door below, were common features of town houses in the West Country. Three were recorded in a recent survey of the Trinity district of Frome, while another survives in the main reception-room of Silver Street House, Bradford-on-Avon.[46] These examples are sub-classical in style and properly belong within a fashionable provincial context, yet they relate to the fitted cupboards characteristic of Devon farmhouses.[47]

PICTORIAL RECORDS

After reading Laycock's orderly account of Devon farmhouse kitchens, it comes as something of a jolt to encounter Wheatley's remarkable watercolour of a farmhouse at Oare on Exmoor, dated 1849, which displays every appearance of being a genuine study but features none of the traditional furniture we have been led to expect (Plate 66). Conceivably its very eccentricity inspired the artist to make a detailed sketch, but I prefer to regard this drawing as a welcome corrective to any neat and tidy interpretation of historical evidence. Presumably farmhouses in the hills were very different from lowland farmsteads, while town houses tell yet another story.

Thomas Rowlandson's lively illustrations to the various *Tours of Dr Syntax* make no claim to topographical accuracy. He was, however, an acute observer and his cottage interior (Plate 67), inn parlour (see Plate 136) and country alehouse (see Plate 121), while generalized, certainly contain information of value to furniture historians. In the kitchen interior *Dr Syntax Turned Nurse*, details such as the wash-tub raised on a stand, the table stationed under the window, the arrangement of plates and jugs on the dresser and many other features, ring far truer than the majority of book illustrations treating rustic interiors.

Travellers who published journals aimed to give an authentic record of the habits and customs of remote communities. Thomas Pennant's *Voyage to the Hebrides* in 1772 is typical of the genre. His precise illustration of a weaver's cottage on Islay (Plate 68) is of capital interest. The husband is seen at a loom and his wife is seated on the bed, partly screened by washing. Children and an old woman huddle round the central hearth and the wretched furniture appears to be home-made, probably of driftwood. The engraving can safely be accepted as a faithful record of living conditions on this Scottish island.

The *Illustrated London News* was renowned for pictorial accuracy, and liberal use has been made of images from this source. The interior of a dwelling on Skye published in 1853 (Plate 69) shows a blackhouse in which the cattle lived at one end and the family occupied the other, partitioned into a fire-room and a sleeping-room, all under one roof. The dresser, which became popular when china plates were easily obtainable, and a traditional long settle are shown, also two low stools, one with a

63. Low stool made of ash, commonly known in the north of England as a 'cricket' or 'buffet'. Reputedly owned by Mary Anne Cotton, the West Aukland murderess, who was hanged at Durham gaol in 1873 for poisoning her children to claim their funeral money. *Beamish Museum*

64. (*Opposite, above, far left*) North Devon cupboard dresser in oak, *c.* 1810, used in the farmhouse kitchen for storing china and groceries. *Courtesy Gabriel Olive*

65. (*Opposite, above, left*) Oak settle from West Somerset with a box seat and cupboard back headed by drawers, eighteenth century, probably third quarter. The cupboard was for hanging bacon or keeping groceries. *Courtesy Gabriel Olive*

66. *Farmhouse at Oare on Exmoor*, watercolour by W.W. Wheatley, dated 1849. This amazing room suggests that many views of domestic interiors are idealized. *Somerset Archaeology Society*

67. *Dr Syntax Turned Nurse* by T. Rowlandson, 1820. A generalized but observant view of a cottage interior.

68. A weaver's cottage on Islay, Scotland, from T. Pennant's *Voyage to the Hebrides* (1772), recording the home of 'a set of people worn down by poverty'.

horseshoe-shaped seat typical of the Celtic fringe. The record of furniture is in fact so exact that it can be accepted as primary evidence for the study of regional design. A somewhat later view (1881) of a fisherman's cottage on the Isle of Man (Plate 70) is especially fascinating because farmhouse kitchens are a much more familiar subject with Victorian artists. That the repertoire of furniture is accurately portrayed can be confirmed by comparison with extant examples. The tall panelled armchair and the two with rail backs are characteristically Manx, as is the small round eating-table, while the soft fabric draped over the mother's rocking-chair is an interesting detail. From this very brief survey of pictorial records it is obvious that, if selected and interpreted with care, they have plenty to offer.

LOUDON'S FURNITURE DESIGNS

69. (*Opposite, above*) The fire-room in a black-house on the Isle of Skye with a sleeping-room beyond, the dresser, bench and stool with a U-shaped seat are typical furnishings. *Illustrated London News* (1853)

70. (*Opposite, below*) Fisherman's cottage on the Isle of Man containing a typical repertoire of Manx furniture. *Illustrated London News* (1881)

J.C. Loudon's prodigious *Encyclopaedia of Cottage, Farm, and Villa Architecture and Furniture* (1833) documents every aspect of building and furnishing rural houses. It is best regarded in the context of the contemporary spate of books containing designs for model farmhouses, which was itself a reflection of the social changes in rural life observed by William Cobbett and others. Loudon employed the term 'cottager' to include 'not only labourers, mechanics and country tradesmen, but small farmers . . . gardeners and upper servants of gentlemen's estates'. He believed that 'a clean,

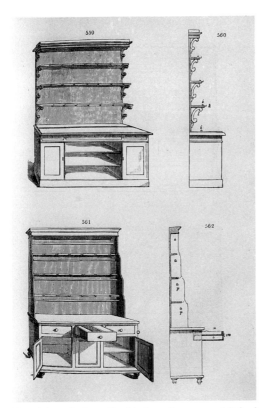

71. Two designs for kitchen dressers published in 1833 by J.C. Loudon who describes exactly how they were intended to be used by the housewife. The lower one was 'used in the better description of cottage dwellings in Cambridgeshire'.

72. Design for a corner cupboard recommended by J.C. Loudon in 1833 as being very convenient in small rooms for china, glasses, the tea-caddy, liquors, etc.

comfortable and well arranged home . . . ought to be sought after and obtained by everyone', and aimed to consolidate recent advances in domestic comfort by describing what an industrious labourer should be able to afford in the way of furniture, rather than advocating a Utopian vision: therein lies the importance of his text and illustrations. The pieces he describes fall into three groups: traditional furniture such as dressers, corner cupboards, simple tables, kneading troughs and settles; articles reflecting commercially fashionable Gothic or Grecian idioms (intended for estate cottages built in these styles), and thirdly items exploiting modern industrial processes, for example tables and chairs with cast-iron supports and wrought-iron bedsteads. The objects displaying 'a more elevated style of design' shed an interesting light on the disintegration of the Georgian vernacular tradition and changing character of the furniture trade.

Loudon's commentary opens with a classic account of kitchen dressers:[48]

Dressers are generally made of deal by joiners, and seldom painted, it being the pride of good housewives, in most parts of England, to keep the boards as white as snow, by frequently scouring them with fine white sand. In old farm-houses, the dressers are generally of oak rubbed bright, and the shelves are filled with rows of pewter plates, &c, polished by frequent cleaning, till they shine like silver. When there is a pot-board affixed to the dresser, it is usually painted black or chocolate colour; and when the shelves and fronts are painted, it is generally white, or, what is in better taste, the same colour as the walls or doors.

The pot-board was for pots, tea-kettles, saucepans, etc., used on the fire (hence the black paint), and the shelves usually had hooks fixed in the front edges 'on which jugs and any small articles having handles may be hung'. Dressers either had cross bars which allowed the plates to lean forward 'so as to protect their faces from dust' or either a bead or groove along the shelves 'to support the plates and dishes in a reclining position against the back'.

Loudon illustrated a dresser in the Grecian style with 'two side-closets, and, in the middle, shelves [Plate 71 top]. There are three drawers above: the centre one for tablecloths, towels, &c.; and the two side ones, for knives, forks, and spoons, and the other for dusters, brushes, &c. In one of the cupboards below may be kept what wines or spirits are in daily use, glasses, &c.; and, in the other, bread, biscuits, groceries, or any other articles of food. The tea-tray and teacups may be put on the upper middle shelf, and the smaller saucepans, &c on the bottom one'. This is by far the most fascinating description one is ever likely to find of how dressers were intended to be used. Loudon also features a design for a dresser found 'in the better description of cottage dwellings in Cambridgeshire' (Plate 71 bottom). The three drawers were for cutlery, nappery and dusters, while 'the cupboard in front is made into two cupboards, in one of which may be kept glasses, teacups, &c.; and in the other, the liquors, fruits, sweetmeats, &c.; in daily use'.

If, according to the author, the dresser lacked cupboards, 'a corner cupboard becomes requisite for cups and saucers, glasses, the tea-caddy, liquors, &c'. They were recommended as being very convenient in small rooms 'as they occupy very little space, and, for a moderate sum, supply a handsome article of furniture' (Plate 72). Loudon illustrated two specimens, remarking that 'the shelves, which are supposed to be of deal, are let into the plaster; and the whole, outside and inside, including the plaster between the shelves, is painted of a wainscot colour. The cost will be considerably diminished by having the upper doors in single wooden panels'.[49]

Kitchen tables, he advised, 'ought to be strong, and, if possible, they should be contrived to fold up, in order to afford more room'. Kneading troughs (Plate 73) apparently performed double duty as 'economical kitchen tables in cottages and small farm-houses in many parts of England':

73. Elm kneading trough for keeping flour and kneading dough; it could also function as a kitchen-table or ironing-board. Early nineteenth century. *Bradford Museums*

The cover, which, when on the trough, serves as a table or ironing-board, either lifts off, or, being hinged, is placed so as when opened it may lean against the wall. Frequently a division is made in the centre of the trough, so that the dry flour can be kept in one compartment, and the dough made in the other. Sometimes there are three compartments, in order to keep separate two different kinds of flour or meal. The board forming the cover ought to be an inch and a half thick, and always in one piece, in order that neither dirt nor dust may drop through the joints. There ought to be four fillets nailed along the underside of each edge of the cover, so as to keep it exactly in its place when on'.[50]

In the West Country, as we have seen, kitchen dining-tables often had a loose top which could be reversed to form a working surface. In other areas it was common for a scrubbed pine or sycamore table-board to be placed on the top to provide a clean surface for kitchen work.

When discussing seat furniture, Loudon commented that forms 'often serve in the scullery as stands for tubs, and for various articles to be washed or cleaned, to prevent stooping more than is necessary'.[51] He also illustrates several benches, one of which has, beneath the seat, a platform 'about three inches from the ground, on which a dog may have a mat for sleeping upon' — it is this kind of detail that makes the *Encyclopaedia* so interesting. However, other ideas, such as the suggestion that high-backed settles might usefully have a towel-roller, bookshelves or a hinged table flap fixed to the back or, alternatively, 'could be ornamented with prints or maps, in the manner of a screen', are likely to be the result of his improving turn of mind, rather than direct reporting of personal observation.

The End of a Tradition

Flora Thompson's famous portrait of rural life blended with autobiography, *Lark Rise to Candleford* (1945), describes the hamlet of Juniper Hill in Oxfordshire in the

1880s. Like the society she describes, none of the buildings now remain, but her chronicle vividly captures the final dissolution of the old cottage economy and contains memorable accounts of cottage interiors. The Revd. Francis Kilvert, curate of Clyro in Herefordshire, has also left a wonderful journal (1870–9) recording the age-old way of life which he did not realize was fast being destroyed by the intrusion of railways. Flora Thompson deserves to be liberally quoted[52] because her written evidence has the ring of truth, and is certainly more authentic than romantic Victorian paintings of cottage interiors. Writing of the homes of agricultural workers she says:

> In nearly all the cottages there was but one room downstairs, and many of these were poor and bare, with only a table and a few chairs and stools for furniture and a superannuated potato-sack thrown down by way of hearthrug. Other rooms were bright and cosy, with dressers of crockery, cushioned chairs, pictures on the walls and brightly coloured hand-made rag rugs on the floor. In the older cottages there were grandfathers' clocks, gate-legged tables, and rows of pewter, relics of a time when life was easier for country folk.

The largest house in the hamlet known as 'Old Sallys':

> . . . was a long, low, thatched cottage with diamond-paned windows winking under the eaves. Of the two downstair rooms one was used as a kind of kitchen-storeroom, with pots and pans and a big red crockery water vessel at one end, and potatoes in sacks and peas and beans spread out to dry at the other. The apple crop was stored on racks suspended beneath the ceiling and bunches of herbs dangled below. The inner room – 'the house' as it was called – was a perfect snuggery. There was a good oak, gate-legged table, a dresser with pewter and willow-pattern plates, and a grandfather's clock that not only told the time but the days of the week as well.

According to Flora Thompson, to visit the homes of the present generation was:

> . . . to step into another chapter in the hamlet's history. In their houses the good, solid, hand-made furniture of their forefathers had given place to the cheap and ugly products of the early machine age. A deal table, the top ribbed and softened by much scrubbing; four or five windsor chairs with the varnish blistered and flaking; a side table for the family photographs and ornaments, and a few stools for fireside seats, together with the beds upstairs, made up the collection spoken of by its owners as 'our few sticks of furniture'. If the father had a special chair, it would be but a rather larger replica of the hard windsors with wooden arms added. The clock, if any, was a cheap, foreign timepiece, standing on the mantelshelf. The few poor crocks were not good enough to keep on show . . . pewter plates and dishes as ornaments had gone.

Sharp insights into these changing social attitudes towards furniture are given:

> The homes of newly married couples illustrated a new phase in the hamlet's history. It had become the custom for the bride to buy the bulk of the furniture with her savings in service. When the bride bought the furniture, she would try to obtain things as nearly as possible like those in the houses where she was employed. Instead of the hard windsor chairs of her childhood's home, she would have small 'parlour' chairs with round backs and seats covered with horse hair or American cloth. The deal centre table would be covered with a brightly coloured woollen cloth between meals and cookery operations. On the chest of drawers which served as a sideboard, her wedding presents would be displayed — a best tea-service, a shaded lamp, a case of silver tea-spoons with the lid propped open, or a pair of owl pepper-boxes. Two wicker arm-chairs by the hearth would have cushions and antimacassars of the bride's own working.

Flora Thompson identified three categories of cottage household in Lark Rise: the old order supporting traditional pre-industrial domestic values (Plate 74); an impoverished next generation in which this inherited rural culture survived in a weakened state and the younger generation who followed modern fashions. The small Oxfordshire community is thus portrayed as socially complex, the differences of each group being reflected in the furnishing of their homes. The author also gives a rare insight into how indifference and the new vogue for antique-collecting (Plate 75) was robbing cottages:

> Sometimes a travelling tinker or casual callers would buy a set of hand-wrought, brass drop-handles from an inherited chest of drawers for sixpence; or a corner cupboard, or a gate-legged table which had become slightly infirm, for half a crown. Other such articles of furniture were put out of doors and spoilt by the weather, for the new generation did not value such things; it preferred the products of its own day, and, gradually the hamlet was being stripped of such relics.

Although manuscript and printed sources contain information of inestimable value about how rural houses were furnished at different times and in various parts of the

74. *The Love Letter* by J. Lomax (1857–1923). This pleasing cottage interior combines traditional furniture with 'parlour' objects such as the geraniums, japanned tea-tray, china dog and prints. *Courtesy Sotheby's*

country, they are less relevant for the study of regional design types. Energetic field-work is the only way to identify local vernacular traditions but, apart from Dr Cotton's outstanding work on regional chair styles and a few exhibition catalogues,[53] published research on this subject has been only sporadic. Gabriel Olive's archive on West Country settles and dressers[54] shows what an important contribution can be made by knowledgeable antique dealers who have 'worked' an area for many years. James Brett of Norwich has identified a distinctive form of East Anglian linen-press mounted on a chest of drawers, the unique feature being either two shallow drawers or a small panelled cupboard between the upper pair of narrow drawers and often an applied wavy moulding beneath the top (Plate 76). David Jones recently drew attention to a particular type of lowland Scottish chest of drawers

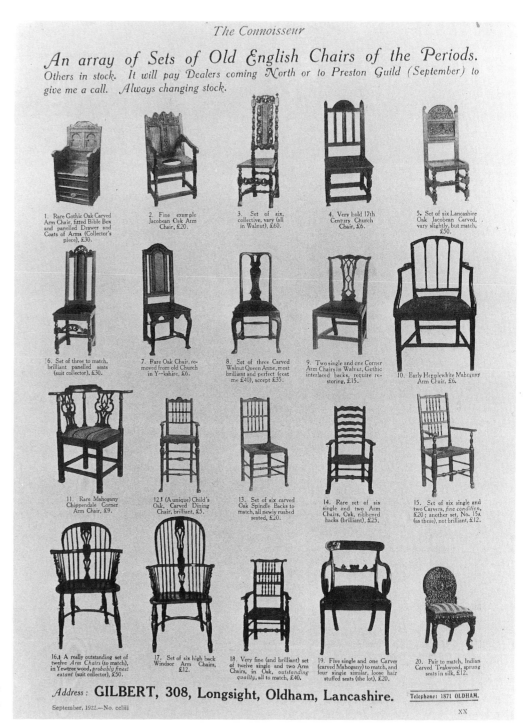

75. This advertisement placed in *Connoisseur* for September 1922 suggests the scale of losses from cottage homes.

76. Late eighteenth-century oak linen-press on chest of drawers from Carrow Abbey, Norwich. East Anglian models are distinctive in having, between the upper pair of narrow drawers, either a small panelled cupboard or a pair of shallow block-fronted drawers and often an applied wavy moulding beneath the top. *Private collection*

characterized by a deep square top drawer used for stowing bonnets.[55] Tom Crispin and Alun Davies have written about Welsh regional furniture, while horologists are becoming aware of strong local variations in the design of provincial clock cases. The result of this and similar research on chairs, beds and Books of Prices has been digested in appropriate chapters; however, much pioneering work remains to be done on charting regional traditions in Georgian vernacular furniture.

5 Urban Working-Class Homes

Because physical evidence of the first major phase of urbanization has mostly been destroyed by slum clearances, and information as to how working-class homes were furnished is, on the whole, meagre, any research programme has to rely mainly on Parliamentary Reports, the writings of journalists, philanthropists and other middle-class observers, scattered pictorial sources and elusive archival material. It is now clear that the Victorian housing problem was, in reality, a poverty problem: the poor simply could not afford to rent decent accommodation and this resulted in appalling overcrowding, squalor and a general lack of possessions. The plight of the labouring classes was described by Thomas Beames in *The Rookeries of London* (1852), by Andrew Mearns in his *The Bitter Cry of Outcast London* (1883) and most memorably in Henry Mayhew's *London Labour and the London Poor* (1861). Although these and other surveys are concerned primarily with social history, authentic information can be gleaned from them about domestic furniture. The possessions of families without regular employment were minimal, but there was also an artisan class with higher earnings who could afford good houses and furniture: handloom weavers in Leeds during the boom years 1780–1820; Nottingham lace workers *c.* 1785–1825; weavers in the Lancashire cotton district *c.* 1785–1815 and coal miners. The compensation claims of victims of the 'Sheffield Flood' of 1864 indicate that the homes of skilled workers in regular employment contained bedsteads, tables, chairs, either a cupboard or chest of drawers and kitchen utensils.[1] This chapter concentrates on the furniture of urban working-class homes without becoming sidetracked into a history of housing.

CELLAR DWELLINGS

Cellars were amongst the most notorious kind of habitation although some had, in fact, originally been designed for residential purposes; they were particularly common in Liverpool, Manchester and the older northern towns. In 1869, Isabella Bird described a coal cellar in Edinburgh: 'the plenishings consisted of an old bed, a barrel with a flagstone on the top for a table, a three-legged stool and an iron pot. A heap of straw, partly covered with sacking was the bed in which father, son and daughter slept'.[2] This damp windowless room with no grate and an earth floor measuring 11 × 6 feet cost 10d. a week. Robert Baker, writing about Leeds in 1842, reported: 'I have been in one of these damp cellars, without the slightest drainage . . . two corded frames for beds, overlaid with sacks for five persons; scarcely anything in the room else to sit on, but a stool, or a few bricks; the floor, in many places absolutely wet; a pig in the corner also'.[3] In 1833 Peter Gaskell estimated 20,000 living in cellars in Manchester and Duncan claimed there were 40,000 cellar dwellers in Liverpool in 1836.[4] At best they were built as servants' quarters with a window, a fireplace, a separate front door and a room at the back for a loom; but many were dark vile places occupied by the most destitute families. A report in the *Morning Chronicle* (1850), after describing the tolerably well-furnished houses of factory

Detail from the back garret of a poor cobbler (see Plate 78). *Illustrated London News* (1863).

77. Cellar and attic dwellings of Manchester operatives, from the *Illustrated London News* (1862).

78. The back garret of a poor cobbler at 10 Hollybush Place, Bethnal Green, London. *Illustrated London News* (1863).

workers in the older parts of Manchester, glanced at the town's cellar dwellings: 'The cellars are, as might be expected, seldom furnished so well. They appear to possess none of the minor comforts, none of the little articles of ornament or fancy furniture which more or less you observe in the parlours. The floors seem damp and unwholesome, you catch a glimpse of a rickety-looking bed in a dark airless corner, and the fire on the hearth is often cheerlessly small'[5] (Plate 77). The cellars of Leeds, Bradford and Halifax were no better,[6] but despite drawbacks, cellars were popular with vendors and outworkers because they were cheap, self-contained and more private than many other lodgings.

ROOKERIES

Tenements, known at the time as 'rookeries', were mostly old buildings subdivided into rooming-houses; they were generally found in the inner-city areas of expanding towns and lacked amenities such as water or sanitation, rapidly degenerating into filthy overcrowded slums. The poorer working classes could not afford to live in houses so they rented a room in one of these buildings. John Simon explained: 'The first hirer of the room may possibly have a pile of rags on which he lies, with his wife and children, in one corner of the tenement, but the majority of his sub-tenants (paying for their family lodging from 6d. to 10d. a week) lie on straw, or on the bare boards'.[7] The common practice of doing 'outwork' such as brush making, matchbox making, sewing or sack making in the poorest houses added to the misery (Plate 78). Street vendors also needed to keep their wares in the apartment. There was little incentive to acquire even basic furniture other than a makeshift bed because families were for ever moving on; hence most rooms were wretchedly bare. Andrew Mearns reported in 1833: 'As to furniture you may perchance discover a broken chair, the tottering relics of an old bedstead, or the mere fragment of a table; but more commonly you will find rude substitutes for these things in the shape of rough boards resting upon bricks, an old hamper or box turned upside down, or more frequently still, nothing but rubbish and rags'.[8]

Poor housing and lack of furnishings seem to have gone hand in hand, so that even families who were not utterly destitute and could have afforded half-decent furniture did not buy any if they lived in rookeries (Plate 79). The above descriptions

79. The room of a widowed paviour from J. Wight, *Mornings at Bow Street* (1824). The children are sleeping head-to-tail, the makeshift furniture includes a packing-case and a barrel.

of how the poor lived is verified many times over in Henry Mayhew's reports. Take his account of a back-garret lodging: 'The boy lived with father (a street seller of fruit), and the room was very bare. A few sacks were thrown over an old palliass, a blanket seemed to be used for a quilt; there were no fire-irons or fender; no cooking utensils. Beside the bed was an old chest, serving for a chair, while a board resting on a trestle did duty for a table (this was once I presume a small street stall)'.[9] It is difficult to find dispassionate evidence about standards of domestic comfort since commentators tended to quote the worst examples; however, Mayhew was resolutely objective and it is clear that in the poorest homes furniture was often improvised from worthless rubbish and 'found' objects. A passage in Peter Gaskell's *The Manufacturing Population of England* (1833) reinforces the impression of squalor:

> The houses of great numbers of the labouring community in the manufacturing districts present many of the traces of savage life. Filthy, unfurnished, deprived of all accessories to decency or comfort. What little furniture is found in them is of the rudest and most common sort, and very often in fragments . . . one or two rush-bottomed chairs, a deal table, a few stools, broken earthenware . . . a bedstead or not as the case may happen to be, blankets and sheets in the strict meaning of the word unknown — their place often being made up of sacking, a heap of flocks or a bundle of straw . . . and all these cooped up in a single room which serves as a place for domestic and household occupations.[10]

BACK-TO-BACK HOUSES

Back-to-back houses, usually one-up and one-down, sometimes with a cellar as well, follow a clear geographical distribution pattern being found in the woollen district of West Yorkshire, south Lancashire and North Midland towns from the late eighteenth century onwards. Nottingham had 7–8,000 out of a housing stock of 11,000 by the 1840s; Leeds in 1886 had 49,000 (71 per cent) and Sheffield 38,000 by 1865. Manchester banned the building of back-to-backs in 1844, and other towns followed: Nottingham (1875); Bradford (1860) and Liverpool (1861)[11] because they were considered unhygienic and lacking in amenities. However, the one family house with a living-room and bedchamber had a solid social tradition behind it and back-to-backs, often known as 'urban cottages', were popular with the working classes, being preferable to cellar dwellings, rooming-houses or lodgings. They were usually part of high-density housing developments, being built in rows facing a yard which contained the communal privy and a piped water supply.

It is no simple matter to discover how early back-to-back houses were furnished, but Robert Baker's report to the Poor Law Commissioners on *The State and Condition of the Town of Leeds* (1842), contains evidence worth quoting: 'A house of this description will contain a cellar, house (living-room) and chamber: there are very few which contain more accommodation than this. The ordinary size of such a cottage-chamber is about five yards square. There are generally two beds in the same apartment where there are families, or even three, and not infrequently instruments of labour, as looms, or the apparatus for combing wool, or for some other kind of handicraft'.[12] Writing of the Irish immigrants (generally noted for their improvidence), Baker recorded: 'A plaid-weaver of industrious habits, will rent a small house, consisting of a kitchen and chamber, at an annual cost of about £4. The kitchen is not only appropriated for culinary purposes, but is the house, the sleeping-room, the hen-house, and the piggery; whilst upstairs are three or four looms, all but touching each other; and perhaps, in a corner, a bed on the floor for one of the owners of those looms, which are employed as follows: one by the occupier of the house, the others by persons to whom they are either sub-let at a weekly rent, or who are relatives, friends of, or labourers for, the owner'.[13] It is likely that Robert Baker described two fairly typical Leeds households. Although handloom weavers in Yorkshire were at this time suffering the effects of factory competition, some weavers' cottages displayed signs of better days. An account of one such West Riding house (possibly a back-to-back) in 1842 shows it to have been nicely furnished although equally overcrowded.[14] It comprised two rooms and a pantry for a man, his wife and nine children. The lower room was clean and comfortable with a painted press bedstead, a chest of drawers, table and chairs, a 'good mahogany case clock', pictures and shelves to display plates. The room above, where the weaving was carried on in a space about 12 feet square, contained three looms, three old stump bedsteads, three chests 'one oak chest used as a child's bedstead' and a quantity of lumber. Five of the children worked as weavers in this restricted space.

SCOTTISH TENEMENTS

The typical form of Victorian working-class house in Scotland was the tenement. Generally of four storeys, they had a communal entrance and stairs with three houses on each landing — two 'Room-and-Kitchen' dwellings flanking a single-end (single apartment) flat. Tenements were built by the thousand, especially in Glasgow, between about 1820 and 1910 and became the standard accommodation for 'respectable and industrious' workers; although not far removed from the concept of minimal dwellings, poorer families could not afford the rents. A characteristic North Country feature was the presence of built-in cupboard beds (Plate 80) until a Glasgow building regulation of 1900 prescribed: 'No dwelling houses shall contain an enclosed bed which is not open in front for three quarters of its length, and from floor to ceiling. This provision shall, after the expiracy of 5 years from the passing of this Act, apply to existing dwelling houses'.

In the typical 'Room-and-Kitchen' tenement house, the front door opened into a lobby containing the W.C. and a built-in press. The Room or parlour contained a bed closet enclosed by a door or, after 1900, by a curtain. This best room was generally well furnished and seldom used except for entertaining. The Kitchen had a fitted sink, range, bed recess, a cupboard larder, a coal-bunker with shelves above and served as the family living-room. The space beneath the bed often contained a low bedframe on casters for the children of the house which was wheeled or 'hurled' out at night, hence its common name of 'hurley-bed' (Plates 80 and 81). The single-end house had the lobby with press and W.C. and one living-room/kitchen; they were popular because the rent was low and few families used their parlour anyway.[15] The tenement at 145 Buccleuch Street, Glasgow, preserved by The National Trust

80. (*Below, left*) Box beds and a 'hurley' bed in the first-floor living-room of a worker's house, 12 Long Row, New Lanark, Scotland. Early twentieth century. *Royal Commission on Ancient Monuments, Scotland*

81. (*Below, right*) The pine 'hurley' bed which was wheeled out at night for children to sleep in.

61

for Scotland, is a very superior four-room dwelling built in 1892, but it contains all the traditional features and the furniture is original to the house.

WORKSHOP-HOUSES

Using the home as a workplace has a long tradition behind it, shoe makers, nail makers, ribbon weavers and many others have always done so. Also, poor families frequently took in 'outwork' such as brush making, matchbox making or sewing which was carried on in the home. However, in many parts of the Midlands and the North, houses specially built for domestic textile weavers combined the function of house and workshop. For example, in Nottingham, where the staple manufactures were hosiery and lace, the stocking workers needed houses with a large well-lit room for their knitting frames and the lace workers required a lace machine-room with space for storing yarn, net and possibly sleeping accommodation for apprentices and journeymen. In the south Lancashire cotton district, prosperous handloom weavers built loom-houses and the domestic system in West Yorkshire likewise demanded special working conditions. An extra storey might be added to a house to provide a separate workplace, as can be seen at Golcar Museum where the top floor is spacious and well-lit. Of course even the upper room of a back-to-back house could be pressed into service as a loom shop.

Valuable evidence as to how a flannel weaver's house near Rochdale was furnished is to be found in Samuel Bamford's *Walks in South Lancashire* (1844).[16] The ground-floor room, measuring about 20 × 24 feet, contained 'a good oaken chest of drawers, prints and drawings in glazed frames . . . a good oaken couch chair, specimens of needlework and other pictures and overhead a breadflake'. Opposite the door was a flight of stairs to the chambers and a passage leading to the cellar and to a small parlour used as a bedroom and a small recess used as a kitchen. 'The chambers above were of two heights . . . flannel weavers require capacious, open rooms, on account of the space necessary for their jennies, their warping mills, looms and other implements of manufacture'. Ascending the stairs, Bamford noted 'In the first chamber was a good bed in an old-fashioned black oaken bedstead. Near that was a loom at which the weaver sat, tying his work. Beyond the loom was another decent looking bed in an old bedstead, next that a warping mill, taking up much room, then a stove with a fire burning, then another loom . . . the arrangements were characteristic of the working and sleeping arrangements of the flannel weavers'. Homes of the skilled Coventry ribbon weavers are described in the *Handloom Weavers' Report* (1840) as 'good comfortable dwellings; some of them very well furnished; many have nice clocks, and beds, and drawers; some ornamented with prints: and some have comfortable parlours'.[17]

Documentary evidence about how working-class houses and domestic workshops were furnished at the time of the Industrial Revolution is scarce because probate inventories cease altogether after 1795. However, when a person applied to the Poor Law Officials for relief, it was customary to make a list of the applicant's household goods and such records can provide welcome insights. In 1832 the Overseer of Ossett, in Yorkshire, inventoried the possessions of a shoemaker and three hand-loom weavers.[18] Isaac Walby lived in a two-room dwelling; the kitchen or 'house' as it was still called, contained, besides hearth furniture: 'five Chairs, I Clock, I set of Drawers, I square, I round table, I Corner cupboard and I teaster bedstead' with bedding and hangings, while his chamber had in it only 'I broad Cloth Loom and a stand bedstead'. James Kempe rented a two-room house with a cellar furnished in a similar style. The main items downstairs (other than the grate and utensils) were: 'five elm Chairs, one Corner Chair, I Cradle, I round table, 2 square tables, 1 24 hour Cloake, I set of oak Drawers, I stump bedstead' with hangings and a pot case. In the Chamber the appraisers found 'I Cotton Loom [e.g. cotton warps] I stump bedstead and a box'. Job Riley, evidently a more prosperous weaver, occupied a workshop-house having a living-room, parlour and dairy downstairs, with a single large chamber on the first floor. The house part was furnished with '8 elm Chairs, I set of Deal Drawers, I Nursing Chair, I Corner Cupboard, I tea table, I square table, I dining table, I round table, I stump bedstead (& bedding), I potcase, I Handweel, I square Cupboard, I Cradle, I Corner Chair' plus ordinary domestic utensils. The chamber above, heated by a stove, contained 'I broad Cloth Loom, 2 Cotton Looms, I stump bedstead, 2 pirn jars, I set of shafts, shuttle & bobings' and various tubs, baskets and boxes. Thomas Johnstone's trade is indicated by the 'shoe makers seat' listed amongst his belongings. Apart from owning a desk and a delf case holding sixteen plates, his furniture was very like his neighbours.

A striking feature of these inventories is the uniformity in the furnishing schemes suggesting that, despite income differences, the four individuals – all apparently widowers of similar age living in the same locality – shared basic assumptions as to how a home should be furnished. None of them owned a traditional long settle, a kitchen dresser with plate-rack, forms, stools or other old-fashioned 'country' pieces; neither had they acquired any modern mahogany furniture which was available cheaply in industrial towns. A set of elm chairs, a corner chair, a corner cupboard, a round table, a square table, chest of drawers (oak or deal), a cradle, a pot case and a stump bed formed the standard repertoire with a few optional extras such as a clock, a tea-tray or chimney ornaments. They all slept in their living-rooms and kept trade equipment upstairs. This analysis tends to confirm the existence of well-established furnishing patterns according to class, region and date. Dales farmhouses in the mid-eighteenth century and Durham miners' cottages during the early Victorian period provide further examples of social conditioning.

MINERS

Information gained from inventories, while authentic, is often rather bare; social reformers tended to emphasize the worst living conditions and the authors of Parliamentary Reports were more interested in the sanitation than the furniture. One therefore turns with gratitude to a major national survey on the state of the industrial working classes published in the *Morning Chronicle* between 1849 and 1851.

Reporting on the pit villages of Northumberland and Durham, where the dwellings often consisted of one large room with an attic over, the correspondent wrote:

We will now enter one of the ordinary class of houses. As a general rule, the furniture is decidedly good; some articles are even costly. The visitor's attention will be especially drawn to the bed and the chest of drawers. In a great proportion of cases neither of these would be out of place in a house of some pretensions. The bedstead is very frequently of carved and turned mahogany, and the bed, clean, soft, and comfortable, with white furniture and a quilted coverlid. The chest of drawers is an article which frequently costs from £8. to £10. It commonly rises almost to the ceiling, only leaving room for a few old-fashioned china or stoneware ornaments to be placed upon the top. The chairs are sometimes deal, and sometimes mahogany. The mantlepiece is generally crowded with little ornaments of china and glass; the plates, cups, and saucers, are usually kept in cupboards; but highly polished brass candlesticks, placed on shelves, or hung upon nails, glitter from the wall. Birds and birdcages abound. The women are the great agents in getting the houses so well furnished as they are. They strive to outdo each other in the matters of beds and chests of drawers, the two great features of their rooms. When a young couple get married, they generally go to a furniture broker in Newcastle or Sunderland, with perhaps £10. of ready money, obtaining a considerable part of their 'plenishing' upon credit, and paying for it by instalments. Like the Manchester mill-hands, the colliery folks have a great notion of clocks; but, unlike the cotton workers, a great proportion of the

82. A large and impressive chest of drawers, *c.* 1850, from Shildon on the Durham coalfield. During the early Victorian period, nearly every miner's cottage contained one of these flashy status symbols crowded with ornaments. *The Bowes Museum*

pitmen's timepieces are regular eight-day clocks with metalic dials. I have good reason to believe that most industrious pitmen can attain to a state of comparative domestic comfort above described. . . .[19]

This picture is confirmed by evidence given by the Relieving Officer of Chester-le-Street, Co. Durham, to Chadwick's *Sanitary Report* of 1842: 'The pitmen's houses generally, in my district, are neat and well furnished, the furniture usually consisting of a good feather-bed, mattress, sheets, blankets, quilts, and a counterpane and hangings, the foot poles mahogany, carved in the modern style, a double chest of drawers, a clock, handsome looking-glass, and half-a-dozen chairs, with other cottage requisites, which altogether will cost from £20. to £40'.[20] A collection of these rather showy status symbols and beautifully worked quilts has been brought together at the Beamish North of England Open Air Museum, Co. Durham (Plates 82 and 83). It is not 'common' furniture, but expresses the pleasure in display in which working people in steady employment with the ability to pay for good articles and ornaments have always taken pride.

The Government Commissioners collecting evidence for a *Report on the Employment of Children* (1842) found that the coal miners' houses at Flockton, a pit village in Yorkshire, were well furnished for the period. Henry Briggs, proprietor of the collieries, described the cottages as having 'seldom but one lodging-room, and one living-room, and a little back-kitchen. Where there is a large family there will be a turn-up bed downstairs'.[21] The detailed case studies[22] record that most of the beds were 'very good and neatly hung'. Simon and Nancy Metcalf, with seven children at home, had three beds in the lodging-room 'one divided off by a curtain for the girls'. Financially, miners were the elite of the industrial workers, hence their living-kitchens were handsome. That of Samuel and Martha Tailor, for instance, contained: 'a bed and 6 chairs, 2 tables, mahogany clock, rocking chair, oak easy chair, cradle, delf case, looking-glass, brass candlesticks, 3 tea trays, steel fire-irons'. The

83. This mahogany tent bed with carved mahogany posts, which descended in the Hope family of Tyneside, is typical of the showy furniture which miners' wives in the area were proud to own. *Leeds Art Galleries*

majority of miners owned in addition to ordinary items, a clock, delf-case, and religious books, the Charlesworths even kept '8 cages of birds' (probably native song birds).[23]

FACTORY OPERATIVES

In Manchester the *Morning Chronicle* reporter made an interesting comparison between the furniture of factory operatives living in Hulme and those dwelling in Ancoats. They earned comparable wages, but because the houses in Hulme were better built they contained superior furniture: 'a very fair proportion of what was deal in Ancoats was mahogany in Hulme'.[24] The observation that a better class of house provided an incentive for buying smart furniture rings true. In Hulme, a typical parlour measured 10 × 8 feet and was hung with cheap wallpaper:

> In at least two of the corners were cupboards of hard wood, painted mahogany fashion, and containing plates, teacups, saucers, etc. Upon the chimney-piece was ranged a set of old-fashioned glass and china ornaments. There was one framed print on the wall. Beside this symbol of art was a token allegiance to science, in the shape of one of the old-fashioned tube barometers, not apparently in a perfect state of order. There were two tables in the apartment — a round centre one of ordinary material, and a rather handsome mahogany Pembroke. Opposite the fireplace was one of those nondescript pieces of furniture a bed by night, a wardrobe all the day. The chairs were of the comfortable old-fashioned Windsor breed; and on the window-ledge were two or three flower-pots feebly nourishing as many musty geraniums.[25]

By contrast, in the 'older, worse built quarter of Ancoats' the correspondent found that although the rooms measured about 10 × 8 feet they were less well furnished, typically containing:

> A substantial deal table in the centre and a few chairs, stools and settles, ranged around. Occasionally, a little table of mahogany is not wanting. Now and then you observe a curiously small sofa; and about as often one side of the fireplace is taken up with a cradle. Sometimes there is a large cupboard, the open door of which reveals a shining assortment of plates and dishes; sometimes the humble dinner service is ranged on shelves which stretch along the walls. A conspicuous object is very frequently a glaringly painted and highly-glazed tea-tray; with a couple of tiny prints, in narrow black frames, suspended above it. A favourite article of furniture is a clock. No Manchester operative will be without one a moment longer than he can help; by far the most common article is the little Dutch machine, with its busy pendulum swinging openly and candidly before all the world. Add to this catalogue an assortment of the used odds and ends of household matters; now and then a small mirror gleaming from the wall; a row of little china ornaments on the chimneypiece; a pot or two of geraniums or fuchsias; other little household appliances giving the small room a tolerably crowded appearance, and you will have a fair notion of the vast majority of the homes of factory operatives in the older and less improved localities of Manchester.[26]

The cottages of the mill workers and weavers in the semi-rural parts of Lancashire contained more traditional furniture. At Saddleworth the reporter found 'ancient yet strong and substantial furniture, the chests of drawers and cupboards of polished oak, chairs with rush bottoms . . . samplers and pictures ornamented the walls' while in every cottage 'a sort of net stretched under the ceiling and filled with crisp oat cakes'.[27] Ammon Wrigley's lovingly remembered verse description of a mid-Victorian handloom weaver's homestead in Saddleworth parish mentions: 'the flagged house-floor, once strewn with sand . . . the chest that polished shone . . . the old oak couch, with panelled back and neat print cushions . . . the bread fleck where the brown oat cake and ropes of onions clung . . . a sampler's picture on the wall, and in the corner nigh a long-cased clock . . . the press where hung a hunting coat . . . and here and there rush-seated chairs with straight and spindled backs . . . a pot shelf by the Kitchen door . . . a corner cupboard in the nook, above my mother's chair, its shelves well filled with dainty stores . . . the mantel shelf with nicknacks rare in quaint and bright array — brass candlesticks and tray . . . there stood upstairs an old hand-loom, close by my parents' bed . . . a cuckoo clock . . . the fifty-jenny . . . skips . . . slubbing creels . . . bobbin wheels'.[28] Verbal descriptions of the homes of well-to-do tradesmen have proved easier to trace than illustrations, which makes the pictorial inventory of household furniture compiled by John Shadford, chairmaker of Caistor, Lincolnshire, about 1860, uncommonly interesting; this is partly reproduced in Plate 84.

In weavers' cottages at Middleton, 'the living room was a sort of country cousin to the same class of apartments in Manchester, furnished a good deal after the same fashion, but in rather a rougher way. In the corners were niched the invariable cupboards. From the wall ticked the invariable clock; beside it hung little miniature sized engravings in black frames'. The 'cottage style' chimney ornaments are then described, followed by a tribute to the 'good substantial furniture . . . strong useful deal tables, an old-fashioned chest of drawers, chairs of different patterns — some of them antique, high-backed affairs, the wood carved into innumerable lumps — others like the ordinary Windsor pattern; and by the fireside the never-to-be-too-highly-honoured rocking chair'.[29]

These splendidly detailed descriptions of interiors show that furniture can be effectively studied in relation to occupational groups, building types and whether the family lived in a rural or urban community. The distinctive repertoires of furniture present in the homes of fishermen, farm workers or crofters are studied elsewhere.

COMMON LODGING-HOUSES

This extremely basic accommodation, found in all industrial towns, was intended for short-stay casual labourers and transient workers. However, cheap lodging-

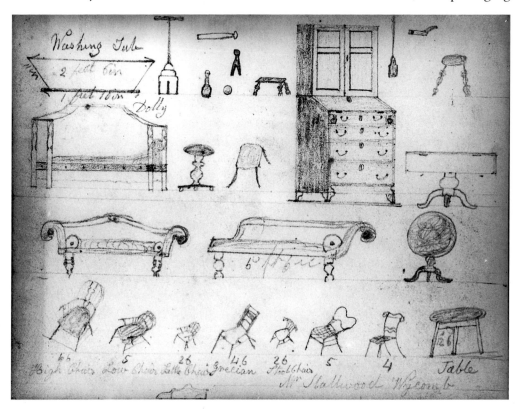

84. About 1860 John Shadford, chairmaker of Caistor, Lincolnshire compiled a pictorial inventory of his household furniture, of which this is a part. The repertoire includes pieces in fashionable and vernacular idioms. *Lincolnshire Archives Office*

houses also served as refuges for poor families for longer periods; they earned a reputation for fever, vice and depravity (Plate 85). The owners normally provided a communal kitchen where lodgers could cook and eat their own food and crammed as many beds as possible into the other rooms. The abominable state of 'these dens of filth, disease and wretchedness' resulted in the Common Lodging Houses Acts of 1851–3 which required them to be registered and inspected. Edwin Chadwick's report to the Poor Law Commissioners on the *Sanitary Conditions of the Labouring Population of England* (1842) contains a harrowing account of such doss-houses,[30] while Henry Mayhew's *London Labour and the London Poor* (1861) also describes the appalling conditions.[31] However, the fullest information about the furniture of such places is to be found in *Santory Progress*, the 5th Report of the National Philanthropic Association (1850), which includes a survey of common lodging-houses in the metropolis.[32] The authors not only describe and illustrate average establishments, but also report on some of the new model lodging-houses erected by the Society for the Improvement of the Labouring Classes.

In Church Lane, St Giles, a furnished room could be rented from 3s. 3d. weekly: 'the furniture consists of a small deal table, two rickety or broken deal chairs, a bedstead without hangings of any kind, flock mattress, two blankets . . . a tub or pail, a pot or pan, and a tea kettle'. In another house they visited the back-room, measuring 11 × 9 feet, let furnished for 3s. a week to a family of eight: 'State of

85. The second-floor front-room of a common lodging-house at 7 Pheasant Court, Gray's Inn Lane, London, 1850. It is a mixed dormitory; notice, too, the street vendor's basket on the wall. *Courtesy Westminster City Libraries*

room — dirty; furniture — bad; windows — 5 whole, 7 broken; number of beds — 3; bedstead, 1'. The beds and their coverings were composed of shavings and rags. A single room on the first floor was shared by three families of Irish labourers and dealers, numbering seventeen persons: 'furniture, only I chair and table; number of beds 3, made of shavings, bedstead, 1'. Impartial evidence such as this (quoted from a *Report of the Statistical Society*, 1848), supported by engravings, is of high value.

In contrast to the 'ragged dormitories' in the neighbourhood of St Giles, the Model Lodging House in nearby George Street (opened 1847) provided hygienic accommodation for 2s. 4d. per week, but few poor people could afford to stay there. It is illustrated and described in *Santory Progress* (Plate 86). Inside the entrance was the Superintendant's counting-house: 'One side of the room is fitted up with bookshelves, to hold the present and future library of the establishment; and on the other side a vast number of keys are arranged; of these keys there are 104, being the number that the house accommodates'. The basement-kitchen was fitted up with 'a large dresser and central table', plus cooking facilities. A small room off the kitchen contained crockery, while the 'Rabbit-hutch room' was fitted up with tiers of meat-safes in which each lodger could keep his food. There was also a wash-house, drying closet and bathroom. The General Sitting-Room, on the ground floor, was furnished 'like a respectable coffee-room with high benches and long narrow tables, made of beech, stained like dark oak . . . here the lodgers, after cooking their meals below,

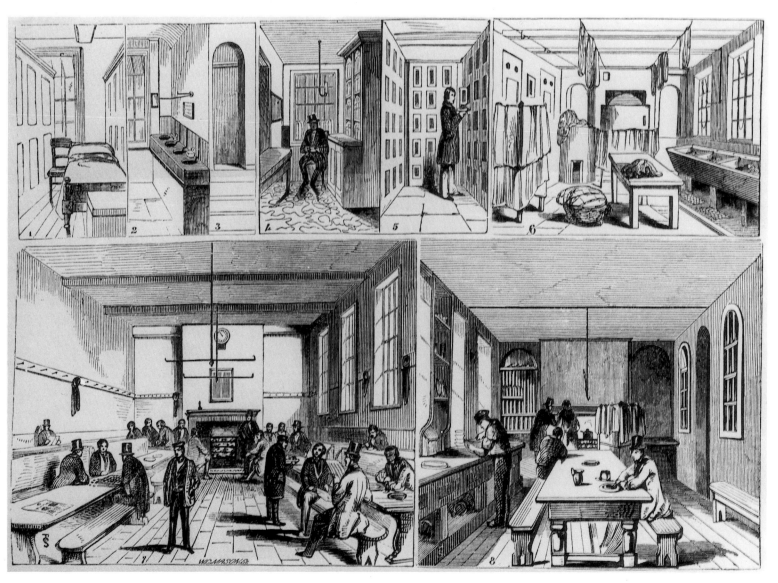

86.   Model lodging-house in George Street, St Giles's, London, 1850. 1 Bedroom. 2 Wash-hand stands. 3 Water closet. 4 Library. 5 Safe. 6 Wash-house. 7 Coffee-room. 8 Kitchen. *Courtesy Westminster City Libraries*

bring them up to dine'. The four upper floors were partitioned off into bed cubicles 'just large enough to take a French bed, a box for clothes and a chair'. The pictorial record of this model lodging-house suggests that it was a cheerless hostel and few were ever built despite permissive legislation.

SALVATION ARMY REFUGES

The Salvation Army and similar rescue organizations, such as the Female Aid Society and the London by Moonlight Mission, set up hostels for the homeless. Many of these Victorian societies catered for special social groups; for example, the Metropolitan Association for Befriending Young Servants provided temporary board and lodging because servants were often dismissed for trifling misdemeanours without a good character reference and needed protection while seeking another job.[33] Night shelters were often like vast warehouses, the floor closely packed with row upon row of 'cribs' containing seaweed-filled leather-cloth mattresses. These gas-lit dormitories with runs of heating pipes survived well into the present century (Plate 87). The Salvation Army also provided relief in its 'penny-sity ups', situated in poor areas such as Limehouse or Whitecross Street. These bare halls filled with rail-back benches were where the destitute could find shelter and maybe listen to a religious address or obtain a free meal (Plate 88).

87. (*above, left*) Salvation Army shelter for the homeless, Burne Street, Limehouse, London, *c.* 1900. *Courtesy the Salvation Army*

88. (*above, right*) A night meeting at the Salvation Army shelter in Limehouse, London, *c.* 1900. The walls are lined with bunks. *Courtesy the Salvation Army*

6 Back-Stairs Furniture

The carefully stratified and subdivided system of household management, which underpinned English country-house society, achieved its most elaborate expression during high-Victorian times. Well-organized Domestic Offices and staff quarters became an increasingly important aspect of house planning — the precise function of every department and status of those concerned with each activity being strictly defined. The architectural principles and lines of communication governing the lay-out of Offices are analysed in fascinating detail in Robert Kerr's *The Gentleman's House* (1864), while the life of domestic servants is vividly recalled in numerous memoirs; however, scant attention has been paid to back-stairs furniture.[1] Many country-house owners have held attic clearance sales or pulled down redundant servants' wings, while at stately homes used as military hospitals or requisitioned during the War, much common furniture was destroyed. However, despite these huge losses, there still remains a sizeable group of great houses with more or less undisturbed servants' quarters below stairs; the attics tell a different story. Some original furnishings such as china cupboards, linen-presses and dressers were built-in or, like kitchen centre-tables, mortars bedded in tree-trunks and box mangles, too massive to be easily moved. So, although a convenient modern kitchen is now the rule, the old Domestic Offices have quite often survived through neglect. This survey concentrates on furniture of known provenance, much of it recorded in inventories.

The questions posed by back-stairs furniture include: was it supplied by fashionable cabinet makers or local tradesmen or the estate carpenter? How does it differ from vernacular pieces produced for farmhouses and cottages? How much sophisticated furniture was relegated when outmoded to servants' rooms? Does back-stairs furniture constitute a genuinely independent sub-group in terms of design, materials and finish within the English tradition? Before tackling such questions, it is necessary to explore the functions of the various Domestic Offices and, with the aid of inventories, contemporary manuals, pictorial sources and field-work, indicate how they were equipped.

THE KITCHEN OFFICES

The Kitchen was devoted to the preparation of food and occupied a primary position in relation to the Dining-Room, Scullery, Larders and Servants' Hall. Besides the range, cooking apparatus and utensils, it was generally furnished with a large, very strong, well-framed centre-table, having a row of deep drawers beneath the top, one or more deal dressers backed by shelves, probably a side dresser placed before the window with either cupboards or a pot-board under, smaller tables, often consisting of hinged flaps fixed to the wall, for occasional use, stout chopping-blocks, pin rails, a towel-roller, a clock, a few wood-bottomed chairs, a marble mortar (for grinding herbs and spices), a meat-screen for spit-roasting and usually a contraption for keeping dishes of meat warm known as a 'haster' (Plate 89). Fine period Kitchens displaying most of these features remain at Raby Castle, Co. Durham; Erddig,

Detail from a watercolour of the Kitchen at Aynhoe, Northamptonshire, by Lili Cartwright, 1847 (see Plate 89).

The Kitchen at Aynhoe. 3d February 1847.

89. Watercolour of the Kitchen at Aynhoe, Northamptonshire, by Lili Cartwright, 1847, showing a haster in front of the fire. *Courtesy Elizabeth Cartwright-Hignett*

90. (*Opposite, above*) The Kitchen at Erddig, Wrexham, showing a large painted pine cupboard, corner cupboard, centre-table with scrubbed top and hooked racks suspended from the ceiling, *c.* 1775. *The National Trust*

91. (*Opposite, below, left*) Haster for keeping dishes warm in front of a fire, painted pine, lined with tin and fitted with iron shelves. From the Kitchen at Ham House, Surrey. *The National Trust*

92. (*Opposite, below, right*) Kitchen table at Harewood House, Yorkshire, with a five-inch-thick sycamore top, the pine frame grained reddish brown. *Courtesy the Earl of Harewood, K.B.E.*

Clwyd (Plate 90); Dunham Massey, Lancashire; Brodsworth, Yorkshire and Manderston in Berwickshire, to mention a few, while several of Thomas Rowlandson's lively sketches portray Kitchen interiors.[2]

There is an impressive Kitchen table at Harewood House in Yorkshire, with a five-inch-thick scrubbed sycamore top, the cracks filled with lead, and a sturdy painted frame (Plate 92). Another memorable example, the size of a billiard-table, made of two huge elm planks raised on eight massive baluster legs, ordered in 1752 for the Mansion House, London, survived *in situ* until the 1960s, but has now, like so many, been broken up.[3] Thomas Webster recommended, in his *Encyclopaedia of Domestic Economy* (1844), that the Kitchen dresser and plate-rack 'are best painted stone or wainscot colour . . . the pot-board is always painted black'. Erddig offers splendid examples of both the towering shelved and side form of painted dresser with whitewood working surfaces. Webster also stated that Kitchen fixtures such as dressers, shelving and closets were normally made by the joiner in finishing the house. Hasters were designed like a shallow cupboard without a back, the interior being fitted with iron shelves and lined with tin; they were mounted on castors so that they could be wheeled in front of the fire to keep joints of meat hot (see Plate 89). The Gillow Estimate Sketch Books illustrate one constructed of deal and elm for a Mr Bailey of Blackpool in 1787.[4] They apparently became popular during the late eighteenth century; good early speciments survive at Ham House in Surrey (Plate 91), and Renishaw Hall, Derbyshire.

The Scullery, used for washing dishes, preparing vegetables, gutting fish, plucking and drawing game, and so on, led directly off the Kitchen and contained, besides sinks and a copper for heating water, a strong plain table, plate-racks, shelving, sometimes a tier of wooden racks for vegetables and perhaps the odd chair. An unforgettable painted pine plate-rack (looking remarkably like a work of modern sculpture) with graduated divisions for eighty-two plates in four tiers may be identified with an entry in the 1792 Newby Hall inventory (Plate 93). In 1780 the Scullery at Appuldurcombe House contained: 'A Copper fix'd, divided into 2;

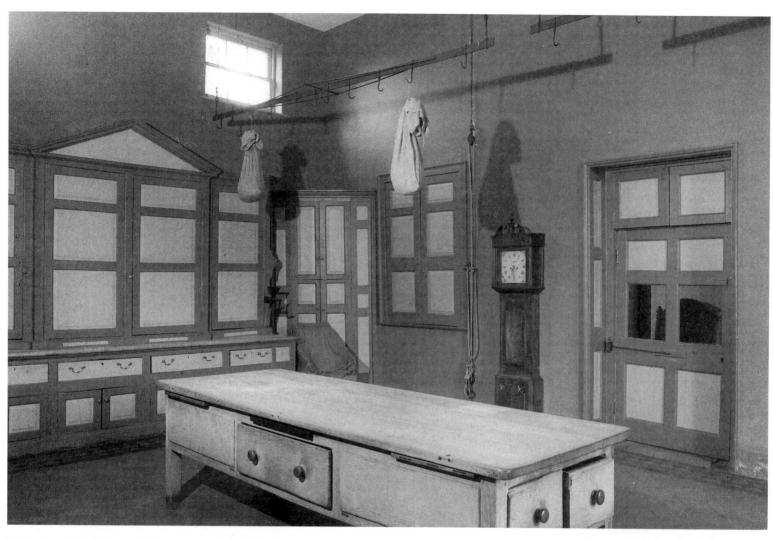

covers and brass cock / A lead sink & brass cock / 2 dressers & shelves, a plate rack / 2 tubs for washing dishes, 1 pail / 2 wash hand bowls / A brass mortar, a dinner Bell / A copper fish Kettle on an iron stand'.[5]

The Dry Larder (or Cook's Pantry), reserved for cooked meats, was usually fitted with a broad dresser without drawers around three sides, a centre-table, marble shelving and possibly a refrigerator of sorts. The Wet Larder, for raw meat, needed bacon-racks, hanging irons, a table, salting trough, chopping-block, scales, a meat-safe and stone shelving. In large establishments separate pastry, vegetable, game and fish larders were customary — a full range can still be seen in the spacious basement at Manderston in Scotland. At Carlton Towers, a handsome mid-seventeenth-century oak dining-table was re-used as a side dresser in the Game Larder where it is recorded in an inventory of 1854; at some time the estate joiner increased its length from 11 to 14 feet to accommodate a marble fish-slab (Plate 95). There was formerly a large eighteenth-century painted pine table at Newby Hall inset with a marble slab either for preparing fish or making pastry (but not both). The endless need for strong tables framing drawers sometimes resulted in pieces designed originally for quite other roles being commandeered and altered for use in the Kitchen Offices (Plate 94). There also existed, at least since medieval times, a bottomless demand for robust stands which could be used for any purpose from drying peas to placing buckets of water or storing bottles upon (Plate 97). The 1795 Harewood inventory lists in the Pastry: 'One Paste Board with Drawers & Marble Slab, 2 Dressers with Drawers, One Cubboard, 6 Shelves, One Dresser with Crooks for hanging Poultry' while the next entry records: 'In the Area — One Marble Fish Slab, one lead cistern'.[6] The Dairy, which might form part of the Kitchen complex, but often occupied an outbuilding, was surrounded by marble or stone shelving for coolness and had an adjoining scullery for scalding milk vessels. It frequently boasted a large stone centre-table with channelled rim to hold water in hot weather. Essential utensils included milk pails, churns, hair-sieves, milk pans, marble dishes for cream, wooden skimmers, butter-moulds, scales, a cheese-press, washing-tubs and a drying-rack. The lavish Regency Dairy at Harewood House is fitted with veined white marble slabs set around the walls on carved stone supports with abundant marble shelving above for cheeses. An elegant watercolour design for the oval centre-table (which no longer survives), signed 'Thomas Cundy 1817', is inscribed: 'Sketch for a Table designed for the Dairy at Harewood House. The top only of

93. Plate-rack designed with one vertical side to stand along the scullery wall. Painted pine, probably late eighteenth century. Formerly at Newby Hall, Yorkshire

94. (below, left) When this mid-eighteenth-century oak writing-table was demoted for re-use in the Kitchen Offices, it received a coat of paint and the top was replaced in sycamore. Formerly at Newby Hall, Yorkshire

95. (below, right) Early seventeenth-century oak table re-used as a side dresser in the Victorian Game Larder at Carlton Towers, Yorkshire, the length increased from 11 to 14 feet to accommodate a fish-slab. *Courtesy the Duke of Norfolk*

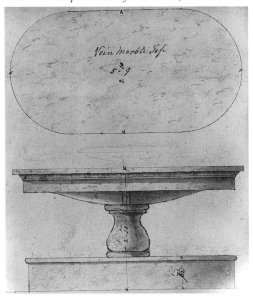

97. A robust multi-purpose X-frame stand with raised metal rim in the scullery at The Grove, Ramsey, Isle of Man. *The Manx Museum*

98. Watercolour design for a Dairy table at Harewood House, Yorkshire, by Thomas Cundy, 1817. *Courtesy the Earl of Harewood, K.B.E.*

vein'd Marble the Plinth and Frame of Oak and Painted in imitation of the Top'[7] (Plate 98). The Bakehouse was another Office related to kitchen work which could be detached from the house, a fine example at Erddig retains its furnishings. Thomas Webster stated that the Bakehouse 'should have a good light and contain the ovens, kneading trough, chest for flour . . . a strong table, presses and cupboards to hold various articles'. A passage in Mrs Parkes's *Domestic Duties* (1825), forcefully describes the essential attributes of furniture made for the Kitchen Offices:

> Furniture which is strictly useful, should be of good quality; strength and durability being generally the chief points to be regarded . . . it is therefore little affected by fashion, whereas the style of drawing room furniture is almost as changeable as fashion in female dress.[8]

THE UPPER SERVANTS' OFFICES

The Butler was responsible for the service of wine, the storage of plate and 'the direction of the various repasts of the family': he had no intercourse with the Kitchen, thus the Butler's Pantry was close to the Dining-Room. His bedroom for reasons of security and the Plate Scullery for cleaning silver were nearby. He needed a small dresser with lead-lined sinks beneath folding covers, a glass-closet, table, napkin-press, linen drawers, shelving and a safe with baize-lined sliding trays and plate chests. At Appuldurcombe in the Isle of White, in 1780, the Butler's Pantry contained a deal press bed set between two cupboards with another large deal press for storing plate, an oak bureau, a tea-table, two beech chairs and a mahogany-framed dressing-glass. It evidently served him as a bed-sitting room, most of the work being carried out in the adjoining Under Butler's Pantry 'Fitted up with cupboards & shelves, dressers & drawers / A lead Cistern & brass cock in Window / 2 round beech stools / 4 Mahogany trays, a Knife do, a plate basket'.[9]

The Housekeeper supervised the whole female domestic staff from Cook to Scullery Maid; she was responsible for the linen, china and groceries, as well as

99. Oak housekeeper's cupboard with shell inlays, signed 'Jos Butler 1814'. Thought to have been made in Tattenhall, Cheshire. The clock by Thomas Joyce of Whitchurch. *Grosvenor Museum, Chester*

100. Armchair, late eighteenth century, from the Housekeeper's Room at Rossall Hall, Lancashire. The beech frame grained to simulate rosewood and a suggestion of bamboo ring turning betray its country-house origin. *Private collection*

ensuring the house was properly cleaned. Her room usually became a social centre for the Upper Servants (Plate 96). It combined the functions of a cosy sitting-room, office and often a store fitted with capacious presses for keeping china, glass, linen, tea, coffee and fancy groceries (Plate 99). An inventory of Hartlebury Castle, Worcestershire, compiled by William Ince in 1781, records that the Housekeeper's Room was provided with three deal linen-presses with shelves and folding doors, a sink and cover, a corner shelf, various trays, tables and chairs (Plate 100), a pair of scales, a marble mortar and pestle, sugar nippers and several hundredweight of soap, candles and cheese, together with lesser amounts of raisins, caster and lump sugar. A large deal press in the passage outside housed stone jars, galley pots, bottles of peppermint, tarragon and rosewater, tin wares, coffee and dinner-services of cream-coloured earthenware.[10] At Harewood the Housekeeper's Room contained, besides the usual comforts, three mahogany china-presses enclosing over 600 itemized articles of tableware, but at other houses a separate China Closet was created with glazed lockable cupboards for the best crockery — one of the most impressive, lined all round with open shelving, is at Penshurst, Kent.[11]

Large country houses maintained a Still Room for the use of the Housekeeper and her assistant – the Still-Room Maid – when preparing tea, coffee or cordials, making jam, jelly, pickles, cakes, biscuits, and so on; in effect, it relieved the Kitchen from pastry work. Necessary items of equipment included a small range, oven, sink, dresser, table and storage units (Plate 102). The excellent, but smaller than average, Still Room at Erddig retains its fixed shelving and drawers painted with the names of spices, sweetmeats and exotic groceries. The 1795 Harewood inventory gives a vivid description of a well-appointed Still Room: '6 Closets with 24 drawers, a lead cistern, stoves, one Dutch oven, one marble mortar with cover, a pair of steps, an oak table, a deal table, one chair, 2 stools, a small winter hedge, copper chocoate pot, coffee mill, 3 tea kettles, 5 sugar canisters, 8 freezing ice pots, 15 ice moulds, 2 tin cheese toasters, 3 tin cake boxes, 5 copper preserving pans, 3 pair of copper scales, a nest of weights, 5 dozen biscuit moulds, tea boards waiters . . .'.[12] In this room the housekeeper and her maid, who was expected to be always 'neat, clean, active and obliging', prepared sweet-flavoured waters for the Cook, aromatics for the dressing-room, cordials for invalids and various delicacies for the table.

The Steward was the Chief Officer who controlled the men servants, paid wages, dealt with tradesmen and collected rents; he had an Office for the transaction of business and keeping estate papers. In 1808 the 'Counting Room' at Temple Newsam contained 'a large deal desk with 2 large drawers on a frame, 2 Deal tables with drawers, a deal cupboard with upright divisions for books and folding doors, a large high nest of Deal Drawers painted buff, a low nest of large drawers with cupboards on ditto, 4 old chairs and counting house stool, 4 old tables on tressells'.[13] A typical early nineteenth-century pine high desk survives from the Office at Broughton Hall, Yorkshire (Plate 101). The Steward lived in some style, his own room functioning as a Dining-Room for the Upper Servants — the Butler, House-

101. Early Victorian high desk on frame from the House Steward's Office at Broughton Hall, Yorkshire. Pine, the interior fitted with letter holes. *Courtesy Henry Tempest*

102. Oak Still-Room cupboard recorded in the 1740 Temple Newsam inventory: 'Large press for China, Glasses, Sweetmeats, etc'. *Leeds Art Galleries*

keeper, Valet, Head Cook, Head Ladies' Maid and visiting servants of equal rank, all of whom enjoyed the right of dining with the Steward on the same fare served to the family. The furniture was generally handsome to match his status. At Osterley Park, Middlesex, in 1782, the Steward's Room included: 'A Wallnuttree Sideboard Table and Marble Slab, A large Mahogany two flap dining table, A large oval ditto, Fourteen wallnuttree matted bottom Chairs, a Scotch Carpet, A Barometer, A large Marble cistron, Two Chair back screens'.[14] In 1771 William Smith supplied '2 dozen of Elm chairs and 2 dining tables'[15] for the Steward's Room at Harewood, several of the chairs still survive, offering a rare instance of fully documented back-stairs furniture (see Plate 196). The 1795 inventory shows that it was furnished in addition with '2 Oak sideboards, a Mahogany Card Table, One Mahogany Tea Table, 2 Fire Screens, one Plate Warmer and one Oval Pier Glass', which must have made it very convenient for Mr Samuel Popelwell's dinner parties. However, the principal pieces in his business Office (with which Thomas Chippendale must have been familiar) displayed a plain utility character: 'One Oak Library Table, One Oak Desk with 2 Drawers, One Oak Case for Maps, One Deal Desk, 2 Stools, One Armed Chair, 2 Elm chairs, one Iron chest, one Brass Candlestick'.

103. Windsor chair, yew with an elm seat, one of a pair made for the new Servants' Hall created in the 1820s at Chatsworth, Derbyshire. *The Chatsworth Settlement Trustees*

THE LOWER SERVANTS' OFFICES

The Servants' Hall, near to the Kitchen, always had a comfortable fireside, was provided with long tables, forms, coat-pegs or a clothes-press, drinking utensils, maybe a clock to aid good time-keeping and perhaps a dresser. One of the most evocative, in the basement at Erddig, is hung with ten Georgian portraits of the staff. At The Grange, Northington, the Servants' Hall in 1795 contained: 'a range of deal clothes presses, a large stout hall table on a frame with a flap, 4 long and one short forms, 2 benches with backs and a three legged stool, a wooden beer waggon, a beer stand, beer pots, a square dressing glass, 4 wig blocks, a dresser, a beer cupboard, boot jack'.[16] Two low-back yew Windsor chairs (Plate 103) are known to have been made for the new Servants' Hall created at Chatsworth in the 1820s,

104. Bench, one of ten recorded in the Servants' Hall at Harewood House, Yorkshire, in 1795. Oak seat, pine frame painted cream. *Courtesy the Earl of Harewood, K.B.E.*

105. Portrait of Edward in the Servants' Hall at Chatsworth, Derbyshire, signed 'Baker 1835'. The long ash table survives. *The Chatsworth Settlement Trustees*

which is glimpsed in a portrait of a liveried servant dated 1835 (Plate 105). The long ash table visible in the background is still on the premises, although now cut in half. Many inventories confirm the evidence of this painting that the essentials comprised long tables, forms (Plate 104) and requisites for the consumption of beer. During the eighteenth century this Office was a common eating-room for all the Lower indoor staff, but later on it became the practice in large establishments to segregate the women domestics in a Maids' Sitting-and Work-Room. There were Maids' Halls at Harewood and Newby, in Yorkshire in the 1790s, the former furnished with linen-presses, a long dresser, a 'winter hedge', an oak tea-table, two large oak dining-tables and seven elm chairs. Victorian country-house plans reveal a multiplicity of Cleaning Offices such as a Brushing Room, the Shoe Hole, Knife Room and Lamp

106. The Victorian Laundry at Beningbrough Hall, Yorkshire. *The National Trust*

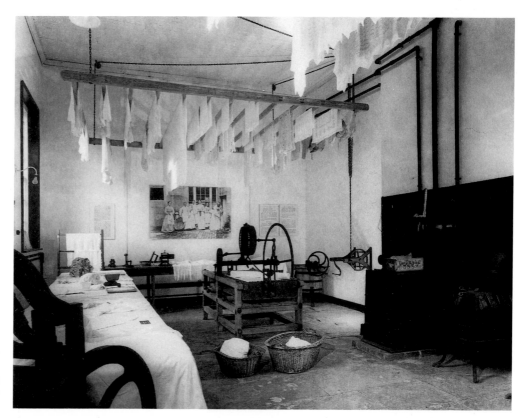

107. The Laundry at Aynhoe Park, Northamptonshire, as depicted by Lili Cartwright in 1847. Notice the large drying-rack, the winter hedge and ironing-table under the windows. *Courtesy Elizabeth Cartwright-Hignett*

Room to name a few — all supplied with strong tables, shelves and cupboards. Gun Rooms were fitted up with lockable presses, a table for cleaning weapons, chairs and racks; the walls were sometimes decorated with animal trophies. Fishing tackle, camp stools (Plate 108) and even bows and arrows (Plate 109) might also be kept here. The Hornby Castle, Yorkshire inventory of 1834 even records a Soap Closet, Rat Catcher's Room and Medicine Room.[17] At Nostell Priory in Yorkshire, Chippendale designed and fitted out an Apothecary's Shop for Sir Rowland Winn, although only the counter survives from this amazing interior.

THE LAUNDRY OFFICES

To avoid unpleasant smells wafting to the family, the Laundry Offices were often located in a building some distance from the main house. This is so at Broughton Hall where the early nineteenth-century Laundry above the Wash-House is almost perfectly preserved, complete with patent washing and wringing machines supplied by Robert Bullman & Son of Leeds in 1831, a box mangle of the same date, a long ironing-table fitted under the windows, a stove for heating irons, spare table and drying closet with cast-iron sliding racks. The Laundry at Broughton could be said to have survived by neglect, whereas the impressive National Trust Laundries at Beningbrough Hall, Yorkshire (Plate 106), Shugborough, Staffordshire, and Erddig, while substantially intact, have in recent years acquired additional items of period equipment.

Country-house records suggest that, by the late eighteenth century, Laundry Offices consisted of a separate Wash-House with adjoining Mangling-and-Ironing-Rooms, where all the laundry for both family and staff was done over a weekly cycle (Plate 107). Most Wash-Houses had a row of wooden sinks or tubs on stands for hand-washing, a big coal-fired copper boiler, often with an iron draining-rack or 'wet horse' over it, large rinsing tubs, pails and perhaps a clothes-barrow for transporting wet laundry. The centre-piece of the Mangling-Room was a large box

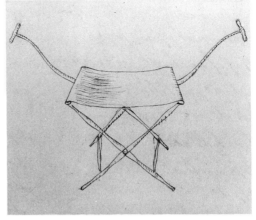

108. A black stained fishing stool with a Wilton carpet seat, from the Gillow Estimate Sketch Books, 1792. *Westminster City Archives*

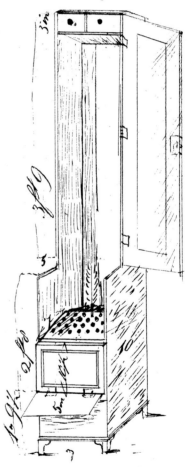

109. Case for bows and arrows made for Dallam Tower, Westmorland in 1790. From Gillow Estimate Sketch Books. This pleasing structure was presumably installed in the Gun Room. *Westminster City Archives*

110. Baker's patent box mangle supplied by Robert Bullman & Son of Leeds to Broughton Hall, Yorkshire, in 1831. Beech frame with a mahogany base board. The box, filled with stones, ran to and fro over the loose rollers. *Courtesy Henry Tempest*

mangle (alongside a scrubbed table), usually made of beech with a mahogany base board. By cranking a chain-driven wheel and pinion the box, weighted with stones, ran to and fro over a pair of loose rollers around which the washing was wrapped (Plate 110). The Laundry Maids folded small articles inside larger ones like sheets or towels and wound them on to the rollers before placing them under the box. The rope-driven 'swiss mangle' which Chippendale supplied to Nostell Priory in 1768 was of this type. J.C. Loudon, writing in 1833, stated 'the common mangle with the improved reversing mechanism known as Bakers Patent' was considered the best. The model at Broughton is by this firm, but many other manufacturers' names occur on cast-iron components. Some less advanced late eighteenth-century proto-types operated by straps are shown in the Gillow Estimate Sketch Books.[18]

If it was fine, the damp washing would be taken in clothes baskets to the drying yard or green, but in the event of wet weather it was hung across large wooden racks with jack-lines and pullies and hoisted to the ceiling, or dried on clothes-horses — known in the north as 'winter hedges'. Two huge wind-up drying-racks, each larger than a field gate, survive at Beningbrough Hall. The Laundries at Broughton and Erddig have special hot-air drying closets with cast-iron racks which slide in and out on wheels running in grooves. The chief furniture of the Ironing-Room (which might well be combined with the Mangling-Room) was long pine tables built-in under the windows, wood-bottomed chairs and stools, a stove with hot-plates for heating flat-irons and a sparetable on which the clean linen was folded and sorted before being returned to the Housekeeper or Lady's Maid.[19]

SERVANTS' BEDROOMS

The Upper Servants by tradition had their own private bedrooms, the Butler next to his Pantry, the Housekeeper and Cook near their domains, the Lady's Maid close to her mistress and so forth. During the eighteenth century they were often provided with neat stained beech bedsteads (Plate 111). The maids who lived-in usually shared

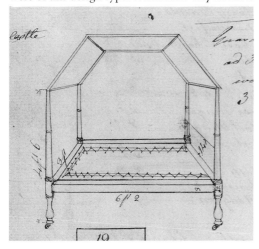

111. Drawing for a stained beech bedstead with 'sacking & cord' bottom, from the Gillow Estimate Sketch Books, 1797. Many servants' beds were of this design type. *Westminster City Archives*

112. The dormitory for visitors' servants at Mamhead, Devon, *c.* 1833. *Country Life*

113. *The Modest Girl in her Bed Chamber*, mezzotint, 1796. Note the morine bed hangings, framed sampler, hybrid chair and list headed 'Duty of Servants' pinned under the window. *Colonial Williamsburg Foundation*

attic bedrooms while the men servants slept on another side of the house. In large well-planned Victorian establishments separate staircases were provided for each sex, but at one manor house near Scarborough, with all the staff bedrooms on the top storey, the male and female quarters were divided from each other by a box bed in which the Housekeeper slept. A photograph of an austere Servants' dormitory in the attics at Mamhead, built by Salvin between 1827 and 1833, shows a row of five painted double-beds each with sloping half-tester, a seat or trunk stand at the foot, built-in cupboards opposite and a peg-board on the end wall (Plate 112). It is one of two such apartments intended for visitors' servants. Mrs Parkes, writing in 1825, advised: 'Let your servant's bedrooms be as plainly furnished as you like, but let the furniture be good of its kind, and such as will render those comfortable by night who have to labour by day'[20] (Plate 113).

Late Georgian inventories with a geographical spread from the Isle of Wight to Scotland reveal that the furnishings of Maids' and Mens' Rooms, and those servants whose Offices were detached from the house (Grooms, Coachmen, Gardeners, etc), exhibit a marked uniformity. Indoor staff were required to share rooms — and often beds. Their furniture is usually recorded as being of wainscot, painted deal, elm, walnut or beech, and frequently described as old or broken (Plate 114). In 1820, at Paxton in Scotland, the Women Servants' Room contained a typical ensemble: '3 Fourposted bedsteads with old printed curtains, 3 Straw mattresses, 3 Feather beds, A chest of painted drawers . . . five handles wanting, A deal table with a drawer, 2 old windsor chairs wanting the backs, 2 Deal stools, an oval dressing glass 9½ × 8in in a gilt frame',[21] while the Men made do with '2 Old square roofed bedsteads, A deal table, a hardwood chair with deal seat'. This is precisely what the Men's Room at Newby offered in 1792 except that a wainscot chest of drawers replaced the deal table. Unmarried estate workers mostly shared rather comfortless apartments; the rooms over the stables at Appuldurcombe were typical in containing '7 stump bedsteads, 7 featherbeds & Bolsters, 28 Blankets, 7 Rugs, 14 old Chairs, 7 do Tables'.

114. Stump bedstead, second half of the eighteenth century, oak, originally with a cord and canvas bottom. From a bedroom in the stables at Hardwick Hall, Derbyshire. *The National Trust*

115. This fine early eighteenth-century burr elm double chest of drawers with a label on the back inscribed 'House maids / Old Furn Hobson' shows how old-fashioned furniture was often demoted to servants' rooms. Formerly at Newby Hall, Yorkshire. *Private collection*

The hierarchical system of household management based on Domestic Offices, which started to emerge after the Restoration, became increasingly amplified over the years. By 1750 the owner of a large country house employed about fifty indoor and outdoor staff, many of whom lived in nearby estate villages, but in the 1890s the Duke of Westminster had over 300 at Eaton Hall while the Earl of Derby employed 727 servants, gardeners and other staff at his death in 1893.[22] The architects of Victorian country houses took great pains to ensure that the paths of the family and their domestics seldom crossed.

Newby Hall, a seventeenth-century house improved by Robert Adam and Thomas Chippendale provides an interesting case history. The comprehensive 1792 inventory[23] reveals that the Upper Servant's Rooms were almost entirely stocked with obsolete furniture from the family apartments, most of which had once been highly fashionable, such as a 'Nonsuch' chest, a walnut double chest of drawers, 4 backstool chairs covered with silk damask, a walnut bureau, a swing glass in a walnut frame, a green porphyry table with ormolu mouldings on a frame, a japanned cabinet on a stand, a table clock in a walnut case, a walnut chest of drawers on a frame and so on. Many of these demoted pieces survived until an attic clearance sale was held in 1986 (Plate 115). Nostell Priory, on the other hand, was a new house, so Sir Rowland Winn, lacking a ready supply of worn-out or unwanted items, commissioned his principal cabinet maker to provide a suitable repertoire of back-stairs furniture including rush-bottom chairs, 2 four post servants bedsteads, a large wainscot double chest of drawers for the servant maids, a turnup bedstead made to fit into a press, a strong large deal table for the laundry, a mangle, a large strong elm chopping block for the Kitchen, 4 deal coal boxes and 3 dozen meat hooks with deal battens — to mention just a few of the mundane items in Chippendale's account.[24] Unfortunately, this common furniture cannot be positively identified, although several likely pieces are rather bigger than equivalent 'yeoman' examples and all are severely plain, although well made (Plate 116). At

116. This may be one of the 'wainscot chest of drawers' which Thomas Chippendale supplied in 1768 for the servants' quarters at Nostell Priory, Yorkshire. *Courtesy Lord St Oswald and The National Trust*

Harewood, another Chippendale house, a similar range was supplied by local joiners. Interestingly, Windsor chairs are rarely listed in servants' quarters, which implies they were only used by the family. Also, oak back-stairs furniture seldom displays the kind of fancy treatment such as crossbanding, stringing, shell inlays or corner colonettes that often features on equivalent 'farmhouse' pieces.

The dramatic increase in domestic staff gave rise to a new generation of painted pine furniture reflecting simplified modern styles (Plate 117). This tradition sprung from earlier painted items rather than the robust oak pieces such as Chippendale had made for Servants' Rooms at Nostell in 1767–71. A late Regency wash-stand at Hardwick Hall, Derbyshire, on turned supports with a simulated marble top, the frame painted olive-green and banded with blue, is typical of these smart but cheap new-style bedroom suites. A slightly earlier straw-coloured chest of drawers, also at Hardwick, is decorated with bamboo mouldings, patterns of black lines in imitation of ebony stringing, playful red blobs and clusters of spots (Plate 119). Large turned wooden drawer handles were at this time more popular than brass hardware. Japanned tin wall lamps were often finished in the same manner (Plate 118). At Brodsworth, there are several complete early Victorian attic bedroom suites, expertly grained to simulate bird's-eye maple, Hungarian ash, satinwood and rosewood. A now not so recent mania for stripped pine has decimated this attractive class of furniture. A pretty painted ladder-back chair from Renishaw Hall, enriched with a festive scheme of red, white and yellow stripes, combined with simple fronded scrolls on a bottle-green ground, is very similar to sets of 'thumb top' rush-seated

117. A Regency period 'French' bedstead (with matching foot and head boards) painted beech and pine, lined in brown, orange and red, on a cream ground. From an Upper Servant's room at Hardwick Hall, Derbyshire. *The National Trust*

118. An early nineteenth-century wall lamp, japanned yellow with black lines, the oil reservoir is set above a drip pan. One of many similar lamps at Chatsworth, Derbyshire. *The Chatsworth Settlement Trustees*

119. A finely painted early nineteenth-century chest of drawers with bamboo mouldings from Hardwick Hall, Derbyshire. This kind of inexpensive furniture is often recorded in servants' rooms. *The National Trust*

120. The festive painted decoration on this beech rush-seated chair is not a product of folk tradition, but an example of 'fancy' furniture encountered in many country houses around 1800. Renishaw Hall, Derbyshire. *Courtesy Reresby Sitwell*

chairs at Dunham Massey and Erddig. They illustrate a popular country-house design type which may be either 'fancy' furniture or intended for staff-rooms (Plate 120). Thomas Webster observed that rush seats 'are much improved by painting with oil paint, as then they can be washed with soap and water'.

Victorian bills, such as Marsh & Jones's account for supplying some exceedingly costly furniture to Titus Salt's new residence at Milnerfield, Yorkshire, in 1866, often include back-stairs items. The Servants' Room No.2 was provided with 'Two 3ft Iron Stump Bedsteads japanned green, a pitch pine wash-stand on chamfered standards, a 3 ft Chest of Drawers, a pitch pine dressing table, a 16 × 20 dressing glass, a dress closet and three birch cane seated chairs'.[25] This suite was very different from the assemblages of old or plain furniture regarded as acceptable a century earlier.

At the end of Queen Victoria's reign, Pratts of Bradford, in a specimen estimate for furnishing a six-roomed house for £150., suggested the following articles for the Servant's Bedroom (the date is 1901)[26]:

3ft Iron bedstead	0	17	6
Felt pad		3	6
Flock Hair Mattress	1	13	6
Bolster and Feather Pillow		9	6
3ft Painted Dressing Chest	1	5	0
Painted Wash-stand		9	9
Toilet Glass		6	0
Cane Seated Chair		4	0
Carpet strip		4	0
	5	12	3

This 'practical scheme', recommended at a time when for social reasons it was becoming increasingly difficult to recruit servants, nicely rounds off our survey of back-stairs furniture.

7 Alehouses, Inns and Taverns

Public houses in Georgian England can be broadly divided under three heads: the alehouse was for those who wanted to drink beer, taverns were for customers who preferred wine and food, and inns were where people stayed the night. Coffee-houses and chop-houses can be considered along with taverns to which they are closely related. Prime sources for studying the furniture and layout of these establishments include building plans and household inventories, together with contemporary illustrations of drinking scenes. Tracing securely provenanced early pub furniture is harder than might be expected.

ALEHOUSES

Until the Regency period, country alehouses were seldom different in plan and character from other village buildings (Plate 132), except for the sign, possibly a sundial, on the wall and benches outside. They were ordinary dwellings, often owned by farming families who brewed their own beer, where it was possible to buy a drink in the kitchen. These 'hedge alehouses' rarely made any special provision for customers other than offering the traditional comforts of a fire-side settle in congenial domestic surroundings. Should the squire call with some friends, they would be entertained in the landlord's private parlour.[1]

It is not easy to identify probate inventories detailing the house contents of these part-time publicans because home-brewing, like dairying, was widely practiced by yeoman farmers and there is usually no way of telling whether a brewhouse functioned on a domestic or a more commercial scale. However, Thomas Morritt of Tadcaster, described at his death in 1722 as a brewer, appears to have combined the trades of alehouse keeper and farmer. He left a barn containing agricultural gear, livestock and horses valued at over £40., as well as a fully-equipped brewhouse. The 'house-body', as living-kitchens were called in Yorkshire, was provided with hearth furniture, cooking utensils, a dresser, tall clock, one bed-pan and no fewer than sixteen chairs and three round tables, for the benefit of customers. Morritt still slept downstairs in the parlour where the appraisers found a bed with hangings, a press, a chest, a box, one cradle and a wanded chair.[2] His inventory gives a valuable insight into the furnishing of an early Georgian alehouse. Christopher Durham, innholder of Bellerby, North Yorkshire, also lived in a typical two-unit house, the contents of which amounted on his death in 1751 to just under £10.[3] The kitchen was sparsely furnished with a long settle, a table and two stools; the parlour contained a bed and a cupboard, while there were two chambers upstairs. His brewery contained a brass kettle, a mash vat cooler, a gile vat and some small casks. It is obvious that at this date, the local pub had not yet emerged as a building type in its own right.

As home-brewing declined and keeping an alehouse turned from a part- to a full-time occupation, the kitchen changed gradually from a place where the family lived and cooked into a drinking-room. At first beer had to be brought in a jug from the brewhouse or cellar as needed. Later, a corner of the public room was partitioned off as a cubicle where barrels of beer could be stored for the pot boys or maid servants to replenish their pitchers (see Plate 127). As a consequence, the room ceased to function as a kitchen and cooking was transferred to a back–kitchen; even so, it generally kept a homely character with a high-backed fire-side settle, chimney ornaments, a display of pewter on the dresser, long kitchen table with forms, common chairs and scatter of round tables. The embryonic bar in one corner operated (if it existed at all) only as a serving-hatch. The idea of a bar counter backed by a splendid array of vessels and bottles, where customers could stand and order drinks directly, originated in London taverns and was only slowly copied by country landlords. One of J.C. Loudon's plans (1833) for a modern Suburban Public House in the Old English Style shows a bar 'with a counter separating it from the shop, or place for standing customers'.[4] This arrangement altered the social environment of the pub and hastened the introduction of tall bar stools.

To recap: the family kitchen became, first of all, a drinking-room which retained, however, many of the amenities of a private house (Plate 121); then a small beer store was established near the cellar steps which was later adapted as a serving-hatch and then, initially in urban pubs, it became a bar counter for dispensing drinks to customers. As specialization and trade increased, the family's own parlour was turned into an apartment for better classes of patron. Even so, Flora Thompson's sketch of the *Waggon and Horses* at Lark Rise in Oxfordshire shows that the traditional alehouse survived in many English villages until a hundred years ago: 'They . . . went as a matter of course, appropriating their own seats on settle or bench. It was as much their home as their own cottages and far more homelike than many for them with its roaring fire, red window curtains, and well-scoured pewter'.[5]

121. *Dr Syntax Reading his Tour in the Kitchen of the Dun Cow*, aquatint by T. Rowlandson (1817). At this date beer was often consumed in the alehouse kitchen.

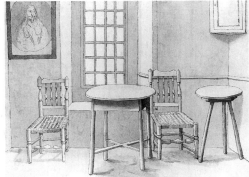

122. *Inside of a Country Alehouse*, mezzotint by W. Ward after George Morland (1797). *Courtesy Christie's*

123. *The Parlour at Kings Weston, Gloucestershire* by S.H. Grimm, *c.* 1788. A public drinking-room furnished with typical tables and common wicker-seated chairs. *By permission of the British Library*

124. Round drinking-table, the frieze drawer, possibly for dominoes, is inscribed 1821. Specifications for this type of pine table, commonly left in the white, occur in many early nineteenth-century cabinet-makers' *Books of Prices. Calderdale Museums Service*

George Morland's *Inside of a Country Alehouse* (1797), shows a group of rustics gathered round a fire.[6] One is seated on a fixed wall bench, another occupies a rush-seated ladder-back chair; a long table stands against the rear wall and there are two small circular drinking-tables, one constructed like a slab-top milking stool, the other of tripod pedestal form (Plate 122). This stone-flagged interior is a public drinking-room, the kitchen function having disappeared. About 1788 the artist S. H. Grimm recorded a typical ensemble of alehouse parlour furniture at Kings Weston, Gloucestershire. His sketch shows two traditional tables, a pair of common chairs, interestingly with wicker seats, and a hanging corner cupboard (Plate 123). By far the most popular pub table at this time had a round plank top supported on a triangular underframe united by stretchers (Plate 124). It was a practical and cheap ancestor of the familiar three-legged ornamental cast-iron table mass-produced for Victorian bars. Built of pine and commonly left in the white, they are described in most of the provincial price books under 'Deal Work'. *The Preston Cabinet and Chair-Makers Book of Prices* (1802), gives a typical specification:

ROUND DRINKING TABLE

For do 2 feet 6 inches, over or under with a triangular frame and lower rails	0	3	6
If without lower rails, deduct	0	0	6
Each inch above 2 feet 6 inches	0	0	1
If a shelf on lower rails	0	0	9

There is no contemporary evidence that they were ever called 'cricket' tables — a term favoured by dealers and collectors. Many late eighteenth-century alehouse scenes also show square-framed tables with forms, others of large oval drop-leaf design or long boards on X-shaped end supports (see Plate 127). This latter pattern was especially popular and several examples bearing the brand marks of Victorian and Edwardian brewers have been recorded[7] (Plate 125).

125. Traditional X-framed alehouse table in pine with iron stays, *c.* 1910. Branded 'WALL CUTLACK & HARLOCK LTD', a firm of brewers from Ely, Cambridgeshire. *Courtesy B.D. Cotton*

126. Two designs 'taken from existing specimens' published by J.C. Loudon in 1833. Left: 'a settle for the veranda of a common public-house'. Right: 'one of a more elevated character, suitable for the hall of a country inn in the old English style'.

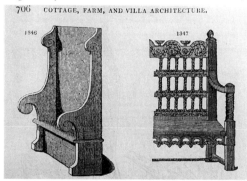

706 COTTAGE, FARM, AND VILLA ARCHITECTURE.

127. Alehouse interior by T. Rowlandson, *c.* 1813. Beer is being served from an embryonic bar near the door. Note the spit-rack over the chimney.

128. (*Opposite, above, right*) Design for a bar-room (viewed over the counter) published by J.C. Loudon in 1833. Fitted with bins for wine and liqueur bottles, shelves for glasses and beer pots, pigeon holes for bottled cordials and accommodation for large store vats and casks.

129. (*Opposite, above, far right*) Loudon's design for a mahogany counter (viewed from the bar-room) with built-in six-motion beer engine connected to butts in the cellar, a 'fountain' or spirit dispenser, sink and drawers for tobacco, biscuits, lemons and so forth.

Farmhouse kitchens with a back door leading directly outside often had a large settle positioned between the door and the fire, the high back extending down to the floor, thus creating a pleasantly warm area around the hearth. Settles long remained a traditional feature in village alehouses, sometimes even being built into partitions.[8] J.C. Loudon published designs for two in 1833, both 'taken from existing specimens' (Plate 126); one was intended 'for the veranda of a common public house', the other 'of a more enriched character . . . suitable for the hall of a country inn in the old English style'.[9]

The way the serving-hatch evolved is recorded in various contemporary illustrations, one of the best being Thomas Rowlandson's lively study *Dr Syntax in the Middle of a Smoking Hot Political Squabble, c.* 1810. The busy interior contains a familiar repertoire of alehouse furniture and kitchen paraphernalia with, in addition, a cubicle in the far corner where a woman is dispensing beer[10] (Plate 127). It was at this time still customary to drink sitting down; the habit of standing or perching on tall stools at a bar counter had not yet caught on.

The section in J.C. Loudon's *Encyclopaedia* (1833), describing every kind of drinking establishment from 'the Hedge Alehouse to the Mansion Inn', contains many architectural designs and abundant information about internal fittings and furniture[11] (Plate 128). He illustrates a modern bar counter with specialized equipment such as 'a six-motion beer engine' or suction pump for drawing ale directly from butts in the cellar and, alongside, a 'fountain' for dispensing spirits via tubes connected to casks (Plate 129). The Beer Act of 1830, which removed all duty on ale and allowed any householder to sell beer without applying to the licencing Justices, led to a huge increase in the number of pubs. Loudon observed that 'the fitting up of public house bars in London forms almost a distinct trade, and the expense incurred in this way by the owners . . . is almost incredible, every one vying with his neighbour in convenient arrangement, general display, rich carving, brass-work, finely veined mahogany, and ornamental painting'.[12] R.H. Bowman, a cabinet maker from Penrith, who kept an illustrated work journal after moving to London, noted in 1838: 'The beer Engine was finished about a week afterwards it took me about 4½ days to do it it was 22¼ long 14 high . . . the man grumbled at

£2. being charged for it'.[13] His drawing of the object is closely similar to Loudon's design.

Competition in the provinces was less feverish according to a dozen or so highly instructive public-house inventories compiled by John Dacre of Otley, Yorkshire, during the 1850s.[14] The average bar had a counter or board fitted with drawers, shelves and a 'motion beer machine'; there might be a dresser behind for measures, jugs, pots and glasses, while lockable spirits cupboards and 'book slates' are sometimes noted. The bar, tap-room and kitchen are most often mentioned as public drinking-rooms. They were always provided with fixed 'long seating' (valued by the foot)[15] and deal 'ale-tables' usually described as round and often having mole-skin or oil-cloth covers. Sets of turned bar stools with comfortable saddle seats did not become widely popular in Yorkshire until high Victorian days (Plate 130).

All the pubs on John Dacre's schedules had at least one parlour or 'snugg', which a generation or so earlier would have been the landlord's private sitting-room for entertaining company. Instead of plain wall seating and ale-tables, the furnishings were smarter, more comfortable and varied. One can discern a standard socially acceptable furnishing scheme in the rooms reserved for the better class of customer. This ensemble, designed to combine interest with a homely veneer, included clocks, weather-glasses, delph-racks, framed maps and prints, boot jacks, chimney ornaments, curtains and sometimes 'Scotch carpet'. Dacre often recorded amenities for recreation such as card-tables, 'bagatelle, cue & balls', a backgammon board or simply 'dice & box'. Shove h'penny does not appear to have been a popular game in the Otley area. The tops of shove-h'penny tables are usually highly polished and about 6 feet long by 18 to 24 inches wide with rounded corners, and of course inscribed lines; some have a swivel cup under the top to hold counters[16] (Plate 131). Domino-tables were generally circular, often with a small drawer or boxed-in underframe for keeping the tablets. As regards seating in the snug, large sets of 'Suffolk' chairs and yew Windsors (with cushions) are regularly listed, plus many ordinary elm, birch, beech, stained and painted chairs. The usual round drinking-tables in oak, sycamore or deal abound, while the occasional 'snap' table, old oak chest, rocking-chair, sofa, dresser and items of mahogany furniture served to give the room a domestic character.

A remarkable group of mainly pre-Victorian alehouse furniture at the old Sun Inn, Bilsdale, on the North York Moors, provides a welcome chance to study objects rather than archives. This remote seventeenth-century cruck-framed thatched cottage, known as Spout House (Plate 132), was licenced to sell beer from 1714 to 1914 when the new Sun Inn was built across the yard. It then survived through neglect until the National Parks Authority embarked in 1980 on a renovation programme. The original kitchen (Plate 133) retains, against the speer or heck, a

130. Bar stool by William Brear & Sons, Addingham, Yorkshire, c. 1900. Stained beech with a sycamore seat and brass foot rail. From one of Joshua Tetley's public houses. *Leeds Museums*

131. Walnut table, early eighteenth century, the top marked out for the game of shove h'penny, a popular pastime in alehouses. *Courtesy Tom Crispin*

132. Spout House, The Old Sun Inn, a seventeenth-century cruck-framed and thatched building in Bilsdale on the North York Moors. *Courtesy N.Y.M. National Park*

133. The interior of Spout House showing a heck seat, early nineteenth-century long settle in oak and elm with a later seat, scrubbed pine table and painted form. All the furniture is original to the alehouse. *Royal Commission on Historical Monuments, England*

built-in seat with shaped slab end forming a traditional ingle-nook; there is a fine early nineteenth-century spindle-back settle which stood on the opposite side of the hearth; a low upholstered couch of similar date stuffed with hay, typical of the region, known locally as a 'squab'; an oak corner cupboard to hold china and glass; a large painted rectangular kitchen table with matching form; a familiar round drinking-table and half a dozen common chairs dating from *c.* 1800 and *c.* 1850 and *c.* 1900 (Plate 134). The scheme pre-dates the introduction of fixed 'long seating' which, when the kitchen became a tap-room, was extended to other parts of the interior. A watercolour painted about 1910 of another small country pub, The Old Lord Nelson at Beck Hole on the east side of the North York Moors, shows a similar arrangement (Plate 135). Although it is now a private house, the ingle-seat and some simple wall benches remain. Like Spout House, it never aspired to a bar counter or even a serving-hatch, and beer was carried up in jugs directly from the cellar.[17]

INNS

Wayside inns were a popular subject with artists. The lively illustrations which Thomas Rowlandson contributed to the various *Tours of Dr Syntax* provide a particularly amusing and well-observed record of English inns during the late Georgian period. Surviving buildings and household inventories confirm that smaller rural inns, often run by a farmer and his wife, differed little from other local houses except that the cellar, stables and brewhouse tended to be larger, the bedrooms rather more numerous and they possessed extra drinking and eating utensils.[18] As a class, innholders were more prosperous than other members of the community. The comfortably domestic 'home from home' character of country inns was exploited in Oliver Goldsmith's comedy *She Stoops to Conquer* (1773), where Tony Lumpkin is able convincingly to dupe Marlow into believing that he is at an inn, and behaving accordingly, when in fact he is in the house of his prospective father-in-law. Large coaching inns, on the other hand, cultivated a 'grander than home' image to catch the eye of the traveller. They provided suites of well-furnished private apartments and often contained impressive dining-rooms, ball-rooms or club-rooms for local entertainments and assembleys. A large staff catered for well-to-do guests while their servants and coachmen had their own communal quarters.

The Crown Inn at Wellington in Shropshire was a typical three-unit yeoman house with lofts, a cellar and farm buildings. When the landlord, John Judgson, died in 1708, it contained twelve beds.[19] The best room, situated as was customary on the first floor, was known as the 'Crown Chamber' and furnished in a traditional style with two feather beds, two large tables, one chest, two joint forms, ten stools and a looking-glass, it was evidently used more often for large gatherings than it was as a bed chamber. His widow, Elizabeth, added a 'Newe Roome' and her probate inventory, taken in 1716, shows the ten stools in the Crown Chamber had been replaced by 'six Green Cloth Chaires and one Joyned Chair'; the furniture in this room otherwise remained unchanged. Mrs Judgson in fact got rid of all thirty-five stools recorded at the time of her husband's death, substituting a trio of 'segg chairs' (rush-bottomed) for the three in the kitchen. She also tripled the value of household linen. The new furniture acquired for the principal chamber put it on a par with the equivalent room at The Swan, the largest inn in Wellington, kept by Rowland Goole who had died in April 1708 — the same month as her husband. His inventory shows that the 'Swan Chamber' contained an almost identical ensemble: 'one Bed, 3 Tables, 12 chairs, one looking glass and 2 pr of Curtains for the windows'.

The Crown passed to William Judgson who died in 1725. During his time the Crown Chamber was left undisturbed, but he turned the 'New Parlour', which ten years before had been very sparsely furnished, into the best guest room. It now

134. A trio of chairs abandoned in the loft at Spout House, illustrating three different phases of furnishing, *c.* 1800, *c.* 1850, *c.* 1900. *Courtesy N.Y.M. National Park*

135. Interior of The Old Lord Nelson at Beck Hole, near Goathland, North Yorkshire, c. 1910. Notice the heck with its ingle-bench, fixed seating beneath the fire window, kitchen range and circular drinking-table. The air of homeliness is typical of village alehouses. *F.A. Brown*

boasted a feather bed, two small tables, a table screen, six leather chairs, a form, a gleaming warming-pan, a clock and case and a bag of hops. He also increased the total number of chairs from twelve to thirty-three. A looking-glass – the fashionable status symbol in his father's day – had evidently been replaced in popular esteem by a handsome long-case clock ticking away in one corner. A series of inventories relating to the same house are of particular value, because even over a short period they often document significant changes in the social use of furniture. One could search for a long time before finding a better instance of a household throwing out all its old joint stools when the head of the family died; furthermore, the fact the Judgson family kept an inn suggests this type of seating had ceased to be acceptable to the community as a whole.

Three mid-eighteenth-century inventories, one describing the contents of a large coaching inn (The Bull at Stamford, Lincolnshire, 1755), another located in a busy market town (The George, Ripley, Yorkshire, 1755), and the third, a modest wayside hostelry kept by John Wilks of Boroughbridge, on the Great North Road in Yorkshire, repay study.

John Wilks, like many country innholders, had a small holding on which he kept livestock — a few pigs, a cow, calf and a mare. Despite possessing three silver gill tankards and a silver pint pot, his estate amounted to only £22. and he died owing two years' rent and lesser sums for malt, hops, porter and cider. His inventory, taken in 1762, is unusually vivid.[20] His 'Housestead' still retained the character of a farmhouse kitchen, although the family now cooked in a back-kitchen. It contained 'one dresser and shelves' arrayed with twenty-one pewter dishes and three dozen plates; there was also a little display of brightly polished utensils including: '1 Warming pan, 5 Brass Candlesticks, a Copper frying pan and a Copper Coffee Pot'. Customers sat either on chairs or the 'Long Settle', there were three 'Tables' and three iron candlesticks to light guests to bed, plus the usual chimney furniture. Private parties might prefer to eat and drink in the 'Little Parlour' which contained '6 Chairs, 2 Tables and some Prints'. John Wilks, a widower, presumably slept in the 'Cellar Parlour' since it allowed access to his (sadly depleted) drinks store. The last ground-floor room was equipped for eating and drinking with '1 Long Table, 4 Chairs and 1 Long Settle', but the provision of '1 Close Bedstead' (which folded

136. (*Opposite, above*) *Dr Syntax at an Inn Copying the Wit of the Window*, aquatint by T. Rowlandson (1817). An excellent record of a smartly furnished guest parlour. Notice the arrangement of glass and china in the hanging corner cupboard.

137. (*Opposite, below*) A Bedroom at an Inn from Eugene Lami, *Voyage en Angleterre*, 1830. The traveller is removing his shoes with the aid of a boot jack, while the maid offers him a pair of slippers.

away into a cupboard), a chest of drawers and '1 pannel chest' meant that if needed, it could also serve as a bedroom. In the 'Best Chamber' upstairs the appraisers listed: '2 Feather Beds . . . 1 pr Chest of Drawers, 1 Round Table & 6 Chairs and a Corner Cupboard'. This must have been where more affluent travellers stayed. There were two other less well-furnished bedchambers each with two bedsteads, a table and chairs or forms. John Wilks, despite some debts, appears to have lived comfortably, brewing, entertaining guests, tending his beasts and haymaking in season. His inventory is a capital document.

The Bull at Stamford, situated 150 miles south of Boroughbridge on the Great North Road, was an important coaching inn with over forty rooms. A comprehensive inventory, made when the landlord, Thomas Darlow, was declared bankrupt in 1754,[21] reveals that the bedrooms were named rather pretentiously after towns: the Grantham/Lincoln/York/Exeter/Wakefield/London or by colour Pink/Rose/Violet and so on. Most were wallpapered and smartly furnished with four-post beds, pictures, window curtains and 'Dutch matting' or 'foot Carpets' on the floor. The inn had a post office (tables and chairs), a post-boys' room (only beds and bedding), an ostlers' room over the stables, a cheese-garret, a well-equipped laundry, maids' rooms and many Domestic Offices. The guest chambers and principal public rooms – bar, dining-room and coffee-room – were fashionably elegant because up-market innkeeping was a competitive business (Plate 136). The element of ostentatious display at The Bull was often palely emulated on the vernacular level in the interiors of humble wayside hostelries.

Coffee, chocolate, tea, punch, wine, ale or spirits, could be ordered at the bar served either in china cups, 'twisted wine glasses' or silver tankards. There was a box of pipes, a supply of slippers, backgammon tables and chamber pots for those in need, also a desk with writing-paper and lignum vitae inkstands; hungry travellers were provided with ivory-handled silver knives and forks to eat food brought in on a mahogany hand-board or served from dumb waiters. Ale came in earthenware jugs, bottles of wine in leather buckets, punch in a bowl and 'a Dutch Tea Kettle and Lamp' was available for those who preferred tea. The presence of looking-glasses with candle arms in the main public rooms and items such as 'a Chapanned Corner Cupboard', a mahogany 'Scallop Tea Table' and a weather-glass created an impression of luxury. The chairs are mostly described as 'leather-bottomed' or matted and there were many 'screen tables', a popular name for 'snap' or small circular tripod pedestal tables with a tip-up top commonly used for eating and drinking.

Thomas Rodwell, landlord of The George at Ripley, a small market town on the road between Harrogate and Ripon, kept a medium-sized inn. At the time of his death in 1755, the 'fore House' was furnished in almost exactly the same manner as John Wilks's 'Housestead', except for the addition of a clock.[22] It contained: 'The Dresser and Plate Case, Clock and Case, A long Settle, one Oval Table, one Ditto, Six Chairs, Three Coffee Potts, one Warming Pan, one large Rainge and Grate, Fire Shovel, Tongs, Poker and Fender'. This was a more or less standard repertoire in the living-rooms of yeoman farmers at the time. Although The George boasted eighteen rooms and Thomas Rodwell's estate was appraised at £256. there are other interesting parallels with John Wilks's much humbler inn. For example his 'Little Parlour' was furnished with '6 Chairs, 2 Tables and some Prints', whereas the 'Little Dining Room' at The George contained 'Six chairs, one Oval Table, three Maps and eight Pictures'. However, there was also, at Ripley, a grander 'Fore Dining Room' for entertaining company.

The guest bedchambers (Plate 137), on the other hand, displayed affinities with those at The Bull in Stamford for not only were they named the Red/Blue/Green Room, but the furniture corresponded. The Blue Room, for instance, had: 'a Bedstead & Hangings, one Dressing Table, one Seeing Glass, Five Chairs, one Rainge, Rod & Window Hangings £9. 17s.' whereas the 'York' bedchamber at

Stamford was equipped with: 'two Bedsteads', curtains & vallances, a Dressing table and Glass, 6 Chairs, a Grate, fender, etc, one Oval Table, Window Curtains and Rods, 2 small foot carpets £9. 9s.'. The amount of bedding: 'One Feather Bed, Pillows and Bolster, one Quilt, two Blankets' was in each case identical. However, The Bull scored heavily over The George in the amenities of the bar. Thomas Rodwell served tea and coffee, dispensed clay pipes from an iron cradle and sought to impress customers by a traditional show of silver tankards, gills, pints, salts, punch-ladles, and teaspoons, appraised at £24. While this parade compared favourably with John Wilks's three silver tankards and a silver pint, valued at £4., it fell far short of the 271 ounces of plate worth £74. at The Bull Inn.

Despite the wide differences in status, analysis of these three mid-Georgian inventories shows that inns shared certain basic attributes. Travellers expected to find a room with pictures on the walls where they could eat either at separate or communal tables. They also required a comfortable bed in a room provided with a table and chairs – for drinking with their companions. The character of the bar, or in the case of small inns the 'house place', was very important. An element of display, be it a clock, gleaming shelves of pewter, brightly polished brass ware or an exhibition of silver, was clearly expected. John Wilks offered the attractions of a congenial farmhouse kitchen, although the cooking was done by his daughter in a back room. Mansion inns lacked this intimate domestic touch but provided an ostentatiously splendid environment where drinks, tobacco and food were dispensed.

J.C. Loudon, writing in 1833 offers, as usual, valuable insights.[23] 'A characteristic of an inn' he observed 'is the bar, or office to which all enquiries are addressed, and from which all orders are issued. The furniture consists chiefly of two or three chairs, with a common round table, a work-table, and a bureau, or writing-desk. There is also generally a clock . . . a cupboard for glass and china, drawers and shelves for tea and coffee urns, the pots, coffee pots, punch bowls . . . vertical divisions for tea trays, waiters . . . a supply of hot and cold water. In presses and drawers in the bar are also kept the table linen, nappery and plate'. This is a pretty fair description of the bars in The George and The Bull, which again underlines the conservative character of inns. Loudon also observed: 'A napkin-press is one of the most useful articles of inn furniture, since table cloths, napkins, towels, etc. after having been used, but not soiled, if neatly folded and pressed, may be made to look as if newly washed and mangled'. At The Bull, the napkin-press was located in the laundry while at The George it was handily kept in the bar.

Two drawings of interiors by S.H. Grimm provide a welcome record of inn furnishings.[24] The earlier, sketched in 1787, is titled: *A part of a parlour at the Saracen's Head at Southwell, called King Charles' Room, Notts* (Plate 138). It depicts a panelled room with six rush-seated ladder-back chairs standing around the walls, a large drop-leaf dining-table stationed beneath a looking-glass at the far end, a circular 'screen table' in one corner and, reflected in the mirror, is an oval gate-leg table, again pushed back against the wall in the approved formal manner. This familiar ensemble had, as we have seen, a long ancestry, and as an added bonus the chairs may well reflect a local Nottinghamshire pattern. The second pen-and-wash drawing, dated 1797, depicts the Assembly Room of an inn at Salthill, Buckinghamshire; with two long trestle-tables laid for company, there are imposing chairs at the head and simple forms down each side. Apart from a reefed window curtain, a huge pedimented press and a stylish chimneypiece, the room is bare (Plate 139). The feast probably followed the ceremony of the Montem, a folk ritual performed on Windmill Hill nearby, shown in other sketches from the same series.

Inventories and illustrations suggest that, when furnishing rooms, landlords observed certain widely understood conventions attuned to their customers' expectations of comfort and style. Inn furniture itself never really acquired a distinctive character, although room arrangements clearly followed traditional patterns. It is, however, worth pointing out that because the furniture needed to be generally fairly robust, many landlords in the Georgian period retained archaic oak pieces because of their sturdy qualities, rather than opting for lightly constructed modern articles, a practice which may explain our national fondness for old-fashioned inns.

TAVERNS AND COFFEE-HOUSES

A tavern was, according to Dr Johnson, 'a place where wine is sold and drinkers entertained'. They were usually found in towns and, like mansion inns, provided not only food, drink, lodging and stabling for travellers, but meeting-rooms for clubs or businessmen, games-rooms and halls for local entertainments. A very thorough research report was published when the Gadsby Tavern Museum in Alexandria, Virginia, was opened in 1980, but no equivalent study of English taverns has been made.[25]

Tavern- and coffee-house owners were less concerned than innkeepers to create the impression of a private home. Thomas Rowlandson's watercolour *The Cock Tavern*, his *Interior of an Eating House* and various coffee-house sketches[26] show parties seated at tables in rows of separate boxes, the divisions formed by the high bench-backs headed by posts and rails supporting curtains, to give a sense of privacy and seclusion (Plate 140). Where the fire continued to be a focal point, room arrangements were less formal with customers seated on chairs at small tripod tables, sometimes partitioned off by movable folding screens, while illustrations of common chop-houses or Ordinaries show diners accommodated on plain forms around a communal table.

In many city taverns and coffee-houses, drinks were dispensed by a pretty barmaid from behind a curved counter backed by a shelved wall-niche for holding china, glasses, bottles and bowls. This urban development, as noted earlier, was the origin of the gin-palace and eventually the pub bar. A rare pictorial record of a London coffee-tavern dating from about 1700 shows groups of men talking, reading, smoking and drinking, while seated at trestle-tables on forms or a long fixed wall bench (Plate 141). One waiter pours coffee and another collects clay pipes from a chest in front of the serving-hatch. There are pictures and notices on the wall and a cheerful fire where customers are ensconced on a settle and in a tub chair. This scene corresponds closely to a description of London coffee-houses published by Henri Misson in 1698: 'These Houses, which are very numerous in *London*, are extremely convenient. You have all Manner of News there: You have a good fire,

138. (*below, left*) *Parlour at the Saracen's Head, called King Charles' Room, Southwell, Nottinghamshire* by S.H. Grimm, *c.* 1787. The furniture in this elegant dining-parlour was paraded against the walls when the room was not in use. *By permission of the British Library*

139. (*below, right*) *Room in an Inn at Salthill, Buckinghamshire* by S.H. Grimm, *c.* 1793. The tables and forms have evidently been specially set up for a feast in this handsome interior. *By permission of the British Library*

140. *Interior of an Eating House* by T. Rowlandson, *c.* 1810. The diners are seated on high-backed settles forming 'boxes'. Note the 'Act of Parliament' wall clock. *Henry Huntingdon Library and Art Gallery*

141. *Interior of a London Coffee-House*, anonymous watercolour, *c.* 1700. A rare early record of what were to become highly popular establishments. *By permission of the British Library*

which you may sit by as long as you please: You have a Dish of Coffee; You meet your Friends for the Transaction of Business, and all for a Penny, if you do not care to spend more'.[27]

8 Regional Chairmaking Traditions

A stimulating recent advance in vernacular furniture studies has been the successful mapping of regional chairmaking traditions. Provincial antique dealers and some collectors were vaguely aware that Windsor chairs occasionally feature a maker's stamp and that local styles existed; but until Dr Bill Cotton started an ambitious programme of research aimed to identify regional designs, no furniture historian had attempted seriously to investigate this subject.[1] Indeed, there was a widespread feeling that apart from defining patterns made in a few centres such as Rockley, Macclesfield and Mendlesham, it would be impossible to establish firm bearings in this field and that 'country' chairs were irretrievably anonymous. Happily, the subject responded well to a fresh approach and, due largely to the exertions of one man, we can now feel reasonably confident about making regional attributions.[2] Having grasped the significance of name-stamped chairs, Dr Cotton, a dealer specializing in turned chairs, was uniquely well-placed to photograph, record and collect them; for other members of the trade, once his interest became known, actively steered named examples in his direction and so on impressive study collection was built up.

Some chairs carry a combined personal and place-name, such as 'AMOS GRANTHAM', others may only bear a maker's name and many just have initials, while a few sport paper labels, stencilled marks or inscriptions (Plates 142–50). By laboriously compiling an index of chairmakers and turners listed in trade directories, Census Returns and similar sources, it proved possible to identify many of the craftsmen who employed a name stamp. The index also, of course, provided a vital bank of precise information about addresses, active dates, apprenticeships and the chair trade in general. Having linked specific chair designs to individual makers and places, local records could be searched for additional biographical details; while a careful stylistic and technical analysis of the chairs themselves revealed how different shop practices interacted with regional design traditions. Having mapped the evidence there remained some areas – Shropshire and Staffordshire, for example – where the industry obviously thrived although no named chairs had been traced. In such cases, paintings and photographs featuring chairs may help to illuminate local styles and energetic field-work sometimes leads to the discovery of seat furniture which has descended in local families or survived in churches or institutions.

At least eight coherent English regional traditions can now be recognized, although their emergence in the eighteenth century is only sketchily documented because name stamps were rarely used before about 1820. Their nineteenth-century development has, however, been clarified to the point where it is now not only possible to place many unstamped chairs within a regional framework, but variant town and even workshop styles can be identified. The subject, at its frontier, is increasingly complex, so an attempt will be made to survey the main traditions and sub-groups in broad outline and take a closer took at the intriguing communities of Windsor chairmakers active in the old Sherwood Forest district of north Nottinghamshire. Much less is known about the makers and regional origin of joiner-made

Detail from the painting of *Sir Roger and Lady Bradshaigh of Haigh Hall, Lancashire*, by A. Devis, dated 1746, showing a park with two Windsor chairs (see Plate 186).

101

142. Mark of William Cole (son-in-law of Philip Clissett) Bosbury, Herefordshire. *Leeds Art Galleries*

143. Mark of Frederick Walker, Rockley, Nottinghamshire, struck on the seat edge of a Windsor chair (see Plate 164).

144. Mark of John Kerry, Evesham, Worcestershire, struck on the back post of a ladder-back chair (see Plate 190).

145. Mark of John Gabbitass, Worksop, Nottinghamshire, branded under the seat of a Windsor chair (see Plate 167).

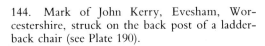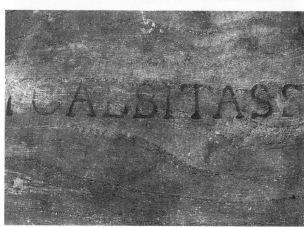

146. Mark of John Hubbard, Grantham, Lincolnshire, struck on the dished seat of a Windsor chair. *Leeds Art Galleries*

147. Trade label of Benjamin Gilling, Worksop, Nottinghamshire, under the seat of a Windsor chair (see Plate 168).

148. Initials of John Steele (?), Middlewich, Cheshire, struck on the front leg of a spindle-back chair. *Leeds Art Galleries*

149. Mark of Charles Leicester, Macclesfield, Cheshire, on the back post of a ladder-back chair (see Plate 156).

150. Maker's mark struck on the fan-tail of a High Wycombe wheel-back Windsor chair (see Plate 178).

common Chippendale and Hepplewhite-style chairs which are treated towards the end of this chapter.

THE NORTH WEST

An occupation abstract published by the government after the 1841 Census includes details of how many chairmakers worked in each county; town totals are also given and there are even Returns for the numbers of chairmakers in workhouses, gaols and lunatic asylums.[3] Statistics from the North West underline the region's status as a major chair-producing area. There were 547 chairmakers resident in Lancashire, with 108 in Cheshire, 55 in Cumberland and 22 in Westmorland; leaving aside London, only Buckinghamshire's 398 approached the Lancashire muster. Ten years later many town totals had increased to give figures such as Manchester (178), Liverpool (106), Preston (42), Blackburn (38), Ashton-under-Lyne (34), Wigan (32), Clithero (28), Congleton (26), Oldham (20) and Stockport (20). The area clearly sustained a highly developed industry producing rush-seated spindle- and ladder-back chairs, mainly for the homes of urban textile workers. They were typically made in stained ash, although alder – also used for clog soles – was employed in certain workshops. Some hybrid chairs combined vernacular styles with elements assimilated from fashionable designs (see Plate 17). The classic patterns have all been provenanced by named examples to towns in the region.[4]

Standard spindle-back side chairs have two tiers of spindles and the armchairs three. The back posts are squared with chamfers below the seat and turned above, ending in nipple finials, while the front legs terminate in pad-and-ball feet. Tight concepts of design allowed only for strictly limited variations in the ornamental turning of front stretchers, profiling of spindles, treatment of the top rail and feet; the overwhelming impression is one of uniformity rather than variety. One of the most coherent sub-groups features a carved fan or shell motif on the crest rail; examples stamped by Charles Leicester of Macclesfield are known (Plate 151) and an interesting early version, dated 1801, is to be found in one of the Gillow Estimate Sketch Books captioned 'Liverpool chair / Stained red'[5] (Plate 152). The ash wood and rushes cost 2s. 2d., 'Staining Wax and Sprigs 6d' and Jno Harrison was paid 2s. 3d. for making it. Sprigs are the thin strips of wood nailed to the seat edge. This widely popular pattern was evidently made in a number of workshops.

151. Spindle-back chair, stained ash with shell motif. Stamped on the back leg 'C. LEICESTER', of Macclesfield, Cheshire, c. 1820–30. *Leeds Art Galleries*

152. Drawing for a 'Liverpool chair' from the Gillow Estimate Sketch Books, 1801. The cost details reveal the ash frame was stained red. *Westminster City Archives*

153. The so-called 'wavy line' ladder back with nipple finials was a popular Lancashire pattern. This stained ash chair probably dates from the mid-nineteenth century. *Courtesy Sotheby's Sussex Sale-room*

154. 'Bar top' ladder-back chair, stained ash, probably made in the Wigan area of Lancashire during the second quarter of the nineteenth century. From Criccieth, North Wales. *F.L. Gilbert*

Few Lancashire ladder-back chairs, known at the time as 'cross splat-back chairs', bear a maker's mark, but the frames are so closely affiliated to spindle forms to leave no doubt regarding their common origin. The tradition produced three easily recognizable but interrelated main models. The largest group, which developed directly from eighteenth-century prototypes, has nipple-top back posts bridged by a set of rungs, its distinguishing feature being the absence of a top bar connecting the two uprights. Armchairs regularly have one more rung than matched side chairs. The graduated and bowed (known at the time as 'sweep') cross splats offered ample

155. Best quality ladder-back armchairs from the Billinge–Wigan area of Lancashire were styled with a handsome scroll cresting. *Courtesy B.D. Cotton*

156. A typical Macclesfield-pattern ladder-back armchair by Charles Leicester, *c.* 1825–50. Stained ash frame, the original rush seat retains its sprigs. Marked on back leg (see Plate 149). *Leeds Art Galleries*

scope for attractive profiling, often with an ogee lower line; ladder backs in fact exhibit rather more variety than their sister spindle chairs. Although evidence for authorship is scanty, it is possible to identify coherent groups, one of the most prolific being the 'wavy line' model (Plate 153).

A second homogeneous family, termed the 'bar top' ladder back, also has its roots in the eighteenth century and survives in large numbers (Plate 154). The common design feature is a slightly bowed top rail fixed across the posts and either shaped to echo the arched splats or, in superior versions, styled with a 'scroll' cresting (Plate 155). Chairs with both head rails have passed to the descendants of John Jackson (1787–1870), chairmaker of Billinge, near Wigan,[6] while one stamped 'P. LEICESTER', who is recorded as working at Hyde and Plumley between 1841 and 1874, provides another point of reference.[7] With the coming of railways, this type was widely distributed; many certainly found a ready market in rural North Wales.

The third main group – Macclesfield ladder backs – are distinguished by a slender turned and curved top rail with 'barrel' or 'reel' terminals dowelled to the back posts (Plate 156). Many are, often rather faintly, impressed 'C. LEICESTER' (see Plate 149), for Charles Leicester who worked at Chestergate and later Derby Street between 1816 and 1860.[8] Virtually identical models were stamped by James Riding, a chairmaker who occupied premises next door to Leicester from 1816 to 1819.[9] The curved rod which joins the tops of the back posts could be used for draping a rug or similar soft fabric (see Plates 49 and 70). Leicester and his peers seldom sold directly to the gentry, but an isolated bill records that in 1810 he supplied Sir John Fleming of Tabley House, Cheshire, with a dozen chairs at 7s. each.

Eighteenth-century spindle-and-ladder-back chairs were more heavily built, often had ornate finials and were sometimes painted green (Plates 157 and 158). None of these characteristics survived into the following century when lightness of construction combined with stained and polished finishes became the rule. Rush seats were, however, occasionally painted as a protection, it was claimed, against vermin. Most seat weavers, matters or bottomers, as they used to be known, were women and children often working in their own homes, although itinerant rush weavers who repaired old chairs were usually men.[10] Rushes came in 'bolts', large

 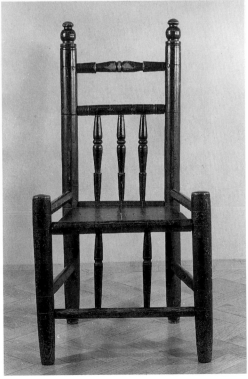

157. *Plucking the Turkey* by Henry Walton, 1776. Detail showing a common turned chair; prominent ornamental finials disappeared by the end of the century. *Trustees of the Tate Gallery*

158. Turned ash chair with original green paint, mid-eighteenth century. The setting-out marks, to ensure accurate drilling prior to assembly, are boldly incised as ornamental rings. *Guiseley Church, Yorkshire*

105

bundles, measuring about 40 inches round, and had to be dampened to make them pliable. Alternatively, seats were worked in wicker (see Plates 13 and 123), but board seats were almost never employed. Because turned chairs were produced in specialist workshops, they do not figure in contemporary Books of Prices. The only sawn parts were the cross splats and arms. These members would be laid out with templates, likewise the turned components were set out with a marking gauge before being lathe-turned. Both workshop practices promoted consistency of design.

The only evidence of a Windsor-chair tradition in Lancashire comes from the Gillow Estimate Sketch Books which contain three drawings, together with a cost analysis, for cherry (1798) and ash (1806) stick-back Windsors[11] (Plate 159). They all exhibit uniform turnery and have a very shallow 'crinoline' stretcher; unmarked examples surface from time to time (Plate 160), but their existence hardly constitutes a tradition.[12]

Little reliable information has so far been gleaned about chairs made in rural Lancashire and the Lake Counties, but the evidence of field-work and one signed ladder-back chair from Penrith suggests they were much less sophisticated than those from urban centres.[13] The Typical 'Dales' chair had a robust turned ash frame with minimal embellishments, the thick posts being united by plain stretchers, those at the front perhaps detailed with a swelling (Plate 161). The back was usually designed with a stay rail and two cross bars supporting a row of three tall spindles. The alternative ladder backs also lacked metropolitan refinements, simply styled cross splats and a little incised turning being normal. The description 'common turned chair' fits these types admirably; they are honest products of the native vernacular tradition with a long ancestry and a wide geographical distribution.

Welcome information as to how a small chair-and bobbin-turner's workshop in Lancashire was equipped comes from a deposition made by Mark Chippindale after his premises at Aighton Bailey and Chaigley were burnt down in 1815.[14] The documents include an inventory of the 'stock in trade, Timber, Machinery, Tools, Utensils and Effects' lost in the fire and reveal that the thatched workshop harnessed

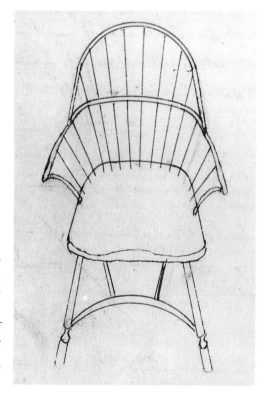 

159. Drawing for an elm and cherry Windsor chair from the Gillow Estimate Sketch Books, 1798. The cost of materials and labour for making such a chair was 9s. *Westminster City Archives*

160. Windsor armchair made by Gillows of Lancaster, *c.* 1800. Ash with an elm seat, originally painted green. One of four from the Judges' Lodgings, Lancaster. *Lancashire County Museum Service*

water power to drive a circular saw, two boring lathes, three turning benches and a press drill; in addition, hand tools to the value of £24. were destroyed. The shop also contained two grindstones, vice, boards, work benches and training benches (to bend steam-heated chair parts). The extent of mechanization is perhaps surprising, since Chippindale employed only two men. The bobbins were reckoned at £151. compared to 'Chair backs and Chairs finished' amounting to £46. The timber lost consisted of deal, ash, eder (willow), birch, crab and alder boards together with 'bobbin wood' — possibly hazel. Chippindale was probably typical in combining chairmaking with other branches of turnery.

SHROPSHIRE

Shropshire is a county of contrasts with industrial towns in the north, and scattered villages to the south. It numbered thirty chairmakers at the time of the 1841 Census, ten being based in Wellington which was the largest urban centre. No turned chairs bearing a name stamp can with certainty be provenanced to the region, but oral testimony, field-work and a study of old photographs has permitted the identification of several local vernacular patterns.[15] The three commonest designs have, typically, either cross splats, a single row of tall spindles or a solid vase-shaped back splat, but the really striking feature which unites these groups and gives the tradition a clear regional identity, is a curved crest rail dowelled across the top of the back posts (Plate 162). Most of the chairs have wooden seat boards, intended to be used with a cushion, although a few were rushed.

Chairs lacking the unique flat top, but otherwise fully expressing the regional character, survive in large numbers. It seems likely that the more elegant examples with pad feet and ornamental 'bell' turning were made in urban workshops, while plainer specimens are products of village chairmakers such as the Owens of Clun in the south of the county. The last active member of this family was J. Owen (d. c. 1900), a self-employed part-time chairmaker who rented a building at a sawyer's yard and turned parts from coppice ash. The finished chairs (said to be spindle backs) were taken to local markets on his hand cart.[16]

NORTH NOTTINGHAMSHIRE

The hamlet of Rockley holds a special place in the affections of everyone devoted to vernacular furniture because the discovery, some twenty years ago, that this tiny settlement supported a thriving community of Windsor chairmakers, inspired the first wave of research into regional chairs.[17] Rockley lies amid fields in the Sherwood Forest district of Nottinghamshire, four miles south of Retford. It had been built beside the Great North Road in 1826–7 by the landowner and named after some nearby rocks.

Valuable information about the Rockley chairmakers comes from Census Returns and trade directories, but these routine sources are supplemented by evidence in local Methodist archives.[18] Thus, we know that William Wheatland, listed as a chairmaker of Beardsall's row, Retford, in 1822, was also a member of the Retford Methodist Circuit and became, in 1821, Leader of the nearby lapsed Gamston Class. Interestingly, three members of Wheatland's small class also followed his trade: John Whitworth, who worked in Gamston as wheelwright and chairmaker until 1851; Joseph Godfrey, recorded at Worksop 1841–51 and Frederick Walker, who was active at Rockley for over four decades. A few years after assuming pastoral responsibilities at Gamston, Wheatland set up as a joiner, wheelwright and chairmaker at Rockley, only a mile away, erecting a workshop beside the main road. It was a long, single-storey brick building which survived until 1971. In 1827 he supplied a tiny adjoining plot on which the first Methodist Chapel was built. Wheatland's new shop attracted an influx of journeymen: he recruited George

161. Common turned ash chair probably from the North West. These plain spindle-back chairs are thought to have been made in the Dales between c. 1760 and 1820. *B.D. Cotton collection*

162. This turned ash chair was probably made in the urbanized Wellington–Telford area of Shropshire during the first half of the nineteenth century. The wooden seat and perched top rail are distinctive local features. *Courtesy B.D. Cotton*

163. Low-back ash Windsor stamped 'NI-CHOLSON / ROCKLEY' for George Nicholson who worked at Rockley, Nottinghamshire, *c.* 1830–40. The 'fleur-de-lys' splat was a popular pattern. *Private collection*

164. Best high-back yew Windsor by Frederick Walker of Rockley, Nottinghamshire, *c.* 1840–50. Maker's mark struck on seat edge (see Plate 143) *Peter Brears*

Nicholson, Frederick Walker, William Fotheringham and John Stocks, while Isaac Fritchley also worked at Rockley for a time. Unfortunately in 1830, Wheatland went bankrupt, resigned as Class Leader and is not heard of again. Despite this setback, Rockley had been successfully launched as a chairmaking centre; Wheatland also deserves credit for initiating the custom of boldly impressing a name/place stamp on the seat edge of chairs. This practice became widespread in the region, but Windsors marked by the Rockley masters outnumber those from other places.

George Nicholson, who had children baptized at the Rockley Chapel between 1831 and 1836, took over the business and workforce (Plate 163), soon to be joined by William Burton. The 1841 Census Returns record Nicholson as aged forty with William Smith, fifteen, resident apprentice. At this date Rockley consisted of thirteen terraced cottages with a population of sixty-two, exactly half being members of chairmaking families. The Census captured the hamlet at its zenith as a Windsor chairmaking community with six active tradesmen. When White's *Directory* appeared in 1844, Frederick Walker had assumed control and many of the workmen had departed, leaving him master of a greatly reduced operation. The reasons for this are unclear, but chairmaking seems always to have been prone to sudden change and upheavals caused by a mobile workforce. However Walker, assisted by his son Henry, was a survivor. During the first ten years, they gave employment to Nicholson's former apprentice William Smith (named as victualler and chairmaker), John Freeborough and William Dukes, while James, the eldest son, joined them for about two years in the early 1860s, before setting up as a chairmaker in Worksop. The Walkers are last heard of in 1871, when the old man was aged seventy-three.

The Rockley Windsor chairmaking tradition can be traced back to Wheatland's Retford workshop and the high degree of stylistic continuity may derive from his marking guages and templates. The popular 'fleur-de-lys' splat pattern, turned profiles and general design attitudes are, however, typical of the region, and it would be misleading to suggest that an easily recognizable 'Rockley' style emerged, although the elegant 'crinoline' stretcher was consistently used (Plate 164). Different grades of chair were produced — the 'best' yew Windsors exhibit refinements not applied to plain stained ash or fruitwood examples and several unconventional designs (but hardly innovative in the context of local work) have been recorded. Because of his long career, Walker's work tends to display more variety, but Nicholson's chairs merit special praise for their fluent lines; examples by Wheatland are comparatively rare. Alone among the Rockley makers, he occasionally omitted a back splat and sometimes morticed spindles through the elm seat.[19]

The impressed marks are almost always struck in large letters along the seat edge (see Plate 143), although stamps in other positions are known and a child's chair simply struck 'WW' exactly matches a fully signed Wheatland example. Chairs by all three masters have descended in local families, indicating an effort to market wares in surrounding villages; by exploiting their position alongside the Great North Road, the Rockley masters also secured sizeable orders from further afield especially, it seems, Yorkshire, which did not have a significant Windsor chair industry. Wakefield Museum owns six matched Windsors by Walker from a large set made for Wakefield Mechanics' Institute; the Masonic Hall in Wakefield contains a fine set of 'best low yew' chairs supplied by Nicholson, while another Walker batch can be provenanced to a Working Men's Club at Haworth.

The village of Wellow, situated twelve miles south of Retford and Worksop, blossomed as a chairmaking centre at exactly the same time that Rockley had done. The population in 1831 was 473 and White's *Directory*, published the following year, names two chairmakers: John Goodwin 'chair manufacturer' and John Ralph 'vict. & chair maker' at The Red Lion: like many country turners, he combined a trade with innkeeping. These bare references hardly anticipate the prolific portrait of Wellow's chairmaking community revealed by the 1841 Census. No fewer than thirty men are recorded either as chairmakers, chairmaker's journeymen or apprentices; furthermore, twenty-one of those listed had been born outside the county. The 1851 Census called for more precise information concerning place of birth, occupation and age, so the returns provide important new details about the workforce and how it was organized. Twenty-four villagers were still directly involved in chairmaking, besides two wheelwrights, one sawyer and a forester. There were three 'chair bottomers', William and Charles Bush, sons of an agricultural labourer and Eliza Cox, an unmarried nineteen year old living with her widowed mother and brothers Charles, a wood turner and William, a journeyman chairmaker. Henry and William Alvey, sons of a farm worker, aged only thirteen and nine, were employed as 'chair grainer' and 'chair polisher' respectively. Evidence regarding subdivisions of labour are always welcome. Other workmen were routinely described as 'chairmaker' (10), 'chairmaker's journeyman' (6) and 'chairmaker's labourer' (1).

The place of birth entries indicate that, with one exception, all ten tradesmen designated 'chairmaker' were born in the Chilterns. Four came from High Wycombe, four from elsewhere in Buckinghamshire and another from Berkhampstead. In contrast virtually all the journeymen, both wood turners and those employed in other branches, were born locally. Further analysis shows that the influx peaked in about 1835 and the majority of newcomers were batchelors who married local girls. One would love to know how and why this colony of chairmakers became established: the answer is, I suggest, linked to the fortunes of the Goodwin family. The Census reveals that John and Anne Goodwin raised a family in High Wycombe where their youngest son, William, was born in 1821. Sometime afterwards, the parents with their daughter and four sons (all to become chairmakers) moved to Wellow, for whatever reason. They were certainly established in the village by 1830 when John Winks of Ollerton was bound apprentice to 'John Goodwin of Wellow . . . and Edmund Goodwin of the same place chair makers'.[20] This indenture is a capital document which reveals they agreed to pay him 'the sum of six shillings weekly' during his first year and then 'one half of the regular and fair journeymens wages' until he reached the age of twenty-one. The course of instruction was also specified: 'namely for the first two years . . . he shall be taught the turning branch of the Trade, for the next following eighteen months to the bench branch . . . and for the last six months the art of framing'. The fact that John Goodwin was described in 1832 as a 'chair manufacturer' implies the existence of a sizeable workshop. He died, aged seventy, in 1840, and is buried next to his wife in Wellow churchyard, the graves being marked by fine headstones.

The business was inherited by John Goodwin, Jnr, who in 1851 employed twelve men including, it is reasonable to assume, his brothers Edmund, James and William, who had all settled in the village. The commercial success of the elder John Goodwin's enterprise evidently attracted other chairmakers from High Wycombe and its environs to join him either as workshop recruits or competitors. One of these was Jabez Hawes of Seir Green, Buckinghamshire who, in about 1834, married a local woman. Their two sons both trained as chairmakers, and the family seems to have set up a rival workshop since Jabez Hawes and John Goodwin are the only firms listed at Wellow in White's *Directory* of 1853; he makes a final appearance in the 1864 edition. By 1871 Goodwin had moved to 122 Newgate Street, Worksop.

The last of the Wellow chairmakers was James Crofts who died in 1883. His great great-granddaughter, Jean Wilson, who has always lived in the village, owns a trade card inscribed 'JAMES CROFTS / Chair Manufacturer / Red Lion / WELLOW'. She remembers hearing that he travelled round the neighbourhood with a horse and cart selling chairs, but following a serious accident the business lapsed. James Crofts is variously described between 1848 and 1879 as a 'chairmaker / chairmaker (broker) / vict & furniture dealer, Red Lion'; he clearly struggled alone and vainly to save the industry from extinction. The main workshop was situated in a yard behind The Red Lion, but only a boundary wall now remains.

A tantalizing, as yet unsolved, riddle concerns the types of chair made at Wellow, since no fully accredited examples are known and documentary evidence is lacking. The *Victoria Country History of Nottinghamshire* (1910), refers to 'the industry of Windsor chair-making, chiefly at Worksop and Wellow'. It is however curious that the Wellow masters seem never to have used a name stamp, because this workshop practice was widespread in the district; also, none of the Wellow tradesmen are designated Windsor chairmakers in the Census Returns. The record does, however, suggest that rush-seated and fancy chairs were produced. The fact that in 1851, Eliza Cox, aged nineteen, gave her occupation as chair bottomer implies she was engaged in rushing or caning rather than adzing elm chair seats. On the other hand, William and Charles Bush, also identified as chair bottomers, could easily have performed this strenuous work. The presence of a chair grainer in Wellow is hard to explain if the trade was geared exclusively to producing Windsor chairs.

Field-work in the neighbourhood has traced a distinguished pair of ash ladder backs with rush seats from the village of Egmanton, which have a strong family tradition of being Wellow chairs[21] (Plate 165). Two others reputed to have been made at Wellow descended in the Rowland family of Scotts Farm: one is a simple child's ladder back, its companion can best be described as a 'fancy' chair — both have rush seats[22] (Plate 166). It seems fair to conclude that Windsor chairs conforming to classic regional patterns, and a range of turned rush-seated chairs, some with a grained finish, were made.[23]

The tradition of Windsor chairmaking in Worksop started when John and Henry Gabbitass from Retford established a shop on the Common about 1822: others followed and within twenty years the town hosted a major chair industry.[24] When, during the third quarter of the century, chair turning in surrounding villages slumped, many redundant workmen secured employment in the town. John Gabbitass, who moved to premises in Eastgate, was the first Worksop master to use a mark — three magnificent low-back Windsors in yew branded 'I. GABBITASS' under the seat are known (see Plates 145 and 167). He died in 1839, leaving his entire stock in trade to his widow Elizabeth[25] who carried on for five or six years, stamping chairs along the seat edge 'E. GABBITASS / WORKSOP'. The illustrious

165. One of six chairs which, according to a strong family tradition, were made by the community of chairmakers working at Wellow, Nottinghamshire, *c.* 1830–50. *W.A. Lacey*

166. Turned ash chair formerly at Scotts Farm, Wellow, said to have been made by James Crofts (*d.* 1883), the last of the Wellow chairmakers. *Private collection*

167. A best quality low-back Windsor armchair made in yew by John Gabbitass of Worksop, Nottinghamshire, *c.* 1830–35. Branded under the seat (see Plate 145). *Tom Crispin collection*

168. Low-back Windsor in yew bearing the trade label of Benjamin Gilling (see Plate 147) active in Worksop, Nottinghamshire, between 1841 and 1851. *Private collection*

quality and coherent design of these chairs suggest that, although the business was continued by her children they stopped using her mark.

John Godfrey of Bridge Street, also active in the 1840s, impressed his chairs 'I GODFREY / MAKER WORKSOP'; a set of eight side and four Windsor armchairs bearing his name can be provenanced to the Servants' Hall in a Lancashire country house.[26] Benjamin Gilling was another early arrival and several chairs are known with a paper label under the seat printed 'WINDSOR CHAIRS / FROM BENJAMIN GILLING / ADJOINING THE GOLDEN BALL INN / WORKSOP NOTTS / TO BE KEPT DRY' — a space is left for writing in the customer's name and address[27] (see Plates 147 and 168). This firm survived into the early twentieth century; their stock included side chairs and an unusual child's weighing and exercising high-chair.[28] Another dynasty was founded by Isaac Allsop, who may have come from High Wycombe to join the Goodwins at Wellow before setting up in Worksop, initially in partnership with Moss, but by 1841 he was trading on his own account. This firm, one of the largest and most productive, closed in 1887. They identified a few chairs either with a brand mark, stencil, punched stamp or paper label; however their illustrated trade card provides an admirable record of six popular Windsor patterns, together with the prices for supplying them in different woods — elm, cherry or yew[29] (Plates 169–71).

169. Trade card of Isaac Allsop & Son, Worksop, Nottinghamshire, late nineteenth century. *Worksop Library*

170. Reverse of Allsop's trade card.

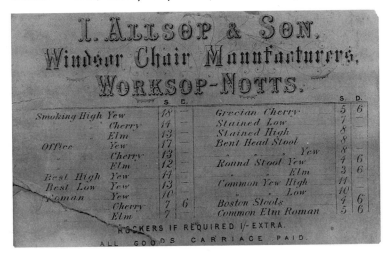
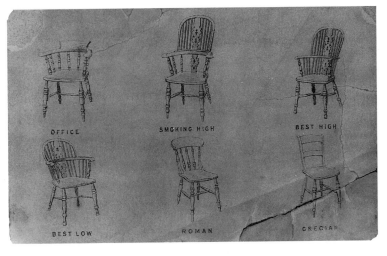

111

Chairmaking in Worksop was virtually finished by the end of the century, its disintegration accelerated by a mass migration of turners to Brighouse in Yorkshire to make bobbins. Nevertheless, John Kelk, who had been apprenticed to I. Allsop & Son, continued to produce Windsor chairs and cricket bats at his 'one man and a boy' workshop until 1936.[30] While it is always satisfying to find name-stamped chairs, care must be taken to ensure they do not distort local patterns of production, because certain large firms, such as Bramers, never identified their work in this way; the practice of sub-contracting also needs to be researched. The survival of the trade in Worksop was assisted, not only by ready access to rail and canal networks, but by the existence of a specialist firm of turners – William Cauldwell – who in 1871 employed twenty-eight, and by 1881, forty men. They were almost certainly mass-producing turned Windsor chair parts to order and are in fact listed under chair-makers in trade directories. Timber was obtainable from two large sawmills and timber yards in the towns, a circumstance which led some chairmakers to rent space at the woodyards so as to be near their source of material. For example, Bramers made chairs on the premises of Godley & Golding until 1887 when, following a fire, they moved to Priory Mill. The commercial infrastructure which developed in Worksop helps to explain why Windsor chairmaking survived there longer than at any other centre in the region.

LINCOLNSHIRE

The strong tradition of Windsor chairmaking that arose in Lincolnshire produced a fine crop of name-stamped chairs. It may be that the unusually large number of Lincolnshire clock-case makers who labelled their work helped to establish this practice. A phase of its early history is perhaps recorded by a group of green painted comb-back examples in the Library at Lincoln Cathedral[31] (Plate 172), and a related pair in Newark parish church, but it was not until the 1820–30 period that marked chairs first appeared. The industry was concentrated on three centres in the south of the county, and although the Wilson workshop in Grantham survived until 1900, the trade was in serious decline by 1860 and nearly extinct twenty years later. The chair masters who employed a maker's mark – an impressed stamp usually combining a personal and town name – were based in Sleaford: Marsh (Plate 174) and Brand; at Boston: Allen; and in Grantham: Amos (Plate 173), Camm, Hubbard (see Plate 146), Taylor and Wilson. Several families were active over more than one

171. Kitchen chair in cherry by Isaac Allsop & Son, Worksop, Nottinghamshire, late nineteenth century. This pattern was called a 'Roman Windsor' (see Plate 170). *Worksop Library*

172. (*below, left*) One of a pair of Windsor armchairs from Lincoln Cathedral Library, painted dark green, probably *c.* 1760–80. *Courtesy the Dean and Chapter*

173. (*below, middle*) Low-back Windsor armchair made by John Amos, *c.* 1825–30. Yew with an elm seat, stamped along the seat edge 'AMOS / GRANTHAM'. The swept arm supports are an early feature. *Leeds Art Galleries*

174. (*below, right*) Ash-framed Windsor chair by Thomas or James Marsh of Sleaford, Lincolnshire, mid-nineteenth century. Stamped 'MARSH' on the dished seat. *Leeds Art Galleries*

generation. Caistor was the only place in north Lincolnshire where a maker's stamp was sometimes used (Todd and Shirley). The picture that emerges is richly complex.[32] To start with, makers in the region favoured many different splat patterns and turning devices, in addition to which the chairs display a stylistic progression from lightness and elegance to heaviness of form. Superimposed on the major design types were individual workshop idioms and, furthermore, there was an interesting escape of influence from the High Wycombe area. The resulting, rather tangled web, is in marked contrast to the stylistic continuity and conservatism of Windsor chairs produced over the same period in the neighbouring county of Nottinghamshire.

Rush-seated ladder-back chairs were made principally at Spilsby, Alford and Louth, by members of the interrelated Ashton, Spikins and Green dynasties. No stamped examples have been found, but their local origin is confirmed by strong family tradition and distribution patterns; it is also significant that the stock in trade of Robert Green, chair turner, who died in 1794, included bolts of rushes. A consistent feature of Lincolnshire ladder-back chairs is primitive squared or 'keeled' cabriole front legs headed by a vase-turned section and united by an ornamental stretcher[33] (Plate 175).

It is clearly not feasible to single out for mention the products of every workshop, but space must be found to describe a remarkable chairmaker's sketch-book kept by John Shadford (*fl. c.* 1843–90). This unique volume contains rough drawings of typical 'Caistor' chairs, trade tools, various items of turnery and furniture, together with eclectic notes and random jottings. It is every furniture historian's dream.[34] Shadford was born in 1828 at Caistor where Windsor chairmaking had recently been introduced by John Todd. In 1843, William Shirley from Grantham also set up a workshop in the town and it is likely that John Shadford was his first apprentice. A Victorian photograph of the small woodyard and shop in Fountain Street shows that he harnessed water power from an overshot wheel. John Shadford worked for Shirley until 1858, when he married and established an independent chairmaking business.

His commonplace book, which is brimful of interest, contains copies of letters, drafts of a trade card and handbill which he considered issuing when setting up on his own account, and what appear to be portraits of himself, his wife and their

175. An early nineteenth-century Lincolnshire ladder back attributed to the Ashton dynasty of chairmakers. *B.D. Cotton collection*

176. Rocking-chair, from the sketch-book of William Shadford, chairmaker of Caistor, Lincolnshire, nineteenth century, third quarter (see Plate 177). *Lincolnshire Archives Office*

177. Chairs of this distinctive pattern are associated with John Shadford of Caistor, Lincolnshire, on the evidence of sketches in his commonplace book. This example in sycamore and ash, stained to resemble mahogany, comes from Willoughton, Lincolnshire, *c.* 1850–75. *Museum of Lincolnshire Life*

house, besides many sketches of Windsor chairs. One of the most illuminating double spreads provides a pictorial inventory of his domestic furniture (see Plate 84), and workshop contents. The latter features all the trade tools, a treadle lathe, vice, straining bench, chair parts and pot of red lead with a stick-back Windsor armchair prominent in the centre. It all adds up to a memorable, if rather quixotic, record. Other pages illustrate various Windsor chairs, many reflecting familiar regional styles such as the 'fleur-de-lys' splat. There are very few side chairs, which is a curious characteristic of the whole North East Midlands tradition. The only highly distinctive design is for a tall-backed kitchen chair with two rows of closely ranked spindles and notches in the yoke (Plate 176). Several examples of this pattern exist, the frames finished in varnished red lead; they are known locally as 'Caistor' chairs and may represent Shadford's personal contribution of the Lincolnshire chairmaking tradition (Plate 177).

HIGH WYCOMBE

Windsor chairmaking in Buckinghamshire was centred on High Wycombe,[35] the trade being well-established by 1800, and a few makers started to identify their work during the early nineteenth century. Distinctive local features at this time include back splats incorporating a pierced-wheel motif, a fan-tail projection supporting twin rear struts on the seats of chairs with single back hoops, and the widespread use of H-pattern stretchers; plus characteristic turnery devices on legs and arm supports (Plate 178). By 1850, there were over 100 workshops in the town. A catalogue of watercolour designs for plain and fancy chairs, produced by Charles and Edwin Skull about 1850, illustrates the range of stock carried by a large High Wycombe firm[36] (Plate 179). Since a quarter of the 119 drawings are for common wood-bottomed Windsor and kitchen chairs, this manuscript serves to clarify regional patterns. It is reasonable to suppose that these elegant sketches display features specific to the Skull workshop. However, the discovery of a closely comparable volume (recently acquired by Temple Newsam, Leeds), with a title page inscribed: 'Mr Amos Catton/Chair Manufacturer/High Wycombe/Bucks/Late Savage', indicates otherwise. Both anthologies include many identical designs, and are likely to be by the same artist. The evidence suggests that large Wycombe firms produced a repertoire of standard local chair designs, as well as a range embodying their own house-style.

The High Wycombe trade came to be organized on the lines of a semi-mass-production industry. Instead of receiving a regular weekly wage, chair workers were paid piece–rates for making components or performing various operations, a

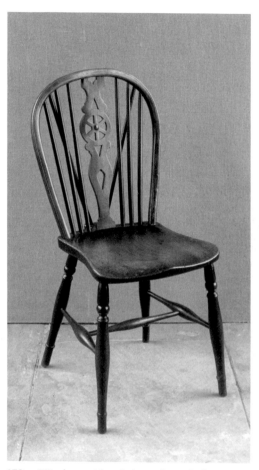

178. Windsor side chair, ash and fruitwood back, elm seat, beech legs and stretchers. A typical High Wycombe pattern, *c.* 1830–50. Maker's mark 'W. LOW' struck on fan-tail (see Plate 150). *Leeds Art Galleries*

179. Detail of a page from the manuscript pattern book of Charles and Edwin Skull of High Wycombe, Buckinghamshire, *c.* 1849. The volume, which contains over 150 designs, is the earliest pictorial anthology of chairs made by a large High Wycombe firm. *Wycombe Chair Museum*

180. Waggon load of church chairs made by the large High Wycombe firm of Thomas Glenister, late nineteenth century. More chairs are visible in the background. *Wycombe Chair Museum*

practice that encouraged the employment of outworkers who simply delivered their parts at an agreed price per gross or dozen to the factory where the chairs were framed up and polished. This led to a reduction in the number of chair manufacturers because tradesmen found it easier to make and sell elements to the large High Wycombe firms than market their own finished chairs. One consequence of this system, which has passed into folklore, was the chair bodgers who lived and worked in the Buckinghamshire beechwoods turning standard chair legs and stretchers on their simple pole lathes for the chair masters (see Plates 11 and 12). Bodging survived until the 1930s, but is likely always to have been marginal to the industry.

Of greater commercial significance is an eight-page *List of Prices*, issued by the Wycombe Chairmakers' Trade Union in 1872, tabulating piece-work rates for every task which a tradesman might be required to perform in making different types of chair in common production.[37] This list, which serves scholars as a kind of Rosetta stone is reproduced in Appendix Three. The headings are as follows: 'Sawyers-out / Benchmen and Bottomers / Turners / Back-makers / Windsor Framers / Cane-seat Framers / Polishers'. The labour cost of carrying out over 250 operations is laid down, creating a factual compendium that not only offers welcome insights into trade practices and the subdivision of labour, but provides a dictionary of current terminology. Who now understands the meaning of 'Quaker back, double list', 'Doffin' and 'Thumb' backfeet, 'Crooked bellows banisters', or 'Fliway stays', or could identify a 'Scotch Roman Chair'? A well-researched edition of this price-list would be invaluable. Account books kept by Pratt's of Bradford show that from the 1850s onwards, they regularly bought for stock quantities of Windsor and other chairs from B. North, E. Hutchinson & Son and Glenisters of High Wycombe[38] — a widely repeated distribution pattern that hastened the decline of many provincial chair centres (Plate 180).

Thomas Sheraton observed in 1803: 'Chair-making is a branch generally confined to itself; as those who professedly work at it, seldom engage to make cabinet furniture. The two branches seem evidently to require different talents in workmen, in order to become proficient'.[39] This traditional separation of the two skills started

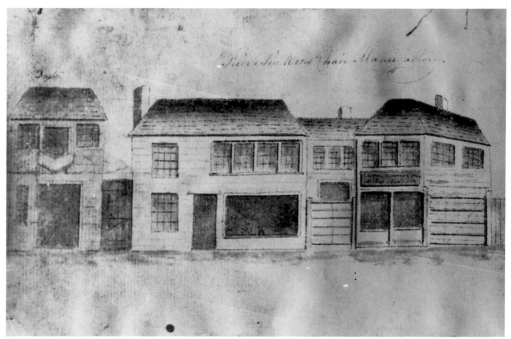

to break down after about 1850 when, nationwide, specialist chair turners were increasingly absorbed into the general cabinet trade. This transition is noted in the memoirs of George Herbert, shoemaker of Banbury, Oxfordshire (1814–1920), who wrote: 'Again there were the chair-makers, many of whom were in this town: now there is not one. There is one or two turners, but they are principally employed by the cabinet-makers'.[40] However, a few small workshops did survive in the county. Hazell's of Oxford made a restricted range of scroll-back Windsors until 1892, and were briefly succeeded by Walter Puddifer — both stamped their chairs.[41] To survive, the business had to be competitive, which required batch production of one or two standard models.

THE PRIORS OF UXBRIDGE

A splendid panorama of the High Street in Uxbridge,[42] drawn about 1810, shows the frontage of a workshop (No.101) inscribed above: 'Prior and Son Wind. Chair

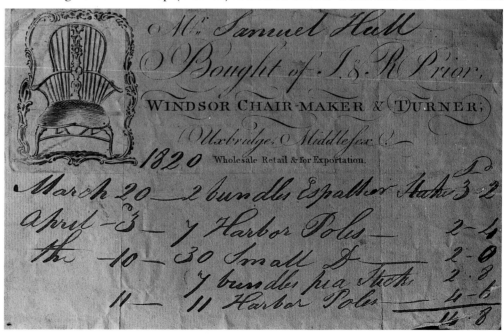

182.   Printed bill head dated 1820 of J. & R. Prior, Windsor Chair-Maker & Turner, Uxbridge, Middlesex, invoicing stakes, sticks and poles. *Hillingdon Borough Libraries*

116

Manufactory' (Plate 181). The next house along, labelled 'J. Prior Jnr' adjoins The Green Dragon, so raising the possibility that the Priors, like many other chairmakers, started up as part timers renting a building in an innyard. The firm was established by John Prior, assisted by his sons John and Robert; they are described in trade directories as 'Chair maker and turner' or 'Rustic chairmaker and hurdle maker'. A printed bill-head of theirs dated 1820 portrays an elaborate Windsor armchair and includes the line 'Wholesale Retail & for Exportation'[43] (Plate 182). However, the invoice, addressed to a Mr Samuel Hall, itemizes only espallier stakes, poles and bundles of pea-sticks, which shows that the Priors, like many country chairmakers, could not earn a livelihood by concentrating exclusively on seat furniture. One of their upmarket customers was Lord Lyttelton of Hagley Hall, Worcestershire, who in 1818 purchased six yew armchairs costing 15s each.[44] Their business was probably similar to that of William Webb of Newington, Surrey, whose trade card illustrates half a dozen Windsor chairs and rustic seats which were also 'for Exportation'. One Windsor bearing Webb's label is known.[45]

More than a dozen yew armchairs stamped on the seat edge 'ROBERT PRIOR / MAKER UXBRIDGE' have been noted (Plate 183). All are of eloquent quality and follow one of two easily recognizable patterns. His routine model combines two sticks and three pierced back splats decorated with disc motifs repeated on supports beneath each arm, which gives the design an impressive unity. The larger and more ambitious version incorporates Prince of Wales feathers in the splats and boasts a 'crinoline' stretcher (Plate 184). The Priors' chairs appear to derive their character from a shop tradition and exhibit little regional content, apart from the front arm support, which is neither turned nor 'crooked' (bent), but interestingly resembles the underarm brace found on the two earliest-known labelled Windsor chairs made by Richard Hewett (Plate 185) and John Pitt of Slough (both chairmakers and wheelwrights by trade) during the mid-eighteenth century. High Wycombe,[46] Slough and Uxbridge are in an area which, it now seems, cradled the famous chairmaking tradition that, from about 1720, derived its name from nearby Windsor — the place from which goods were shipped to London.

From an early date, Windsor chairs seem to have been associated with gardens and were often painted 'grass green' to blend with their parkland setting[47] (Plate

183. Stamp on seat edge of chair in Plate 184.

184. (far left) Windsor armchair, yew with an elm seat stamped along one edge 'ROBERT PRIOR / MAKER UXBRIDGE', early nineteenth century. The Prior workshop is shown in Plate 181. *Roger Warner*

185. (left) Windsor armchair bearing the label of Richard Hewett, chairmaker and wheelwright of Slough, Buckinghamshire (d. 1777). Various woods stained red. *Trustees of the Victoria and Albert Museum*

117

187. One of six elm and beech Windsor chairs made for the garden created at Claremont, Surrey, *c.* 1772–5. The original 'grass green' colour is visible under a later coat of dark green paint. *The National Trust*

188. Lettering beneath the seat of the chair shown in Plate 187. It is rare to find such well-provenanced Windsors, together with evidence of date and social use.

186). A fine set of six, now at Powis Castle (Plates 187 and 188), are painted under the seats 'GARDEN CHAIRS FROM CLAREMONT' — the country house in Surrey built by Clive of India in 1772–3 and landscaped by Capability Brown at the same period. In addition to being admired as picturesque rustic furniture, Windsors also possessed antiquarian associations and were considered appropriate for libraries. During the early nineteenth century, stick-back Windsors became fully integrated into the native vernacular tradition, although they never entirely lost a sense of social identity being found, for example, in army barracks (see Plate 367), canteens, pubs and reading-rooms — but not in workhouses, prisons or schools.

MENDLESHAM

Square-backed 'Mendlesham' Windsors force their way into this survey because of their status as the only distinctive East Anglian turned chair. Tradition asserts that they were made by Dan Day of Mendlesham in Suffolk, and indeed, in 1838, a chairmaker named Richard Day died, aged fifty-five, in the village.[48] The structural form of these armchairs is remarkably consistent and most are of uniformly high quality; however, the sheer numbers and existence of variant design clusters make it unlikely that only a single workshop was involved.[49] The majority are constructed either of fruitwood or yew with an elm seat. The square-framed backs typically display pale inlaid stringing lines, a short pierced splat flanked by spindles, a bowed lower stay rail, and have two rows of small turned balls – a feature shared with East Anglian joined chairs (Plate 189). There is no other evidence for a tradition of common turned chairs in the region which, adding to the intriguing wisps of mystery surrounding their date and exact origin, gives the Mendlesham type a special interest. Possibly a group of tradesmen from the High Wycombe area moved to Suffolk, just as the Goodwins and their followers migrated to Wellow in the 1820s and started making chairs in a local idiom.

KERRY, CLISSETT AND BREAR

There is no urgent need to examine regional chair traditions in the complex South West area, the subject of an excellent recent exhibition catalogue.[50] It would, however, be satisfying to know more about chairs from say Staffordshire and rural Lancashire. What local patterns, for instance, were favoured by the twenty-eight makers working at Clithero in 1851? Instead of trying to map the whole country – a project bravely attempted in Dr Cotton's forthcoming book – this survey concludes with some notes on three interesting workshops situated in areas not so far covered.

Directories mention two John Kerrys, uncle and nephew, chair turners, active in Evesham, Worcestershire, between *c.* 1820 and 1854. Several plain ladder-back chairs are known stamped 'KERRY' in large letters on one back post (Plates 144 and 190). Dr Cotton's exciting discovery of a vertical spinning-wheel in elm impressed 'KERRY EVESHAM' confirms that chair turners sometimes made these instruments.[51] Spinning-wheels not infrequently bear a maker's name, especially in Scotland where a Guild of Spinning-Wheel Wrights was established.

Philip Clissett (1817–1913) was also from Worcestershire, but at the age of twenty-one moved to Bosbury in Herefordshire, where he worked for seventy years as a chairmaker becoming, in contrast to the obscure Kerrys, something of a cult figure. The cleft coppice ash Clissett used was, in the traditional way, turned while still green on a pole lathe. He is said to have produced six rush- or elm-seated chairs weekly which were sold in neighbouring towns. Several of his relatives worked as chairmakers in the district, sometimes stamping their initials, like him, on the end grain of the back posts[52] (Plate 142). Clissett became famous after being 'discovered' in 1880 by a leading member of the Arts and Crafts Movement, and thereafter championed as 'a real survival of village industry'. In 1890 Ernest Gimson spent a few weeks at Bosbury learning chairmaking skills.[53] Clissett's fluent spindle- and ladder-back chairs express inherited design attitudes current in the West Midlands and the Welsh Marches (Plate 191), although after 1890 his work included various 'improvements' suggested by the architect James Maclaren who 'found' him, and are not entirely honest products of the native vernacular tradition.[54]

The firm of Brear & Sons, Addingham, Yorkshire, demonstrates how a traditional chairmaking business in Wharfedale survived long after the Windsor chair

189. 'Mendlesham' Windsor chair, fruitwood frame with elm seat, the back inlaid with whitewood strings. Chairs of this pattern were made in Suffolk during the first half of the nineteenth century. *Trustees of the Victoria and Albert Museum*

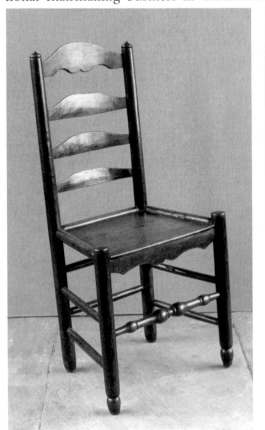

190. (*far left*) Chair stamped 'KERRY' on each back post (see Plate 144). Made by John Kerry, Evesham, Worcestershire, *c.* 1825–50. *Leeds Art Galleries*

191. (*left*) Armchair by Philip Clissett of Bosbury, Herefordshire, ash frame with sycamore crest rail, the top of each back post impressed 'PC', nineteenth century, second half. *Leeds Art Galleries*

119

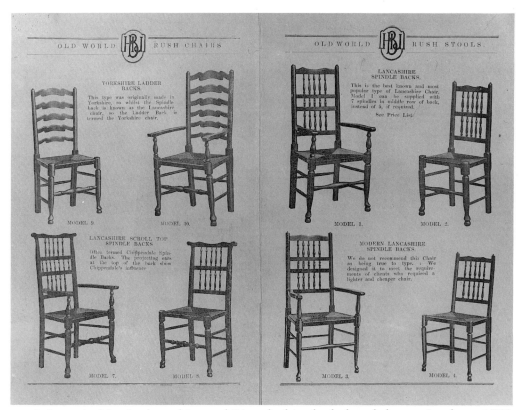

192. Trade catalogue illustrating 'Old World Lancashire . . . Chairs', issued *c.* 1920 by H.J. Berry & Sons of Chipping, Lancashire. *H.J. Berry & Sons, Ltd*

193. Trade catalogue of *Chairs, Stools, Peggy Sticks, Hay Rakes &c,* issued *c.* 1900 by William Brear & Sons, Addingham, Yorkshire. *Private collection*

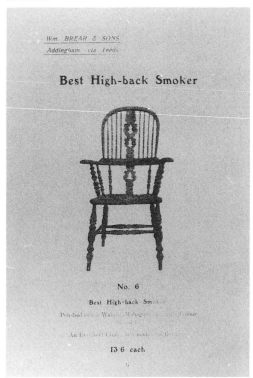

workshops in Nottinghamshire and Lincolnshire had closed down. In about 1860, William Brear, the owner of a water-powered sawmill on Silsden Moor, moved to the nearby village of Addingham where he set up as a sawyer, timber merchant, chairmaker and general turner. In addition to selling timber, the firm made field gates, fence posts, mallets, hay rakes and small domestic turnery; supplied shafts, felloes and naves to local wheelwrights; provided thousands of bobbins for woollen mills in the area and produced a range of ordinary turned chairs which evidently proved a commercial success, because two illustrated catalogues of chairs and stools and so on, were issued about 1900 and 1920[55] (see Plates 16, 20 and 400).

The catalogues show that Brear's stock consisted of routine stick-and-splat-back Windsors[56] (Plate 193), smokers' bows, stick- and lath-back kitchen chairs, rockers, stools, go-carts and babies' common chairs. All were very cheap and conservative in design. They catered for the needs of the neighbourhood and also supplied workhouses, schools, public halls and chain stores such as Timothy White's. The family retains a long run of old ledgers which await detailed study. Before the Great War up to thirty workmen were employed, but chairmaking had ceased by 1940.[57] The history of William Brear & Sons provides a classic illustration of how a country firm, engaged in diverse branches of the woodworking trades, survived to produce traditional wood-bottomed chairs well into the present century.

H.J. Berry & Sons of Chipping, a village on the edge of the Forest of Bowland in Lancashire, whose early history is in many ways comparable, followed a different route to survival by specializing in reproductions of 'Old World Lancashire Rush Seated Spindle and Ladder Back Chairs' for middle-class homes (Plate 192). One of their catalogues is extant,[58] and it is interesting that no overlap occurs between their repertoire and Brear's stock. The firm now makes modern and traditional chairs by high-tech methods.

JOINERS' CHAIRS

Chairmakers who had been apprenticed to joiners very seldom identified their work with name stamps (Plate 194); accordingly the study of vernacular Chippendale and

Hepplewhite-style chairs is much less advanced than research on regional turned chairs. Although a few hybrid chairs which combine turned lower members with fashionably styled backs framing decorative splats are known (Plate 195), seat furniture in which the parts are locked together by mortice and tenon joints and the work of chair turners really represent two separate traditions. This point can be pressed home by analysing a typical specification from the *Leeds Cabinet and Chair-Makers Book of Prices* published in 1791:

'COMMON elm chairs, with four holes in the bannister, rounded backs, and low rails, bottoms slipt, each	0	2	8
If bottoms nailed on, deduct each	0	0	3
If backs canted, low rails square, deduct each	0	0	2
If loose seat, each	0	0	4
If stuff'd over rail, deduct loose bottom			
If elbow chair, extra	0	0	3
A pair of elbows	0	2	6
If OG head	0	0	6

The opening statement describes a routine joiner's chair, the elm frame united by pegged mortice and tenon joints and with a pierced 'fan' splat; the back posts 'rounded' behind (with a rasp), straight legs united by stretchers, and the seat board housed in a groove along the rails. This was evidently a basic 'Leeds area' design type, the labour cost being 2s. 8d. compared to the 2s. 3d. which Gillows paid a workman for making one spindle chair. Various choices are then listed: the seat board could be directly nailed to the rails, the back posts simply chamfered behind (with a spoke shave), and the stretchers squared rather than given a rounded top. If adopted, these labour-saving options represented a saving of 7d. Rabbetting the rails to accept a loose seat involved extra workmanship and cost 4d. more; alternatively a 'stuff'd over' upholstered seat, the cover secured by a row of brass nails, might be preferred. Because armchairs are always slightly larger than side chairs, fashioning

194. Walnut armchair stamped 'S. SHARP NORWICH', probably 1760s. An interesting case of a provincial maker using an unfashionable timber to make a stylish chair. *Trustees of the Victoria and Albert Museum*

195. (*far left*) Chair stamped 'BANCROFT' on the top of one front leg, an interesting late eighteenth-century ash and alder frame which combines the techniques of the turner and joiner. From the Lancashire–Cheshire area. *B.D. Cotton collection*

196. (*left*) Fan-back elm chair from a set of twenty-four supplied by William Smith in 1771 for the Steward's Room at Harewood House, Yorkshire. *Courtesy the Earl of Harewood, K.B.E.*

197. (*right*) This elm and oak chair is inscribed beneath the seat: 'William John / Carpenter fecit / October 21 1778'. *J.H. Hill collection*

198. (*far right*) One of four early nineteenth-century joined chairs, inscribed in pencil under the seat: 'These chairs are made from black cherry-wood from Whixley nr York'. *Hornsea Museum*

199. Elm rocking-chair, early nineteenth century. Low chairs with a work or 'knitting' drawer were particularly convenient for nursing mothers. *Bradford Museums*

200. (*Opposite*) A corner chair made for the Bell family of The Hall, Thirsk, Yorkshire, from remnants of a venerable elm tree that was burnt down in 1819. *Private collection*

the frame took longer, the extertion involved being reckoned at 3d., while making a pair of arms was expensive (2s. 6d.) because these members had to be laid out with templates, then sawn and shaped. Lastly, an 'ogee' or curvelinear 'cupid's bow' crest rail cost 6d. more than a standard serpentine profile. Adding carved embellishments was time consuming – therefore expensive – and required specialist training; accordingly it is rarely seen on Georgian vernacular seat furniture.

In 1771 William Smith, thought to be a local tradesman, made '2 dozen of elm chairs / 2 dining tables £21. 2s.' for the Steward's Room at Harewood House, near Leeds.[59] It is satisfying to find the pattern he supplied (Plate 196) accurately described twenty years later in the *Leeds Price Book*; the compilers evidently still regarded it as a standard model, which says something about design attitudes. A plain oak and elm chair, although unprovenanced, is significant because of an inscription beneath the seat: 'William John / Carpenter fecit / October 21 1778'[60] (Plate 197). The chair perhaps originated in a rural community which could only support one, possibly part-time, woodworker trained as a carpenter, but required to cater for the wider needs of local families. A somewhat later set of four chairs is of comparable interest because one is pencilled under the seat: 'These chairs are made from black cherrywood from Whixley nr York'[61] (Plate 198). A pair of corner chairs made from the remnants of a famous elm which stood on the Green at Thirsk, in Yorkshire, until it was burnt down on mischief night (4 November) 1819, are carved along the top rail 'OLD ELM TREE 1820' (Plate 200). They show how deeply a love of elaborately fretted splats (inspired originally by Chippendale's *Director*) became embedded in the native tradition.

Although disappointingly few provenanced and datable joiners' chairs have been traced, documentary sources provide a little additional information. It is clear from furniture bills that common chairs were often made in urban workshops. They occur for instance in several of Chippendale's accounts,[62] and in 1800 Elwick & Robinson, the leading Wakefield cabinet makers invoiced 'An Elm Nursing Chair with Drawer and Rockers' to the Wentworths of Wooley Hall[63] (Plate 199). Furthermore, the fact that so many *Books of Prices* regularly used in large urban workshops include costings for 'common elm chairs', confirms that they were not thought of as 'country' chairs.

201. One of three elm chairs from a single-storey cottage at Doll's Hole, Beetley, Norfolk. A popular East Anglian pattern described in *The Norwich Chair Makers' Book of Prices*, 1802, as a 'square, back, stay rail, hollow seat, wood bottomed chair... plain Marlbro' feet'. *Norfolk Museum Service*

202. Shetland armchair, nineteenth century, pine and beech (probably driftwood) with traces of blue paint; side and front stretchers missing. From a deserted croft at Brough, the curved arms are a distinctive Scottish feature. *D. Learmont collection*

The *Norwich Chair-Makers' Books of Prices* (1801), provides detailed specifications for a dozen 'common' chairs and examples of most have been found in East Anglia.[64] A typical description reads:

> 'For framing a square back, stay rail, hollow seat, wood-bottomed chair; elm ash, beech or walnut-tree, with straight top and stay rail, single pitch back feet, plain taper above the seat, with two rails on a side, Marlbro' feet, without banisters or splats . . . 2s. 6d.'.

A list of optional refinements and 'extras' follows. Hollow seats nailed to the rails, and backs incorporating rows of ornamental balls (termed 'buttons') are amongst the most distinctive regional features (Plate 201). Chairs displaying these characteristics later spread to the North: John Dacre, when valuing pub furniture in Otley, Yorkshire, in 1852, several times lists sets of 'Suffolk' chairs,[65] while a slightly earlier Chester furniture-maker's cost book depicts a cherrywood chair of East Anglian design.[66] The history of English furniture is always less clear-cut than it would be convenient to believe.

THE CELTIC FRINGE

In sparsely populated areas of the Scottish Highlands and Islands, the Isle of Man, West Wales and rural Ireland, chairs were frequently made by the householder or local handyman rather than trained craftsmen, resulting in the emergence of regional traditions that are often wholly independent of English vernacular idioms. Many peasant families could not afford any seat furniture, making do with logs, stone blocks, turf baulks; or, if they lived on the coast, a whale's vertebra might serve as a stool. Some crofters, however, produced home-made chairs from whatever timber was available — usually bog wood, driftwood or scrub. Family life centred around a peat fire on the floor in the middle of the room, smoke escaping through a hole in the roof; chairs and stools (known in Scotland as 'creepies') tended to be small and low, so that everyone could gather round the fire for warmth, their heads below the dense smoke canopy.[67] This is why chairs are often soot-blackened.

Several primitive chair types have been recorded in the almost treeless Caithness and Sutherland areas of the Scottish Highlands, where they acquired a distinctive character from the versatile use of naturally bent branches for the main members; birch, blackthorn and orchard trees being employed where available.[68] The archetypal 'Sutherland' chair consisted of two naturally angled 'elbows' connected by cross splats, with short sections of branch stuck in to form legs, and a flat piece of wood fastened across as a seat board. A specimen from the West Highlands, made of blackthorn, has rungs (two are now missing) which slot into holes bored with a red-hot poker — not drilled (Plate 203). An even more rugged example found on a deserted croft at Achlipster, Caithness, has a top rail made from the handle of a turf-flaying spade; the cross bars are, as usual, whittled, not lathe-turned. The Highland Folk Museum at Kingussie has assembled a collection of such chairs including two known to have been made about 1900 by Samuel Clarke, a shepherd on the Assynt estate, west Sutherland.[69] Their late date is betrayed by higher seats and the fact that the rungs are secured to the 'knee' members by dowelled sockets, rather than open wedged joints.

'Caithness' chairs belong to the same tradition, but often display a number of technical advances: the seat rails are tenoned into raked back posts which continue down to form the rear legs, the front supports are squared and the back is typically filled with a panel of turned spars (Plate 204). Ash and elm were commonly used. It is said that the front seat bar was for drying knitted socks. Some Caithness chairs are constructed with natural 'knees' as the main frame element, while others feature ladder backs which relate them to Sutherland patterns. The geographical spread of this Highland chairmaking tradition has not been precisely charted.

203. Low chair made from two elbows of blackthorn. *National Museums of Scotland*

204. A pattern of chair (traditionally the wife's) widespread across the north of Scotland during the last century. *Highland Folk Museum*

In the Northern Isles and the Hebrides, driftwood was plentiful in the era before lighthouses and much furniture was made from timber cast up on shores, usually pine left in the white, although occasionally painted[70] (see Plates 46–48). Many old chairs on Shetland are joiner-made and reflect Anglo–Norwegian styles; some have panelled backs and arms to provide draught proofing, many are of simple yoke-back design with either a single cross bar, or flat upright banisters, and all have wooden seats[71] (Plate 202). Typically, Scottish bowed arms are common, while several examples exhibit an archaic 'William and Mary' character, although dating, almost certainly, from the nineteenth century.

A basic, almost timeless, style of vernacular chair found throughout the Celtic fringe is the stool with a stick back. This classic pattern has a slab seat raised on three or four legs, while the back struts support an armbow made from a naturally curved branch (Plate 205). Documented or dated examples are unknown, but they are native to such remote areas that the type must have evolved independently of the English Windsor chair tradition: they were produced well into the nineteenth century. Many utilize peeled scrub wood – gorse stems form the legs of one Isle of Man stool (Plate 208) – while the wood is sometimes so unworked that bark remains. Others are fashioned from cleft branches and in Ireland, where they are today quaintly called 'famine' chairs, late versions incorporate turned members.[72] Rather clumsy, heavily built ash and elm chairs of this type are indigenous to West Wales, especially Cardiganshire. The backs nearly always combine three flat staves and two pairs of

205. Stick-back chairs of this type were widely used in the living-kitchen of houses on the Isle of Man, nineteenth century. *The Manx Museum*

125

206. Low stick-back chair utilizing naturally curved spars of wood; a brace across the seat front is missing (see Plate 69). *Highland Folk Museum*

207. A classic Welsh stick-back chair. Hewn elm seat and naturally curved armbow, whittled ash legs and splats with traces of green paint. From the Cwm Tudu area of Cardiganshire. *Tom Crispin collection*

208. (*below, left*) Manx stool made by C. Kelly of Peel, nineteenth century. The legs are gorse stems. *The Manx Museum*

209. (*below, right*) Manx stool, the seat board made from a forked branch, nineteenth century. *The Manx Museum*

sticks supporting a massive rough hewn armbow; this design is sufficiently consistent to form a distinctive sub-group within the broad tradition[73] (Plate 207). Equivalent chairs from the Scottish Highlands are much smaller, lower and more lightly constructed to suit crofts; some utilize a horseshoe-shaped piece of wood for the bottom (see Plates 69 and 206). Seat boards contrived from the V-fork of a branch were also employed on three-legged Manx stools (Plate 209). In fact, the exploitation of naturally curved and angled scrub wood is the most distinctive feature of Celtic chairs and agricultural implements.

Two other chair types must force their way into this brief survey. The first (which takes its name from Sligo in north-west Ireland), has a tall back post in the form of a flat stave, the open triangular seat is framed by three blades of wood into which the two arm supports are tenoned, while the cleft front legs are united to the rear post by a T-stretcher.[74] This very striking design is distantly related to the ancient tradition of triangular turned chairs although the members are improvised from cleft or sawn timber. Sugan chairs from the rural west of Ireland owe their name to the ropes made of sugan or twisted straw which form the seat (Plate 210). The frames are of a simple, largely international, rectangular ladder-back pattern with two cross bars, squared posts and turned stretchers.[75] Ash was the traditional wood, although other timbers and variant styles occur. Like most Irish vernacular furniture, surviving examples date from the nineteenth century. Chairs of closely similar design, with marram-grass seats were made in the Hebrides and west of Scotland, although many now possess later driftwood seat boards.[76]

210. Ash sugan chair, *c.* 1850, the seat made from ropes of twisted hay (sugan). Simple rail-back chairs of this pattern were common along the Celtic west coast of northern Britain and Ireland. From County Limerick. *The National Museum of Ireland*

9 Regional Beds

SCOTTISH HIGHLAND AND ISLANDS

It may seem eccentric to start by drawing attention to the Neolithic hut dwellings at Skara Brae in Orkney, but the primitive wall-cavity beds and sleeping pens, enclosed by upright flagstones either side of the central hearth, do provide antecedents for types of bed space which survived in Orkney and the Outer Hebrides until well into the last century: it is certainly to the far north that one must turn to find evidence of primitive sleeping accommodation. There are many eye-witness accounts of the ancient practice of transhumance — the annual migration of menfolk and livestock to upland summer pastures known as 'shielings'. This system prevailed longest in north-west Scotland, finally dying out on Lewis only two generations ago. Shieling huts were built of stone and turf on either circular or rectangular plans, at least half the floor being occupied by a rough bed of heather and dry grass. This area was usually fronted by a low retaining wall of stones topped by turf which served as a fireside seat (possibly the origin of the long settle); alternatively, the bedding was raised on a low earth bank reminiscent of sleeping platforms in early Viking houses.[1]

Thomas Pennant described such a bed in a conical hut, constructed of branches and covered with turf, which he saw on a visit to the island of Jura in 1772: 'the furniture a bed of heath, placed on a bank of sod; two blankets and a rug; some dairy vessels, and above, certain pendant shelves made of basket work, to hold the cheese, the produce of the Summer'.[2] Similar beehive or wigwam shelters built by itinerant charcoal burners and bark peelers in the New Forest, the Furness District of Lancashire and South Yorkshire also embody age-old traditions. Owing to their transient nature none survive, but early twentieth-century accounts and illustrations indicate that, like the shieling huts, they often had a central hearth and roughly formed sleeping 'lairs' consisting of brushwood covered with bracken, grass or straw.[3]

W.T. Dennison, one of the Commissioners reporting on *The Conditions of the Crofters and Cottars in the Highlands and Islands of Scotland* (1884), described a stone bed in a cottar's house on Orkney: 'parallel to, and about two feet from the horribly damp north wall, a row of flags was set up on edge, fixed to the earthen floor. The trough formed by the damp wall, for back, the damp earth covered with a little straw or heather for bottom, and having the cold flagstones for front, was the bed of the Orkney peasant during the greater part of the last century'.[4] A traveller to Mull in 1800 recorded a similar arrangement in the cottages: 'Around the sides of the room are ranged little cribs for the beds, which are generally composed of heath, with the roots placed downward and the tips upward'.[5] Certain long houses on Orkney at Nether Benzieclett, Mossetter and Langalour, retain their traditional *neuk-beds* housed in a projecting outshut. These alcoves have internal stone ledges or corbels at the head and foot to support bed boards, often a shelf or recess in the end

211. Underside of bed tester decorated with birds. This extraordinary bed cannot be related to a local tradition of painted furniture. The bed itself, dated 1724, is shown in Plate 220. *Leeds Art Galleries*

129

walls to hold personal articles, and the entrance is narrowed to a slit by two vertical flagstones[6] (Plate 212). The *neuk-bed* at Langalour is set entirely within the thickness of the wall and is therefore related to the *crûb* or wall-cavity beds described in Captain F.W.L. Thomas's account of eighteenth-century Hebridean blackhouses published in 1870.[7]

The *crûb* was entered by crawling through a hole into a conical recess in the immensely thick wall. Thomas reported that the older houses on Lewis usually had one, perhaps two *crûbs* near the hearth, and occasionally one in the barn. 'If there were more in the family than these beds would hold, they lay in a corner upon the floor, railed in by a plank on edge'. The Revd. Neil Mackenzie, who was Minister on St Kilda in early Victorian days, recalled a visit to one of these strange island dwellings: 'Now you had to creep along on hands and feet, as it was only in the centre of the house that you could even sit upright. In this way you arrived at the edge of the steep slope above the bed opening (i.e. a *crûb*, or recess in the thickness of the wall), down which you went head foremost, nothing visible above but your legs, while you spoke and prayed with the sick'.[8] The houses on St Kilda consisted of byre and living-room with a central hearth under one roof. Two plans survive recording the arrangement of furniture in a *crûb* dwelling (Plate 214), and a house containing one narrow box bed and larger fixed bedstead (Plate 213). The black-house in a more modern style, now preserved as an Ancient Monument at Arnol on the west coast of Lewis, contains three timber box beds fronted by curtains which point to a great improvement in living standards during the nineteenth century (see Plate 48). The Tankerness House Museum on Orkney also retains a fairly late pair of box beds with panelled sliding doors. The wall or cupboard-bed tradition was so deeply implanted in Scottish culture that the bed recess or 'bed in the wall' (enclosed behind doors or screened by curtains), became an established feature even in large urban tenement blocks built throughout lowland Scotland in Victorian days (see Plate 80).

212. The kitchen of a farmhouse at Kirbister, Orkney, showing a central hearth and a *neuk-bed* recess in the south wall. *Courtesy the Royal Commission on Ancient Monuments, Scotland*

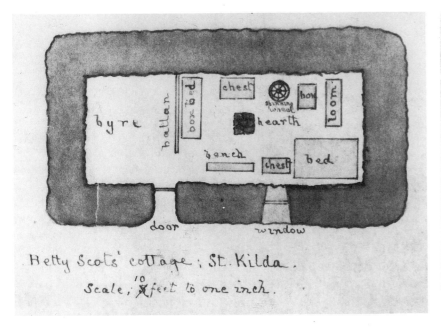

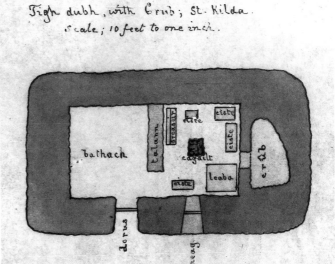

An early freestanding box bed from Badenock, now at the Highland Folk Museum, is incised '1702 DMP' (for a member of the McPhearson clan), and the pine doors bear graffiti of stags (Plate 215). Alexander Fenton quotes a memorable account of how large families squeezed into such beds:[10]

In March 1847, a visitor to a house measuring 14 by 12 ft. observed in it a single box bed. He asked where the man and his wife and six children slept at night. The answer was: 'Weel . . . jeust look i' the inside o' the bed, an' ye'll say it's weel

213. (above, left) Drawing published by Captain Thomas in 1867 recording Betty Scott's cottage on St Kilda which was typical of the houses built and furnished c. 1840. The single room contains two box beds, a bench, loom, spinning-wheel and various chests arranged round the central hearth. *Courtesy the National Museums of Scotland*

214. (above, right) Drawing published by Captain Thomas in 1867 recording the only blackhouse he found on St Kilda with a traditional boot-shaped *crûb* or sleeping cell in the thickness of the wall. The furniture is named in Gaelic: *leaba* (box bed), *ciste* (chest), *dreaseir* (dresser). *Courtesy the National Museums of Scotland*

215. Free-standing pine box bed dated 1702 and initialled 'DMP', from Badenock, Scotland. *Highland Folk Museum*

131

planned tae haud eight o' us. The wife and I lie wi' our heeds at the head o' the bed, the two eldest lie with their heads at the foot o' the bed, the peerie (little) t'ing – that is the baby – lies i' his mither's bosom, the ain next the peerie t'ing lies i' mine, and the middle two lie on a shelf in the foot o' the bed, over the heads o' the eldest twa. An' truth I can tell you we are no' cauld gin I close the bed doors.'

WALES

Bed outshuts, created by stepping out a short length of wall to form an alcove, are unknown to students of English vernacular architecture, but an interesting concentration has been recorded on the Gower peninsular in South Wales; they are also found in north-west Ireland. The Welsh examples occur in houses of typical regional plan dating from the late sixteenth to the mid-nineteenth centuries and are usually adjacent to the main fireplace.[11] One of the finest is from Kennixton, Llangennith, where the bed is boxed-in behind a panelled oak screen with pierced ventilation panels above the sliding doors; a long bench fixed against the front of the partition serves as a fireside settle (Plate 216). An early nineteenth-century outshut bed of tongue and grooved plank construction in a farmhouse at Delvid, Llangennith, occupies the same position in relation to the hearth.

In North Wales, movable box beds were once common. F.H. Norman reported them from one-roomed cottages in Anglesea and Caernarvon in 1867:[12]

216. Oak cupboard bed of *c.* 1760 with ventilation panels and sliding doors from Kennixton, Llangennith, Gower. *Welsh Folk Museum, St Fagans*

This room is unceiled and paved with stones and is used as a living and sleeping room. It is generally partially divided by two box beds which are placed nearly across the centre of the room, leaving only a narrow passage to connect the portions of the room which are used by day and night respectively. Although only one room, the cottages with the beds thus disposed have the appearance of having two rooms, the backs of the beds being fitted with shelves, on which the household crockery, etc. is placed.

If additional sleeping accommodation was required for children, it was customary, according to the Welsh folk historian Iorwerth Peate, to place boards across the tops of the box beds creating what was known as a *croglofft*, reached by means of a ladder.[13] A typical standing box bed of pine with sliding doors from Cardiganshire is preserved at St Fagans, the framework being held together by iron hooks so that it could be dismantled if the owner moved house.

IRELAND AND SETTLE BEDS

Turning briefly to Ireland, a cottier's house from Duncrun township, north Derry, now reconstructed at the Ulster Folk Museum, has a bed outshut or *cuilteach* in one corner of the kitchen near the fire; it contains a stump bedstead divided from the room by curtains. The Ordnance Survey Memoir (prepared about 1835), reporting on 'the habits of the people' of Upper Clumber, Londonderry, stated that in most rural houses 'the only bedstead consists of bog timber, supported on large stones with a bundle of straw, or rushes, for a pallet, a canvas sheet and a blanket'.[14] The Memoir for Templecorran, Co. Antrim, noted a distinctive form of rural Irish bed: 'The furniture of the kitchen is very plain and homely. The servants not infrequently sleep in settle beds'.[15] This widely distributed article of dual-purpose furniture was designed like a panel-backed settle having a boxed-in seat and solid ends; on the release of two hook catches the front falls forward to create a sleeping crib (Plate 217). Bedding was stored inside the box seat. Scattered inventory entries reveal that settle beds, which were apparently unique to Ireland, evolved during the late seventeenth century, although the fourteen examples collected by the National Museum and ten acquired by the Ulster Folk Museum are all thought to date from the nineteenth century. The vast majority of surviving specimens are of pine, usually painted dark brown, red or with a grained finish; sometimes the backs are faced with simulated rather than framed panelling. A few have seats which are much too high for sitting comfortably. Little is known about their social status, although oral tradition suggests they were commonly used by servants, children or tramps seeking shelter. They have been recorded in Canada from areas of Irish settlement.[16]

217. Settle beds were found throughout rural Ireland. This painted pine example shown in the folded-down position is from Ulster, nineteenth century, second half. *Ulster Folk and Transport Museum*

GREEN BEDS FROM THE CHANNEL ISLANDS

Vernacular furniture from the Channel Islands displays a strong regional character, one of the most striking items, found mainly on Guernsey, being the green bed, known locally as a *lit-de-fouaille* (fern) or *la joncquière*.[17] During the last century nearly every rural dwelling owned one; however, they rapidly fell into disuse following the German Occupation, and a census undertaken in 1971 traced only sixty-nine examples. Cochrane's *Guide to the Island of Guernsey* (1826) stated: 'An ancient custom prevails throughout the country farm-houses and cottages: in the kitchen, there is what they term a green bed, about two feet high from the ground, covered in the dry fern or pea haulm, upon which the tired labourer reposes'. These beds, made in the form of a shallow box raised on square legs, with a narrow ledge around the top, traditionally stood against the wall at one side of the fireplace. It was customary to store peat under the green bed, which suggests that the bedding was originally placed on a stack of peats before pine frames were introduced.

218. (*above, left*) A Guernsey *joncquiere* or green bed, filled with *jonc* (soft rush) which, with *fouaille* (braken) were traditional early fillings. *Courtesy J.H. Lenfestey*

219. (*above, right*) A Guernsey green bed filled with *peahaulm*; pine with a plank bottom, probably nineteenth century. *Courtesy J.H. Lenfestey*

The shallow trough could be filled with various bedding materials: bracken was widely used in upland parishes, but where *jonc* or green rushes were plentiful, they were preferred (Plate 218). Peas formed part of the Islanders' staple diet, thus *pea haulm* (dried pea-stems) offered a popular alternative (Plate 219); on Alderney bags of dried seaweed were favoured, but during the present century most families employed sacks filled with oat husks. There are no recent records of green beds being regularly used as a sleeping place; in modern times they served the family as a couch where the men could rest or the women sit and knit. Dally's *Guide to Guernsey* (1860) mentions that 'on festive occasions, such as *vraicing* (seaweed harvesting) feasts, it was customary, above this lit, to suspend a canopy which was tastefully decorated with flowers and fern leaves'. On the much more cosmopolitan island of Jersey, similar beds, known colloquially as a *lit-de-veille*, had all but disappeared by 1920; only one specimen survives.

THE BUILT-IN BED TRADITION IN ENGLAND

This tradition appears to have been restricted to – or at least lingered longest – in the northern counties, particulary the Lake District, the North York Moors and Northumberland. A famous literary account of a bed closet occurs in Emily Brontë's *Wuthering Heights* (1848); the action of her novel, set in the Yorkshire Dales, is supposed to have taken place in 1801. Mr Lockwood, snowbound at the remote farmstead of Wuthering Heights, is shown to his room:[18]

> I fastened the door and glanced round for the bed. The whole furniture consisted of a chair, a clothes-press, and a large oak case, with squares cut out near the top, resembling coach windows. Having approached this structure, I looked inside, and perceived it to be a singular sort of old fashioned couch, very conveniently designed to obviate the necessity for every member of the family having a room to himself. In fact, it formed a little closet, and the ledge of a window, which it enclosed, served as a table. I slid back the panelled sides, got in with my light, pulled them together again, and felt secure against the vigilance of Heathcliff, and everyone else.

This very precise description raises two points: firstly, no cupboard beds with outside windows have been recorded and secondly, it is rare for bed closets to be situated upstairs, because they mostly date from a time when families slept on the ground floor. In fact, the only region where such beds are known on upper floors date from the period of the Great Rebuilding in the Lake Counties.

A house at Kirkbride on the south side of the Solway Firth, which has a lintel carved 1721 and formerly contained a spectacular painted standing bed dated 1724

220. Headboard of a painted oak bed from Kirkbride, Cumbria, dated 1724 and initialled F^HA for Francis and Anne Hall. The panel opened to reveal a wall niche (see Plate 211). *Leeds Art Galleries*

(Plates 220 and 211), still retains an original panelled partition with double doors enclosing a bed space which projects over the stairwell.[19] The RCHM volume on Westmorland illustrates two fixed beds with hinged doors headed by open panels in the first-floor bedchamber of a house at Waitby, dated 1690,[20] and another alcove bed upstairs in a house dated 1674 at Troutbeck.[21] In Yorkshire the recess under the staircase was a popular position. A fine example from the now-deserted farm called Start House in Baldersdale, a side valley of Upper Teesdale, is carved 'HH DH 1712', the initials standing for Henry and Dorothy Hutchinson (Plate 221). Henry Hutchinson's probate inventory of 1735 shows he was a yeoman sheep farmer but, sadly, his furniture is lumped together under 'Household Goods £6'.[22] Had the appraisers itemized this bed, it would most likely have been listed as a 'close bed', the local name for a panelled sleeping recess. Built-in cupboard beds are also known from farmhouses at Harwood, Winston and Dalton in Teesdale. One of the few references to box beds in the lowland zone comes from the inventory of Thomas

221. Front of an oak cupboard bed built-in under a staircase at Start House, an isolated farmstead in Upper Teesdale, Yorkshire, dated 1712. The carved initials HH DH stand for Henry and Dorothy Hutchinson. *Courtesy Beamish Museum*

Linton, a shoemaker at Pocklington in the Vale of York whose inventory (1697) notes '2 beds in the cupboard in the house'.[23] At Firby almshouses, near Bedale, the remains of six pine wall beds with planked doors were photographed before this row of one room, single-storey cottages was converted into a private residence[24] (see Plate 312).

On the North York Moors cruck-framed long houses were the predominant regional type, and several cottages in Farndale preserve the built-in beds once common in this area.[25] At Cotehill a recess in the kitchen contained, until recently, a wide bed cupboard enclosed by two solid doors. At nearby Oak Crag a similar bed was housed in a space beneath the staircase, while Duck House, a farm further down Farndale, contains a loft with twin bed cubicles occupying a bay between the two central pairs of crucks. The latter are open at the front, with the boarded backs and ends following the slope of the roof. Two beds of the same pattern with chamfered posts and corded bottoms survive in the original sleeping loft at Spout House, Bilsdale, a thatched cruck-framed hedge alehouse (Plate 222). James Walton suggests that in the older single-storey cottages on the North York Moors, built-in beds were normally sited near the hearth in the living-kitchen which at this date was still open to the thatch; then, in the eighteenth century, sleeping lofts with fixed bed cubicles were constructed in the roof space over the lower end, and during the following century the whole house was chambered over by extending the half loft, allowing beds to be placed more centrally.[26] A very interesting oak bedstead from a farmhouse in Iburndale, near Sleights, started life under the thatch in a loft, corresponding almost exactly to the beds at Spout House, which explains why one headpost is much shorter than the other (Plate 223). When sleeping lofts became outmoded, instead of discarding the bed the foot posts were cut down, the rails hinged and provided with extra legs, thus converting it into a turn-up stump bed (Plate 224). The cross bar at the head of the mattress frame is housed in grooves and fitted with tensioning bolts.

222. Pair of beds, originally with corded bottoms, built into the sleeping loft at Spout House, Bilsdale, on the North York Moors. *Courtesy N.Y.M. National Park*

223. This oak bedstead, originally built into a sleeping loft (see Plate 222), was later converted into a space-saving turn-up bed. From Iburndale, near Sleights, on the North York Moors. *Trustees of the Ryedale Folk Museum*

224. The bed shown folded up.

The Revd. J.C. Atkinson of Danby, author of *Forty Years in a Moorland Parish* (1891), gives several accounts of what he called the 'sleeping arrangements' of his parishioners. About 1870 he visited a cottage at Egton which sheltered both beasts and family under one roof: 'The floor was of clay and in holes, and around on two sides were cubicles, or sleeping-boxes – even less desirable than the box beds of Berwickshire as I knew them fifty years ago – of the entire family. There was no loft above, much less any attempt at a "chamber"....'[27] On another occasion, a farmer's wife at Liverton took him upstairs to see their sleeping place: 'What I found was one long low room partitioned off into four compartments nearly equal in size. But the partitions were in their construction and character merely such as those between stalls in a stable. These four partitioned spaces were no more closed in the rear than the stalls in an ordinary stable and the partitions were not seven feet, hardly six and a half in height, while the general gangway for all the occupants was along the open back'.[28] Atkinson was told that the first space was used by the parents and their two younger children, the next allotted to the older children, the third to the farm girls and the fourth to the man and farm lad.

LOWLAND SCOTLAND AND THE BORDERS

The real stronghold of the box-bed tradition (as the Revd. Atkinson hinted) was Scotland and the Border Counties (see Plate 57). They were mentioned by many witnesses from the northern part of Northumberland who gave evidence to the Royal Commissioners whose Report of 1868 has already been quoted.[29] Mr Borthwick of Kirknewton dwelt in a two-roomed cottage 15 × 15 and 12 × 12 feet: 'the kitchen is fitted up with two large box beds which form small bedrooms, as the occupant dresses there in the morning'. The Revd. J. Allgood of Ingram stated that in the cottages in his parish: 'the one room when occupied is divided into two apartments by two box beds being placed across the room, leaving space for a doorway in the centre'. Mr Hughes of Ilderton reported 'the usual construction is an oblong ground floor divided into kitchen and sleeping room 12ft square each by frame partition beds'. A mid-nineteenth-century watercolour of a barn-like interior containing three box beds almost certainly records a bothy in the Border Counties. One of the beds is enclosed by a sliding door, the others have limp curtains across the opening (see Plate 378); lodging boxes, the end of a rail-back bench and a Scottish-type chair with panelled arms are also visible. However, bohemian farm labourers preferred such free and easy living conditions to the improved fixtures and furnishings which Loudon considered suitable for the ploughman's room. These included cast-iron bedsteads 'the invention of Mr Mallet of Dublin (which) have been extensively used in Ireland' (Plate 225). They are indistinguishable from surviving beds in contemporary prison cells in York Castle and Northleach (see Plate 289).

J.C. Loudon, who grew up near Edinburgh, included an illuminating (if rather long-winded) paragraph about box beds in his *Encyclopaedia* (1833):[30]

> Box beds are common in the better description of cottages in Scotland. This bed is of the usual length, and in general four feet wide within. There are four square posts, at the four corners; and the back and ends are filled in with boarding grooved and tongued; while the front is formed into panels, one of which at top and another at bottom are fixed, and two between them slide in grooves, and form the door of the bed. The roof is of boards, and the bottom of laths. There is generally a shelf, and sometimes two, fixed to the inside of the bottom of the bed, just above the bedclothes; and sometimes there is one at the top, close under the roof. There are also sometimes one or two shelves against the back of the bed; so that this piece of furniture not only serves as a bed, but as a wardrobe and linen chest. In some parts of the country the bed doors fix within by bolts, or have a lock to fasten them on the outside; so that a person going to bed, with all his

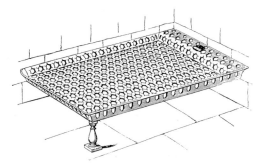

225. Design for a cast-iron bedstead by Mallet of Dublin, illustrated by J.C. Loudon in 1833 as suitable for a ploughman's room. They were also used in prison cells (see Plate 289).

treasure round him on the surrounding shelves, may secure it while he is asleep at night, or going out to work in the daytime, by bolting or locking the doors. These box beds can be easily taken to pieces, and put together again. Besides serving as a wardrobe &c a box bed may be made to supply the place of a partition, two of them being often placed, in Scotland, across any apartment, which they thus divide into two rooms, leaving a passage between them. In roomy cottages four are sometimes placed back to back; thus giving two beds to be entered from the kitchen, and two from the parlour. A bed of this sort, well-made, was formerly considered the principal article in a Scottish cottagers furnishing . . . but they are too costly, and too cumbersome, for a tenant at will, or on a short lease.

Turning from written sources to material evidence, the curtained bed recess in the cottage at Doon, where Robert Burns was born, still looks much as it did when illustrated in 1859[31]; and at Auchindrain, a unique farm town in Argyll, now preserved as a site museum, the main sleeping accommodation in the older houses took the form of a box bed in the kitchen. An ingeniously contrived complex of built-in beds in a deserted farmhouse on the island of Stroma in the Pentland Firth, Caithness, represents a sophisticated final phase of the box-bed tradition. W. Ashley Bartlam, who visited this three-roomed house in 1977, reported that the centre unit contained:[32] 'two box beds with space between for a third bed. The two sides of the box beds are open and either side is capable of being closed by a removable boarded panel set into a check and held in place by wooden turn buttons. The panel can be mounted on either side of the bed allowing a large number of possible combinations of sleeping arrangements'. These beds are similar to, although wider than, ships' bunks and are panelled below to create a storage space.

PRESS BEDSTEADS AND FOLD-AWAY BEDS

In the mid-Georgian period press beds, that is bedsteads designed to fold away into a cupboard, were sometimes made by leading cabinet makers for fashionable clients. For example, in 1772 Thomas Chippendale supplied a lavish press bedstead disguised as a break front bookcase for David Garrick's apartments at 5 Royal Adelphi Terrace; it no longer survives, but the shell of another press bed contained in a large japanned cabinet, which Garrick commissioned from Chippendale for his Villa at Hampton, still exists.[33] The space-saving character of press beds made them very suitable for town houses.

Cabinet maker's *Books of Prices*, published in London and provincial centres from 1788 onwards, nearly all give costings for press and related types of fold-away beds. For instance, the *Leeds Cabinet and Chair-Makers Book of Prices* (1791) contains details of the rates for constructing not only a 'Four Feet Press Bedstead . . . £2.' but also Table Beds, a Toilet Table Bedstead 'the Fronts and Ends covered with a Curtain, to appear as a Toilet Table when the Top is down' and a Bureau Bedstead 'all solid, common Brackets, to represent Four Drawers in Front . . . to turn out behind'. The Gillow Estimate Sketch Books illustrate a 'Buro bedstead made of deal with 5 sham drawers in front' which took John Crowdson twelve days to make in 1788[34] (Plate 226), also a simple beech and elm turn-up stump bed (Plate 227);[35] both were almost certainly intended for servants. Common turn-up beds, not housed in a cupboard, were presumably the ancestor of enclosed press beds. A collection of inventories from Horbury, near Wakefield, dated between 1688 and 1757, record 'turn up bedsteads' or 'turn up bedstocks'[36] while the 'faling bedstead' which Christopher Binks, joiner, of Shelton Moorhouse, Yorkshire, bequeathed to his daughter in 1749, may well have been of this form.[37] Loudon illustrates both types (Plate 230), and a trade catalogue issued by Heal & Co. in 1853 advertised four 'Servants' Press Beds' with folding beech frames and laced canvas bottoms.[38] Beds of this pattern were widely popular in working-class homes in Scotland until the

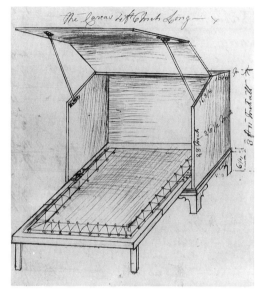

226. Drawing for a bureau bedstead in deal with five sham drawers and a corded canvas bottom. From the Gillow Estimate Sketch Books, 1788. *Westminster City Archives*

227. Drawing for a turn-up bedstead in beech and elm from the Gillow Estimate Sketch Books, 1788. *Westminster City Archives*

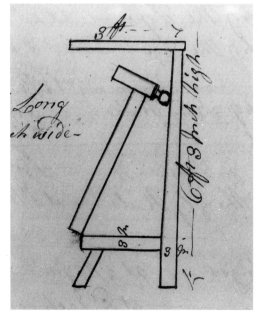

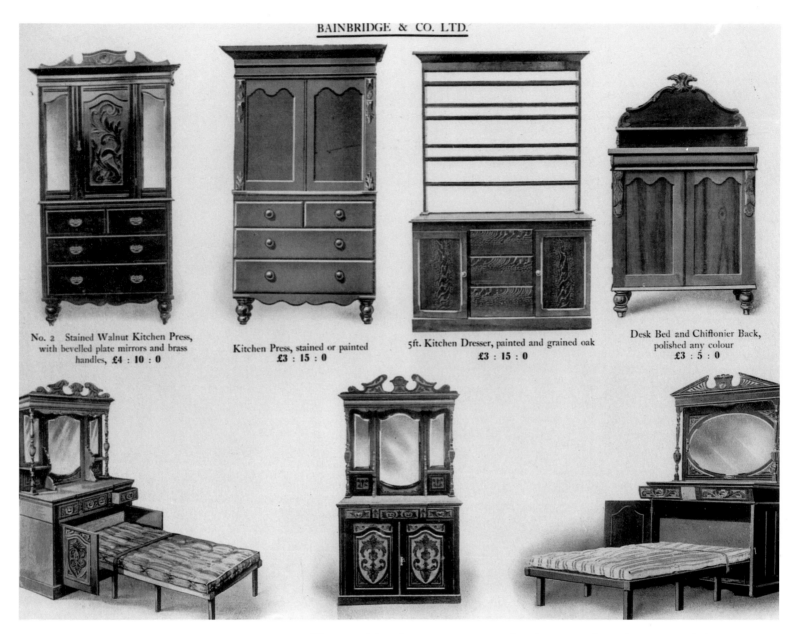

No. 2 Stained Walnut Kitchen Press, with bevelled plate mirrors and brass handles, £4 : 10 : 0

Kitchen Press, stained or painted £3 : 15 : 0

5ft. Kitchen Dresser, painted and grained oak £3 : 15 : 0

Desk Bed and Chiffonier Back, polished any colour £3 : 5 : 0

228. Chiffonier or 'dess' beds from a trade catalogue of c. 1910 issued by Bainbridge & Co., Newcastle-upon-Tyne, Northumberland. *Beamish Museum*

1920s.[39] Inevitably, the vast majority of such presses have been gutted, but an intact example was collected in 1967 from the kitchen of a cottage in Little Kildale, Cleveland (Plate 229). Loudon observed that they 'are very common in kitchens, and, sometimes in parlours . . . but they are objectionable as harbouring vermin, and being apt soon to get out of order when in daily use', adding they 'are not held in much repute; because they indicate a deficiency of bed-rooms'.[40]

Despite Loudon's strictures, an entirely new generation of fold-away beds emerged in the North East before social changes eventually led to their demise. Before the Great War most miners on the Northumberland, Durham and Yorkshire coalfields lived in small cottages, but since they earned above-average wages, the front room was often stocked with showy mahogany furniture which included a fold-up 'dess' bed concealed in a chiffonier or sideboard (Plate 228). The local word 'dess' meaning 'to pile up in layers' was later corrupted to 'desk bed'; Edwardian examples are usually fitted with wire spring mattresses. Frank Atkinson has recorded oral evidence about dess beds[41] and collected examples from Spennymoor, Pity Me and Stockton in Co. Durham, now at Beamish and the Bowes Museums. A manuscript account book kept by John Wainwright, joiner, of Skelmanthorpe in South Yorkshire, contains numerous references (dated between 1883 and 1911) to

140

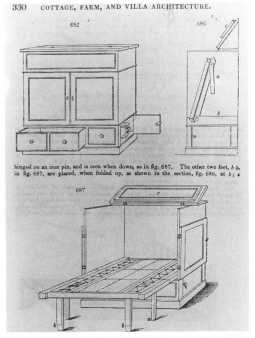

229. A painted pine press bed, mid-nineteenth century, from the living room of a cottage in Little Kildale, Yorkshire. The hinges stamped 'BALDWIN PATENT'. *Trustees of the Ryedale Folk Museum*

230. Designs showing a press bedstead, published by J.C. Loudon in 1833 as suitable for the kitchen of a cottage dwelling. They were also often used by servants.

grained or mahogany 'chiffonier bedsteads', many of the entries being accompanied by diminutive sketches.[42] He charged up to £6.10s. for models with pillars, carved panels and a shelf, but some of his customers in the 1890s paid him for removing unwanted bedstocks, a fate that has now overtaken almost all the survivors. While they are too elaborate to be accepted as products of the vernacular tradition, dess beds offer a logical point at which to conclude this section.

TRUCKLE BEDS

Household inventories from all parts of the country record 'truckle' or 'trundle' beds although their use declined during the eighteenth century. They were low-framed beds on castors traditionally wheeled under the parents' bed and pulled out at night for children or servants to sleep on. At his death in 1729 Robert Townend, gardener, of Horbury, near Wakefield, owned 'one truckle bed and some bedding 6s. 6d.'; twenty years earlier the appraisers of the estate of his neighbour, Joseph Cawtheron, listed in the parlour 'One stand bed & one trundle bed & ye bedding';[43] it was presumably used by some of his five children. The only surviving truckle beds are Welsh: an oak-framed specimen with a corded bottom from Gelli, Glamorgan, is now at St Fagan's Museum, while another is preserved at Wern Newydd, Cardiganshire.[44] In Scottish tenements, a similar kind of bed on wheels called a 'hurley' bed was kept under the bed recess and brought out at night for the children (see Plate 81); they were common well into the present century, but although many adults still alive slept in them when small, none of these beds have been traced.

10 Straw and Wicker Furniture

STRAW FURNITURE

J.C. Loudon's observations on the uses of matting in furnishing cottage dwellings can serve to introduce the subject of straw, rushes and flags as traditional furniture-making materials. In 1833 he wrote: 'Matting is manufactured, in many different manners, out of the straw of corn, rushes, or other long, narrow, grassy or sedgy leaves. In Monmouthshire, easy chairs with hoods, like porter's chairs in gentlemen's halls, are constructed of straw matting on a frame of wooden rods, or stout wire; and chairs are made entirely of straw in different parts of England, in the same way as the common beehives'.[1] In the past, many farm and domestic articles were made of straw, including baskets, seed-lips, bee skeps, mats, chairs, hassocks, chair-back screens, palliasses, cradles and even beds. The generic term for this ancient craft is 'lip-work' and unthreshed winter-sown wheat or rye straw was considered best for making the rolls which were coiled and bound with strips of bramble or split withy. The most suitable bramble grew in shady woods and was cut in winter when the sap was down. The prickles were taken off, the stem split and the pith removed with a knife to produce long, tough, smooth strands. The only other tools were a cow horn guage for ensuring the straw was drawn into rolls of uniform thickness and a bone awl for opening the weave when binding the coils.[2] Straw crafts were often a spare-time activity: a well-documented lip-work chair at Gressenhall Museum is known to have been made about 1860, by a farm labourer named Brown, as a fire-side chair for his wife (Plate 231). He worked on the Wattlefield estate in Norfolk and supplemented his meagre wages by producing straw bee skeps.

Dorothy Hartley, writing in the 1930s, described and illustrated a traditional straw bed in the form of a shallow trough; it was of a type constructed by shepherds for use in their lambing sheds or by harvest workers in their bothys.[3] Thus, when farm labourers were allowed 'two trusses of straw each for their bed' it was not simply thrown down in a heap,' but skilfully drawn into long ropes to make a thick mat with a raised edge and extra coils at the head. Such beds are also said to have been widely used by children and servants, particularly at inns, but none are known to survive which makes the example contrived by 'a Dalesman shepherd' and sketched by Dorothy Hartley rather significant (Plate 232). Straw plaiting was a cottage industry in parts of West Yorkshire and William Smith, looking back to earlier times in his *Rambles About Morley* (1866) wrote: 'Straw was the material of the bed, from which came the phrase, once common in Morley and the neighbourhood "My wife is in the straw" applying to her confinement'. Rushes were widely used for making low drum-shaped stools known as pesses or hassocks. The ever informative J.C. Loudon noted that in England footstools were 'very commonly formed by covering a bundle of bulrushes with rush matting';[4] a group of such hassocks in the Chapter House at Lincoln Cathedral were sketched by S.H. Grimm in 1793 (Plate 233) and several pesses are preserved at Strangers' Hall, Norwich.

231. Chair made from thick bands of unthreshed drawn straw. Made about 1880 by a farm labourer on the Wattlefield Hall estate, Norfolk. *Norfolk Museums Service*

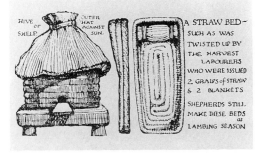

232. Drawing of a straw bed, contrived by 'a Dalesman shepherd', published by Dorothy Hartley in the 1930s.
(*Opposite*) Detail from the painting *Night* by Francis Wheatley, 1799, showing wicker cradle (see Plate 241).

143

233. Four rush pesses or hassocks sketched by S.H. Grimm in the Chapter House at Lincoln Cathedral in 1784. They were also used by cottagers as stools. *By permission of the British Library*

Straw chairs are of three main types. One has a round seat raised on a circular 'beehive' skirt with a comfortable gondola-shaped back. Another, accurately described by Loudon as resembling a hall-porter's chair, had either a square or half-round 'box' seat supporting a high canopied hood with deeply recessed arm-rests. Specimens which have aged well are very impressive and possess a beautiful smooth, golden complexion. The third sort, popular in the Orkney Isles, consists of a conventional timber-framed lower stage and arms with tall uprights supporting a high curved straw-work back, often with a domed hood. They are the peasant equivalent of a winged easy chair and enjoyed a reputation for being very warm, so were generally given to old or sick members of the family or nursing mothers; the seats of some are fitted with a night commode. The design of straw chairs broadly follows the pattern of wicker furniture; sometimes they were reinforced by an inner structure of poles or set on a base frame of wooden rails, to protect the foot rim from wear, but often rigidity was achieved entirely by means of the stiffness of the tightly coiled straw ropes.

One of the earliest references to 'beehive' chairs is John Aubrey's allusion to Ben Jonson's 'studyeing chair, which was of strawe, such as old women used'.[5] An Oxford inventory of 1678 mentions 'one great straw chayre'[6] which sounds very like 'a great chair made of rushes' described in a West Country inn-scene in Henry Fielding's *Tom Jones* (1749), where it serves the hero as a sleeping chair. John Smith, an innkeeper at Iron Acton, Gloucestershire, had 'a Holm chair' (*helm* is a dialect word for stalks of straw) in the best chamber in 1728, and another Gloucestershire inventory of 1727 records 'one Straw Chair', also in a bedroom.[7] This branch of furniture appears in fact to have been widely popular in counties bordering the River Severn, perhaps as an offshoot of the fishing industry which sustained a vigorous demand for putcheons, baskets, kipes and various traps. East Anglia was another region where the tradition lingered on, although recorded examples are of low-backed form.

A survey of provenanced lip-work chairs confirms that the tradition persisted longest in South Wales, the Welsh Marches and Gloucestershire. Roger Warner, an antique dealer who has 'worked' this region since the 1930s fully agrees, whilst examples and photographic records at St Fagan's, Gloucester and Brecknock Museums, endorse this distribution pattern. They have also been reported from the Forest of Dean, the New Forest, the Channel Islands, and Ireland, while a charming painting by Alfred Provis, titled *A Wiltshire Cottager's Fireside*, dated 1853, portrays a

234. *A Wiltshire Cottager's Fireside* by Alfred Provis, 1853. Canopied straw chairs were customarily used by nursing mothers. *Illustrated London News* (1853)

235. Canopied straw chair which belonged to the physician Edward Jenner (1749–1823) of Berkeley, Gloucestershire. *Museum of the History of Science, Oxford University*

236. This straw chair from Painswick House, Gloucestershire, which retains its original ticken cover and padded seat, probably dates from the 1830s when straw furniture was briefly fashionable. *Leeds Art Galleries*

home-made hooded specimen (Plate 234). The earliest securely dated, canopied straw chair, which is in the Museum of the History of Science at Oxford, was owned by the physician Edward Jenner (1749–1823) of Berkeley, Gloucestershire, where he spent most of his life (Plate 235). The straw tends, during use, to be compacted to a smooth glossy surface, but low-backed chairs were sometimes provided with a close-fitting cotton case for comfort and protection. A well-preserved model cased in its original striped ticken, formerly at Painswick House, Gloucestershire, is thought to date from about 1830 when the mansion was enlarged (Plate 236). Such chairs were socially acceptable in country houses around this time: there was one in the drawing-room at Aynhoe, Northamptonshire, in 1835, while a watercolour of the saloon at Howsham Hall, Yorkshire, painted by Mary Ellen Best in the 1830s, shows a pair without fabric covers but sporting decorative crestings.[8] Furthermore, Thomas Webster's reliable *Encyclopaedia of Domestic Economy* (1844) states: 'The beehive chair, made of straw , has been long used in Wales and Scotland, as well as in some places in the north of England. But it is only of late that they have appeared among our fashionable furniture. They are, however, warm and cheap, and are admired by some persons for their simple, homely, and snug appearance'.[9]

Straw-backed Orkney chairs remained in customary use until well into the age of photography and have, during the present century, been the focus of a craft revival (Plate 237). They are thought to have evolved from a low round stool which in time acquired a half-circular shoulder-high back and eventually a tall domed hood. The

237. Orkney chair; the frame, built of oak from St Magnus Cathedral, bears the label of D.M. Kirkness, 'Joiner & Orkney Chair Maker', Kirkwall, dated 1921. *C.G. Gilbert*

146

238. Making a low-back Orkney chair from unthreshed oat straw secured to a pine frame, *c.* 1910. *Courtesy Tankerness House Museum*

fully developed version (akin to orthodox West Country models) was known as a 'heided stül' and had a light inner skeleton entirely overlaid by bands of oat straw or bent grass. According to W.T. Dennison, writing in 1905, the idea of replacing the base with a timber box seat incorporating a drawer emerged about the middle of the eighteenth century; in his day the drawer was used by 'the goodman' for keeping liquor, snuff and books; 'the goodwife' traditionally sat in a low-backed chair.[10] From about 1878, D.M. Kirkness, a Kirkwall joiner, built the wooden frames and employed local fishermen to make the straw backs in their spare time (Plate 238). Before leaving Scotland reference must be made to an unusual nineteenth-century settee from a farmhouse in Strathdearne, Inverness-shire, with a pine and ash frame, a corded bottom and hay stuffing which, when a later textile cover was removed, was found to be upholstered in rush matting (Plate 239). This remarkable survival

239. Settee having a pine frame and corded bottom stuffed with hay and upholstered with rush matting (found beneath a later fabric cover). From a farmhouse in Strathdearne, Inverness-shire, Scotland. *Highland Folk Museum*

again illustrates the versatile uses to which 'rushes or other long, narrow, grassy or sedgy leaves' were put by rural craftsmen.

WICKER FURNITURE

Willows need fresh running water at their roots so, although the tree is widely distributed, its main strongholds are the river systems of the Midland Counties, East Anglia and the Somerset Levels. Methods of working this light, strong material have varied little over the centuries, robust structures being created by interweaving a stout framework of rods or stakes with thin osier withies.[11] Down the ages poor families, unable to afford wooden seat furniture, have fabricated wicker chairs from locally grown willow wands.

When discussing a rudimentary tub chair, of staved-barrel construction, Randle Holme wrote in 1649: 'There is another kind of these chaires called Twiggen chaires because they are made of Owsiers, and Withen twigs: having round covers over the heads of them like to a canapy. These are principally used by sick and infirm people, and such women as have bine lately brought to bed; from whence they are generally termed, Growneing chaires, or Child-bed chaires'.[12] A painting in the National Gallery by Jacob Jordaens (c. 1620) portrays the Virgin as a nursing mother seated in a spectacular hooded wicker chair of this description (Plate 240). The inventory of Joan Trew, widow, of Corfe Castle, Dorset, dated 1681, actually lists, 'a Groaning Chaire' in one of the bedrooms.[13] In Holland, a curious tray-like basket seat with a low rounded back, known as a *bakermat*, was woven for mothers engaged in feeding and swaddling their babies before the fire.[14] The 'nurse twige chayre', recorded in an Oxford inventory of 1673, may refer to a seat of this type.[15]

Wicker chairs were used at all levels of society until replaced by even more comfortable unpholstered winged easy chairs which first appeared in the late seventeenth century; but due to the perishable nature of the material, one has to rely heavily on documentary and pictorial sources when studying early wicker furniture. Basketwork was widely used to make cradles (Plate 241) and bird cages, sometimes

240. Many early inventories record twiggen, wanded or wicker chairs. This detail from a painting by Jacob Jordaens of *The Virgin and Child* (c. 1620) shows a fine hooded example. *Trustees of the National Gallery*

241. *Night* by Francis Wheatley, 1799. Because of its lightness, wicker was popular for cradles. Notice, too, the basket and straw hat hanging on the wall. *Yale Center for British Art*

screens,[16] occasionally for the side panels of food cupboards (Plate 242), in districts where timber was scarce, as in Iona, for coffins and in Welsh slate quarries for stretchers (Plate 243). Writing in 1838, William Howitt recalled having seen, in the sleeping loft of a shepherds' but in the Cheviots, beds made from 'pieces of wicker-work, like the lower half of a pot-crate cut off, about half a yard high, filled with straw, and a few blankets, laid upon it'.[17] However, because of its lightness and natural flexibility, wicker was particularly suitable for chairs. Chairs were frequently woven by general basket makers, known in the Midlands as 'wickermen' and in North Yorkshire as 'wand weavers'. They are described variously as twiggen-, wanded-, wicker-, willow-, rodd-, withy-, basket-, or owsier-chairs to name the commoner regional terms. Some basket makers are listed in early nineteenth-century trade directories under the heading chairmakers; George Joyce of Basing-stoke, Hampshire, was particularly versatile, being described in 1823 as 'turner, ch. & basket m.'.[18]

Analysis of 185 rural inventories from mid-Essex, compiled between 1638 and 1700[19] shows that twenty-eight households possessed a wicker chair, usually only one, often kept in a bedroom. A smaller sample from North Yorkshire, dated 1750–70,[20] yields a lower incidence, but they are mostly located in the housestead or living-kitchen, while collections of eighteenth-century inventories from Gloucester-shire and Shropshire[21] confirm this change of station. A schedule of furnishings in an inn at Cowbridge, Glamorgan, dated 1765, lists, 'six Twig Chairs' in the kitchen, another six in the best guest chamber and two more in other bedrooms: however, they are, perhaps, likely to have been common turned chairs with basketwork (see Plate 123) or conceivably rush seats.[22]

There is evidence that, whereas in the seventeenth century wicker chairs performed a useful social role as a bedside seat[23] for old and infirm people or nursing mothers, they came later to be regarded as particularly suitable for baby chairs. Georgian artists certainly often portray them serving this purpose.[24] J.C. Loudon, in

242. Wicker panels have been used to ventilate the sides of this nineteenth-century pine food cupboard from Acharacle, Argyll, Scotland. *Highland Folk Museum*

1833, illustrated a child's commode chair 'made entirely of wickerwork, which costs, complete, about London, only 4s. 6d.' (see Plate 398). 'Everyone', he continues, 'who can make a basket can make a chair of this description. In England the cottager's child is placed in a chair of this sort after he is a week old'.[25] A painting by George Morland features a chair of precisely this pattern (Plate 244). The two holes in the elbows were for holding either a restraining rod or a tray-top table with pins in the ends and a single front leg. The longevity of this design is proclaimed by several models illustrated in a trade catalogue issued by Morris, Wilkinson & Co., wicker-furniture manufacturers of Nottingham in 1909[26] (Plate 245). The familiar winged child's chair with a high boarded back and box seat, which survives in large numbers (see Plate 401) is clearly a timber version of this routine wicker type which suggests that the rather similar, but puzzling, so-called lambing or shepherds' chairs – once common in the Pennine Dales – may also be based on earlier wanded chairs translated into wood, rather than originating in a tradition of joined furniture (see Plate 35).

A rare publication titled *A List of Sizes and Prices of Baskets, Hampers, Chairs and Carriages of the Newark and Farndon and Sutton-on-Trent District*, compiled 'by a Committee of Journeymen, and Agreed to by the Employers, June 1878'[27] contains a wealth of information about articles woven in white, buff of brown willow. It not only describes square peak-backed, round peak-backed, common round-backed, fitched-back, double-staked and lounging chairs, but includes items such as perambulator carriagework, Stilton-cheese baskets, eel traps, randed chaff baskets and prices for 'chair bottoming'. A similar Price Book regulating the piece-work rates for wickermen in the Basford district of Nottinghamshire (1891) also survives;[28] the specifications however relate mainly to drawing-room, conservatory and garden chairs. This fanciful, often rather flimsy range, known at the time as 'art wicker furniture' marks a genuine break with the native vernacular tradition which favoured a few proven patterns rather than novel styles. The chance discovery of a dozen or so trade catalogues illustrating wicker furniture made by leading Midland firms during the Edwardian period[29] gives a wonderful insight into the diversification of forms and variety of decorative styles, as well as more conservative chairs, produced for middle-class homes. Because of its light and yielding character, this material was also popular for invalid carriages (see Plate 365).

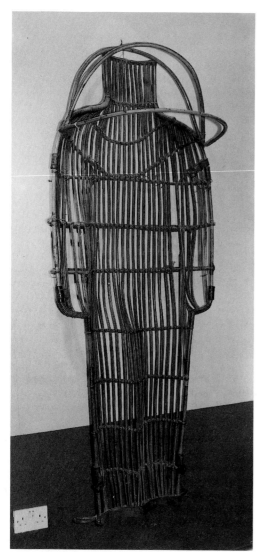

243. Wicker stretcher used to lower injured men from perilous places at the Dinorwic slate quarry, Llanberis, North Wales. *National Museum of Wales*

244. Detail from George Morland's *Comforts of Industry*, 1790, showing a cottage interior with a nursery chair strikingly similar to one illustrated by J.C. Loudon in 1833 (see Plate 398). *Trustees of the National Gallery of Scotland*

245. A nursery chair with a vase and table flap, from a trade catalogue of wicker furniture issued by Morris, Wilkinson & Co., Nottingham, in 1909. *Leeds Art Galleries*

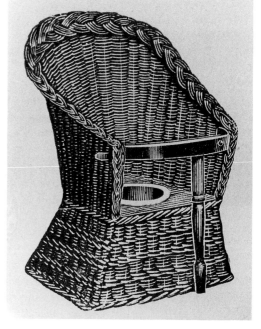

150

11 Schools

By the early eighteenth century a network of small schools existed in towns and villages throughout the country. Many had been built and endowed by local benefactors, others were held in part of the church; there were also Charity Schools and, of course, Dame Schools. However, before the Sunday School Movement started in the 1780s, very few poor children received an elementary education. While many old school buildings survive few retain their original furniture, so any study of this topic must to a great extent rely on pictorial and documentary evidence. Some large private schools such as Eton, Harrow, Westminster and Winchester provide better returns for the furniture historian.

In 1752 the Trustees of Isleworth Blue Coat School (funded by public subscription) ordered 'a writing form as plain as can be made and two forms to sit on', the latter to be constructed 'in as frugal a manner as possible'. In the following year there were two writing-desks, five forms, two shelves and two rows of hat-pegs for forty pupils.[1] At this date schools consisted of one big classroom; the well-preserved Grammar School at Hawkshead (which William Wordsworth attended) was typical in having seats fixed along the side walls fronted by narrow slope-top desks for the upper standards, backless forms for the younger children and a master's rostrum at one end where pupils could be called out one at a time for their lessons to be heard. At Heptonstall Free Grammar School, founded in 1642 and closed in 1889, the following survive: the headteacher's desk, some sturdy forms and a long freestanding plank-top desk at which scholars sat face to face[2] (Plate 246). One of Thomas Bewick's woodcuts portrays a very similar ensemble of furniture in a schoolroom (Plate 247). A very instructive engraving of the Quaker schoolroom under John Bunyan's Meeting House shows a row of boys seated at long desks fixed down one wall, a group of girls in bonnets writing at a double desk and forms for the infants; the master, presiding at his raised desk, and a female assistant, are giving individual tuition (Plate 248). The Meeting House at Gildersome, Yorkshire, has a small room at the rear which contains a traditional school desk for ten pupils with a row of inkwell holes drilled in the central flat.

Some of the best preserved furnished interiors are to be found at famous public schools. The original hall at Harrow is typical in having lines of backless forms ranged down each side with an imposing pulpit-like desk at one end. Similar traditional layouts survive at Eton and Shrewsbury while others exist on a more modest scale at Courteenhall, Northants and Corsham, Wiltshire, or are portrayed in old views of Sedbergh, Westminster and Charterhouse (Plate 249). An interesting item of equipment used from an early date by scholars at Winchester, known as a 'scob', was designed like a square box raised on legs for keeping books — a primitive forerunner, in fact, of the modern locker desk.[3] An engraving of the dormitory at Westminster shows a barrack-like room partly subdivided by curtains and furnished with stump beds along both sides, each having a wooden trunk at the foot and by the head a large bureau with a supporting cast of Windsor chairs and wash-stands.[4] Similar tall narrow bureaux with drawers in the lower stage and a cupboard above were provided at Eton, know as 'Etonburrys'.[5] They were made

246. Long double-sided pine desk with a central flat housing lead inkwells, probably late eighteenth century. From the Old Grammar School, Heptonstall, Yorkshire. *Calderdale Museums Service*

247. A village school, woodcut by Thomas Bewick (1753–1828).

248. Charity school under Bunyan's Meeting House in Southwark, from *Londonia Illustrata*, 1882. *Guildhall Library, City of London*

249. Schoolroom at Charterhouse. *Illustrated London News* (1862)

locally to order for the boys and became their own property when they left. It is clear that even in aristocratic establishments eighteenth-century school furniture was robust to the point of being spartan.

DAME SCHOOLS

These infant schools were usually run by an elderly, often barely literate woman who, for a weekly fee, would look after small children and teach them a little reading and sewing; writing or arithmetic was rarely attempted. They were mostly held in cottage kitchens or dingy town basements where 'the children were as close as birds in a nest, and tumbled over each other like puppies in a kennel'. Another observer reported: 'Scholars may often be seen sitting round the sides of a four-post bed, on low forms, the sides of the bed forming a back to the seat, sometimes on the sides of the bed'.[6] The probate inventory of 'Ann Bainbridge, School Dame of Stillington in the County of York', dated 1766, reveals that besides routine domestic furniture her cottage contained two long tables and forms 'one Bible, one Common Prayer Book & other School Books'.[7] John Harden's charming water-colour of a rustic Dame's School at Elterwater in the Lake District, sketched in 1806, portrays a homely kitchen with children seated on simple plank forms and low stools, three boys are looking at books, one girl is occupied with needlework, an older girl amuses an infant while the mistress in her fireside chair is teaching a small boy (Plate 250). Another drawing of 1810 by Thomas Unwins shows a dame surrounded by her school of young lacemakers at Quainton, Buckinghamshire.[8] Although Dame Schools remained popular into the late nineteenth century, it is now virtually impossible to identify any common furniture definitely used in such establishments.

SUNDAY SCHOOLS

Sunday Schools were a product of the late eighteenth-century Evangelical Revival, and although the earliest were founded by middle-class philanthropists – notably Robert Raikes of Gloucester – the movement rapidly became part of, not imposed on, working-class culture. They were always local organizations, usually controlled by ordinary working men (national bodies such as the Sunday School Union played a marginal role) and they never became the monopoly of any one denomination. The geographical spread and enrolment figures – 200,000 by 1785, 450,000 in 1818, 1,400,000 in 1833, 2,100,000 in 1851 and 6,000,000 by 1914 – suggest that by the 1820s nearly every working-class child benefited from this popular mass literacy movement. The children, placed in graded classes, were taught reading, writing and religion for about four and a half hours each Sunday over a period of roughly four years. After the Education Act of 1870, most schools provided only religious instruction.[9]

Early classes were held in cottages, barns, workshops or warehouses, but as numbers grew, many governing bodies built or rented their own premises, or met in day schools, church or chapel halls. By 1818 the mean enrolment in Lancashire was 248 pupils, but Stockport Sunday School at its peak exceeded 5,000, while many others taught over 1,000 children under one roof. Unfortunately, owing to urban renewal, the architectural heritage of this great working-class movement that provided millions with their only elementary education in fast vanishing, and it is increasingly difficult to trace Sunday School furniture.

251. Victorian class box, grained pine, from Macclesfield Sunday School. *Macclesfield Museum Trust*

252. An original stained pine trestle-desk with hinged flaps from Hurdsfield Sunday School, near Macclesfield, built in 1811. The cupboards behind are late Victorian. *Macclesfield Museum Trust*

Macclesfield Sunday School, an imposing four-storey block erected by public subscription in 1814, is an honourable exception. Ten years after it closed in 1973, the building was reopened as a museum dedicated to the local silk industry and as a Sunday School Heritage Centre; happily, all the best features have been preserved, including the architect's original model. There are many huge plank benches, up to 24-feet long, with cast-iron frames, foot rests and narrow desk ledges, with pencil grooves and inkwell holes, hinged to the back rails. Also some tables, cupboards and typical grained pine class boxes in the form of a chest above two deep drawers (Plate 251). A research team has surveyed other Sunday Schools in the area recording interesting items of equipment and furniture. Hurdsfield Chapel and Sunday School (built 1811), for example, has two upstairs classrooms which still contain a remarkable pair of early nineteenth-century trestle-desks with long flaps supported, when raised, on hinged wooden brackets and plain pine forms to match (Plate 252).

253. A late-Victorian painted pine seat box from the Sunday School of a Wesleyan Chapel at Sowerby Bridge, Yorkshire. Similar locker stools are shown in Plate 261. *C.G. Gilbert*

One is unlikely to come across inventories of Sunday School furniture; however some late-Victorian trade catalogues published by Educational Suppliers include relevant illustrations (see Plate 261), and scattered documentary references have been noted.[10] In 1784 the Trustees of the Westgate Unitarian Chapel in Wakefield purchased '2 New Forms for the Sunday school scholars' and later ordered '100 quills, a bottle of ink, 3 slates, reading books, slate pencils and paper'. The Committee Minutes of the Macclesfield Sunday School refer in 1821 to buying 'The Superintendants Desk & Drawers £6.6.', but such allusions are rare. Marion Lawrance, author of a handbook *Housing the Sunday School* (1911) refers to 'The basement Sunday School widespread in Victorian days — damp floor, low ceiling, half windows, furnace in one corner, step ladder, brooms and broken furniture in another'. She recommended purpose-built premises adjoining the church providing a large central area with the Superintendant's desk on a raised dais, a piano and stand for song rolls, so the whole school could join in the opening and closing worship. Individual alcove classrooms lining three walls should, she advised, be equipped with tables, chairs, blackboards, perhaps a sand-table, cupboard for books and handwork, maps and charts. The original (disused) Sunday School at Birstall Methodist Chapel (1864) is planned along these lines, while a forsaken painted pine locker stool stencilled 'B3' (Boys Class 3) from the nearby Wesleyan Chapel at Sowerby Bridge, Yorkshire (Plate 253), typifies the kind of furniture found in Victorian Sunday Schools and, sadly, the degree of interest it arouses.

Schools 1800–1870

The period from 1800 until the introduction of State education in 1870 saw a steady growth in the number of schools for poor children; while new ideas about the organization and layout of classrooms were pioneered by the British and Foreign School Society (established by Joseph Lancaster in 1808), and the National Society for Promoting the Education of the Poor (founded by Andrew Bell in 1811). The Lancastrian system[11] was based on the principle of simultaneous teaching by one master with the aid of monitors. His model schoolroom for 304 pupils contained nineteen rows of benches seating sixteen children; the back rail of each supported a long desk-slope having a bead along the lower edge to stop the slates from sliding off, and a book ledge under the top; the corners of the desks and forms were rounded to reduce the risk of accidental injuries (Plate 254). The front row of seats were provided with sand-trays for beginners to practice finger-writing. Instead of being ranged along the side walls the desks and seats, securely fixed to the sloping floor, were aligned across the room in a central block, all facing the master's platform. The wide side aisles were marked out with semicircles where small classes of between nine and twelve received instruction from older children, aided by lesson boards hung on the walls. Baize curtains suspended from the ceiling were designed 'to check the reverberation of sound'. This practical, if rather rigid, system enabled

254. Interior of the Lancastrian School at Borough Road, London, *c.* 1825. *Courtesy M. Seaborne*

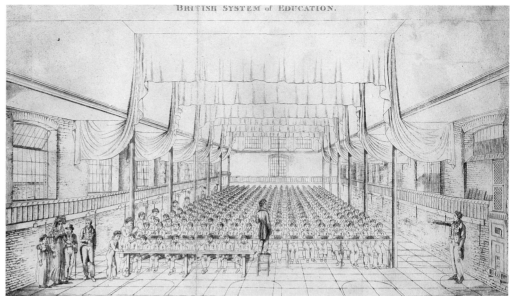

255. Interior of the Madras School designed by Andrew Bell at Clapham, London, *c.* 1810. Note the infants using a sand-table at the front. *Courtesy M. Seaborne*

one master to control the whole school although the pupils, assembled in small groups, were still taught singly by monitors.

Dr Andrew Bell's system of education, known as the Madras School because he first experimented with it in India, was promoted by the National Society set up in 1811. These schools were also conducted by a single master through the agency of monitors, the children being arranged into classes and taught by senior pupils. Dr Bell's scheme of self-tuition or mutual instruction allowed for greater flexibility than the Lancastrian system: instead of desks immovably fixed in a central block, the schoolroom was laid out in open squares defined by forms with writing-desks placed against the walls; since the furniture was free-standing, other patterns could be created. An early nineteenth-century engraving of the London Central School of the National Society in Baldwin's Gardens shows lines of children standing in open squares formed by benches on cast-iron legs, each of which seated twelve scholars, while a continuous writing-desk and form, both with cast-iron supports, extends round the walls. The combined desk and seat unit was apparently unknown at this date. J.C. Loudon, who visited this school in 1832, observed a book-box in the centre of each square and a cupboard for books and papers in one corner; the master had a 'movable desk and seat on castors so that he can fix his position in any part of the room'.[12] A capital engraving of the Clapham Madras School, c. 1810, portrays infants learning the alphabet at a sand-tray and other pupils with slates, seated at wooden slope-top desks, being taught individually by monitors (Plate 255). There is a large brick stove in the centre of the room and a high double-sided master's desk in the background.[13]

The monitorial system was challenged by Samuel Wilderspin and David Stow who opened model infants' schools at Spitalfields in 1820 and at Glasgow in 1826 respectively.[14] They introduced the revolutionary idea of having either a small separate classroom or a steeply raked gallery at one end of the main room where children could be taught collectively directly by the master (Plate 256). This communal teaching, known as the 'simultaneous method' or 'gallery lesson', was strikingly different from the monitorial system whereby children were taught one at a time by older pupils, or the traditional Grammar School technique where they recited their lessons in turn to the master; it proved, in fact, to be so successful that

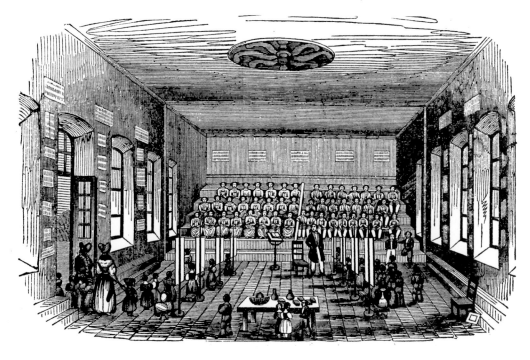

256. Stow's model infant school, 1836. There is a gallery lesson in progress; other children are being taught around lesson-posts. *Courtesy M. Seaborne*

257. Watercolour of the village school at Aynhoe, Northamptonshire, by Lili Cartwright, c. 1846, showing gallery seating, forms, lesson-posts, blackboard, map-stand, writing-desks and many improving texts. *Courtesy Elizabeth Cartwright-Hignett*

simultaneous teaching eventually became the norm in all schools. During the experimental phase, monitors still played a supportive role in teaching the three R's to small groups of infants standing around lesson-posts (Plate 257), but a decisive break had been made and by the middle of the century opinion set in strongly against the Lancastrian and Madras systems. The next step, taken in Wesleyan and other progressive schools, was to replace unqualified monitors by trained, paid assistants and pupil teachers who taught in separate classrooms or conducted general gallery lessons. Large school halls were at first divided up only by curtains, but the pattern of separate rooms furnished with forms and desks accommodating classes of up to thirty had become the gererally accepted practice when, following Foster's Education Act of 1870, the great national school building programme started.

Although some of the buildings which housed Lancastrian, Madras and model infants' schools remain, no furnished interiors survive, so it is fortunate that educational literature of the time illustrates plans of approved classroom layouts and engravings showing lessons in progress. After about 1840, the design of schools became a recognized branch of the architectural profession and some cabinet makers started to specialize in supplying educational equipment. J.C. Loudon published a valuable account of school buildings and furniture 'according to the present most improved practice' in his monumental *Encyclopaedia* of 1833.[15] Of seating and desks in Lancastrian schools he remarked 'cast-iron legs are preferable, as they support the desk-board with equal firmness, occupy less room, and have a neater appearance . . . a form twenty feet long will require five'. At eighteen-inch intervals, slates were fixed by means of screws and short lengths of string to the desk tops, while slate pencils were kept in drawers placed under the first desk of each class. Teaching aids at this date included printed copy sheets pasted on thin strips of wood, alphabet boards 'from twenty to thirty feet long, and two feet broad', fixed to the wall behind the master's rostrum and large lesson-boards with printed texts hung on the aisle walls for monitors using pointers to teach reading.

The 'simultaneous method' of instruction, pioneered in infants' schools, came to be universally adopted; so Loudon's illustrated account of the furniture he saw when visiting six London infants' schools in 1832 is of special interest as a record of first-generation teaching aids, many of which remained popular for the best part of a century. One engraving shows a large double-sided swivel blackboard supported between standards, set on castors and fitted with a wire strung with black and white beads to teach numeration. He also noted an 'alphabet frame' with narrow ledges on which sets of letters painted on small square tablets were arranged for teaching single letters, syllables and words (Plate 258). Another line drawing depicts a portable abacus on a cruciform base with twelve rows of different coloured beads 'for teaching the first four rules of arithmetic'. The 'infants' show box' contained a long roll of paper bearing pictures, figures, names, etc., which, by turning a handle, appeared in succession at the opening; the stand on which it was set had an object shelf with a box for books below. There are also illustrations of a teacher's 'pulpit', seats, desks, a gallery and classroom layouts. He stated that furniture for infants' schools could be obtained from Mr Beilby, Chelsea, 'those for the Madras system, from central school, Baldwin's Gardens . . . all those for the Lancastrian system from the Borough School'.

The diversity of schools in England during the period leading up to Foster's Board School Act of 1870 is apparent from G.T.C. Bartley's panoramic *Schools for the People: History, Development and Present Working of Each Description of English School for the Industrial and Poorer Classes* (1871), which catalogues each kind of educational establishment in welcome detail (with illustrations). A now wholly unfamiliar pattern of educational services also emerges from other books such as Mary Carpenter's *Reformatory Schools for the Children of the Perishing and Dangerous Classes and Juvenile Offenders* (1851) or C.J. Montague's *Sixty Years in Waifdom: or the Ragged School Movement in English History* (1904). Although schools for idiots and imbeciles (like army, workhouse and prison schools) were funded by public money, those for the blind, deaf and dumb, cripples, orphans and schools catering for the 'destitute and depraved', relied entirely on charity for their buildings, rent, furniture, books, etc., and were often staffed by volunteers.

'Ragged' schools was the name given to free evening or day schools intended for children who, owing to the poverty of their parents, lack of clothing or dissolute habits, did not attend other schools in the area. These typically consisted of one large schoolroom, perhaps divided for boys and girls with smaller rooms off for separate classes (Plate 259). Furniture, depending on subscriptions raised by the organizing committee, could either be simple forms and a chair for the master or aspire to one of the model systems. Ragged schools were directed to children utterly unprovided

258. Ledged reading-stand with a case below to hold letter tablets and a blackboard at the back, hinged fall-flap missing. Made by the North of England School Furnishing Co., Darlington, *c.* 1885. Formerly at Willington R.C. Primary School, Co. Durham. Similar to an apparatus illustrated by J.C. Loudon in 1833. *Beamish Museum*

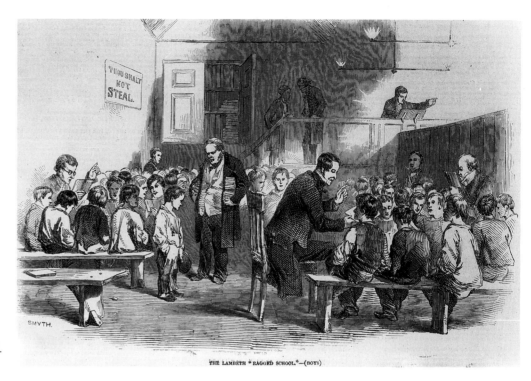

THE LAMBETH "RAGGED SCHOOL."—(BOYS)

259. Boys' class at Lambeth Ragged School. *Illustrated London News* (1846)

260. Infants' dual desk, pine and cast-iron, *c.* 1880, a standard model ordered by the Leeds School Board (see Plate 267). From Beecroft Primary School, Leeds.

261. (*Opposite*) School and Institute furniture from a trade catalogue issued by George Hammer & Co. Ltd, London, *c.* 1900. *Beamish Museum*

for by other institutions, but there remained some children – vagrants, beggars, juvenile offenders and the homeless – beyond the pale even of free ragged schooling. Industrial feeding schools, where children were given meals and taught a trade as a means of encouraging attendance, were an attempt to cope with this problem. Magistrates sometimes sent young criminals to residential Reformatory Training Schools instead of prison.

Because poor children were often forced to work long hours at an early age, many free schools were held in the evening. Mechanics' Institute Schools, designed to assist young adults, were first founded by Dr Birkbeck and by 1840 over two hundred such centres, where the labouring classes received instruction in Arts and Sciences, existed throughout the country. Evidence about the furniture used in various kinds of school is widely scattered through contemporary publications, notably the *Illustrated London News* which shows the interior of a school for the indigent blind (14 June 1851), the Brook Street ragged, industrial, sabbath and free day school (17 December 1853), the shoemaking department in a school for training destitute boys (1 January 1858) and an orphanage school (2 April 1870), to mention a few engravings accompanying reports designed to prick the conscience of the nation.

SCHOOLS 1870–1914

The establishment in 1870 of a State system of elementary education supervised by specially appointed local School Boards created a huge demand for school equipment. Prior to the Act it had been common for money spent on school fittings to be deducted from the master's stipend, a practice that discouraged the purchase of furnishings. To serve this new market, Educational Supply Companies able to fulfil large contracts sprung up in growing industrial towns (Plate 260). School attendance was made compulsory in 1880 and the appointment of Attendance Officers further increased the numbers of children in government-inspected schools. The leaving age was ten (which is why early desks are so small), and government grants were made on the basis of attainment in the three 'R's' and attendance records. The 1902 Education Act, which replaced School Boards with 318 new Local Education Authorities financed from the rates, generated additional funds for school buildings

School and Institute Furniture.

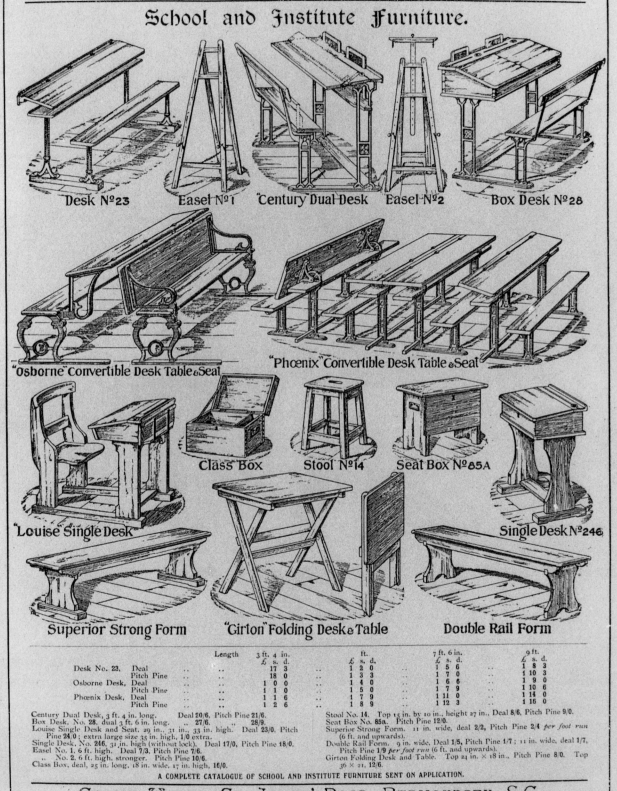

Desk Nº 23   Easel Nº 1   "Century" Dual Desk   Easel Nº 2   Box Desk Nº 28

"Osborne" Convertible Desk Table & Seat   "Phœnix" Convertible Desk Table & Seat

Class Box   Stool Nº 14   Seat Box Nº 85A

"Louise" Single Desk   Single Desk Nº 246

Superior Strong Form   "Girton" Folding Desk & Table   Double Rail Form

		Length	3 ft. 4 in.		ft.		7 ft. 6 in.		9 ft.
			£ s. d.		£ s. d.		£ s. d.		£ s. d.
Desk No. 23,	Deal	..	17 3	..	1 2 0	..	1 5 6	..	1 8 3
	Pitch Pine	..	18 0	..	1 3 3	..	1 7 0	..	1 10 3
Osborne Desk,	Deal	..	1 0 0	..	1 4 0	..	1 6 6	..	1 9 0
	Pitch Pine	..	1 1 0	..	1 5 0	..	1 7 9	..	1 10 6
Phœnix Desk,	Deal	..	1 1 6	..	1 7 9	..	1 11 0	..	1 14 0
	Pitch Pine	..	1 2 6	..	1 8 9	..	1 12 3	..	1 16 0

Century Dual Desk, 3 ft. 4 in. long.   Deal 20/6, Pitch Pine 21/6.
Box Desk, No. 28, dual 3 ft. 6 in. long.   ,, 27/6.   ,, 28/9.
Louise Single Desk and Seat, 29 in., 31 in., 33 in. high. Deal 23/0, Pitch Pine 24/0 ; extra large size 35 in. high, 1/0 extra.
Single Desk, No. 246, 31 in. high (without lock). Deal 17/0, Pitch Pine 18/0.
Easel No. 1, 6 ft. high. Deal 7/3, Pitch Pine 7/6.
  ,, No. 2, 6 ft. high, stronger. Pitch Pine 10/6.
Class Box, deal, 25 in. long, 18 in. wide, 17 in. high, 16/0.

Stool No. 14. Top 15 in. by 10 in., height 27 in., Deal 8/6, Pitch Pine 9/0.
Seat Box No. 85a. Pitch Pine 12/0.
Superior Strong Form. 11 in. wide, deal 2/2, Pitch Pine 2/4 *per foot run* (6 ft. and upwards).
Double Rail Form. 9 in. wide, Deal 1/5, Pitch Pine 1/7 ; 11 in. wide, deal 1/7, Pitch Pine 1/9 *per foot run* (6 ft. and upwards).
Girton Folding Desk and Table. Top 24 in. × 18 in., Pitch Pine 8/0. Top 36 × 21, 12/6.

A COMPLETE CATALOGUE OF SCHOOL AND INSTITUTE FURNITURE SENT ON APPLICATION.

CROWN WORKS, ST. JAMES' ROAD, BERMONDSEY, S.E.
Showrooms :—430, STRAND, LONDON, W.C. (First Floor.)

262. Pitch pine cupboard for books or work-baskets from St Anne's Higher Grade School, Leeds, opened in 1898.

263. School globe-stand by W. & A.K. Johnstone, London and Edinburgh, c. 1890. *Bradford Museums*

and furniture. In Leeds (which after London ranked as the largest Board in the country) the principal firms were E.J. Arnold & Son, Ltd, J.W. Bean & Son, Illingworth, Ingham & Co. and McCorquodale & Co.; the leading Sheffield company was Redmayne, May & Co.; and in County Durham, the North of England School Furnishing Co. Ltd (NESFCO), established in Darlington about 1870, enjoyed a dominant position. The trade was effectively monopolized by large educational suppliers, most of whom rapidly developed lines in stationery, textbooks and teaching aids. General cabinet makers were seldom able to compete with these tycoon firms, although country joiners continued to equip village schools. HMI Sneyd-Kennersley wrote disapprovingly of a small Welsh village school in the early 1870s '. . . the light is scanty. There is a tiled floor; there are desks for the upper standards only; the other children sit on benches with no back-rails: both desks and benches are evidently the work of the carpenter on the estate'.[16] School Boards also tended to place lucrative contracts with local firms, but a list of major commissions appended to NESFCO's 1885 catalogue shows that their business was by no means restricted to counties north of the Humber.[17]

The NESFCO trade catalogue of 1884 mentions recent 'large additions to our Works and Plant, the erection of a Foundry and the establishment of a London showroom'; by 1903, following further 'enlargement and modernisation', the Company was trading not only as furniture manufacturers but complete School Outfitters stocking requisites of every description with depots in Newcastle, Sunderland, Middlesbrough and Norwich. Their 1909 catalogue features a bird's-eye view of the factory in Darlington (which by then exceeded 100,000 square feet), and includes photographs of the foundry and wood-working shops. After 1889 Councils were empowered to spend money on vocational secondary education; accordingly NESFCO started to supply Technical and Art College equipment, securing a contract to furnish the prestigious Technical Institute, Belfast. About the same time, they fitted out Westminster City Library, Hull Central Library and added banks, boardrooms, canteens, churches and mission halls to their repertory.

E.J. Arnold's of Leeds stocked a smaller range of school furniture than NESFCO, but offered a wider selection of stationery, books and accessories. In 1870 Edmund Arnold had opened a general stationer's shop in Briggate with a warehouse and factory behind; favourable market conditions led to such rapid growth of the schools department that in 1895 the firm was able to build spacious new premises and achieved a national reputation as educational contractors. Extensions in 1907 trebled the 20,000 square feet of the original factory which suggests that the firm was on much the same footing as their Darlington rivals. Both companies identified their furniture with an inscribed metal tablet between about 1895 and 1910. Copiously illustrated catalogues[18] provide an excellent pictorial record of available stock and contain invaluable descriptive information (Plate 261). The amazing variety of pupils' and teachers' desks, easels, abaci, reading-stands, work-tables and store cupboards, often marketed under fancy names such as 'Chaucer', 'Emmerson' or 'Invincible', illuminates the keen commercial world of school suppliers after the Foster Act established the right of every child to an elementary education. A publication titled *Rules to be Observed in Planning and Fitting up Schools*, issued by a government committee in 1883, provides details of approved classroom layouts and furniture, while E.R. Robson's *School Architecture* (1874) contains useful general chapters of furniture and apparatus.

Externally, the new Board Schools presented the countenance of red-brick palaces and the interiors, if not quite so grand were, in the best Victorian tradition, stocked with suitably substantial furniture ranging from desks with decorative cast-iron frames and imposing pitch pine cupboards detailed with stop chamfers, V-joints and handsomely moulded cornices (Plate 262), to lofty map-stands (Plate 264), museum cabinets (see Plate 268), wall charts, globes (Plate 263), abaci (Plate 265) and an extraordinary range of equipment and teaching aids. In 1885 NESFCO stated that their large locker desks, being 'entirely of wood, and being massive and highly finished, were suitable for buildings of high character'.

Photographs showing classroom activities are rich in human interest (Plates 268 and 270), but contemporary trade catalogues provide an even better, if rather arid, record of old school furniture (Plate 266). Victorian concern with health and hygiene naturally influenced design. Single desks as opposed to dual, four, six or ten seaters, were advocated by NESFCO in 1885 'on account of the important Educational and Sanitary advantages resulting from the isolation of students when engaged in study'. Medical men pointed out that since scholars using ordinary long desks vary in stature, it was essential to provide individual desks and seats 'exactly proportioned to the figure'. A certain Dr Liebreich maintained that short-sightedness, spinal curvature, flat chests and other 'evil deformities' were caused by poorly designed desks. The 'perfect instrument of Education' was apparently to be found in Glendenning's Patent 'Adjustable' Desk combining Dr Roth's chair (Plate 269). The patent, taken out in 1880, was renewed in 1883 when NESFCO secured exclusive rights to their manufacture. The locker section was made to slide horizontally to or from the scholar seated on a specially fashioned chair fitted with a movable spine-

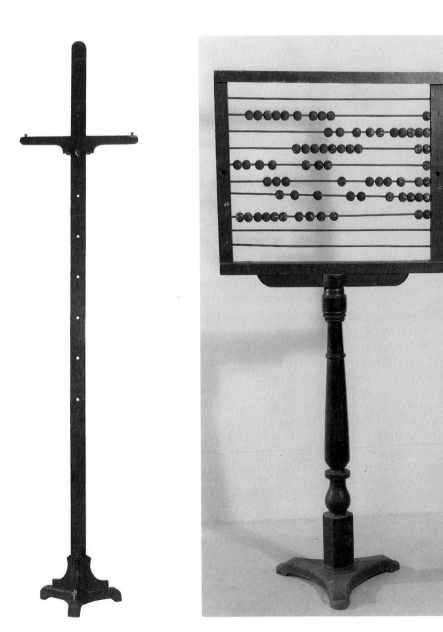

264. (far left) Map-stand, by the North of England School Furnishing Co., Darlington, c. 1890, the 9-foot pine post is bolted to a cast-iron base. Impressed 'NCC' (Northumberland County Council). *Beamish Museum*

265. (left) Abacus by E.J. Arnold & Son Ltd, Leeds, c. 1900. Pitch pine with a cast-iron base. From Bearing Street Junior School, South Shields, Co. Durham. *Beamish Museum*

266. (*Opposite, above*) Daily attendance board from a trade catalogue issued by the North of England School Furnishing Co., Darlington, Co. Durham, 1885. In the days when children were often absent from school many incentives were used to encourage regular attendance. *Leeds Art Galleries*

267. (*Opposite, middle*) Glendenning's modern locker desk, patented in 1880, pine, beech and cast-iron, designed on scientific and medically approved principles, including an adjustable spine-pad. Individual desks proved too costly for most schools. *Wakefield Museums*

268. Science lesson, *c.* 1880, from an album of photographs produced for the Leeds School Board illustrating different phases of school life. *Leeds Schools Museum Service*

269. (*Opposite, below*) Advertisement for a fully adjustable desk and chair from a catalogue issued by the North of England School Furnishing Co., Darlington, in 1885 — the year after they had purchased the Glendenning's patent. *Leeds Art Galleries*

270. Handwork lesson, *c.* 1880. The children are seated at standard Leeds School Board desks (see Plate 260), the tops marked with a grid. From a photograph album illustrating different phases of school life. *Leeds Schools Museum Service*

pad (plate 267). The writing suface was inclined on scientific principles at an angle of 15° and the desk top incorporated a reading-slope set at 40°. Later improved models included a folding copy-rest, fixed foot board and allowed for vertical movement of the seat and locker. An example displaying all these refinements is in the Museum of the History of Education at Leeds University.

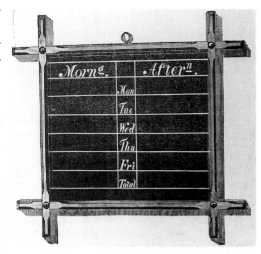

Medical acceptability was only one, and not necessarily the most important, criterion of desk accommodation. Educational suppliers were eager to convince customers that their models enjoyed unique advantages. Some, it was claimed, occupied less floor space, others were fitted with improved patent hinges or made with seats that tipped up noiselessly allowing standing space for drill sessions; certain desks included safeguards against trapping children's fingers, permitted 'free arm work' or even possessed turn-up tops coated underneath with a patent slate finish, while George Hammer pointed out that his reversible desks and seats, 'have no loose screws, pins or wedges to be lost, nor chains or springs to be broken'. The trade literature reflects a fiercely competitive market, but basically school furniture was required, as always, to be simple in construction, practical in use, virtually unbreakable and inexpensive (Plate 271).

Many of the firms which vied for commissions were largely dependent on conservative design types; the demand for 'improved models' and patented innovations seldom degenerated into a craving for novelty. Thus most mass-produced late-Victorian school furniture evolved from traditional prototypes, and despite refinements of detail, continued to express the solid attributes of utility and durability which have always informed common furniture (Plates 272 and 273). The fact that, for example, William Brear & Sons – general turners and chairmakers in the Dales village of Addingham, Yorkshire – supplied hundreds of chairs to Bradford Education Committee before the Great War emphasizes the overlap between the output of traditional and industrial workshops making school furniture. When NESFCO diversified its products, the firm introduced a range of plain furniture for public houses, chapels, cafés, offices, parks, welfare centres and working-men's clubs — all distinct non-domestic or institutional sub-groups expressing the same robust character as their educational stock-in-trade. Today, Victorian school furniture is not infrequently encountered, serving as churchyard or bowling-green benches, village seats (Plate 277), or in pubs — impressive evidence of the versatile, interchangeable pattern of usage which, despite varying degrees of specialization, is commonplace on the vernacular level.

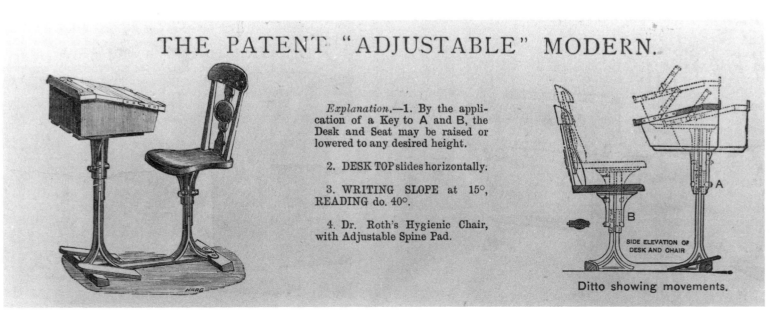

THE PATENT "ADJUSTABLE" MODERN.

Explanation.—1. By the application of a Key to A and B, the Desk and Seat may be raised or lowered to any desired height.

2. DESK TOP slides horizontally.

3. WRITING SLOPE at 15°, READING do. 40°.

4. Dr. Roth's Hygienic Chair, with Adjustable Spine Pad.

SIDE ELEVATION OF DESK AND CHAIR

Ditto showing movements.

271. Schoolmistress's work-table by Illing-worth, Ingham & Co., Leeds, *c*. 1900. Oak, with a half-hinged enclosed top, front flap, graduated yard measure marked out on the working surface and three lock-up drawers. Impressed under-neath 'DCEC' (Durham County Education Com-mittee). *Darlington Railway Centre and Museum*

272. (*right*) Blackboard easel with map slide, pine, *c*. 1900, by the North of England School Furnishing Co., Darlington. From West Stanley Junior School, Co. Durham. *Beamish Museum*

273. (*far right*) Teacher's chair, beech and elm, raised on a pine frame, by the North of England School Furniture Co., Darlington. Formerly at Hendon Junior School, Co. Durham. *Beamish Museum*

The Museum of the History of Education in Leeds houses a large and important archive, together with an impressive collection of teaching accessories. Their holding of school furniture is at present limited to a monumental six-seater locker desk with attached form from Bristol Grammer School, two four-seater desks, a teacher's desk of about 1900 by the giant firm ESA (Educational Supply Association) of Stevenage, two high chairs, a swivel blackboard and a fully adjustable Glendenning's patent desk bearing NESFCO's plaque. Easily the largest provenanced

274. (*above, left*) A late-Victorian convertible desk/seat of pine and wrought iron, designed on the same principle as Plate 275, but evidently made by the local joiner and blacksmith. From the village school at Addingham, Yorkshire, which closed in 1892. *Bradford Museums*

275. (*above, right*) A late-Victorian three-seater convertible desk/seat by George Hammer, London, pitch pine and cast-iron. Formerly at Armley Road Church of England Primary School, Leeds.

276. (*left*) Dual desk in oak with slate slots, inkwells, a book ledge, foot rail, tilt-seat and back-rest. Illustrated in the North of England School Furnishing Co., Darlington, catalogue for 1909. *Beamish Museum*

277. (*above*) A convertible desk/seat from Thorpe School, Fylingdales, Yorkshire, now serving as a park bench at Robin Hood's Bay.

278. (*right*) Assistant-teacher's pitch pine desk, intended to be used with a high chair (see Plate 273). Formerly at St Anne's Higher Grade School, Leeds, which opened in 1898.

279. (*far right*) Pupil-teacher's desk, formerly at St Anne's Higher Grade School, Leeds, which opened in 1898.

assortment of obsolete school furniture was rescued in the early 1960s by Beamish Museum, Co. Durham, as a record of a vanishing phase of community life in the area. Many of the items are branded DCEC (Durham County Education Committee) or NCC (Northumberland County Council). Most museums with 'folk life' interests — Leeds, Bradford, Shugborough Hall in Staffordshire, the Museum Education Department at Glasgow and elsewhere — can muster enough equipment to create a Victorian classroom. Alford Civic Trust, Lincolnshire, maintains a School Museum, The National Trust have a Museum of Childhood at Sudbury Hall and some enlightened headteachers retain old movables for sentimental reasons when their school furniture is upgraded, but these holdings cannot disguise the fact that very little survives. Many vintage items illustrated in trade catalogues – sand-tables, mistresses' work-tables, map cupboards, even first generation Board School desks – are now almost impossible to track down.

A five-seater convertible desk/bench from the village school at Addingham (Plate 274), evidently the result of collaboration between the local joiner and blacksmith, attempts to copy industrial models by firms such as George Hammer & Co. where the desk top, when turned over, forms a seat with a back[19] (Plate 275). Bradford Museums also possess a cheap desk and seat from a Dame School at Baildon which have been blacksmithed together.[20] The equivalent Board School desk was a handsome two-seater with a cast-iron frame, slope-top drilled for inkwells and provided with a pencil groove, slate slots, book ledge, a foot rail, tilt seat and back-rest (Plate 276). Different types of desk were produced for headmasters, assistant teachers and pupil teachers — fine examples from St Anne's Higher Grade School, Leeds (opened 1898), are still in use at Our Lady's Roman Catholic Primary School in the city (Plates 278 and 279). The Board School centenary celebrations in 1970 briefly encouraged the preservation of historic equipment, while field-work in schools can still yield unexpected discoveries; but the long-term future of what remains outside museums is obviously at risk.

12 Workhouses

Elizabethan welfare legislation, culminating in the Poor Law Act of 1901, placed responsibility for looking after the poor on each local community. The Act called on parishes to appoint an Overseer and levy a rate for relieving the aged and infirm poor. The rate could be used to build a 'poorhouse' to shelter those unable to support themselves, but many paupers were given 'out-relief' in their own homes. Knatchbull's Act of 1723 authorized parishes to provide a workhouse or 'house of industry' in which able-bodied paupers were made to work for their keep, and within a few years some 150 had been set up. These institutions were intended to deter vagrants from seeking parish relief by combining harsh conditions with tedious labour. Orphans, the old, sick and insane might be lodged in a common workhouse, but most parishes continued to maintain benevolent poorhouses which gave food and shelter to deserving paupers. In 1782 Gilbert's Act allowed groups of parishes to combine for this purpose. Sir Frederick Eden's three volume survey *The State of the Poor* (1797), provides a wealth of detailed information about different kinds of workhouses or poorhouses. They ranged from the large well-regulated establishment at Liverpool for 1,200 persons, to oppressive squalid institutions in remote farmsteads or small homely refuges akin to village almshouses.

In 1832 the soaring expense of coping with all categories of the poor led to the setting up of a Commission of Enquiry to look into the practical operation of the Poor Laws. The most influential figure in drafting the Poor Law Amendment Act of 1834 was Edwin Chadwick, the 'architect' of the Victorian workhouse system. Parishes were merged into 'Unions', administered by an elected Board of Guardians who were supervised by Government Commissioners to ensure national uniformity. The average Union embraced about thirty parishes centred on some market town, serving a population of roughly ten thousand. Inmates were rigidly segregated into children / able-bodied males / able-bodied females / the sick, aged and other impotent poor. Life for the able-bodied was to be 'wholesomely unpleasant' based on a degrading regime of plain living, discipline and hard labour such as stone breaking, oakum picking or sack making, the aim being to ensure that their circumstances were more disagreeable than the lowest paid labourer. Out-relief to the able-bodied ceased; if a man entered the workhouse, his family (from which he would be separated) must join him; life, in fact, was to be so repellent that many paupers who were 'offered the house' refused to enter it.

Following this legislation grim, prison-like workhouses rapidly sprung up all over the country. In the first two years, 127 were approved with an average of 300 beds each, while many enlargements to existing parish houses were made. The Act resulted in one of the most ambitious public building programmes of the century; by 1840 an estimated 350 new Union workhouses had been erected at an average cost of £5,000. They were usually two-storey blocks built around a courtyard, the basic rooms being dormitories for each category of inmate, dining-rooms, work-rooms, wash-rooms, kitchen, laundry, a ward for the chronic sick, nursery and sometimes a schoolroom.[1] Our knowledge of workhouse furniture comes mainly from scattered inventories, contractors' estimates for fitting out new Union workhouses, the Board of Guardians' minute books, pictorial sources and surviving provenanced items, some of which bear brand marks recording their origin (see Plate 288).

The parish books of St Botolph's, Cambridge, show that in 1741 the workhouse contained sixteen inmates and in 1750 nine. The records, which include inventories for 1739 and 1747,[2] also suggest that the goods of paupers were sometimes taken into the workhouse. In 1747 the ground floor accommodation consisted of a comfortably furnished 'Officer's Parlour', a day room with chairs, stools, a table, six spinning-wheels, candlesticks, fire-irons, etc., and a well-equipped kitchen. Upstairs there was a bedroom for the Master and four unheated chambers for paupers containing a total of seven feather or straw beds together with an equal number of chamber-pots, chairs or stools, one trunk and a looking-glass. That St Botolph's was typical of small humanely run early-Georgian parish houses is confirmed by a short inventory made in 1755, when Elizabeth Barningham became mistress of the poorhouse at Arkengarthdale, a rural parish near Richmond in North Yorkshire.[3] The building was provided with six chaff beds, six stools, two tables, four coffers, a dresser, one long settle, equipment for carding and spinning wool, two washing-tubs and a picturesque assortment of kail pots, piggins, brass pans, supping pots, wooden bowls, trenchers, and other utensils. Apart from the absence of chairs, the furnishings differed little from the household goods found in neighbouring farmhouses, which suggests that the local community regarded it more as an almshouse than a place of shame. The two-storey workhouse built in the local vernacular style at Witham, Essex, in 1714, and converted into cottages in 1841,[4] illustrates how traditional poorhouses merged naturally with domestic village architecture, in contrast to the fortress-like Victorian institutions designed to inspire fear and dread. There is good evidence that furnishings too reflected the transition from parish poorhouse to Union workhouse.

The workhouse built at Charlton Kings, Gloucestershire, in 1872 at a cost of £466, was transferred to the Cheltenham Union in 1834 and closed down in 1847. Before handing it over to the Cheltenham Guardians a detailed schedule of 'Furniture, fixtures, utensils and other effects' was compiled.[5] This list reveals that the Charlton Kings workhouse accommodated about a dozen residents and was more austerely furnished than poorhouses at Cambridge and Arkengarthdale. The Committee Room, where applicants for relief were interviewed, contained a square deal table, a set of two elbow and twelve ash chairs, four stools, two built-in cupboards, a tailor's bench and a shoemaker's stall. The domestic offices included a kitchen/eating-room sparsely furnished with a 'Long Deal framed Table, four Deal Forms, Deal Dresser and shelves', a pantry, laundry, bakehouse and storeroom. The one ground-floor bedroom contained 'an Iron Turn-up Bedstead, a Straw Bed & flock Bolster, an elm box and Maniacs Chain' — a reminder that even in 1834 lunatics were sometimes confined in workhouses. The bedrooms were provided with a varied assortment of eleven iron, half-tester, turn-up, sacking or lath-bottom bedsteads; six elm clothes boxes, two night commodes, two deal dressing-tables, an oak chest of drawers and a basin-stand. The absence of chairs on the premises (except in the Committee Room) and minimal comforts are typical of the plain living to which paupers were increasingly subjected even under the old Poor Law.

In 1836 the newly elected Guardians of Ledbury Union in Herefordshire drew up a specification for furnishing their new workhouse; this document is of capital interest because it features marginal sketches of several articles.[6] The Board Room was to be supplied with an oak table 14 feet by 3 feet 6 inches raised on shaped end supports, two elbow and sixteen ordinary chairs 'as per sketch' and '1¼ in. segment edge oak seats all round the walls framed with legs &c as the chair pattern . . . the corners near the doorways to be framed quadrant'. The Clerk's Office and waiting-room required a table containing lockable drawers, three rows of shelves, '20 strong Windsor Chairs Grecian pattern' and 100 feet of deal rail with iron hat pins. The four day rooms were to have 'deal seats 11 in wide fixed all round the walls on elm or oak bearers', a long table and two forms 'on strong framed legs'. Other items on the schedule included thirty towel-rollers, 300 feet of deal shelving, a deal bath 'dovetailed and put together with white lead' and fitments such as sinks, plate-racks and dressers. Details of furniture for the schoolroom, chapel, larder, laundry and refractory rooms follow. This orderly contract demonstrates the efficiency with which the New Poor Law was administered after the old system of parochial relief was abolished. The creation of large, odious institutions was in some ways a successful solution to the problem of pauperism.

A comprehensive inventory of the Buxton workhouse, belonging to the Aylsham Union, Norfolk, taken by Mr Lawrence, the master, in 1839, provides another insight into how the new 'Bastilles', as they were popularly known, were furnished.[7] The Government Commissioners who controlled local Boards of Guardians, attempted to impose national uniformity, so this record is likely to be typical of the new generation of Union workhouses. Leaving aside the well-appointed Master's Office, sitting-room and sleeping apartment, accommodation was provided for 281 new residents who, in obedience to the new regime, were strictly segregated according to sex. The women and men each had their own day room, dining-hall, dormitory and probationary ward, while there were separate day rooms and schoolrooms for boys and girls respectively. These quarters contained a basic repertoire of long or short tables, forms, seats with or without backs and stools, the only novelties being cradles in the womens' day room, a chaplain's desk in the female dining-hall and educational paraphernalia in the schoolrooms. The usual Domestic Offices can be passed over, leaving the four 'paupers' sleeping rooms', each of which had a night stool and between them seventy-four double and twenty-four single wood bedsteads supplemented by thirty-seven double and thirty-five single iron bedsteads making up a total of 170 designed to sleep 281 inmates. The schedule of clothing reminds one that paupers were required to wear a degrading uniform.

In their report, the Poor Law Commissioners recommended that workhouse children should be housed separately and treated more humanely than adult paupers. It was their intention that youngsters should receive the same education being offered in elementary schools — namely instruction in reading, writing and religious knowledge; in 1842 arithmetic was officially added to the syllabus. In rural Unions it was normal to send pauper children to local schools, but in densely populated urban areas many Boards established separate workhouse schools. In County Durham, for instance, the Sunderland, South Shields, Stockton and Gateshead Unions all provided schools.[8] The Buxton inventory, quoted in part above, records the contents of the Girls' and the Boys' schoolrooms. The latter was equipped with '1 long Table & 5 inkstands, 2 Long Forms, 4 Stools, 1 Coal Box, Stove, Fender & dustpan, 4 doz Large Slates, 1 doz Small do., 2 doz school Bibles, 40 Testaments, 40 Lesson Books, 69 Copy Books, 15 Reading Tablets, 5 doz Arthmetical Tablets, 3 doz Prayer Books, 2 doz Hymn Books, 2 maps, 4 doz Alphabetical and Spelling Cards, 6 Catechism Books & 4 doz Primers'.

Two inventories dated 1812 and 1817 survive from the old 'House of Industry' at Ampthill in Bedfordshire,[9] while the first Union minute book reveals how the new workhouse was equipped. The early building contained a room with a cross-framed deal table and a dozen Windsor chairs which was also used by the local community as a Sunday School. The main room sported a long dining-table and six deal forms, twelve Windsor chairs, a round tripod table, looking-glass, fire-irons, a warming-pan, tinder-box and extinguisher; it was modestly comfortable. Besides the kitchen and pantry there was a sick-room and three sleeping wards for ten men, boys and women. The evidence points to a small fraternity enjoying decent standard of living. A diary kept by the Master of Knaresborough workhouse between 1788 and 1792 paints a lively picture of day-to-day life in a comparable small parish house, reflecting his touching concern for the inmates' health, welfare and Christian behaviour.[10]

In 1835 the Guardians of the big new Ampthill workhouse ordered[11] '2 dozen Iron Bedsteads' from Ride and Colman, which were no doubt similar to a surviving example of about the same date from Thetford workhouse (see Plate 286). Two weeks later they resolved 'that an advertisment be inserted in the Northampton newspaper to 'Upholsterers, Carpenters and others for plans and estimates of Bedsteads either Wood or Iron for the use of the Ampthill Workhouse'. At their next meeting the clerk was instructed 'to order from Wm Battison, George Battison, John Spring and Wm Northwood a Bedstead of each of the large size of good seasoned wood for the inspection of the Board' and a week later he minuted their approval of 'the Pattern Bedstead . . . by Mr George Battison' and ordered '50 double Bedsteads and 50 single to be delivered in six weeks time'. In due course the Board paid for the samples and in February 1839 George Battison received a cheque for £58. One of his plain elm stump beds with pine slats is preserved at Bedford Museum (Plate 280).

The invaluable evidence gleaned from workhouse inventories can be usefully supplemented by pictorial sources, particularly during the Victorian period. One of the earliest views is a plate from Rowlandson and Pugin's *Microcosm of London* (1808), of the day room at St James's workhouse. It shows a vast, rather stern interior containing large tables, forms, a few chairs, a wool-winder and clothes-horse, peopled by some fifty, mainly elderly, women either sewing, gossiping in groups or simply resting (Plate 281). Sir H. Van Herkomer's romanticized oil-painting titled *Eventide – a Scene in the Westminster Union* (1878) at Liverpool Art Gallery also portrays a spacious, depressingly institutional room crowded with old ladies engaged in reading, sewing, supping tea or sitting quietly on benches. Their gloomy surroundings are brightened by a vase of flowers, a few pictures on the walls and a pussy cat.

An engraving of the West London Union, dating from about 1860, records the women's short stay casual ward in which the only furniture was a sloping two-tier

280. Stump bedstead, elm with a pine head-board and slats, one of fifty made in 1836 by George Battison, a local joiner, for the work-house at Ampthill, Bedfordshire. *Bedford Museum*

281. The women's day room at St James's workhouse, furnished mainly with large sewing-tables and forms. A rare view of an 'unreformed' workhouse from *Microcosm of London*, 1808.

sleeping platform constructed of bare boards with no visible bedding.[12] That this type of accommodation was not unique is proved by a slightly earlier illustration of a Refuge for the Destitute and Houseless Poor in Whitecross Street, London,[13] where inmates slept together on immense open platforms spread with straw, no attempt being made to provide individual beds. At the West London Union, one wall of the barn-like men's casual ward was partitioned into rows of byre-like stalls with loose straw on the floor where groups of men and boys huddled like cattle;[14] it would be hard to contrive more degrading conditions. An engraving of a new ward at Marylebone workhouse, published in the *Illustrated London News* on 29 September 1867, shows a long room with sleeping platforms ranged down each side subdivided, by low board partitions, into narrow beds, each with a mattress and hinged compartment at the head for storing clothes. The walls and roof bear religious texts such as 'In God I Put My Trust', painted in red letters on a blue ground[15] (Plate 282). Some late-Victorian lantern slides of the Otley workhouse[16] include a view of the sleeping quarters which shows what appears to be the original cattle-stall type of accommodation (Plate 283).

A rare photograph of the female dining-room at St Pancras workhouse depicts long rows of uniformed women[15] seated at narrow, closely regimented tables

282. (*right*) The new casual ward for women at Marylebone workhouse, London. The central grille covered heating pipes and beyond the doors was a bathroom. *Illustrated London News* (1867)

283. (*below*) Stall-type sleeping accommodation for casual vagrants at the Wharfedale Union workhouse, Otley, Yorkshire, built in 1873. *Courtesy the Walker family*

284. Detail of a grained deal bench fitted around three sides of the waiting vestibule outside the Board of Guardian's Room at Ripon workhouse, Yorkshire, opened in 1855.

285. Oak chair of 'Grecian' design from a large set made for the workhouse at Wincanton, Somerset, in 1838. Branded 'WINCANTON UNION' under the seat. *Leeds Art Galleries*

(designed like school desks on cast-iron supports), eating rations off tin plates. Other equally depressing early twentieth-century photographs record day rooms, work-sheds, sick-wards and dormitories.[16] One of the few illustrations of a workhouse board room occurs in Mrs Trollope's novel *Jessie Phillips: A Tale of the Present Day* (1844). It shows the Guardians in session seated on handsome chairs around a large table.

Following abolition of the workhouse system in 1930, many buildings found a new role, often as old people's homes, orphanages or hospitals, while Gressenhall now houses the Museum of Norfolk Rural Life. The destruction of furniture has inevitably been colossal and unless items happen to bear a brand mark proving their origin, it is seldom possible to confirm the ancestry even of pieces which still survive in former workhouses. The gatehouse of Ripon Union (1855), until recently, contained the Guardians' boardroom table and chairs, but now only a fixed wall seat of painted pine with turned legs and ramped arm rests survives in the adjoining waiting-room (Plate 284); the vagrants' cells and bathroom have been stripped, but in the main block two robust work- or sewing-tables from the female day room are preserved, one of which is built-in under a window of take full advantage of the light. The Museum of Lincolnshire Life possesses a provenanced set of routine late-Victorian smoker's bows; a severely institutional oak 'Grecian' Windsor chair branded 'WINCANTON UNION' datable to 1838 is now at Temple Newsam House (Plate 285), while Bedford Museum retains one of fifty elm stump bedsteads which George Battison supplied to the Ampthill workhouse in 1835.

A large collection of accredited workhouse furniture is held by the Norfolk Museum Service. One of their most striking acquisitions is an austere iron bedstead made for the Thetford Union about 1836 which must be typical of many recorded in contemporary inventories[17] (Plate 286). For example in 1839 the paupers' sleeping-rooms at Buxton workhouse, Norfolk, contained seventy-four iron bedsteads and

in 1835 the Guardians of Ampthill ordered '2 dozen iron bedsteads' from Ride & Coleman. J.C. Loudon, writing in 1833, described as a recent innovation 'Stump bedsteads made entirely of wrought iron; the place of the canvas or sacking bottom being supplied by interwoven iron hooping which is manufactured by Messrs Cottam & Hallen of London'.[18] The Thetford model is painted grey and would have supported a chaff or straw mattress, the feet are pierced by screwholes. Other, more traditional provenanced examples of workhouse furniture at the Museum of Norfolk Rural Life include a locally made banister-back armchair branded 'FOREHOE UNION' (Plates 287 and 288), a long scrubbed pine dining-table and group of archaic splat-back chairs indigenous to Gressenhall; the grained high-master's desk from Wicklewood workhouse and a standard early nineteenth-century East Anglia pattern square-backed cross-rail chair incorporating three balls from the same institution. Needless to say all these chairs have wooden seats. By combining documentary evidence with pictorial sources, and a search for extant items, a reasonably full picture of this neglected vernacular sub-group has emerged, although undoubtedly many specimens of workhouse furniture remain to be identified.[19]

288. Branded mark on the armchair (see Plate 287).

13 Houses of Correction, Bridewells and Prisons

Houses of Correction (popularly known as bridewells), established under an Act of 1576–7, were not originally part of the prison system. They were intended to punish sturdy beggars, vagrants and other disorderly or idle members of society by forcing them to work for their keep. Houses of Correction were the direct responsibility of Justices of the Peace in quarter sessions and about two hundred were erected under the statute. However, by the late seventeenth century, magistrates increasingly regarded them as places of detention and hard labour for petty criminals rather than institutions for providing work for the unemployed able-bodied poor.[1]

The authorities provided a building and paid the master's salary on the understanding that no further charge was made on the rates — a system which inevitably led to wretched conditions and harsh regimes since the master's main concern was to avoid incurring expense and maximize profits from the prisoners' work. Following the reforming crusade of John Howard, parliament attempted between 1774 and 1791 to improve conditions and reduce overcrowding by introducing systematic inspections and other measures. By 1789 a start had been made on building over forty new gaols and Houses of Correction, and it is at this point that bridewell furniture can, for the first time, be identified and studied as an institutional sub-group.

Under an Act of 1784, which provided for the remedying of grossly inadequate accommodation, the North Riding Justices ordered a new House of Correction to be built in Northallerton, Yorkshire.[2] At their meeting on 7 November 1788, the Committee of Visiting Justices 'ordered that sacks be made of Harden to be filled with Straw for Bedding to fit the Bedsteads of the different Cells according to the pattern already made by Thomas Winsper. That a Blanket and Rug be provided for each of the Beds according to the Pattern produced by John Marshall. That Nine Suits of Bedding for large Beds and the like number for Small ones be provided and also Six spare Blankets for the use of Prisoners, in case of Sickness'. They also ordered blue and brown kersey uniforms and proposed that 'the Prisoners Confined to Labour' should comb wool, prepare warps for worsted goods and spin wool in their cells. An inventory of the Northallerton House of Correction taken in 1800 reveals that each cell contained a bedstead, bedding and blankets, a stool, night stool, a pail and fire-grate. There was also in the building a kitchen and back-kitchen for preparing prisoners' food, a jury-room, Under Gaoler's-room, a reading-desk and table with prayer books in a room which served as a chapel, various leg irons, body irons, neck collars, shackles and handcuffs, plus items such as a bathing-tub, boilers, ladders, stoves and two hand bean mills. Although none of this furniture survives, the documents provide a precise record of how a well-regulated House of Correction was equipped at the close of the eighteenth century.[3]

In Gloucestershire, a model House of Correction was built at Northleach in 1791, for thirty-seven prisoners, each of whom had a ground-floor day cell and a first-floor night cell. There were also three workrooms, an infirmary wing, a kitchen,

Detail from *A Rake's Progress* by William Hogarth, showing the Prodigal in the Fleet Prison, London, 1735. Debtors were required to pay for their comforts (see Plate 293). *Leeds Art Galleries*

289. Cast-iron cell bed supported on stone blocks, the head raised 6 inches; prisoners were allowed a pallet, hemp sheets and two blankets. The Northleach House of Correction opened in 1792, but this bed base probably dates from *c.* 1830 (see Plate 225). *Cotswold District Council*

290. Timber-block stool and sleeping platform in one of the old cells at Lancaster Castle. *Lancashire County Council*

291. Prisoners being weighed at Clerkenwell House of Correction. *Illustrated London News* (1874). This was a short-term institution for untried criminals after they had been committed by a magistrate.

bathroom, chapel and Keeper's house.[4] It was a forerunner of grim, purpose-built Victorian prisons. Each night cell contained a heavy cast-iron bed in the form of a flat grid with a raised head-sill supported by stone blocks, on which a straw or horsehair pallet was laid (Plate 289). Two of these frames survive, and there are closely similar bed bases in the gaol at York Castle Museum. The only other 'furniture' was a square stone which served as a seat; one of the old cells at Lancaster Castle still has an equally primitive wood-block stool (Plate 290). Littledean House of Correction, also in Gloucestershire and built at the same time as Northleach, retains some original built-in timber bedsteads with raised wooden head rests at one end, wall-mounted flap tables and plain forms.[5] A similar form is visible in a much later engraved view of the Clerkenwell House of Correction which also records a typical warder's high stool, a weighing machine and other stern items of furniture (Plate 291). Clearly a bureaucratic concern for the welfare of prisoners did not admit concessions to comfort. Even the condemned ward at Newgate was uncompromisingly institutional (Plate 292).

Although the National Government assumed some responsibility for the confinement of criminals in 1779, the maintenance of prisons continued on the whole to be the duty of Local Authorities – county justices and municipal corporations – until the Prisons Act of 1877 transferred their administration *en bloc* to the Home Office. Because in the past punishments were mainly whipping, death, transportation, the stocks or fines, common gaols or 'lock-ups' were for many centuries places of temporary safe custody such as part of an old castle or cellars under a court house, rather than special buildings where prisoners served long sentences.

The two hundred or so common gaols existing in mid-eighteenth-century England bore no resemblance to monolithic Victorian prisons; they were run as private profit-making ventures by gaolers whose sole legal responsibility was to prevent prisoners from escaping. So it is not surprising that conditions were generally atrocious. Fees were charged for bedding, light, fires, food (other than a meagre diet of bread and water), removing irons, discharge and indeed any services or privileges. Depending on the ability of a prisoner (or his friends) to pay, accommodation ranged from a dark insanitary, overcrowded dungeon to a private cell

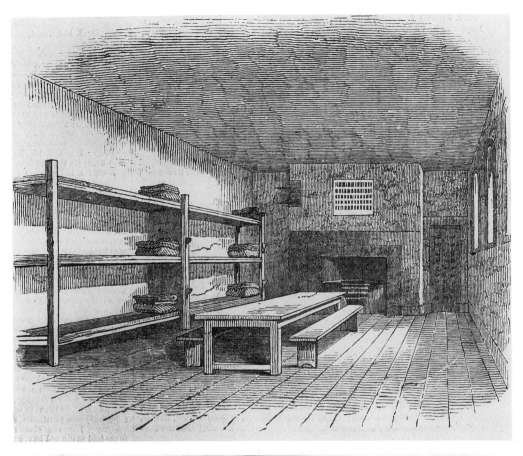

292. Ward for condemned prisoners at Newgate, London. *Illustrated London News* (1850)

293. *A Rake's Progress* by William Hogarth, showing the Prodigal in the Fleet Prison, London, 1735. *Leeds Art Galleries*

179

or a well-furnished apartment in the gaoler's house. Under such an unregulated system it is impossible to categorize prison furniture, except to point out that for the majority it was minimal or non-existent. The seventh scene in Hogarth's *A Rake's Progress* (1735) shows the Prodigal in the Fleet Prison seated on an upholstered chair beside a tripod tea-table in a roomy cell with a curtained four-poster bed, a stove and a barred window in the background (Plate 293). A gaoler and a pot boy, who has just brought in a mug of ale, are demanding payment for these amenities and refreshment.[6] A series of prints published by Carington Bowles in 1787 representing the contrast between Vice and Virtue in the character of two brothers, shows Frederick imprisoned for debt in a sordid room furnished with a stump bedstead, a broken ladder-back chair and a table with a pitcher standing on it[7] (Plate 294). He too was fortunate in being able to rent a private room. Thomas Rowlandson's well-observed prospect of the pass-room at Bridewell in London is certainly more typical of prison life (Plate 295). It shows a large bare interior peopled by eighteen women and infants, the only 'furniture' being bed berths or stalls divided by low wooden partitions filled with loose straw along each side of the room.[8] Another rare eighteenth-century prison print portrays the sick-ward at Marshalsea as a lofty chamber with, on each side, a row of men lying on the stone floor beneath a raised sleeping platform on which other ill prisoners recline, while hammocks slung from the ceiling form a third tier of human suffering[9] (Plate 296).

Very few specimens of prison furniture survive from the Georgian period,[10] but one of the cells in the Tollbooth or lock-up at Aberdeen still contains a pine crib bed designed like a shallow trough raised on square corner-posts, originally with a slatted bottom (Plate 297). This is the only known example of a once common type of crib bedstead, also found in asylums and barracks; it was intended to sleep two or three men. Two fearsome items of prison furniture at Lancaster Castle are of capital interest.[11] The most shocking of these is a hanging chair adapted from an old

296. The sick-ward at Marshalsea Prison, London. Detail of a print published in 1729.

297. Crib bed of *c.* 1800 in a cell at the Tollbooth, Aberdeen, Scotland, originally with a slatted bottom. This is a very rare survival of a once common type of institutional bed designed for more than one occupant. *Aberdeen Museums*

counting-house stool by adding a back, arms, arm supports and castors, the new members being screwed to the original pegged frame (Plate 298). This chair was made specially for Jane Scott of Preston, aged twelve, who was hanged in March 1828 for the murder of her mother. A disability prevented her from walking to the gallows, so she was strapped into this chair and wheeled to the drop. The Castle also houses two remarkable lunatic restraining chairs of heavy plank construction painted dark green. Each is fitted with a commode beneath the hinged seat board and three screw-operated iron bars through which a wide leather strap was passed to confine the struggling occupant. One arm rest is carved 'I BROWN 1837' and 'E.K. 1837' (Plate 299). These chairs served as a grim reminder that before County Asylums were established under an Act of 1808, the criminally insane were sent to gaol in exactly the same way as other prisoners.

These two grisly relics, in fact give a misleading impression of Lancaster Castle, because throughout the eighteenth and nineteenth centuries the majority of prisoners were debtors, many being taken into custody by amicable agreement in order to clear their debts; and providing they had friends outside prepared to pay for their comfort, they could expect a congenial life. On entry the debtor or his friends paid anything from 5s. to 30s. for his quarters which were given nicknames such as 'The Constables' (5s.); 'The Pin Box' (15s.); 'The Chancery' (15s.); 'The Belle Vue' (15s.); 'The Pigeons' (16s.); 'The Top' (£1.) or 'The Snug' (30s.) Many of the debtors were Quakers who refused to pay Tithes or the fines imposed on them for failing to attend services of the Anglican Church. Their quarters, known as 'The Quakers', cost 25s. Visitors were allowed from 8 am to 8 pm, the prison library was available at a fee of £1. per year and between 1752 and 1794 there was even a bowling green within the walls for the prisoners' entertainment; indeed, the Castle was at one time affectionately known as Hansbrow's Hotel, after the Governors James and Arthur Hansbrow who held the post successively from 1833 to 1867. A prospect of

298. Hanging chair adapted from an old counting-house stool; pine painted greyish brown. In 1828, at Lancaster Castle, Jane Scott, aged twelve, was strapped into this chair and wheeled to the drop. *Lancaster County Council*

299. Lunatic restraining chair in the prison at Lancaster Castle, constructed of pine painted dark green with a commode beneath the hinged seat board and iron bars through which a wide leather strap was passed. One arm is carved 'I BROWN 1837'. *Lancaster County Council*

300. *The Quakers 1ˢᵗ Class Day Room for Debtors, Lancaster Castle,* 1856. Many Quakers were taken into custody for refusing to pay tithes or fines to the Anglican Church; these congenial quarters cost 25s. *Lancaster City Museums*

The Quakers 1ˢᵗ Class Day Room for Debtors, Lancaster Castle, dating from this time, demonstrates the privileged life that certain debtors enjoyed (Plate 300).

Between 1774 and 1791 parliament attempted, through permissive legislation, to reform the prison system by the provision of secure and sanitary buildings, transforming the gaoler into a salaried public servant, subjecting criminals to a reformatory regime of hard labour, plain food and religious worship and introducing periodic inspections. Because the legislation was not statutory, it was only implemented sporadically; but these measure, inspired by John Howard, mark the beginnings of prison reform. The increased pressure on gaols, following the loss of the American colonies where convicts had been transported, forced the government to keep them on hulks and local justices to build new gaols, some of which embodied Howard's principles. Thus, during the nineteenth century prison furniture starts to emerge as a distinct institutional sub-group.

An engraving in Henry Mayhew and John Binny's important study *The Criminal Prisons of London and Scenes from Prison Life* (1862) reveals how the original cells in the female convict prison, built by the government at Brixton in 1819–20 were furnished (Plate 301). Each contained a gas jet, three triangular corner shelves, a square table, a boarded stool, little deal box for storing clothes and a hammock with bedding which was kept rolled up during the day but slung wall to wall on staples at night.[12] Other illustrations of scenes at Brixton show the cheerless convict nursery[13] with mothers seated on little beds nursing infants — children born before the sentence started were sent to the workhouse. Mayhew also included views of the wash-house and ironing-room,[14] where the women laundered their own clothes and those belonging to the prisoners at Millbank and Pentonville as well; others worked in the bakehouse, kitchens and infirmary.

Pentonville was built in 1840–42 as a model institution for 520 long-term prisoners. Inmates were not allowed to associate or talk with each other but worked, ate and slept in separate cells. Even in the chapel prisoners were isolated in individual box pews to prevent intercommunication[15] (Plate 302). Every cell contained a water-closet and copper wash-basin, a round three-legged stool, a shaded gas-burner, small table, corner shelves for stowing a mug, tin plate, wooden spoon, soap box, bible, etc., and a canvas hammock bed for slinging at night between

301. Cell in the old wing of the female convict prison at Brixton, built 1819–20. The hammock and bedding, shown folded up, was slung wall to wall at night. *The Criminal Prisons of London* (1812)

183

302. Divine service at Pentonville where the 'separate system' which prevented prisoners from associating or communicating was rigorously enforced; even the chapel had individual box compartment pews. An identical scheme of c. 1845 survives in the gaol chapel at Lincoln Castle. *The Criminal Prisons of London*, 1862

staples fixed to the walls.[16] Many cells also housed a loom or shoemaker's last because prisoners were expected to work for their keep[17] (Plate 303). The dark punishment cells were bare of furniture except for a narrow bench with a sloping headpiece and a rug. The cell furniture must have been supplied under contract to the Surveyor General of Prisons, but it is not known who designed or made it. At Millbank, built in 1812 for prisoners awaiting transport to Australia, the cells were provided with a square table of plain wood, a stool and either a hammock or a bed board resting on stone supports which served by day as a shop board for tailoring.

Convict prisons were government institutions for criminals sentenced to penal servitude or transportation. Correctional prisons were managed by magistrates, supported by county rates and housed persons serving shorter terms; the inmates were subjected to strict discipline and hard labour. In Mayhew's day, the cells in London Houses of Correction contained much the same furniture as those in the convict prisons. Some had flap tables or corner cupboards with a drawer in place of open triangular shelves, or the lid of the water-closet offered the only seat, but by and large provision was remarkably uniform. What distinguished Houses of Correction was the punitive labour such as the dreaded treadmill, the crank and tedious oakum picking in huge rooms watched over by warders seated on high stools to enforce silence. The gaol at Beaumaris on Anglesey, built in 1829, is the only one left in the country where the treadwheel is still in position. It also contains a shallow crib-style bedstead and one narrow infirmary bed; cell fittings include a wash-basin, typical corner shelves, hammock staples and a few tables. Engravings of Tothill Fields House of Correction for juvenile offenders, published by Mayhew in 1862, depict the boys' and girls' schoolrooms equipped with long desks and forms, a teacher's high desk, alphabet boards, maps and religious texts. Each child received an hour's schooling a day.[18] Views of the boys' oakum-room and the girls' sewing-room[19] show closely ranked rows of long forms for the prisoners, watched over by warders perched on stools. Another illustration shows the female clothes store at Tothill Fields — a lofty room lined from floor to ceiling with numbered open lockers containing bonnets and bundles of garments with a large office desk in the centre at which the clerk stood to write.[20]

It only remains to mention the hulks at Woolwich, which in 1841 held 3,550 convicts. Once again, Mayhew provides a pictorial record of the accommodation. Aboard the *Defence*, the lower decks were divided up by grilles into living quarters; long tables and forms used during the day were stowed away at night to make space for hammocks.[21] There was a chapel, schoolroom and kitchen, but washing for the whole fleet was done aboard the *Sulphur*, while the *Unité* was fitted out as the hospital ship.[22] During the day convicts worked ashore in stone-breaking gangs or at the dockyards.

303. Separate cell for long-term prisoners at Pentonville, built 1840–42. The loom was for day work; at night the hammock was slung for sleeping. *The Criminal Prisons of London*, 1862

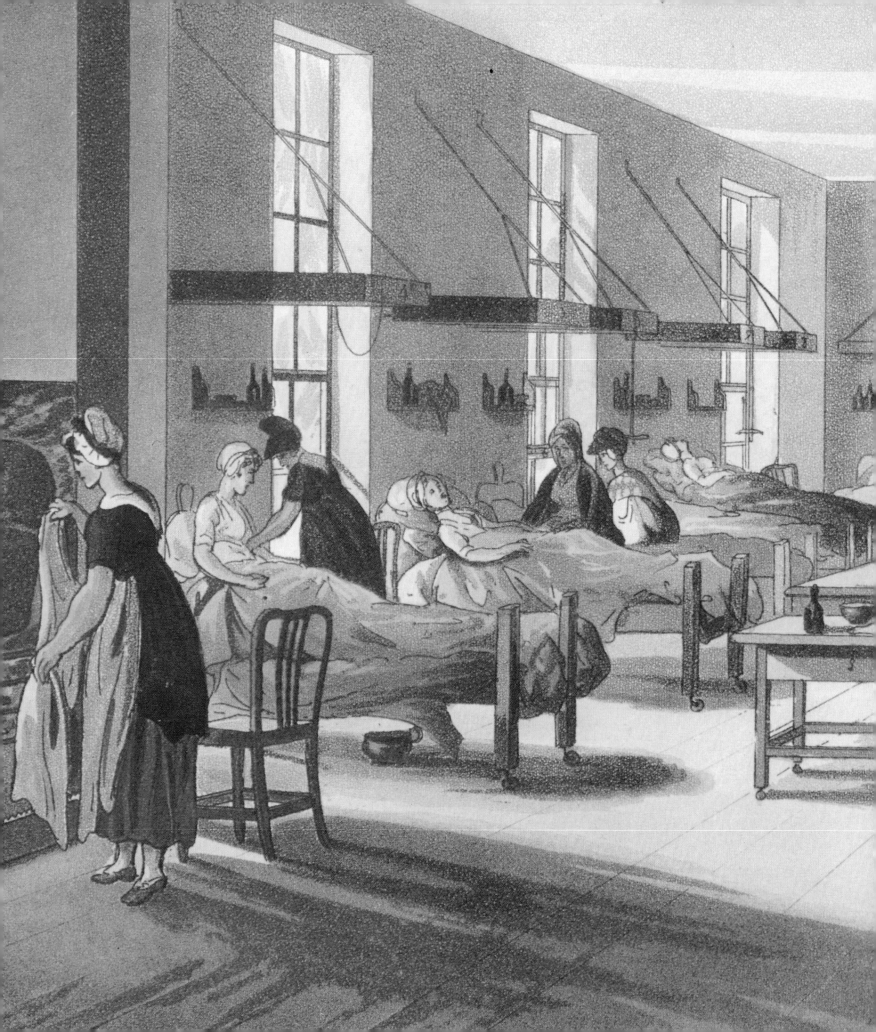

14 Lunatic Asylums and Hospitals

During the first half of the eighteenth century disgracefully little special provision was made for insane members of the community. If, as often happened, acute mental disorder reduced individuals to poverty, they were classed as 'pauper lunatics' and sent by the Parish Overseer under the Poor Laws to a workhouse. If illness caused them to break the penal law, they were liable to be imprisoned with common criminals in a county gaol (Plate 299), and sufferers who wandered abroad, begging outside their legal place of origin, transgressed the vagrancy laws and were sent by magistrates to the local House of Correction. A madman who lived in London might be confined in Bethlem Hospital (known popularly as 'Bedlam'), an institution financed by public subscription and the only old-established lunatic asylum in the country. Some private madhouses existed where wealthy patients were sent or 'put away' by their relatives, but these were invariably squalid and inmates were treated harshly by the attendants, since it was believed that gross cruelty would drive out the evil spirit. However, families who could not afford to pay for private care might attempt to cope by confining solitary lunatics at home, often chained like animals, in a cellar or attic.[1] The conditions under which the insane were kept in bridewells and poorhouses are sketched in the chapters dealing with prisons and workhouses. The following account explores the not very promising subject of how lunatic asylums during the Georgian period and County institutions, established eventually by legislation, were furnished.

St Luke's Hospital for the Insane, London, founded by public subscription in 1751, was a palatial building in the tradition of grandiose charitable institutions. An excellent description of the sleeping accommodation was sent in 1794 by John Bevans to his friend, William Tuke, then involved in building the Retreat, a well-known Quaker asylum in York: 'The walls of the lodging rooms are lined with deal framing in small panels of what we call bead & flush. The Bedsteads close, deep sides & end 2½ in thick close to and fixt to the floor — a close boarded bottom, upon the declevity towards the feet, with a groove across full of holes, where the wet drains into a Drawer that's under it for the purpose, which is drawn out when necessary — there is a Chain I saw fastened to the foot of the Bedstead, I suppose to fasten each leg when they are very bad; I did not think of looking at the Head, but suppose the same to be there. They have considerable quantity of straw under a flock mattrass — but Jn Howard particularly recommends Hair Mattresses as preferable to any other tho: they may cost something more, as the wet passes through them readily. There were pretty good Blankets, and everything were I was, remarkably sweet and clean'.[2]

Each gallery at St Luke's had two day rooms; one for quiet, the other for frantic patients. In 1904 the Medical Superintendant, describing conditions a century earlier, stated: 'There was no furniture beyond bare tables and wooden forms . . . each patient had a wooden trough-shaped bedstead fixed into the wall and containing loose straw . . . covered with sacking in the cases of convalescing patients only'.[3] A print, published in Rowlandson and Pugin's *Microcosm of London* (1808), shows the interior of the womens' gallery at St Luke's Hospital — a vast hall with attendants busy scrubbing the canvas bottoms of crib and stump bedsteads which have been pulled out into the middle of the room (Plate 304).

The non-mandatory Asylum Act of 1808 allowed for the provision of County asylums for criminal and pauper lunatics: during the first two decades nine counties built mental hospitals and various Parliamentary Committees reported in 1807, 1815–16 and 1828. Little is at present known about how these new institutions were equipped, but there was an emphasis on restraint because keepers were liable to be fined if patients escaped. The Committee of 1828 heard that pauper lunatics confined at the White House, St Pancras, slept in 'A crib room . . . a place where there are nothing but wooden cribs or bedsteads; cases, in fact, filled with straw and covered with a blanket, in which these unfortunate beings are placed at night; and they sleep most of them naked on the straw, covered with a blanket'. Patients were placed in the bed boxes at 3 o'clock, their arms and legs secured, and left there until 9 o'clock the following morning, and at weekends from Saturday afternoon until Monday morning. No examples or even images of these cot-like beds are known to survive, but they were evidently related to the crib beds used in some eighteenth-century prisons and Salvation Army Refuges until about 1900 (see Plates 87 and 297).

In 1792 the Quaker tea-merchant William Tuke, revolted by the brutal treatment of patients at the York asylum, resolved to establish a humane hospital known as the Retreat. This, by enlightened example, helped enormously to improve conditions nationwide. In 1794 he wrote to John Bevans: 'a subscription has been set on foot for providing a retreat for Persons afflicted with Disorders of the Mind, under the care and management of Members of our Society'.[4] It was proposed that the Retreat should house thirty patients who paid between 8s. and 15s. weekly. The regime was based on kindness rather than cruel restraint and the original accounts show that John Carr's dignified building was equipped more like a home than an institution. Most of the furniture was made by local tradesmen: in 1796 Benjamin Boocock supplied 24 elm chairs, 12 wood bedsteads, 6 deal dressing-tables, 12 bedsteads 'boarded round', plus chests of drawers, an oak dining-table, two looking-glasses and 'four Large Washing tubs'. William Cobb invoiced a Kitchen dresser and William Parkinson fitted out the laundry, while John Bevans procured, from James

304. The womens' gallery at St Luke's Hospital for the Insane, London, founded in 1751. Attendants are scrubbing down stump and crib bedsteads. *Microcosm of London*, 1808

Fisher in London, three replicas of the special beds at St Luke's Hospital on which he had reported. The accounts also provide details of commode chairs, night stools, deal tables, desks and furniture ordered for staff apartments.[5]

A schedule of work to be put in hand at the Oxford Lunatic Asylum in 1823, records that each day room contained a strong table with forms, while the sleeping galleries had beds and forms only. In these and the wet patients' room, the fire-grates were enclosed by iron guards and the windows protected by wire grilles. One room was fitted up as an apothecary's shop, another designated for storing blankets and waistcoats, and a plumbing system supplied the washing troughs, a lead-lined bath and water-closets. The offices included a drying-room, laundry and wash-house.[6] These facilities show that the patients' health and hygiene, if not their domestic comfort, were being considered. The kitchen contained a 'Dresser with shelves over . . . Large table on castors in the centre and a Table with proper Knives fixed for cutting bread'. The diet of inmates is hinted at in the provision of 'Copper Boilers for Gruel and Milk'. Some comparable evidence exists for the West York-shire Pauper Lunatic Asylum at Wakefield, which came into being as a result of the County Asylum Act of 1808 and opened in 1818. The hospital, now renamed Stanley Royd, together with the East Suffolk Health Authority at Felixstowe, are among the few to maintain museums which include asylum furniture.

An inventory of Horton Road Lunatic Asylum, Gloucester, taken in 1845 is rewarding because it reveals how a well-regulated early Victorian asylum was furnished.[7] The institution was subdivided into six sectors, each consisting of an unheated sleeping gallery with between fifteen and twenty-six wooden or iron bedsteads, a night commode and chamber pots. The adjoining day rooms contained deal tables and forms, a clothes-press, one press bed (presumably for a night attendant), a coal-box and fire irons, also eating utensils such as wooden trenchers, tin soup bowls, pints, spoons, bone knives and forks, roller-towels and wash-stands. The Keeper in charge of each ward had a comfortably furnished room where the cooking was done and hazardous articles such as razors, tinder-boxes and injection instruments kept.

Information about conditions at Bethlem Hospital, London, can be patched together from various sources,[8] starting with Hogarth's famous representation of the Incurable Ward in the eighth scene of his *Rake's Progress*, painted in 1733. Inventories of the old building, compiled in 1788 and 1795, also exist and when a new hospital opened in 1815 an auction catalogue titled *Household Furniture Contained in the Officers's and Servants' Part of the Establishment* was issued, although regrettably cell furniture is not listed. For particulars of the patients' accommodation it is necessary to consult the minutes of evidence taken by a Parliamentary Committee in 1815 and the Charity Commissioners' Report of 1837. Later in the century there are engravings and finally photographs which portray furniture in the wards, day rooms and elsewhere. Bethlem Royal Hospital moved to Beckenham in 1930.[9]

In 1795 the wards, described as galleries, were identified by the name of the Keeper in charge. The patients' sleeping-rooms were small cubicles leading off them, but their contents are not noted: presumably the wretched furniture was considered not worth listing. Bean's Gallery contained a typical ensemble: 'An Elbow Chair with a Close Stool / A water pump and stone sink / An Inscription Board / A deal press bedstead / 2 Table Boards / 3 Trussells / 5 forms / a deal press'. There were also Side Rooms which patients occupied during the day. Hawkins's Side Room was provided with: 'A Grate fixed / A Guard Iron / A Table / A Settle & 4 Benches / lock and Key'; some also had long roller-towels and a close stool chair. Patients who were not chained up could go to Stove Rooms to get warm or take a hot bath. These were each supplied with a grate and guard iron, benches, a copper and bath. The two 'Green Yards' were for exercising and drying washing, the mens' yard was provided with '2 Skittle Grounds / 8 Benches / a table'.

Evidence taken in 1815, by a Parliamentary Committee Enquiring into the State of Madhouses, is more helpful about cell furniture.[10] Violent or dirty lunatics slept in 'crib' beds, elsewhere called 'troughs', filled with straw and changed weekly; the others had 'Tolerably good Hessian beds, a flock bed, three blankets and a coverlid'. The same Committee heard about similar beds in a private madhouse at Fonthill, Wiltshire: 'The furniture of these cells was a long box, about six feet long by two and a half wide, raised from the ground for a bedstead, to which the patients were chained; in some of them the patients had blankets and coarse rugs, in others only straw'. In 1837 the Charity Commissioners reported that in Galleries Nos 2, 3 and 4 at Bethlem 'The furniture of these bed-rooms consists of a stump iron bedstead, with a canvas stretcher, flock bed, sheets, three blankets, and a rug and bolster. A wooden seat is fixed to the wall near the bedstead'. However, on visiting the basement they found that traditional beds, 'a wooden frame grated at the bottom and filled with straw', were still in use.[11] Engravings of the Men's and Women's day rooms published in the *Illustrated London News* in 1860 show spacious interiors with ferneries, house plants, gas light, busts of philosophers, pictures, carpets, cabinets and comfortable domestic furniture (Plate 305). Standards of amenity obviously rose sharply during the Victorian period. Photographs of Bethlem and other asylums confirm that the quarters occupied by quiet long-stay patients took on a pleasant club-room character.[12] An estimate by Bell and Coupland, of Preston and Lancaster, for furnishing a new Annexe at Lancaster County Asylum (now Moor

305. The womens' gallery for quiet long-stay patients at Bethlem Asylum. *Illustrated London News* (1860)

Hospital) in 1863, is illustrated by a fine series of designs attributed to Bruce Talbert for furniture in a progressive baronial Gothic style.[13] Small wonder that some inmates suffered delusions of grandeur!

306. A print of one of the wards at Guy's Hospital for Incurables, London, published the year of its opening, 1725. *Trustees of Guy's Hospital*

HOSPITALS

Turning now to medical hospitals, a remarkable prospect of a ward at Guy's, London, engraved by Thomas Bowles in the year of its opening in 1725, shows a large bare interior with rows of open-sided built-in box beds ranged against the walls; a low locker seat is fixed beside the head of each bed (Plate 306). By contrast, a print of the Middlesex Hospital, published in 1808, is at once familiar as a sick-ward (Plate 307). It portrays a spacious, well-lit and ventilated room with stump bed-steads raised on large wooden castors around the walls. Each bed stands beneath an angel half-tester (some with curtains), from which hangs a pulley device to help patients raise themselves into a sitting posture. Individual medicines are placed on a

307. This splendid record of a womens' ward at the Middlesex Hospital was published in *Microcosm of London*, 1808.

308. The Military Hospital at Portsea, Hampshire, showing a typical arrangement of iron-framed furniture, not unlike a barrack-room. *Illustrated London News* (1855)

shelf over the bedhead and chamber pots are stowed under the beds. Ordinary splat-back chairs for visitors abound, while the tables and forms in the centre of the ward were presumably intended for convalescing patients to use at mealtimes. A doctor is shown examining one of the female patients, another is in conference with relatives and a nurse airs linen in front of the open fire. The whole minutely observed, richly animated scene, conveys a vivid impression of how a well-ordered subscription hospital ward of the period was furnished.

A monograph on *Hospitals, Infirmaries and Dispensaries, their Construction, Interior Arrangement and Management*, published in 1867 by F. Oppert, physician to the City Dispensary, contains forthright descriptions of interior arrangements in existing institutions.[14] The author recommended: 'The best material for bedsteads is iron, because it is more durable than wood, and less apt to harbour vermin; a light blue or green paint, although more expensive than a darker tone, should be preferred, because it looks much more cheerful ... sacking bottoms are generally used'. 'Horsehair' he advised 'is a better material for mattresses than wool, because it can be disinfected by steam at a moderate cost. Over the bed should be a rope with a hand-grasp, near it a chair and side table, with, if possible, a marble top. Instead of curtains, which interfere with supervision, low screens, not higher than four or five feet, should be used whenever they are needed; their colour should be dark green. In the middle of the room there should be a long table, with a marble top, for holding all the necessary things. A side-board, and a few easy-chairs complete the furniture'. One could search for a long time before finding a better description of a hospital ward of the period. A prospect of the barrack-like military hospital at Portsea, published in 1855, records a typical furnishing scheme (Plate 308).

A fine repertoire of early hospital furniture survives, rather surprisingly, at the Dinorwic Slate Quarry Hospital, Llanberis, opened in 1876, which was only downgraded to a first-aid post in the 1940s and is now an outstation of the National Museum of Wales (see Plate 309). The ward contains strong iron-framed beds, each with a 'stirrup' pulley and a multi-purpose bedside chair: the box seat serves as a locker while the back flap, supported when raised on hinged wooden brackets, also functions as a convenient bed-table. They were originally painted brown and are said to have been made in the joiner's shop. The principal furniture in the surgery consists of a shaped wickerwork stretcher (see Plate 243), a padded operating-table, an adjustable examination couch, a robust armchair with a sliding head rest used for dentistry and a tall chamfered pine stand bearing an optician's alphabet cube — eye injuries caused by slate splinters were common (Plate 309). This archaic furniture is a moving reminder of the hardship and danger to which quarrymen were exposed.

Another rather late, but satisfyingly complete, suite of hospital furniture was collected by Bradford Museums from Scalebor Park Asylum, Yorkshire, in 1970. Pratts of Bradford won a contract in 1902 worth £9,062 to equip this new mental hospital, each patient's room being supplied with a fumed oak bed, a chair, single-door wardrobe framing a mirror, a combination wash-stand cum dressing-table with marble slab and tile splash-back, a bedside pedestal, a circular table and a printed fabric bed-screen. This suite is representative of inexpensive functional institutional furniture made under competitive tender in the machine age; its homely domestic scale and character is a nice touch because the majority of patients were long-stay residents.

The prodigious Wellcome Collection, consisting of medical material, now housed at the Science Museum, includes items of hospital furniture. One of the displays reconstructs part of Lister's Ward at the Royal Glasgow Infirmary (built 1861), featuring a bed, day bed, circular table, bible-box and stool. There is also a late Victorian operating-table, a wicker bath chair and various continental curiosities such as early parturition chairs with horseshoe-shaped seats used by midwives to assist delivery and an Italian Hypocratic table, designed like a rack for stretching the body to restore dislocated joints.

Finally, although invalid furniture – an interesting subject in its own right – is not treated in this survey, a strangely haunting stretcher-settee from Ireland deserves

309.   Optician's stand, dentist's chair with sliding head rest and a bedside locker seat with table flap from the Dinorwic Slate Quarry Hospital, Llanberis, opened in 1876. *National Museum of Wales*

310.   This Irish beggar was carried from door to door by neighbours on a well-contrived stretcher seat. *Illustrated London News* (1843)

311. Receiving ward at Hyde Park, London, for reviving people apparently drowned in bathing or skating accidents on the Serpentine. *Illustrated London News* (1844)

notice as a rare vernacular example of this genre. The helpless occupant was carried about on it by neighbours from door to door seeking shelter and food (Plate 310). Another, perhaps marginal, but nevertheless compelling illustration, shows a patient, medical attendant and nurse in an establishment run by the Royal Humane Society in Hyde Park for reviving people apparently drowned in bathing or skating accidents in the Serpentine (Plate 311). The building contained two wards for men and women with beds warmed by hot water, hot tables for heating flannels, and a bath.

15 Almshouses

The terms 'hospital' and 'almshouse' were in the past used interchangeably to describe every type of charitable refuge from leper houses to homes for poor widows, the elderly, sick and infirm. Many were founded by Guilds to shelter destitute members in their old age, or by wealthy individuals to benefit their local community. Numerous almshouses were established after the Dissolution of the Monasteries and performed a valuable welfare service to back up the various Poor Laws. Most medieval hospitals, such as St Mary's, Chichester, followed the monastic plan of a large infirmary hall with bed cubicles and an adjoining chapel where the residents lived as a single community. After the Reformation the collegiate system emerged, which provided separate living-rooms for the inhabitants, and by the eighteenth century almshouses typically took the form of a row of cottages with a communal chapel, often a refectory and perhaps a wash-house. A Master or Warden and a clergyman were normally appointed to look after their worldly and spiritual needs. Almshouses were popular because residents enjoyed an independent status compared to the institutional life of poorhouses maintained by Parish Officers.[1]

The almshouses at Firby, near Bedale in North Yorkshire, built and endowed by John Clapham in 1608, comprise a single row of six one-room dwellings with a central two-storey chapel and Master's house, chambered over. An inventory of 'Christopher Conyers late maister of Christes Hospital at Firby', taken in 1660, records that he owned 'some bookes, a bed, a chaire, 2 old chests, one reckon pan, a frying pan' and that he kept 'apples in the Chamber', valued in all at ten shillings.[2] The building has recently been converted, but some long pine benches with rail backs and hinged box seats, also several double cupboard doors of plank construction, which enclosed recesses containing built-in stump bedsteads in each cottage, still survive (Plate 312). They appear to date from an early nineteenth-century up-grading of the amenities. By about 1720 the one-up one-down almshouse was the standard adopted for new refuges because that had become the minimum socially acceptable accommodation in villages.

While many almshouses were built in the local vernacular idiom, others reflect the architectural pretensions of the gentry class who founded them. For instance, the Aberford almshouses, established in 1844 by the Gascoigne family, are in a picturesque Gothic Revival style. The chapel, refectory and cloister were provided with impressively 'monastic' architect-designed oak tables and benches with chamfered rails and tusk tenons (Plate 313), but the eight dwellings were uniformly furnished with 'common' elm chairs (Plate 314), plus a repertoire of painted pine furniture comprising a circular three-legged table, kitchen sideboard, chamber-table, chest of drawers, cupboard, dressing-table, wash-stand and iron bedstead. These pieces, made by Atkinson & Barker of Leeds, display a severe, semi-institutional character that set them aside from ordinary domestic furniture.[3] Sometimes almspeople were required to supply their own furniture: this rule

312. From the row of six single-storey, one-room almshouses at Firby, near Bedale, Yorkshire, built in 1608; each had a bed-recess enclosed by pine double doors next to the fireplace. *Courtesy Hambleton District Council*

313. Corridor bench made for Aberford almshouses, Yorkshire, in 1845. The style reflects the ornate Gothic character of the building. *Leeds Art Galleries*

314. (*right*) Elm chair, from a set made in 1845 by Atkinson & Barker of Leeds for Aberford almshouses, Yorkshire. *Leeds Art Galleries*

315. (*far right*) Oak chair, probably from a set of thirty-six ordered in 1777 for the Manor Court at Temple Balsall, Warwickshire. *The Governors of Temple Balsall*

prevailed at Morden College, Blackheath, and the catalogue of effects sold by the Trustees in 1800 to defray debts left by two deceased members reveals that their rooms contained elegant mahogany items.[4]

An interesting assortment of furniture survives at the almshouses at Temple Balsall, endowed in 1679 by Lady Katherine Leveson for twenty poor widows.[5] The original accommodation was provided with ten tables, twenty stools, twenty mats and twenty beds. Several plain oak tables with chamfered legs formerly used by the almswomen are extant, although they probably date from a rebuilding of 1725–7. The finest indigenous furniture is a massive oval gate-leg table and set of chairs used by the Steward and Governors at their bi-annual meetings. The splat-back armchair is carved with the initials and dates of successive Stewards, the earliest being 'FW 1775' for Francis Wheeler, who was appointed in that year. It is very traditional in design, but then such bodies often favoured conservative styles, so in context this date is plausible (Plate 316). The ten oak side chairs, of a slightly different pattern, may originally have belonged to a set of '36 Good Oak Chairs' ordered for the Manor Court and Jury Chamber in 1777 at a cost of 3s. 8d. each[6] (Plate 315). Now in the church at Temple Balsall, there is also a long pine X-framed table said to have been used for 'Parish breakfasts'.

Basic furniture commissioned for almshouses has proved depressingly hard to trace or document. A seventeenth-century oak stump bedstead made for Trinity Hospital, Castle Rising, Norfolk, where each almswoman had a bed sitting-room, is preserved at Strangers Hall, Norwich; there is a routine painted pine chapel bench at the Geffrye almshouses, London,[7] and photographs exist of a robust early eighteenth-century oak table and two matching chairs from a row of six almshouses in Snowdonia (Plate 317). Some tables and chairs at Dowell's Retreat almshouses, Birmingham, are understood to date from 1831, and there is an ensemble of rather grand high-Victorian furniture at Archbishop Holgate's almshouses, Hemsworth, Yorkshire; even so, our knowledge of this branch of furniture is disappointingly

316. Oak armchair, *c.* 1775, carved with the initials and dates of successive Stewards of the Manor Court at Temple Balsall, Warwickshire, who were responsible for the local almshouses. *The Governors of Temple Balsall*

317. Oak table and pair of chairs, one of six matching ensembles from a row of almshouses in Snowdonia, Wales. Early eighteenth century. *Roger Warner*

318. Soup kitchen set up in St Mary's Hall, Coventry. *Illustrated London News* (1861)

slight. It seems that, like almshouse architecture, the furniture could express an ostentatious, an institutional or a vernacular character.

SOUP KITCHENS

Soup kitchens, classic products of Victorian philanthropy, were set up, usually by religious or charitable organizations, in any convenient building to dispense nourishment to the poor, destitute or unemployed. They proved a popular subject with artists and journalists who wished to prick the conscience of the nation, and so were often featured in magazines. A view of Spitalfields soup kitchen published in the *Illustrated London News* of 16 March 1867[8] shows a man using a step stool to ladel broth from a row of huge boilers into large buckets with pouring lips which in turn supplied four metal cauldrons set on low square tables. The soup was then served with dippers into jugs and cans brought by a waiting hungry crowd. This scene is one of many which portray the basic essentials of a soup kitchen — all record boiling vats and sturdy well-framed tables. A view of the kitchen set up in St Mary's Hall, Coventry, in 1861, to sustain striking weavers, shows in the foreground a long counter with women cutting up fresh vegetables and potatoes[9] (Plate 318).

16 Meeting Houses and Chapels

Church, as opposed to chapel, furniture offers a large and rewarding area for study which might be thought to fit comfortably into the present survey. There is, however, a long tradition for the separate treatment of ecclesiastical furnishings – more particularly fixtures such as choir stalls, pews, pulpits, altars, screens, etc. – and in any case much of the church woodwork commissioned during our time-frame is hardly vernacular in character. A few payments in country joiners' account books for re-pewing churches or making inscription boards are noted and one splendid painted parish chest is illustrated (see Plate 29), but no sustained effort has been made to cover this field. Unpretentious Nonconformist chapels and Meeting Houses tell a different story. It must, however, be acknowledged that collectively, parish churches contain a huge reservoir of common furniture which offers abundant opportunities for exciting discoveries (see Plate 158). Vestries, dark corners under the tower or side chapels frequently contain domestic chairs, tables, cupboards and chests which have slumbered for centuries.

QUAKER MEETING HOUSES

Friends do not believe in sanctified places, but they become emotionally attached to their historic buildings; and since their form of worship has changed little, many old Meeting Houses survive with fine original interiors.[1] Early gatherings were often held in private homes, but after the Toleration Act of 1689, large numbers of public Meeting Houses were erected by local subscription; there was another marked spell of building activity in the 1790–1830 period. Quakers never favoured a particular architectural style; Meeting Houses were rarely professionally designed and always simple, generally reflecting regional building patterns.[2] Some advice from the Leeds Preparative Meeting held on 28 August 1706 helps to illuminate contemporary thought about furnishings: 'it is the general sense of this Meeting that at least all such as buy any furniture into their houses, that it is plain as becometh the truth'.[3]

The internal fittings and furnishings of Meeting Houses display a certain uniformity of plan. The main room was filled with rows of benches, normally free-standing, but sometimes fixed, and often arranged around three sides of a square with a platform at one end (see Plate 321). This was the Minister's Stand which could be a single built-in seat raised one step, or a three-tier panelled structure for the Ministers, the Elders and the Overseers (Plate 319). If additional seating was needed, a gallery might be inserted. From the early eighteenth century, women Friends were encouraged to hold their own Business Meetings, and for this purpose a separate area was provided, often on the balcony or in a chamber below it, the space being divided from the main hall by large wooden shutters. Some screens were built with simple lift-out sections; the panels might, however, be designed to slide sideways or operate with counter-weights on the principle of a sash window, while the shuttered variety either folded down or were hinged at the top and held open by iron stays or hooks set in the ceiling. Democratic changes have made the Minister's

319. Brigflatts Meeting House, Cumbria, showing the gallery, Minister's Stand and oak forms of 1714 to which backs and arms were added in 1720. *Courtesy Library of the Society of Friends*

Stand and shuttered partition obsolete, but they survive in many older Meeting Houses. A long double-sided grained pine desk in a back-room at Gildersome, Yorkshire (1756), is a reminder that such areas were frequently used for schooling, as a library or committee room. Fine hat rails and, less often, stick-stands were provided in cloakrooms or passages. The only other articles of furniture likely to be encountered are bookcases or shelves, chandeliers and quite often a table and chair used by the Committee Clerk at the Monthly Business Meeting.[4] The tradition is far more versatile than the rather static, and self-consciously honest, American Shaker furniture with which it has sometimes been compared.

Quakers were enjoined 'to choose what is simple and beautiful as becometh the truth' and the rows of plain sturdy seats which are a memorable feature of Meeting Houses reflect these sincerely held views. The benches, commissioned countrywide over a period of about two hundred years, make a handsome contribution to the native tradition of functional furniture. Being, as a rule, moveable, they are only distantly related to church or chapel pews and since they also have little in common with ordinary domestic settles, these large open-backed pine benches form a genuinely independent branch of seating furniture. The absence of carved decoration, even during the late seventeenth century when so much regional woodwork was embellished, is characteristic of Quaker attitudes; while the fact that the Victorian Gothic Revival fashion, so popular with other religious groups, passed them by, is further evidence of their respect for simplicity.

Early seats were often made without backs or arms, an omission which later generations frequently remedied: benches may thus be the work of two joiners. For instance, at Brigflatts, Cumbria (1675), the original oak forms with plank seats resting on splayed legs were provided with robust back rails and open arms by John Holmes in 1720[5] (Plate 319). The forms at Grayrigg, Cumbria (1696),[6] were fitted with backs in 1732 and those at Rookhow, Cumbria (1725), have also been adapted. At Colthouse, Cumbria, in 1841, comfort was further increased by the purchase of moreen and curled hair which Joseph Gill made up into seat cushions[7] (Plate 320).

Friends' Meeting House, Colthouse, Near Hawkshead.

320. Meeting House at Colthouse, Cumbria. The pine benches illustrate the design problem of adding a back and arms to simple forms. *Courtesy Sanderson & Dixon*

Two bench patterns evolved; the earlier was of slab-ended construction with twin back rails, the seat ends often being vigorously profiled: Variations on this model continued to be favoured by some Friends until well into the nineteenth century; excellent examples are found at Nailsworth (Gloucestershire) (Plate 322), Gainsborough (Lincolnshire), Skipton (Yorkshire), and many other places (Plate 321). The second type is of rectangular design having a broad top rail, frequently a middle rail for children to sit against, and open arms. The members, united by wooden pegs, are usually squared except perhaps for scrolled arm rests raised on vase-turned supports. A set of twenty-two magnificently restrained benches of this sort are preserved at High Flatts, Yorkshire (Plate 322a). Victorian influence is sometimes betrayed by the use of stained and varnished finishes or the presence of heavy machine-turned legs, while the fixed wall seats with high backs and tall winged ends found in many Meeting Houses relate to contemporary alehouse seating.

321. Friends Meeting House at Uxbridge, Middlesex (1755), with the original slab-ended pine benches. *Courtesy Library of the Society of Friends*

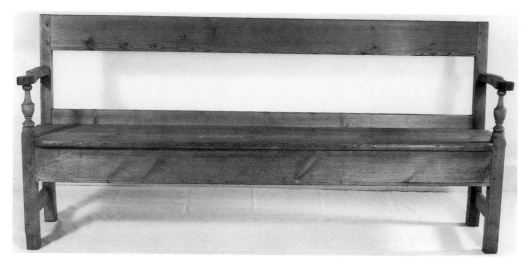

322. Oak bench from the Friends Meeting House at Nailsworth, Gloucestershire, perhaps mid-eighteenth century.

323. Varnished pitch pine pew door with stencilled number from the Shelley Methodist Chapel, Yorkshire.

William Alexander of York, who published *Observations on the Construction and Fitting up of Meeting Houses* (1820), advised Friends not to paint their furniture which 'may be kept very neat, by the application of a little soap and hot water, once in a year or two'. If, however, a painted finish was desired he recommended 'Oak or wainscot colour, neatly done, is preferable to any other, from its durability, and its capability of being repaired, without painting all over again'. Imported pine left in the white was most often employed by Friends for Meeting House furniture.

Although scattered references to ordering benches exist in various minute books, explicit documentation is elusive. In 1821 the London Gracechurch Street Meeting was rebuilt and fitted out with new seats, 'the result of great care bestowed on their shape and size'. The Friends commissioned several trial models, eventually selecting a plain traditional example which quickly became a standard pattern for Meeting Houses in the capital.[8] Seats of this improved design can be seen at Friends House, London. When the Kendal Meeting House was rebuilt in 1816, William Fisher, a Quaker joiner with a workshop nearby, provided all the woodwork, including the well-finished Minister's Stand and rather ordinary slab-ended benches. A set of twelve stained cherrywood chairs with upholstered seats was provided for the Committee Room and cloakroom where they are still to be found.[9] The old furniture at Lancaster has been entirely removed but the archive contains references to the purchase of seats between 1789 and 1790.[10]

A census of datable benches confirms the conservatism of Quaker designs and suggests the existence of certain regional preferences. Seats of more than one style and period often co-exist in Meeting Houses; they may all be indigenous or some may have belonged to a nearby abandoned Meeting[11] as at Countersett, Yorkshire, which includes benches from Carperby, also in Yorkshire. Such variety avoids the sometimes institutional character of the seating in some large town Meeting Houses. Thomas Rowlandson's busy view depicting a Quaker Meeting in Pugin and Rowlandson's *Microcosm of London* (1808), provides an excellent record of the interior of one of the big London Meeting Houses. If one had to use a single word to describe the special quality of Quaker furniture, 'sincere' is perhaps most apt.

NONCONFORMIST CHAPELS

Nonconformist chapels are a familiar feature of the English landscape. They were built, often in a vernacular style, by local tradesmen for congregations who rejected the religious symbolism of the Established Church. During the nineteenth century many rather showy architect-designed chapels were erected in towns, but we are concerned here mainly with the plain 'preaching house' and its furnishings. Since elaborate ritual played no part in their services, early dissenting congregations met for worship in almost any suitable building – barns, stable lofts, workshops or converted cottages – because they needed to be provided only with a simple pulpit and seating. This historical background explains why, even after the Act of Toleration in 1689, Nonconformist chapels only slowly developed a characteristic form.[12]

The oldest chapels are those established by Congregationalists, Baptists and Unitarians; the Methodists came into existence much later, and their buildings were influenced in part by the traditional Dissenting Meeting House, and partly by the Anglican Church. However, despite denominational distinctions, early chapels were all basically preaching houses and their interiors share many common features. The pulpit was generally placed centrally against the long wall opposite the entrance and facing rows of loose forms or fixed pews arranged in two equal sections for men and women, often with a hat rail on the mens' side. The pulpit might have a canopy or sounding board, a chair for the preacher and below a small railed rostrum with a Communion table. Unlike the Established Church seats were free; early comers sat down first, the benches for rich and poor alike being of the same construction. Pew doors sometimes have finely stencilled numbers (Plate 323) and wrought-iron latches, while candlesticks fixed to the pew fronts occasionally survive. A number of chapels still preserve original chandeliers (Plate 324); a beautiful example composed of a wooden orb supporting six scrolled candle-arms is to be seen at Walpole, Suffolk. Many interiors were provided with a gallery reached by a staircase with turned banisters. The gallery in the thatched Congregational Chapel at Hornings-ham, Wiltshire, has a set of wooden candlesticks along the front edge and there is a rail with over thirty hat pegs on the mens' side; while a music-stand shows that the seats facing the pulpit where occupied by the choir. A wall clock was frequently placed on the front of the gallery where it was visible to the Minister but not the congregation. Sometimes chairs or tables associated with famous long-dead preachers are proudly preserved.

Simplicity suited the spiritual needs of early congregations, but where ornamental trappings do occur – such as the carved dove perched on a globe over the pulpit in the Unitarian Chapel at Framlingham, Suffolk – they display the vigour of folk art. The fact that most of the woodwork in chapels is fixed does not make it less interesting as furniture, but its artistic value clearly depends rather more on the survival of a unified scheme than on individual items (Plate 326). So, if furnishings are taken in a broad sense to embrace pulpits, pews, hat rails, light fittings, etc., and are studied in the context of such architectural features as wall panelling, staircases and galleries (made in all probability by the same joiner), then many well-preserved pre-Victorian chapel interiors can be appreciated as a coherent vernacular statement reflecting local traditions.

Chapels that succeed on this level include Walpole and Horningsham (both rural Congregational), already mentioned. The Old Baptist Chapel at Tewkesbury retains, among many original furnishings, a bookcase in its customary position beneath the gallery, chandeliers and a Communion table, while other fine example are to be found at Cote, Oxfordshire; Great Horwood, Buckinghamshire; Church Lench, Worcestershire, and Maltby le Marsh, Lincolnshire — each with a baptistry concealed under the floor.[13] Early Methodists often gathered for fellowship in private houses or held open-air Meetings. An unspoilt early chapel occupying a small room over a stable at Raithby, Lincolnshire, was dedicated by John Wesley in 1779. The wayside chapel at Sneed in Wiltshire and another tucked away amongst outbuildings at Shelley, near Huddersfield (1785), also preserve typically straight-forward Georgian furnishing schemes. By 1784 there were over 350 Methodist chapels.[14] The New Room, Bristol, built in 1739 and reconstructed in 1748, is believed to be the earliest and contains many original fittings including some backless forms. John Wesley's advice to chapel builders, 'let there be no pews, and no backs to the seats,' was not always heeded.

324. Chandelier (one of a pair) from a Presbyterian Chapel in Perthshire. The turned beech stem, painted buff, supports six scrolled iron candle-arms. *Private collection*

325. Preaching chair owned by John Nelson (1707–74), a pioneer of Methodism in West Yorkshire. *Birstall Methodist Church*

326. Interior of Bethel Chapel, Durham, built 1853. *Courtesy Beamish Museum*

Nonconformist chapels in urban centres – Friar Street Unitarian, Ipswich (1700), is representative – tended to be more refined architecturally than those serving isolated rural congregations, and so fall outside the scope of this survey; as do the increasingly elaborate chapels built for wealthy congregations during Victorian days. This is not to say that resplendent Mission Halls never contain interesting pieces of common furniture: the proud Methodist Chapel at Birstall, Yorkshire (1846), preserves the remarkable elm preaching-chair with a book rest on the crest rail and hinged kneeling ledge used at open-air meetings by John Nelson (1707–74), who brought Methodism to the district and founded the first chapel on this site (Plate 325). His tiny brick study dated 1751 with a window, fireplace and homely reading-desk, still stands in the graveyard.[15] A slightly later oak pulpit chair, used at services held in a farmhouse near St David's, is now at the National Library of Wales.[16] This, however, is a rare survival, for by 1840 even the sensible varnished pine furnishings in the grey four-square Nonconformist chapels which abound in the Welsh countryside hardly express a true vernacular character; their self-conscious dignity marks the end of a long tradition.

17 Factories and Workshops

Although this broad subject can be narrowed down by excluding machinery such as looms or knitting frames, it still embraces items like teazle-dressing tables, bobbin bins and certain kinds of workbench which might be regarded by some as sub-furniture. The threshold is not always easy to define. In many trades workmen used a 'horse', consisting of a low bench on splayed legs, often with a seat at one end. Cobblers' stools incorporating a partitioned tray for tools and nails on the worker's right-hand[1] (see Plates 78 and 330), sheep-shearing cratches, the long seat-cum-workbench traditionally used by sailmakers and the nailer's anvil horse are typical specimens. Three-legged examples of the same general pattern include marquetry donkeys, the saddler's clamp stool and the shaving horse, mare or brake, fitted with a pedal-operated jaw to hold billets fast while being shaped with a drawing knife[2] (see Plate 11).

Custom has always played an important part in equipping workshops. Thus, to allow complete freedom of movement, basket makers sit on a low platform on the floor, a lap board placed across their knees serving as a bench;[3] for the same reason tailors traditionally sew seated cross-legged on their broad cloth-cutting table (Plate 327), while in Welsh quarries slate splitters used low home-made backstools, the slabs of stone propped against their outstretched legs (Plate 328). In Sheffield file cutters[4] and scythe sharpeners were provided with little stools for working at their anvils and grindstones, while hammermen in the tilt shops sat on suspended seats, which swung freely around the hammer head, when forging blades.[5] Other specialist seating ranges from one-legged stools favoured by some potters working at their wheel, to low apple-sorting chairs — all were designed to facilitate the performance of a particular job.

Charles Tomlinson's copiously illustrated *Cyclopaedia of Useful Arts* (1854), contains an outstanding pictorial record of how trade workshops were equipped at the time. The wood engravings show a profusion of sturdy tables, workbenches, horses and seats, including such novelties as a glass maker's chair with long slanted metal arms 'for rolling the blowing-iron with the hot glass backwards and forwards with the left hand, while the pucellas, held in the right hand, give the glass the required form'.[6] It is clear from Tomlinson's survey that the posture of workmen, whether they stood, or how they sat, was largely a matter of function governed by tradition. The archetypal workshop stool was of high three-legged form (so it could master uneven floors) with a D-shaped slab seat. A fairly late example, from a firm of Lincoln brush makers, eloquently expresses the character of factory furniture; it is made of cheap timber (painted pine) and betrays evidence of hard usage, frequent repairs (later stretchers, nails driven through the socket joints). There is no sign of personal ownership (Plate 329). Cast-iron stools with circular adjustable wooden seats used with Singer sewing machines survive in large numbers.[7]

A charming engraving, published in 1810, of the burnishing shop at the Worcester Porcelain factory shows ten girls seated at work tables on rush-bottomed ladder-back chairs (Plate 331). The bare room, functional furniture and bowed heads indicate that conditions, although more light and airy, were not so different from

327. Tailors made clothes for men and boys and riding habits for ladies. To allow free movement they customarily, when sewing, sat cross-legged on their large cutting-out tables. From *The Book of English Trades* (1806)

328. (*above*) Slate-splitter's stool (*blocyn tîn*) and baitbag from the Dinorwic Quarry workshops, North Wales. The man worked with the block of slate resting against his outstretched legs. *National Museum of Wales*

329. (*below*) A typical workshop stool in pine, the legs painted black; from the premises of Singleton and Flint, brush makers of Lincoln, *c.* 1900. *Museum of Lincolnshire Life*

330. (*Opposite, above*) Late Victorian cobbler's stool, pine with turned beech legs and a leather seat, used by the Tallant family of Leeds who established their business in 1892. *Leeds Museums*

331. (*Opposite, below*) The burnishing shop at the Worcester Porcelain factory, 1810. *Dyson Perrins Museum Trust*

332. (*left*) Burnishing room at the Worcester Porcelain factory, 1881. The original ladder-back chairs have been joined by local spindle backs and the girls work without bonnets; otherwise the scene is much the same. *Dyson Perrins Museum Trust*

those of other artisans. It is one of twelve engravings 'descriptive of the works of the Royal China Manufactory, Worcester' which provide an admirable record of how the various departments were furnished.[8] The later *A Guide Through the Worcester Royal Porcelain Works* (1881), reveals that the burnishing-room had changed little in essentials, although the original ladder-back chairs were supplemented by local spindle backs[9] (Plate 332). Chairs of both patterns are also visible in a workshop photograph dating from *c.* 1900 showing that their height and stability were increased in a rather makeshift way by attaching slabs of wood to the feet[10] (Plate 333). The ladder backs display striking similarities to patterns made by the Kerrys of Evesham between *c.* 1820 and 1850 (see Plate 190).

Regional industrial museums contain growing collections of Victorian factory and workshop furniture, but space allows only a sampling of typical examples from

333. Workshop at the Worcester Porcelain factory, *c.* 1900. The height of the chairs has been increased by fixing slabs of wood to the feet. Strong tables set under windows and plenty of shelving was clearly important. *Dyson Perrins Museum Trust*

334. Burling tables at Bean Ings Mill, Leeds. Bales of cloth were passed over the sloping tops and inspected for small imperfections known as burls. *Courtesy Leeds City Libraries*

West Yorkshire woollen mills. Burling sheds were provided with scores of robust six-foot pine tables, having hinged slope tops and slatted platforms underneath, at which women sat inspecting bales of cloth for small imperfections known as burls and knots; these were picked out with fine irons and the damaged spot then mended (Plate 334). A set of burling-tables from James Ives of Yeadon, now at Armley Mills Museum, Leeds, were probably made by millwrights, because the frames are held together by coach-bolts instead of mortice and tenon joints — a method of construction traditionally used to build looms. Darning bags, sometimes embroidered with a girl's name, are nailed to the tables, while the plank benches are given a homely touch by padding in the form of cloth wound around the back rails and colourful loose seat cushions.

Each weaving shop had an Overlooker's bench, designed rather like a sideboard with two drawers above cupboards in the base, a worktop and rear stage housing racks for spanners and other tools. These plain, oily structures were used by foreman mechanics who serviced the machinery and, by making small adjustments, programmed looms to create different patterns in the cloth. A battered pine specimen is preserved at Bradford Industrial Museum, which also owns once common items such as a belt-mending donkey and bobbin bin. The latter, which bears abundant scars, is in the form of a long narrow trough with profiled slab-ends and three divisions strapped with iron (Plate 335). To cater for different types of loom, operatives needed to keep by their spinning frames various types of pirn to fit different shuttles; hence, compartmented bins were placed on the spinning floor to store the pirns and small bobbins required by cloth manufacturers at the time. Hide containers and small skips on wheels were also used.

A teazle-dressing table from Messrs Wormalds & Walker, blanket manufacturers, Dewsbury, Yorkshire, is very crudely made of bare pine (Plate 336). In use, the top was piled with teazles which needed to have the stems trimmed before the heads were packed in rows and locked into iron frames resting along the front edge. When filled, the rods were mounted on a gig mill which raised the nap on woollen cloth as it passed over rollers. The foregoing examples illustrate the spartan character of factory furniture: bakeries, nail shops, jewellers, printers, confectioners, tailors,

335. Victorian pine bobbin bin from Bradford, Yorkshire, in the form of a trough with divisions strapped with iron. These bins, which held various pirns and small shuttles, stood by spinning frames in woollen mills. *Bradford Museums*

saddlers, button makers, etc., all required their own repertoire of equipment and furniture.[11] This tradition was entirely functional, making no reference to fashionable styles.

The Book of English Trades and Library of the Useful Arts (rev. ed., 1823), conceived as a career book for youngsters, the text illustrated by engravings, is a mine of information about different working environments[12] (Plate 337). These range from an elegant domestic interior with the female members of a family of straw-hat makers busy around a circular tripod table, surrounded by bonnet-stands and hat-boxes, to the apothecary standing at his counter which is decked out with pestle and mortar, pill-rolling slab, scales, treen measures, chopping board, etc., behind which lie nests of drawers and open shelves for storing bottles and canisters (Plate 338). Other instructive plates record a baker working at a big kneading trough with a flat top for shaping his loaves and an engraver confronting a large looking-glass angled above his bench to reflect the image. Many illustrations emphasize the vital importance of good natural daylight for tradesmen such as watchmakers, jewellers

336. Late Victorian pine teazle-dressing table from Messrs Wormalds & Walker, Blanket and Rug Mfrs of Dewsbury, Yorkshire. This class of furniture was often made by millwrights; a drawer beneath the top on the right-hand side is missing. *Bradford Museums*

337. A tin-plate worker making culinary and domestic utensils from tin plates drawn out on a rolling mill. The finished articles are displayed for sale. From *The Book of English Trades* (1823)

338. Apothecaries prepared and sold pills, ointments and drugs used in medicine and administered them either on their own judgement or according to the prescription of a physician. From *The Book of English Trades* (1823)

and tailors, performing fine work; the lacemaker is actually portrayed seated in her garden.

Before the Industrial Revolution many trades, particularly spinning and weaving, were carried on at home as cottage or outwork industries.[13] In weavers' houses bedrooms often doubled up as loom shops, but many home-based tradesmen kept one room as a workshop, although the contents are frequently lumped together by appraisers under the head 'tools and utensils'. Vernacular building research, such as J.C. Timmins's survey *Handloom Weavers' Cottages in Central Lancashire* (1977), can give a useful lead into the subject of domestic workshops. Samuel Bamford's splendidly detailed account of his visit in 1844 to the home of a flannel weaver living near Rochdale is quoted in the chapter on urban workshop-houses (see p. 62). Most cotton weavers worked at cellar or ground-floor level because vegetable fibres needed a damp atmosphere, whereas in the Woollen District of Yorkshire, loom shops were normally on the upper floor where natural light was less restricted; space existed for storage and extra window openings could if necessary be added.[14] When space was severely restricted weavers with large families sometimes built beds on top of the loom frames, creating a sleeping loft. Joiners' account books occasionally mention workshop furniture: in 1845 William Dawson of Otley provided 'a New Work Board for Tailor's shop, wood, making £1. 13s. 6d.'[15] and in 1829 James Pratt of Bubwith, near Howden, charged Philip Richardson for 'a Shoe Makers seat 10s. 6d.';[16] such references are, however, few and far between. It would be possible to multiply descriptions, but hopefully enough has been said to define the essential character of factory and workshop furniture.

18 Offices and Shops

Anyone may be forgiven for assuming that the subject of office furniture is largely devoid of interest, tedious and dull. This negative view, provoked by the often boring nature of office routines, should be resisted, because the history of how small counting houses were replaced by the large-scale departmental offices of late Victorian commerce is an unfairly neglected aspect of the Industrial Revolution. Pictorial and documentary sources reveal how small offices, known as counting houses, were furnished. For example, Thomas Rowlandson's watercolour sketch of 1789, titled *A Merchant's Office*, shows four clerks perched on high stools poring over ledgers lying open on a long double-sided slant-top desk. An oil lamp rests on the flat between the slopes, there are bookshelves on the wall and the owner, seated in an upholstered armchair before a small table, works alongside his staff (Plate 339). This kind of cramped unhealthy setting remained the norm until about 1870, because early workplace legislation applied only to factory premises and was not concerned with improving the conditions endured by thousands of white-collar workers employed by the business and financial community.

An inventory taken in 1760 of the stock-in-trade and furniture on the premises of Paul Saunders, a leading London upholsterer,[1] reveals that the 'Compting House' contained: 'A Mahog. Desk in 2 parts with Frames &c / 2 stools / a Nest of Pigeon Holes by the side of the Desk / a Case for Compting House Books with Partitions / A Wain't Table with a Drawer'. That this was a standard repertoire is confirmed by an inventory made three years later listing items in the office of William Linnell, a rival cabinet maker[2] (Plate 340). The furniture was mostly in painted deal or oak, except for the desk slopes, which it was customary to make from mahogany boards. A well-contrived oak merchant's desk at the Museum of London dating from the early eighteenth century expresses the compact, utility character which came to typify office furniture (Plate 341). The neat façade of letter holes, folio divisions and small drawers is enclosed by double doors above a fall flap, supported, when open, on three sliding lopers. A sale catalogue of contents in the counting house of Captain Jones,[3] the Quay, Bridgnorth, Shropshire (1832), shows that conditions improved little during the next seventy years. The lots included: 'Large and convenient mahogany writing desk / Large painted ditto with drawers / Mahogany Cat / Chest / Capacious bookcase with sliding partitions / Letter racks / Map of England and Wales'. This ensemble is closely similar to the furniture depicted in an engraving of a typical merchant's counting house published in Edward Huzen's *Panorama of Professions and Trades* (Philadelphia, 1837) (Plate 342).

Unfortunately, the subject cannot be advanced very far by studying isolated early survivals; however, much rewarding information about counting-house furniture is contained in the various Price Books issued by London and provincial tradesmen from 1788 onwards. These volumes record in precise detail the agreed labour cost of making routine articles of furniture in common production, and most devote several pages to describing and pricing standard counting-house desks, bookcases and

339. *A Merchant's Office*, watercolour by Thomas Rowlandson, dated 1789. A typical small counting house with the owner working alongside his clerks. *Yale Center for British Art*

340. A cabinet maker in his counting house, anonymous late eighteenth-century oil-painting. The wall unit would have been described at the time as 'a case for compting house books with partitions'. *Trustees of the Victoria and Albert Museum*

212

341. An early eighteenth-century oak merchant's desk; the façade of letter holes, folio divisions and small drawers is enclosed by a fall-front and double doors secured by a single lock. It stands on a much later table. *The Museum of London*

stools. For instance, *The Leeds Cabinet and Chair-Makers Book of Prices* (1791), fixed the piece-work rate for manufacturing two sizes of single and two double-sided desks. The basic labour charge for making 'A Three Feet Six Inches Single desk, all solid, One Flap, square clampt, Three small Drawers in the Inside and Six Letter Holes, no Arches, to stand on a Frame' was calculated at 16s. There follows a list of additional charges for increasing the size, making a pedestal base, and optional extras such as document sliders, a gallery around the top, mitre-clamping the top, etc. The frames were often put together with bed screws to give them added stability. A fine double-sided desk on turned supports, made for the office of the Keswick Pencil Lead Company in about 1840, is now at the Museum of Lakeland Life (Plate 343). The central flat supports a polished brass book rail across which the ledgers were passed for double-checking by the clerk seated opposite. *The Edinburgh Book of Prices for Manufacturing Cabinet-Work* (1821), included costings for a slope-top table desk with lifting handles and a drawer in the end for ink and sand glasses, similar to the one shown in Plate 342.

The Cabinet-Makers' London Book of Prices (1793), is one of many that gives a specification and breakdown of costs for making a typical counting-house bookcase: 'Three feet long, and three feet high to the top of the cornice, the ends nine inches wide, two flat-pannel'd doors, the panel plow'd in . . . 13s. 6d.'. There follows a scale

342. The junior clerks in this counting house were expected to stand at their desk; the master has a small slope-top table desk and a comfortable chair. From E. Huzen, *Panorama of Professions and Trades* (1837). *Courtesy Indiana State Museum*

213

343. Double-sided counting-house desk of *c.* 1840 from the Keswick Pencil Lead Company, Cumbria. Mahogany top, the central flat was for inkwells, the brass posts and rails to park ledgers on. *Museum of Lakeland Life, Abbot Hall, Kendal*

of charges for internal fittings and optional refinements according to the customer's requirements. These include 'Each shelf across the book-case 8d. / Each upright ditto for books 5d. / Scolloping ditto, each 2d. / Each letter hole 4½d. / Each plain arch 1½d. / Each drawer not exceeding twelve inches long or three inches deep 1s.' and so forth. Cabinet makers did not engage in the production of seat furniture, so it is necessary to turn to a related publication, *The London Chair-Makers' and Carvers' Book of Prices for Workmanship* (1802), to discover that the basic cost of 'Framing a counting-house stool, (either square or to spread) with square or turn'd legs, straight seat-rails, four lower rails, and open braces; height of the seat from twenty-two to thirty-six inches' was reckoned to be 2s. 5d. Each extra lower rail cost 2d. and an additional charge was incurred 'if the end rails be framed on the slope', while tapering each leg on two sides cost 1½d. A Regency period desk stool converted by the addition of a back, arms and castors into a child's hanging chair, is illustrated in Plate 298. High stools were not always provided and junior clerks often had to stand at their desks[4] (see Plate 342).

As commerce expanded so the amount of paperwork increased; but change was slow to come and 'sombre little counting houses, with a table in the centre, a raised desk where a clerk may sit on a high stool, some cupboards and an iron safe built in the wall', as described in Mortimer's *Mercantile Manchester* (Manchester, 1896), persisted well into the present century (Plate 345). An authentic suite of offices created about 1820 for two clerks and a book-keeper survives at Quarry Bank Mill, now an industrial site museum at Styal in Cheshire. The outer office, with an adjoining waiting-room and communicating with the manager's sanctum, retains many original fittings and furnishings which consist of two slope desks with mahogany tops on soft wood frames set under the windows, several high stools, wall-mounted ledger racks, timber filing cabinets, built-in book cupboards, drawers, open shelving and a number of iron safes. All the woodwork is grained. The inner office has flat-top partners' desk, comfortable chairs, bookcases, a clock and appropriate status symbols. Another well-preserved Victorian clerk's office is to be found at the Llanberis Quarry Museum in Wales, while the astonishingly cramped and gloomy office of Robert Hall & Sons, Textile Machine Manufacturers of Bury, has been reinstated at the Higher Mill Museum, Helmshaw, Lancashire. The space, partitioned by timber and frosted-glass screens, accommodates double-sided counting-house desks with brass book rails, clerks' stools, book cupboards, safes, a telephone booth and a time clock. This depressing environment, dating from about 1900, illustrates a phase of transition between small counting houses and large well-ordered modern offices where traditional furnishings and procedures were replaced by specialist equipment and new systems.

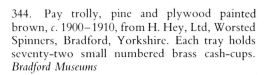

344. Pay trolly, pine and plywood painted brown, c. 1900–1910, from H. Hey, Ltd, Worsted Spinners, Bradford, Yorkshire. Each tray holds seventy-two small numbered brass cash-cups. *Bradford Museums*

Two plates in Pugin and Rowlandson's *Microcosm of London* (1808), show how the Stamp Office at Somerset House and the Post Office were furnished — although these interiors are not typical except in so far as they are staffed exclusively by men. Few women were employed in commerce before the rapid late Victorian expansion of offices provided a range of low-status typist and telephonist jobs for females.[5] Although steamship companies, insurance firms, banks and the railways employed thousands of white-collar workers,[6] very little of the furniture used in their offices during the last century survives. Much of it was of course built-in. A few solid Victorian items made for the London Merchant Banking House of Barings still exist,[7] and venerable pieces sometimes survive in wayside railway stations, but the losses have been enormous. A once familiar, but now utterly obsolete article, is the 'omnibus' or pay trolley. An Edwardian example, from H. Hey Ltd, Worsted Spinners, Bradford, Yorkshire, is of painted pine and resembles a chest of shallow drawers mounted on two cast-iron wheels; each drawer contains a plywood tray fitted with seventy-two small numbered brass cash-cups (Plate 344). The trolley was wheeled around the factory on Fridays when the mill operatives, on production of a tally, collected their wages — the empty cups being dropped down a chute into a lockable compartment below as tacit acknowledgment that the amount was correct.

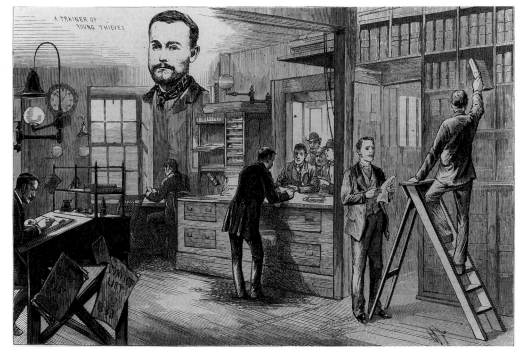

345. The convict office at Scotland Yard for ticket-of-leave men under police supervision. A fine record of an unmodernized Victorian office in use. *Illustrated London News* (1883)

This procedure ensured that a minimum of working time was lost during the distribution of wages. It would be hard to find a better instance of a once practical but now quaintly archaic item of office furniture.

It was not until the last quarter of the nineteenth century that firms specializing in the manufacture of office furniture were established. Educational suppliers, who catered for the huge demands created by the government school building programme, sprung up in large numbers at about the same time and some of them produced both types of furniture. This was the great age of exhibitions and innovation, and late Victorian office furniture reflects a sharply competitive world of ingenious patented designs, labour-saving equipment and multi-purpose furniture, each firm claiming that their improved models were the most efficient, versatile or elaborately styled on the market. Many of these new ideas were introduced from America where business men seem first to have appreciated the need for orderly systems to cope with the massive growth in paperwork. An aristocrat in the American office was the Wooton Cabinet Secretary incorporating 'everything that ingenuity can suggest or devise to facilitate desk labour'; it was, the makers further claimed, 'a MINIATURE COUNTING-HOUSE, with a combination of such conveniences as are found best adapted for the manipulation of office work, and these *all under one lock and key*'. A range of ostentatiously splendid Wooton desks was available in various expensive woods and they are now prized collectors' items.[8]

It is unlikely that quite such extravagant desks were ever made in England, but they inspired a more professional attitude towards the design of office furniture in this country, where the roll-top desk became widely popular. Superior models manufactured by W. Angus & Co., London, in oak, walnut or mahogany, cost up to £45 each in 1905[9] (Plate 346). Special features included a stationery rack, a letter file and movable partitions in the pedestal drawers; a letter-drop near the top of the roll; extension slides; a leather lining to the writing bed; an automatic central locking mechanism, plus numerous pigeon-hole pockets, small drawers and book spaces. A model with a special low roll was available which 'allows an unobstructed view where oversight of an office is required'. Besides offering thirty-two patterns of desk, the 1905 Angus trade catalogue illustrated a range of typewriter tables; various grades of boardroom table; traditional single and double-sided slant-top

346. An extra choice grade 'Angus' roll-top office desk available in finely figured oak, walnut or mahogany, *c.* 1905. *Leeds Art Galleries*

clerks' and book-keepers' standing desks with brass rails; revolving bookcases; office wash-stands; wardrobes; umbrella stands and copying presses. The firm published separate catalogues devoted to filing cabinets, office chairs and their newly patented 'Gunn' sectional bookcase.[10]

Shannon Ltd, Office Fitting Experts of London, with branches in six large cities, published a bumper general catalogue about 1910, which is prefaced by a humorous drawing of a chaotic Dickensian counting house opposite a photograph of a well-laid out modern Shannon office.[11] The contrast in working environments, although exaggerated, makes a valid point. The catalogue illustrates an impressive array of roll-top desks fitted with rotary ends; a range of revolving and tilting chairs; adjustable typists' seats and various office stools. Imposing cabinets with decorative crestings and a many-tiered façade of file drawers for storing documents flat now appear unbelievably cumbersome (Plate 347), but Shannon also supplied modern-looking vertical filing systems in polished timber or cold rolled and pickled steel cabinets with a japanned finish. The latter material, it was pointed out, protected valuable papers 'not only against the ravages of fire but in Eastern climes against such destructive vermin as the white ant'.

Shops

John Evelyn wrote in his *Diary* that the Restoration of the Monarchy 'brought in a politer way of living which soon passed to luxury and intolerable expense'.[12] He was referring to court circles, but an increase in prosperity was felt throughout English society, one symptom being the appearance of village shops which stocked a much wider range of goods than travelling chapmen were able to carry. As country shopkeepers multiplied so farmers became less dependent on market towns, local craftsmen and domestic skills to supply their needs. This change in trading patterns is reflected in scores of inventories. M.W. Barley claims that the village shopkeeper 'set in train a revolution in living standard and domestic comforts, and so contributed to new modes of thought and behaviour in which medieval survivals could not flourish'.[13]

A comparison of the basic mercery and haberdashery wares left by Elizabeth Lawrence, chapwomen by Donington, Lincolnshire, in 1672,[14] with the astonishingly diverse stock of two shopkeepers active in the 1690s, underlines this change in the retail trade. The splendidly detailed inventory of Joshua Johnson, who lived at Wellington, Salop, and died in 1659,[15] reveals that he stocked an extensive range of cloth, tape, ribbons, buttons and thread. Also ink-horns, paper, card, bibles, school books, various spices, sugar, salt, hosiery, curtain rings, herrings, soap, candles, tobacco, spirits, etc. Joseph Clarke, grocer and draper of Roxwell, Essex (d. 1692),[16] stocked very similar goods, but also sold dyestuffs, snuff, nails, brooms, gunpowder and shot, mouse-traps, bedcords, pipes and corks. If there was no apothecary nearby, general mercers often supplied drugs and medicines as well. A census of inventories[17] suggests than Johnson and Clarke were fully typical of shopkeepers descended from the chapman tradition and precursors of the general store.

Shopkeepers usually had a front shop for serving customers and an inner or back shop for warehousing or, in the case of craftsmen, a workroom. Joshua Johnson's premises contained three counters, one of which was boxed in and fitted with six drawers, there were also two nests of drawers, eleven deal and oak boxes, a press, a set of five drawers, pewter measures and three scales with brass weights. In 1725 Daniel Bridges, an Essex grocer,[18] stored his merchandise in drawers, tin canisters, pots, bottles, boxes and casks or on shelves. The appraisers noted 'the nest of drawers containing small quantety of severall sort of things amounts to 11s. 7d.; sugar and plumbs in the drawers under the counter, 10s. 9d.'. A mezzotint published by Carington Bowles of about 1770, titled *The Chandler's Shop Gossips or*

347. A sixty-drawer 'Shannon' filing cabinet with raised veneered panels and hand-carved fancy cornice, c. 1910. Cabinets containing 120 drawers were also available in oak, walnut or mahogany. *Leeds Art Galleries*

348. *The Chandler's Shop Gossips*, mezzotint, published *c.* 1770. A marvellous shop print showing counter, nest of drawers, shelves for cheese and canisters, ham and candles hanging. *Colonial Williamsburg Foundation*

349. Confectioner's shop where comfits, jams, jellies, candies, sugarplums, gingerbread and pastries of various kinds were sold. *The Book of English Trades* (1823)

Wonderful News, provides a marvellous record of a shop interior (Plate 348). It portrays a small uncarpeted room cheered by a fire, chimney ornaments and a picture over the mantlepiece; a slicer and chopping block rest on the counter which is backed by a large nest of drawers. A ham and bunches of candles hang on one side, the other being occupied by a glazed corner cupboard containing canisters, while cheeses and a storage jar are displayed on an open shelf. 'Dame Prattle' the shopkeeper is shown clutching a pair of scales and talking to 'Doll Drab' whose dress is about to catch fire, meanwhile 'Jack Filch' purloins a pile of coin on the counter. *The Book of English Trades* (rev. ed., 1823) illustrates many typical shop scenes; the Apothecary (see Plate 338), and the Confectioner (Plate 349), show particularly interesting arrangements with a high stool and chair for the convenience of customers. Other tradesmen, such as the Clockmaker and Tin-plate worker, are depicted in their workrooms with wares ranged around the walls, no counter being provided (see Plate 337).

A mid-nineteenth-century account book kept by James Brumfitt, general cabinet maker of Skipton in Yorkshire, contains several references to fitting-up shops.[19] A typical entry, dated 18 February 1856, relates to Mrs Phillip of Embsay who commissioned a 'Bing [dresser with shelves]; Nest of 24 Drawers; Counter; 4 Shelves; Desk and Sign Board'. William Dawson of Otley, joiner, provided similar fixtures to William Todd in 1845:[20]

To a new Counter & fitting up for shop	1	2	0
Fitting up board at end of counter for scales to rest on		1	3
To a Nest of Drawers for shop		19	0
Pin Rail, Railing and shelf for Windows		10	0
A new Desk for Counter		8	3
Drawers making and fitting up in Counter		10	9
A rail and fitting up to hang Bacon on		1	3

Much the same picture emerges from an inventory and valuation of John Rayner's

218

shop in Harrogate, compiled by John Dacre in 1860:[21] 'Long Counter 4 Drawers with Mahogany Top / Counter of 2 Drawers / Cupboard with flap Drawers / Nest of Drawers / Shelves and bearers / Rack and Iron Holdfasts / Large Store Canisters / Scales & Weights / Chair and Stool'. The last item may have been a step-stool, used to reach high shelves (Plate 350).

Co-ordinating evidence from late seventeenth-century inventories, Georgian pictorial sources and early Victorian accounts, suggests that shop fittings were remarkably static except for the introduction of a desk for writing, keeping papers and perhaps serving as a till. An old-fashioned rustic shop at Shere in Surrey, sketched in 1885,[22] illustrates many traditional features (Plate 351), although by this date commercial firms specializing in fitting-up shops existed in most large towns, offering a stylish range of professionally designed shop fronts, counters with elaborately carved trusses, impressive wall fixtures and smart show cases. Typical late Victorian shop interiors have been re-erected in many regional museums of community life.

CORN EXCHANGES

Pugin and Rowlandson's *Microcosm of London* (1808), contains a fine interior view of the corn exchange opened in Mark Lane in 1804. The caption to this plate explains: 'There are fifty boxes or stands which let from fourteen to twenty guineas per annum. The corn factors each have a kind of desk before him on which are several handfulls of corn, and from these small samples are every market day sold many thousand quarters'. Magnificent corn exchanges were built in many cities and towns during Victorian days, although most are now empty or serve different purposes. The vast trading halls were copiously furnished with matching sets of desk-stands for the factors, and those which survive are capital examples of batch-produced commercial furniture (Plate 353).

The *Illustrated London News* of 1 April 1851 published a view of the busy new corn exchange at Northampton with, down each side, a long row of table desks on turned legs designed with a shallow well for corn at the front, a raised central till and a flat top behind for doing paper work; there was no seating. The same magazine portrayed in its issue of 16 April 1859, the Sleaford corn exchange, featuring box-like

350. Oak step-stool, used in shops for reaching high shelves, probably early nineteenth century. *Bradford Museums*

351. This view of a shop at Shere, Surrey, featured in a series of Rustic Interiors published by the *Illustrated London News* (1885)

stands with tray tops and writing slopes. A very powerfully designed and strongly made desk from Bury St Edmunds corn exchange, built between 1861 and 1862, is now in the Norfolk Rural Life Museum (Plate 352), which also owns examples from Norwich and Beccles. The last user was a merchant from Diss, his painted name board being displayed on the front above the corn tray; the factor stood on a low platform base with a narrow perching seat on the left-hand side. It is constructed of oak stained black, with pine drawer linings.

The Leeds corn exchange, built by Cuthbert Broderick in 1864 housed, until very recently, scores of black-painted table desks with hinged flaps, trays and the unusual feature of screw-in posts which, when erected, support a raised ledge; and when collapsed were stowed in the deep frame and securely locked away with the merchant's books, papers, cash, ink, pens, etc. Some corn-exchange desks may have been architect-designed, but whoever conceived them, they nevertheless make a memorable statement about the functional qualities and original character of the best Victorian institutional furniture. It could be claimed that just as in the 1930s manufacturers often responded with innovative brilliance to the challenge of designing wireless sets, so their predecessors reacted in equally versatile ways to the challenge of devising these corn-merchants' desks for which no precedent existed.

AUCTION ROOMS

The interiors of Georgian auction rooms can best be pursued in prints and drawings of the period.[23] Thomas Rowlandson's coloured aquatint of Dr Syntax at a book auction, published in 1820, is probably an actual view of the premises of Robert Saunders, the founder of Hodgson's. It shows a large book-lined room with a few paintings hung on the walls and some works of art displayed on a shelf; the floor is occupied by a long narrow table arranged around four sides of a square at which the bidders are seated. The auctioneer sits in a large chair at one end next to his clerk. A similar scene, but with a big oval table and a continuous fixed form around the outside, is represented in another Rowlandson watercolour dating from the late

352. One of the original stained-oak corn-factor's desks from Bury St Edmunds corn exchange, Norfolk, built 1861–2. *Norfolk Museums Service*

353. Norwich corn exchange (built 1863); the locker desks, raised on platforms, have a seat at the side and a corn tray in front. *Norfolk Museums Service*

eighteenth century; here the auctioneer is standing at a rostrum to command the room (Plate 354). Other views portray the clerk seated at an elevated desk and often an easel on which the painting being offered for sale was exhibited. Christie's auction rooms in Pall Mall are featured in Pugin and Rowlandson's *Microcosm of London* (1808); they moved in 1823 to their present King Street address, and a painting by J. Gebgaud of a fashionable picture sale held there in 1828 shows a much grander interior with glass chandeliers, carpets on the floor and comfortable chairs.

354. *The Auction Room*, watercolour by Thomas Rowlandson, late eighteenth century, showing a typical rostrum and seating-plan of the period. *Yale Center for British Art*

19 Railway Premises

Railway literature contains disappointingly little information about the original furnishings of platforms, ticket and parcels offices, waiting-rooms, signal-boxes, goods depots, porters' lamp-rooms or lineside cabins. Important stations were ostentatiously splendid with 1st, 2nd, 3rd Class and Ladies' waiting-rooms, large booking halls, palatial refreshment-rooms and numerous offices. On the other hand, wayside stations were often built of local materials in familiar architectural styles and provided with robust functional furniture which displays its own character and deserves to be treated as an independent sub-group.

The National Railway Museum at York has assembled dozens of substantial platform and waiting-room benches inscribed with the initials of long defunct companies or bearing station names. One of the most striking, from Yarmouth South Town, has a painted cast-iron frame ornamented in low relief with fish and shells against a fish-net ground (Plate 356). Some companies incorporated their monogram in the openwork design of cast-iron bench ends, 'GWR' and 'GER' being amongst the most familiar; platform seats on the Caledonian Railway combined an interlaced 'CRC' and a thistle, while those on the Furness Railway which skirts the Lake District, featured a squirrel amongst vines.

Waiting-room seats were often contructed of painted or stained and varnished hardwood with heavy turned legs and stuffed-over seats covered in leather cloth or horsehair; some were lettered along the back with initials such as 'MS & LR' (Manchester, Sheffield and Lincolnshire Railway) or 'O I J R' (Otley and Ilkley Joint Railway; Plate 357). The degree of comfort depended on the importance of the station or the class of passenger. Waiting-rooms at country halts were generally provided only with plain wall seats and possibly a centre-table, while at the other extreme, accommodation for 1st Class ticket-holders at a large station might include a carpet, leather sofas, armchairs, an umbrella stand, and travelling rugs. At Garsdale, a remote station on the Settle–Carlisle line, the waiting-room contained an harmonium and a bookcase for the occasions when it served the local farming community as a chapel and lending library;[1] on rural lines, station buildings not infrequently became a social centre akin to a village hall. There is evidence that some big companies designed and made passenger seats themselves; the Great Western, for instance, relied on their carriage shops at Swindon to cast the iron supports, construct timber frames and do upholstery work.[2] A census would doubtless identify different company styles and chart developments in design.

Rowley Station in Co. Durham, built in 1867 and now re-erected at Beamish Open Air Museum, is a typical example of mid-Victorian wayside railway architecture. The Ladies' waiting-shelter has fixed wall seating, a centre-table and the original closet. The combined booking-clerk's and parcels office contains a complete range of fitted and loose furniture, creating a cosy interior with a comfortable fireside (Plates 358–9). The fixtures include an L-shaped counter with cupboards and cash drawers, a wall-mounted ticket-rack enclosed by an upwards-sliding shutter, a shelf unit with vertical ledger divisions, a nest of pigeon holes

356. Victorian platform seat with appropriately decorative cast-iron ends. *National Railway Museum, York*

357. Station seat, painted brown, the back rail incised 'O & IJR' (Otley and Ilkley Joint Railway, opened 1865). *National Railway Museum, York*

355. *(opposite)* Signal man's chair from Leek Brook Junction box on the North Staffordshire Railway. *National Railway Museum, York*

for luggage labels and a notice-board. There is also a writing-table, stool, two smoker's bows, a wash-stand, mirror and office requisites. The booking office at Monkwearmouth (now a site museum), which dates from 1866, is larger and more impressive, although the internal arrangements are very similar. The woodwork of both interiors is grained. Plans of stations, although seldom informative as regards furniture, at least show the disposition of buildings and confirm that a huge demand existed for furniture to equip goods depots with their associated locker-rooms, weighbridge house, offices and warehouses; freight departments once generated as much revenue as passenger traffic. An oak slope-topped clerical desk, designed like an outsize davenport with a spindle gallery, now at the National Railway Museum, is known to have been used by a stores superintendant on the Stockton and Darlington Railway (Plate 360).

The workshop books of Owen Fitzpatrick, employed by Pryce and Delany, cabinet makers of Birkenhead, document some basic office furniture made for the Wirral Railway Company in 1884–5.[3] They commissioned a 'Drawing Table . . . with Bible front Supported on 6 Square legs framed with cross bottom rails and put together with bedscrews' and a 'Screen for end of drawing table 7ft high 5ft wide with 2 wood Panels at bottom and 2 glass Panels at top'. They also ordered a large deal press having sliding doors in the upper stage and an arrangement of trays and drawers with flush handles below. Other specifications are for towering pitch pine cupboards incorporating shelves, pigeon holes, a fall front desk, sliding trays, etc. These and similar entries provide a brief insight into the kind of functional furniture which Railway Companies required in vast quantities.

The National Railway Museum has an impressive array of well-provenanced Victorian tables and chairs from stations, railway hotels, refreshment-rooms, buffet cars and offices. Most are well finished and reflect popular period styles; they can be described as respectable rather than fashionable (Plate 362). Stained beech, birch, oak, elm and cheap mahogany were the favourite woods. Nearly all display company emblems or initials either decoratively carved (Plate 361), inlaid or painted on the backs or impressed under the rails. For instance, a basic balloon back chair is stamped 'L Y R' (Leeds and York Railway) and bears a metal tab inscribed 'Goods Yard Leeds'; a few even retain maker's trade labels. The museum also houses a

360. A late Victorian stores superintendant's desk from Stooperdale Locomotive Works, Darlington. *National Railway Museum, York*

361. Detail of a mid-nineteenth-century oak table in the Gothic style, the frieze carved 'NSR' (North Staffordshire Railway). *National Railway Museum, York*

362. (*far left*) Oak balloon-back chair, carved 'B & E' (Bristol & Exeter Railway). A sturdy version of a popular Victorian design. *National Railway Museum, York*

363. (*left*) This late Victorian elm armchair is of a type widely used in offices and signal-cabins; the back is carved 'LB & SC' (London Brighton & South Coast Ryl.). *National Railway Museum, York*

358 and 359. Two views of the combined booking-clerk's and parcels office at Rowley, Co. Durham — a typical wayside station built in 1867, now re-erected at the North of England Open Air Museum, Beamish.

364. The signal-box at London Bridge Station staffed by a signal man, a registering clerk and a telegraph clerk. *Illustrated London News* (1866)

collection of the invalid chairs which were provided by many companies at large stations. A wicker example by Carters, New Cavendish Street, London, is typical (Plate 365). Stretcher trolleys and coffin carriages were also available on some platforms.

Signal-boxes offer an interesting field of study; the one from Rowley is furnished with a high-backed fireside settle, a table, smoker's bow and slope-top desk with companion stool. The Darlington Museum owns an oak corner chair of traditional late Georgian pattern, but betraying Victorian details, from the Bowes box on the Stainmore line where there were sidings and the signal man needed to turn both ways. Well before the end of the century, corner chairs had been replaced by rounded smoker's bows (Plate 363). Good visibility was vitally important, and a blue-print of a standard L M S brick and timber signal-cabin at Kilmalcolm in the Scottish division,[4] shows the postition of the signal lever frame and wheel for operating level-crossing gates; the desk is located in a small projecting bay-window, so the man on duty could look up and down the line while making entries in his train journal; a long locker seat stood near the stove. Major stations such as London Bridge had large, lavishly equipped and well-staffed boxes (Plate 364).

A spectacular signal man's chair, of framed panel construction painted crimson lake, survives from Leek Brook Junction box on the North Staffordshire Railway (Plate 355). This unusually capacious chair, intended to protect incumbents from draughts which rose through holes in the cabin floor, was deemed by the Inspecting Officer to have contributed to a night collision at Stoke Station in February 1872.[5] He reported:

> When visiting the cabins at the North and South ends of the station (which are large and comfortable cabins), I observed in each cabin a large armchair with high back and sides and cushioned seat. The sides of the armchair have glass windows so that the signal man while enjoying himself may look right and left. I submit it is not desirable that such comfortable means should be provided for the men to go to sleep on duty and I recommend the chairs should be removed at once.

Happily, at least one of these chairs survived at Leek Brook Junction until L M S days, and was eventually acquired for the nation.

365. Invalid carriage chairs were formerly available at many large stations; this one was supplied by Carters, New Cavendish Street, London. *National Railway Museum, York*

226

20 Army Barracks and Campaign Furniture

The English Army was slow to accept direct responsibility for providing quarters for soldiers. By the early eighteenth century barracks were few, small and scattered, the majority of regular troops being billeted in tiny detachments in inns, livery stables and victualling houses. For political reasons Ireland and Scotland were comparatively heavily garrisoned, so in these territories the Army was compelled to build or rent barracks. After the 1715 rebellion, £9,300 was voted for extra accommodation, the estimates allowing for five beds per room, each bed sleeping two men. An English military dictionary of 1702 described barracks as 'A hut like a little Cottage, for Soldiers to lie in the Camp. They are generally made by fixing four strong forked Poles in the ground, and laying four others across them; then they build the Walls with Wattles, or Sods, such as the Place affords. The Top is either thatched, if there be straw to spare, or covered with Planks or sometimes with Turf'.[1] These temporary hovels probably contained only makeshift beds, but the stream of complaints about the permanent barracks, where they existed, suggest living conditions were not much better.

As the size of the Army increased some new barracks were built by the Board of Ordnance; the largest, at Fort George, Inverness-shire, was designed by William Skinner in 1748 for 1,600 men. It followed the traditional prison-like, three-storey courtyard plan encircled by a high wall; the men's quarters contained little furniture, other than four double beds per room. However in the Ravelin Guardhouse a sloped sleeping platform was constructed against the long wall, on which palliasses could be laid out.[2] Officers were provided with individual rooms and closets. Before the major barrack-building programme which started in 1793 and continued throughout the Napoleonic Wars, it has been estimated that in all the forts and barracks, dormitory accommodation existed for about 20,000 soldiers.[3]

Documentary or pictorial evidence about how eighteenth-century barrack-rooms were furnished is scarce. The Army Regulations of 1785 contain instructions to Barrack-Masters respecting the issue of kitchen utensils,[4] but it is not until after 1794, when a Barrack-Master General was appointed, that a clearer picture emerges. According to John Williamson, author of *A Treatise on Military Finance* (1796), the following articles were supplied to every room occupied by eight men: 'bedsteads, mattresses, blankets, sheets, rugs, round towel, table, racks for arms, fire-irons, iron pots, pot hooks, iron trivets, ladels, flesh fork, frying pan, grid-iron, large bowls or platters, small bowls or porringers, trenchers, spoons, water bucket, coal tray, bellows, candlestick, tin can of three gallons, large earthen pan for meat, basket for coals, drinking horns, earthen chamber pots, broom and mop'. Officers' rooms were 'furnished with a table, two chairs, a coal box, coal tray, bellows, fire-irons and fender'.[5] The notion of a basic barrack-room kit had evidently arrived. By 1805 troops were concentrated at over 200 stations, barracks were still being put up after Waterloo and these buildings provided the regular quarters of the Victorian Army. What was to become a familiar barrack-room pattern of closely ranked individual beds lining each wall, and a common dining-table with forms in the centre, was a

366. Interior of a barrack-room at the Royal Military Academy, Woolwich, 1810. Notice the range of lockers, the turn-up beds and the cadet at his 'Woolwich' trunk.

367. Soldiers' recreation-room at Aldershot camp from the *Illustrated London News* (1868). The army purchased large quantities of Windsor chairs, always specifying that they be made from riven timber.

legacy of the Napoleonic Wars. In the absence of married hostels, wives and children were forced to share these cramped quarters, a small sleeping area often being separated off by means of a blanket thrown over a rope.

A coloured print showing the interior of barrack-room at the Royal Military Academy, Woolwich, in 1810, allows a glimpse of the furnishings and (rather superior) standard of comfort available to ensigns at the time[6] (Plate 366). The lofty, flagged room with plaster crumbling off bare walls, has a coal-tub beside the hob-grate which is equipped with fire-irons, a cooking pot and fender. Two beds headed by valanced half-testers, suspended from hooks in the ceiling, are visible; one is shown folded away against the wall with the curtains drawn around it. A plain dining-table stands in front of the partly shuttered window, there are ordinary square-framed stools, a small wash-stand, a hat rail and a large fixed locker for storing utensils. One cadet is busy at his 'Woolwich trunk', the 'Neux' is at his cupboard going for water; personal touches include a wicker bird cage and two caricatures over the hearth.

A growing public concern for the welfare of troops, prompted by the Crimean War, was reflected in books and magazines. The *Illustrated London News* (12 May 1855), published engravings of barrack interiors and Officers' huts at Aldershot, while George Godwin's *Town Swamps and Social Bridges* (1859), describes various London barracks. Most soldiers still lived in over-crowded, ill-ventilated dormitories, which served both for sleeping and eating. At some barracks, a separate cookhouse and dining-room were provided, while regimental recreation-rooms (Plate 367) and schools to teach children and adults were not unknown.[7] The Guard-

368. The Guard-room, Portman Street barracks, at night, 1859. Inclined sleeping platforms were an old established feature of barrack-rooms. *Courtesy Westminster City Libraries*

228

369. Sale of a deserter's kit in army barracks. *Illustrated London News* (1875). At this date, soldiers ate and slept in barracks, the furniture is all standard issue.

room at Portman-street had a traditional inclined sleeping platform with wooden boxes, 'like those in the casual wards of workhouse', for the men of rest upon[8] (Plate 368). During the post-Crimea period, photographs offer an increasingly valuable record of Army life. The picture of a typical barrack which emerges shows a long room closely lined with iron bedsteads which fold back to create more space, and provide a row of comfortable seats (Plate 369). Each bed is normally shown with a kit shelf and peg board at the head and an Army-issue wooden chest parked under the foot, while a central gangway is occupied by dining-tables and forms raised on cast-iron supports[9] (Plate 370).

Thomas Sheraton's *The Cabinet Dictionary*, published in 1803 at the height of the French Wars, includes an interesting section on camp furniture, which was then in great demand from soldiers on active service. Such articles, he observed, 'required

370. Royal Irish Regiment barrack-room of other ranks laid out for inspection, *c.* 1898. Notice the *trompe l'oeil* painted chimney-piece. *National Army Museum*

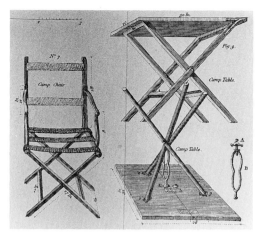

371. A camp chair and two tables from Thomas Sheraton's *Cabinet Dictionary* (1803). Campaign furniture was designed to fold up and lie flat.

372. Station life in Burma from a photograph by A.G. Newland, *Illustrated London News* (1891). The Army and Navy Co-operative Society Catalogue, 1908 (under Furniture Bombay Depot), records that the 'Ratnagiri' chair shown in the foreground cost £1. and weighed 28 lbs.

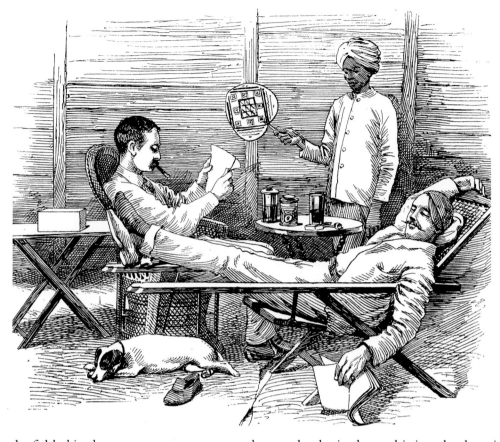

373. Campaign trunk dated 1797 which belonged to Robert Dalrymple of the 3rd Foot Guards, killed at Talavera, 1809. The maker's label of J. Pritt, Lancaster, is pasted under the lid. *Trustees of the National Museums of Scotland*

374. This postcard of *c.* 1910 illustrates the standard of comfort enjoyed by army officers in the field. *C.G. Gilbert*

to be folded in the most compact manner that can be devised; yet this is to be done in such a way as, that when they are opened out, they will answer their intended purpose . . . most of the things which are of this nature, will also suit a cabin or sea voyage'. Sheraton described and illustrated camp or field bedsteads, camp chairs, desks, stools and tables (Plate 371). This was a highly competitive market and many ingenious pieces of compact campaigning furniture were patented by firms such as Morgan & Sanders, Thomas Butler and William Pocock. Being intended for Officers they were generally made of mahogany with brass-bound corners, recessed handles and similar refinements, so strictly fall outside this survey.[10] The National Army Museum has a small collection of trunks (Plate 373), writing-boxes, folding chairs, tripod wash-stands and patent collapsible military beds with sail-cloth bottoms used by Officers in the field.[11] Ordinary soldiers on campaign improvised furniture from whatever was lying around such as tree branches, ammunition boxes or planks. Lt Richard Goodman, 5th Dragoon Guards, wrote home from the Crimea in 1854: 'I have got a small table and camp stool made by the artillery wheeler, which makes me much more comfortable'.[12] After the Crimean War, Army General Orders laid down the maximum sizes for brass-bound chests of drawers and imposed weight restrictions on baggage. Heal & Son's first trade catalogue (1848), illustrates portable tubular iron bedsteds intended for Officers on foreign service; in fact, troops in India often enjoyed a higher standard of comfort than those at home. The *Report of the Kabul Committee on Equipment* (Calcutta, 1882), considered the question of camp furniture for Officers, reproducing approved patterns of beds, tables and chairs. As the Army and the Empire it ruled expanded, an increasingly diverse repertoire of camp furniture became available. One of the most comprehensive pictorial sources from this period is the massive Army and Navy Co-operative Society Ltd *Bombay Depot Catalogue* (1908),[13] although it must be conceded that, while fascinating, the line drawings and text lack the human interest of records showing soldiers using camp furniture in the field (Plates 372 and 374).

21 Bothies, Chaumers and Mine Shops

The bothy system grew up in the early 1800s on big farms in the arable districts of Scotland and north-east England, where large numbers of unmarried agricultural labourers were hired annually in return for their board and lodging, plus a cash wage. Although harvest bothies for female farm workers were sometimes established, maid servants invariably continued to live in the farmhouse. The typical bothy was a sparsely furnished barrack-like shed or loft over stables where the men both ate and slept. The farmer gave them rations of milk, oatmeal and potatoes which they cooked themselves. Bothies earned a reputation for being comfortless and squalid, especially in the Lothians where farms were large (Plate 375). A series of newspaper reports on 'The Scottish Peasantry' includes a description of a bothy in 'a dilapidated biggin' near Kerriemuir, Forfarshire:[1]

> The fire, which presented the appearance of having been a 'roaring' one, was being allowed to die out, and two or three of the men were lounging leisurely on the form in front of it, awaiting the call from the foreman. Ranged along the back wall were three box beds, the clothes in which were lying just as the sleepers had left them. In front of these were four chests and a couple of rickety old chairs – rareities in a bothy – while two other chests were placed along the end wall near the furthest off bed from the fireplace. From a strap of wood on the end wall above these chests hung an array of wearing apparel, consisting of trousers, jackets, &c. Immediately opposite the fireplace, near the end wall, lay a heap of hagwood or small tree branches, while a bing of coals occupied the front corner, and between these and the door were a slop pail and a tin basin. The space at the opposite side of the door was occupied by the indispensable pot and a bucket containing clean water, the corner next the fire being taken up by a rude looking table, which it was explained was never used at meal times. A small paraffin lamp was hung above the fireplace, while the shelves on either side of it contained a miscellaneous cargo of all sorts of articles. The floor, which was laid with flagstones, was in a frightfully dirty state.

By the end of the century, cooking and cleaning might be done by a 'bothy-maid' and conditions had improved greatly when the system eventually died out about 1940.

Smaller farmers, particularly in the north-east Lowlands of Scotland and in Yorkshire, preferred the chaumer system, whereby labourers ate their meals in the farm kitchen and enjoyed a customary right to sit by the fire until 9 o'clock, when they retired to the chaumer or mens' room in the steading. These dormitories were very like the bothies, except that the farmhands did not have to cook for themselves. A bothy which William Cobbett saw near Dunfermline, in 1832, was a bare room measuring 16 by 18 feet with a door and one window. It had an earth floor and contained three beds to sleep six men, six brose-bowls, a large iron cooking pot, ten bushels of coal piled in a corner and a heap of loose potatoes under one of the

375. A typical bothy interior, Angus, 1906–14. One man perches on his lodging box, the other two are seated on a bench, they each have a *cappie* or brose-bowl. *Courtesy National Museums of Scotland*

376. These lads are seated on a bothy bench (Perthshire) with their most treasured possessions. *Courtesy National Museums of Scotland*

232

377. Interior of a bothy for six plowmen at Mains of Dun, Forfarshire. From an undated newspaper feature about the Scottish peasantry, *c*. 1880. *Courtesy National Museums of Scotland*

beds.[2] In 1891 the Midmar doctor described a typical chaumer as being: 'a loft above the stable . . . inside the room are two or more beds, according to the size of the farm; and if any space is left, it is nearly all taken up with trunks, which also serve as seats'.[3]

The farmer provided basic bothy furniture (Plates 376 and 377) which consisted generally only of beds and a bench often heavily carved with the initials of previous occupants. The plowmen's own wooden kists contained their Sunday clothes and treasured possessions such as show harnesses or melodions. Classic pine lodging boxes and benches with rail backs have been collected by the Country Life Section of the National Museums of Scotland. Surviving beds are rare, although some masters provided box beds (Plate 378), and a mid-century account of a bothy in Easter Ross makes it clear that the long apartment housing twenty-four men contained two rows of deal crib beds.[4] Another description records: 'There are three beds, six chests, belonging to the men which contain their clothing, and six barrels to hold the oatmeal which is supplied every four weeks. The only furniture supplied by the master in addition to the beds, consists of a pot or kettle, six wooden *cappies*

378. Victorian watercolour of a bothy or chaumer interior containing box beds. An armchair, a typical rail-back bench and three lodging boxes are visible in the left foreground. *Trustees of the Ryedale Folk Museum*

233

or bowls, six spoons and a short form or seat. There is no chair and no table. In as much as the form, a seat without a back, can accommodate only four persons, two must seat themselves on the top of their chests or meal barrels'.[5]

Scottish fisher girls who followed the herring fleets, gutting and packing the catch, lived in bothies in the main ports. A hundred years ago, crews of girls from Nairn regularly sailed each summer to Lerwick in Shetland for eight or ten weeks. Their pine kists, made by the local joiner, were generally painted either brown or maroon, or occasionally grained and varnished (Plate 379). They held Sunday and working clothes, sheets, blankets, towels, knitting wool, an oilskin coat, crockery, cutlery, etc. The boxes always incorporated a small till (known as a *shottle*) at one end, with either a hinged lid or pair of small drawers for keeping personal articles like knitting needles, a wisker, bandages, gutting knives and loose change. The only other furniture in the one-roomed bothies at Gremista near Lerwick, where the girls lived, were a table and bunk beds. The crews slept three to a bed and cooked their own meals.[6]

Single estate workers and gardeners employed by country-house owners frequently lived in bothies. William Barker remembers one at Bywell Hall, Northumberland, in the 1920s. It had once been a workman's cottage and contained three bedrooms, a bathroom and living-kitchen with a range 'where we did all our cooking, it was plainly furnished with a scrubbed table and wooden forms to seat eight people. We slept two to a bedroom, we each had a bed, chest of drawers, bedside chair and mirror. We were supplied with clean linen and towels once a week. A women came in the mornings to clean, make the beds and cook our mid-day meal, the rest of the meals we all had to take turns to prepare. I think a racing hostel might be the nearest to a bothy as I knew it in the 1920s and 30s'.[7] Obviously, standards had much improved since the days when the master looked upon his labourers as being little better than beasts of burden.

The bothy system lasted until the tractor era. Many farms in Yorkshire have an outbuilding still known as 'Paddy's bothy' from the itinerant Irish harvest bands. There is a well-preserved example over a field barn at Foss Ings, Abbotside, near Askrigg.[8] Mine shops were a type of industrial bothy and large numbers of mill workers in Lanarkshire were housed in similar barrack-style accommodation during the early Industrial Revolution, although little is known about how these buildings were furnished.

MINE SHOPS

Owing to the isolated position of lead mines in the northern Pennines and the Lake District, many miners stayed during the week at mine shops or lodging shops provided by the company. A few of these plain substantial two-storey buildings (Plate 380) still stand as empty shells in the Nenthead area of Co. Durham and one, at nearby Killhope, has been restored as part of a site museum. The *First Report of the Commission for Inquiring into the Employment of Children in Mines and Manufactures* (1842), contains a first rate description of how mine shops were furnished. Dr Mitchell reported in evidence:[9]

> The first one of them which I saw was about nine miles across the fell, south from Stanhope. On entering the door it was seen that the lower part was one room . . . and had a great fire burning at the east end. Along the one side, that next the window, was a deal table, extending the whole length of the room, and alongside of it was a form, and there were two other forms in the room. All along the other side on the wall were little cupboards, 48 in number, in four tiers above each other, six of the cupboards with the doors off, but most of the rest carefully locked with padlocks, and in which the several miners had deposited their wallets, with their provisions for five days.

379. Fisher-girl's kist from Nairn, Scotland, painted pine; early twentieth century. The *shottle* was for keeping the gutting knife, bandages, wisker and other small personal articles. *Jean Bochel*

380. (*Opposite, above*) Lodging shop at Manor Gill Mine, Teesdale, Co. Durham. *Courtesy Beamish Museum*

381. (*Opposite, below*) Interior of a miners' lodging shop, Rookhope, Co. Durham, late nineteenth century. Several men are seated on the end of their sleeping berth, there is a coal bunker, also a table behind the stove. *Courtesy Beamish Museum*

234

Other articles included a pitcher, a tea-kettle, a pan for boiling potatoes, two pans for frying bacon, fire-irons, a besom and a large box containing the clothes which the masters put on when they came to see the mines.

> On ascending to the upper room by a ladder, it was seen to be a sleeping-room. Along one side of the room were three beds, each six feet long, by about four feet and a half wide; then there were three other beds on the other side; and at the farther end was a seventh bed, extending from the one line of beds to the other. Immediately over these seven beds, and supported on posts, were seven other beds, placed exactly in the same way. Each of these 14 beds was intended for two persons . . . but they might be made to receive three men each; and, in case of need, a boy might lie across at their feet. There was no opening of any sort to let out the foul air. The beds were stuffed with chaff. There were blankets, but no sheets. The furniture of the lodging shops is supplied by the masters. The beds and blankets are supplied by the miners themselves.

This lodging shop, consisting of a cooking and eating-room on the ground floor, with a dormitory above, was typical of others visited by Dr Mitchell, although some had a separate drying-room for wet clothes, and he visited one with a bed 'suspended from the top of the room, which economically filled up a space which otherwise would have been vacant'. The miners interviewed considered these lodging shops 'most destructive to health' and 'not fit for swine to live in'. *The Kinnaird Report on the Condition of Mines* (1862–64), revealed that conditions had changed little,[10] while a graphic late Victorian photograph of the miners' lodging shop at Rookhope, Co. Durham, shows a desperately crowded interior serving as dormitory, kitchen and drying-room (Plate 381).

In the Welsh slate quarries, workmen who either did not live in the neighbourhood or could not find local lodgings lived during the week in similar 'barracks' provided by the owners. At Dinorwic, barrack accommodation was given to about 420 quarrymen until the daily workmen's trains led to their decline.[11] Most employers provided a *caban* near the bottom of the quarry where the men could eat their 'snap'. At the North Wales Quarry Museum, Llanberis, the *caban* or mess-room is furnished with plain pine X-framed tables, simple benches, a range of lockers for 'bait' boxes fixed to the wall, chests and cooking facilities. The original storeroom still contains massive tiers of drawers for nuts, bolts and other hardware and cupboards for machinery parts; a fully equipped hospital also survives at this memorable industrial site museum.

22 Ships

The history of ship furniture, although little studied, is surprisingly rewarding and unexpectedly complex, because the subject covers not only passenger ships, but men o'war, merchant vessels and fishing boats, each of which had different kinds of accommodation.[1] Ships designed specially for conveying passengers were first built in early Victorian days; prior to that time, passengers were carried in merchant ships, the captain undertaking to provide living space and very little else in the way of fittings, furniture and comforts. Wealthy passengers could afford to equip their cabins with fine furniture and paid to eat at the Captain's table. William Hickey, who voyaged in the East Indiaman *Plassey* in 1769, described the Captain's cabin as 'painted a light peagreen with gold beading; the bed and curtains of the richest Madras chintz, one of the most complete dressing tables I ever saw, having every useful article on it — a beautiful bureau and bookcase, stored with the best books and three neat mahogany chairs'.[2] The very rich might hire the entire stern cabin and furnish it to the same standard as their London house, but this commodious space was normally partitioned into separate 'state-rooms' around 12 by 12 feet — large enough to contain a bed, desk, table, chest of drawers and seating. Cabin furniture was often taken ashore on arrival and used in the owner's new home. However, the majority of emigrants endured spartan conditions in the 'steerage' – the empty cargo hold – sleeping on their own straw mattresses and cooking in family groups on a small brick hearth. On some ships there was also a long dark 'tween decks cargo space with narrow bunks built in two or three tiers where those steerage passengers able to afford a berth slept[3] (Plate 382).

Because cabin furniture was traditionally brought aboard from the passenger's own house, it was slow to emerge as a type and assume a distinctive character. Obviously plain domestic pieces capable of fitting into a confined space were most suitable, and a limited range of specially designed travelling furniture such as compact 'military' chests and 'knock-down' beds was available. Sometimes the presence of fittings such as brass lifting handles on small chests of drawers which could also be used to lash the piece down enable one to recognize ship furniture;[4] many cabin tables were bolted to the deck or fixed by iron stays, rather like guy ropes, and may retain eyelet plates under the top; indeed, any devices for securing articles against shifting are significant for identifying cabin furniture[5] (Plate 384). The tops of large dining-tables were often made with a perimeter gallery and grid of slats over which the cloth was laid to prevent everything sliding off; alternatively, thin sand bags were use for the same purpose.[6] Chests of drawers might be raised on stump feet to protect them from wetting if water came aboard and several illustrations show small tables and cot beds hanging by cords from the ceiling to compensate for the motion of the ship[7] (Plate 383).

The workshop books of Owen Fitzpatrick, a cabinet maker employed by Pryce and Delany of Birkenhead, contain interesting particulars of furniture ordered for steamers, gunboats and troop ships between 1879 and 1886.[8] Most of it was made in

382. Between decks on an emigration vessel, *Illustrated London News* (1851). The roughly fashioned double box berths served as living as well as sleeping spaces.

383. *HMS Caesar, Baltic Fleet*, from the *Illustrated London News* (1856). Suspended trays were common in ships' dining-rooms.

hardwoods such as mahogany, teak, American walnut or Danzig oak and included dining-tables, sideboards, bookcases, settees, benches, camp stools, wash-stands, glass trays and bottle-racks. Special design features included cross-blocking table pillars and legs for fixing to the deck, fitting rims or guards by clip plates to the edge of dining-tables and sideboards, the provision of braced cross-stretchers allowing the frames to be bolted down and clamping basins within wash-stands. Rounded edges and corners were normally specified, bookcases featured sliding doors and case furniture often had pine ends for screwing to the bulkhead. Racks and trays for drinking glasses, bottles and decanters were invariably designed with holes or wells to secure the vessels (see Plate 384).

The captains of merchant ships found the hiring out of space to 'cabin' and 'steerage' passengers very lucrative, but it was not until the mid-nineteenth century that ocean-going packet ships with a fixed date of departure and destination started to operate on the North American route. First-Class travellers were provided with fully furnished accommodation, their private cabins or state-rooms being equipped with curtained bunks, a padded locker seat, wash-stand, table, chairs, carpet and other comforts, all supplied by the ship's owner and no longer the passenger. Meals

384. *Come Youngster Another Glass of Grog Before You Go on Deck*, engraving, *c*. 1830. The cabin table is anchored to the floor, the sideboard is provided with bottle and glass stands. *Trustees of the National Maritime Museum*

were served by a Steward in the saloon, containing a long table and benches, which also functioned as a recreation area (Plate 385). In contrast, the crew's quarters, generally 'for'ard below deck', contained a bare minimum of furniture — built-in bunks, space to stow sea chests and a table to eat at. Naval-style hammocks (which originated in the West Indies) were provided in some sailing vessels. Conditions in fishing boats were often even more cramped and squalid, although the tradition of bunks built into the side of the vessel, central table and locker seats lived on.

The world's first large iron screw propeller-driven steam ship, the *Great Britain*, was built in 1839-43, but it was not until about 1860 that sail suddenly gave way to specially constructed passenger-carrying steam ships. The well-lit, ventilated and decorated cabins were fully equipped with luxurious and convenient multi-purpose furniture in a style reminiscent of Victorian suburban houses (Plate 386). Under the stimulus of competition, the interiors became even more ostentatiously splendid until they resembled floating palaces. Even Artic exploration ships had respectably comfortable cabins (Plate 387).

Gentleman captains of men o'war were permitted by Admiralty regulations to have a retinue of servants, and lived in the highest style of elegance. William Hogarth's well-known conversation picture, *Captain Lord George Graham at Table* (*c*. 1740), portrays the stern cabin furnished with a carpet, looking-glasses between the windows and fashionable cabriole-legged chairs placed around a table set for dinner.[9] Lord Nelson's flagship HMS *Victory*, one of very few early sailing vessels to survive, gives an idea of the handsome accommodation, although the interiors were not particularly grand by the standards of the day. Fighting ships had gun ports along each deck, and since the cannon were lashed down in the cabins, all furniture had to be cleared away when the ship was made ready for action. Captain Mizzen in *The Fair Quaker of Deal*, a play of 1710, boasted 'I have an invention which makes the great guns in my cabin appear to be elbow chairs covered with cloth of tissue'.[10] The sailors who manned the guns lived communally below decks in dark damp spaces, as recorded in a rare early nineteenth-century watercolour showing a lower-decks scene on a man o'war with hammocks and sea-chests visible (Plate 388).

The sea-chest is a classic article of ship furniture. Leather-covered trunks with decorative brass nailing patterns and lining paper were used at an early date, but the traditional sailors' chest at the time of the Napoleonic Wars was of robust boarded

239

388. Lower-deck scene on man o' war at Gravesend, anonymous watercolour, *c.* 1810. *Trustees of the National Maritime Museum*

389. A ship's dispensary fitting in teak, *c.* 1830, bars passed across the openings to retain the bottles. *Trustees of the National Maritime Museum*

390. Pine sea-chest with rope lifting handles, the lid painted with a clipper in full sail, nineteenth century, second half. *Trustees of the National Maritime Museum*

pine construction with dovetailed corners, a deep lid, internal till and wooden skids underneath. Many had splayed sides (the 'wedge' shape giving greater stability) and a rope lifting handle at each end threaded through a block which was often carved with simple motifs such as a heart, a diamond, a star or fish scales, etc.[11] The exterior was commonly painted some dark colour or had a grained finish; examples with elaborate decorative painted surfaces are mostly fakes. However, during the late Victorian period a genuine popular tradition emerged for featuring colourful, if rather primitive, nautical scenes inside the lid (Plate 390). A typical example in the National Maritime Museum is brightly painted with a clipper flanked by a sailor with an anchor and the figure of a woman, accompanied by the inscriptions: 'Homeward Bound / Welcome Home / Thomas Ray Barr Greenock'. The same collection includes a curious trapezoidal profiled chest,[12] clearly purpose-built to fit into an awkward space, several little ditty boxes in which sailors kept small personal items, a repertoire of ships' carpenters' tool-chests and a long narrow chart-box divided internally. Sailmakers' benches were also found aboard wooden ships together with various wall-racks such as the ship's dispensary, designed with a bar across the openings to retain the medicine bottles[13] (Plate 389). Pictorial and written sources, together with the few surviving vessels such as HMS *Victory* at Portsmouth or the *Cutty Sark* and the *Reliant* at Greenwich, combine to convey a rewarding impression of what accommodation was like on board ship in the past.

23 Caravans, Narrowboats and Living-Vans

During the eighteenth century, itinerant tradesmen and showmen journeyed from place to place on foot; the caravan, or 'house on wheels', first made its appearance between about 1820 and 1840 with the general improvement of roads. The earliest users were travelling showmen; Romanies did not take to the *vardo* or living-waggon until about 1850, but thereafter they became increasingly common. Gypsy caravans were often very magnificent with skilfully planned interiors to cater for sleeping, living and cooking (Plate 391). Certain design types evolved with distinctive coachwork and layouts such as the 'Ledge', 'Bow-Top', 'Brush' or 'Burton', but the finest of all were Reading caravans favoured by Romanies.[1]

A description of the interior of a traditional Reading caravan must serve to illustrate the general patterns of fittings and furnishings. Immediately to the left of the half-doored entrance was a tall narrow wardrobe with a small brush cupboard below; the cast-iron stove came next with an airing cupboard above and a shelf fronted by polished brass rails; then came the window having a built-in double locker-seat beneath it, usually with a lift-up top but also provided with drawers. On the right or off-side, as one entered, was a quarter-round china cupboard with glazed doors set above a lower stage which had solid panelled doors for keeping boots and cleaning things (Plate 394). Another upholstered locker seat, this time with a shallow cupboard overhead incorporating three small cutlery drawers, faced the fire and the remaining space on this side was occupied by a handsome bow-fronted chest of drawers under the window. The rear of the caravan was fitted up as a two-tier bed space filling the whole width of the far end (Plate 393). The top bunk was curtained and had a long galleried shelf overhead for displaying crockery; the lower berth, enclosed by hinged or sliding doors (sometimes faced with mirrors), was intended for children and might be a little shorter and narrower. An 'angel' paraffin lamp supported on a scrolled brass arm provided the main source of light. Soft furnishings included curtains, cushions, bedding and perhaps rugs on the linoleum floor covering. Caravans were custom-built by specialist firms who favoured their own styles of coachwork and decoration, but in vintage models the interior woodwork is always resplendent with painted, grained, scumbled or French polished surfaces lavishly embellished with stencilled motifs, gilding, and lining. Horses, flowers, classical foliage and elaborate scrolls were the most popular decorative motifs. Waggon-painters and carvers were inspired by the same flamboyant Victorian folk tradition as fairground artists, creating an impression of Baroque extravagance. The interiors of gypsy caravans are interesting as an illustration of how skilfully designers overcame the problem of furnishing a very small space and as a rare authentic example of folk art applied to furniture.

Another brightly painted kind of horse-drawn transport (also a by-product of the Industrial Revolution) are narrowboats which, until the 1940s, navigated the canal system in large numbers. The basic design of the cabins, which formed the boatman's home, remained almost unchanged, certainly since mid-Victorian days, when the well-known tradition of decorating barges with castles and roses became firmly established. The standard cabin layout is now seldom seen in working craft, but early examples survive in narrowboats at the waterways museums at Ellesmere Port, Cheshire and Stoke Bruerne, Northants. The interiors were, if anything, even more confined than those of gypsy caravans, seldom being more than 9 feet long with an effective width of about 6 feet. The cabins followed a standard design that made maximum use of the available space, the furniture being built of pine with numerous mouldings and panels for displays of decorative painting.[2]

Double entrance doors at the stern led down into the cabin via a wide step with a hinged tread which served as a coal-box. Forward of the doors, immediately to the left, was the cast-iron cooking stove with a brass drying rod above and, in the corner below the deckhead, a small ticket drawer where lock passes and toll-tickets were kept, a richly painted dipper was usually hung under this drawer screened by a

391. Interior of a gypsy caravan, Notting Hill, London, before the standard arrangement of furniture and traditional decoration had become fully established. *Illustrated London News* (1879)

392. (*opposite, below*) Narrowboat cabin showing the cupboard flap open, a crocheted lace pelmet, angel lamp, brass rail over the stove and a traditional display of china plates. *The Boat Museum, Ellesmere Port*

piece of crocheted lace. The oil lamp, supported on a scrolled brass arm, was fixed between the stove and a wall unit consisting of an arched and panelled cupboard door ornamented with castles and roses hinged at the bottom so that when opened the flap let down to form a kitchen-table (Plate 392); below this food cupboard was a cutlery drawer, and beneath that, a further storage compartment. The far end served as a bed alcove with a double bunk which folded away into a recess between the food cupboard and the forward bulkhead; at night, the bed hinged down across the end of the gangway and was screened by curtains (Plate 396). A large clothes cupboard filled the space over the 'bunk hole', and there was a drawer below facing a similar one on the other side of the cabin. The wall opposite the stove accommodated a locker bench which provided a seat by day and a side bunk at night.[3] Other seat furniture consisted of a gaudily painted slab-end stool (Plate 397), and a seat board that bridged the front of the bed alcove when the bunk was stowed away.

Although the internal paintwork displayed local variations, it conformed to certain basic rules. The standard ground was buff comb-grained to a light oak scumble and varnished, mouldings were picked out in bright colours and fancy work included geometrical patterns, stencilled ornament and lining, besides the famous castles and roses.[4] The panelled entrance doors, which opened outwards, always featured a castle in a romantic landscape above a cluster of roses. The table-

393. Interior (facing front) of a 'Ledge' caravan by Duntons of Crane Wharfe, Reading, dated 1907. *Reading Museum and Art Gallery*

394. Interior (facing rear) of a 'Ledge' caravan by Duntons of Crane Wharfe, Reading, dated 1907. *Reading Museum and Art Gallery*

395. View of a living-van showing the fitted furniture, from an early twentieth-century catalogue of Fowler & Co., Leeds, Yorkshire. *Leeds City Museums*

396. Narrowboat cabin looking forward; the arched cupboard door-cum-table flap is decorated with a castle, with a drawer below and cross-bed space beyond. *The Boat Museum, Ellesmere Port*

397. Boat stool, probably painted by Bill Evetts of Manchester about sixty years ago. *A.J. Lewery collection*

cupboard also had a castle on the front with flowers above, while the cutlery drawer, ticket drawer and often the crossbed flap almost always bore a display of roses usually on a green or wood-grained ground. The boatman's stool, his watercan, dipper and bucket were also gaily painted. The precise source of this folk-art tradition has never been properly explained, but it was certainly very different from the Baroque character of the Romany caravan. Gypsies and canal folk were both members of insular trade communities with their own artistic traditions.

Another traditional type of mobile home, known as a living-van, provided accommodation for contract ploughing teams, who travelled from farm to farm with pairs of traction engines which hauled their cable plough back and forth across the field. It was obviously an advantage for such crews to live close to the plant so that working hours could be kept as long as possible; pairs of steam engines with their trailers were a common sight on country roads from about 1860 until the 1920s. A team normally consisted of a man on each engine, a ploughman and a skivvy to do the cooking. The standard living-van was fitted up with two pairs of bunks, individual wall lockers, a flap table, seating, a cooking stove, store-chest, a workbench for small repairs and large boxes for spare parts and tools. Most vans were strongly built of pine planks set on big steel wheels, but unlike horse-drawn gypsy caravans, they never sported festive painted decoration.

An early twentieth-century trade catalogue of Cultivating Machinery published by Fowler & Co. (Leeds) Ltd, Steam Plough and Locomotive Works, illustrates a sectional view of a small living-van for three men showing the arrangement of fitted furniture[5] (Plate 395). A fine example, dating from this period, built by Fowler and used on farms in the Sleaford area is preserved at the Museum of Lincolnshire Life. Road workers used similar vans, although they were less often equipped for sleeping; there is one at the Castle Museum, York, while the Museum of Farming at Murton has a small shepherd's hut mounted on old reaper wheels, furnished with a stove, seat and rough bed which was towed into the fields at lambing time.

24 Children's Furniture

Although nursery furniture is popular with amateur collectors and writers on antiques who are beguiled by small-scale versions of fashionable adult designs,[1] it is seldom studied seriously and little interest has been shown in products of the vernacular tradition. Prior to about 1800, furniture for children was by and large restricted to cradles, cribs, chairs and baby-walkers; it was not until the nineteenth century that more attention was paid to the needs of infants. The repertoire of nursery furniture illustrated in J.C. Loudon's account of cottage dwellings, published in 1833,[2] is of special value because he was clearly reporting on articles he had seen personally, and claims that such items were generally made by the cottager himself (Plate 398).

Loudon starts his description of the 'various contrivances in use in England to enable a mother who has no servants, to relieve herself at pleasure from carrying her child', by explaining how to build a simple swing chair. The most original feature of this home-made contraption was the use of 'ten piece of elder tree, six inches long, with the pith burnt out with a redhot poker' through which four knotted cords were strung 'tied together and hung from a hook in the ceiling'. Elder is generally thought to be a worthless timber, but in this instance was perceived by countrymen to have the right technical properties for the job. Another practical apparatus, 'a go-gin for a child who can stand, to teach it to walk', consisted of 'a perpendicular shaft, long enough to reach from the floor to the ceiling, which turns in a hole in a brick or flagstone, and within a staple driven into the side of one of the ceiling joists'. A short arm morticed into the shaft ends in a circular ring with a gate made of wood or twisted withy which encircled the child's waist and gave some support enabling the happy infant to stagger round and round in circles. Several go-gins of this kind have been recorded: one from Devon, now at Temple Newsam, is of ash with an iron spike at each end and displays every sign of having been fashioned by a wheelwright or wagon builder, the arm is adjustable for height within a slot by means of a peg and holes (Plate 399). A form of baby-walker used in England, but not mentioned by Loudon, consisted of an oblong frame set on four splayed legs, grooves in the long side rails held a sliding board with a circular aperture in which the infant was placed and allowed to toddle to and fro within the frame. A good specimen is preserved at Stranger's Hall, Norwich, while there are others at Hertford Museum and the Cambridge Folk Museum.

A primitive item of child-minding equipment, akin to a playpen, which Loudon noted on his travels, was 'a hollow cylinder, nothing more than the section of the trunk of an old pollard tree, commonly to be met with in England; the inside and upper edges are smoothed, and a child just able to stand is put into it, while its mother is at work by its side, or going after the business of the house'. He also illustrates a familiar go-cart or baby-cage consisting of a light framework on castors with splayed struts supporting a ring often with a hinged section secured by a hook and eye. These contraptions had been popular in England since late-Tudor times and several fine seventeenth-century examples with elaborate turnery, sometimes

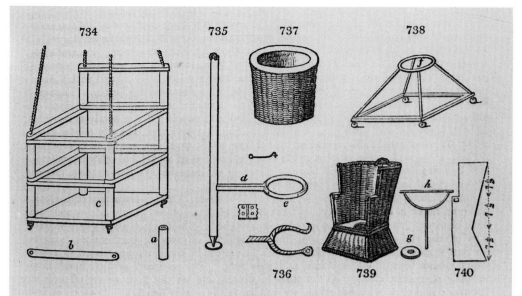

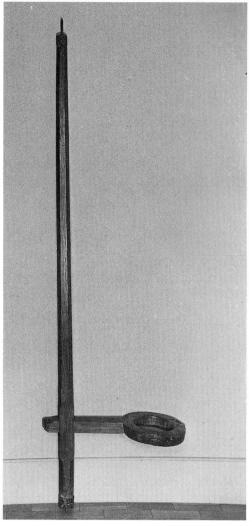

399. This early nineteenth-century ash go-gin from Devon was fixed between a beam and the floor to teach a baby placed in the ring to walk. *Leeds City Art Galleries*

400. Walking stool or go-cart, varnished birch with pottery castors. Wm Brear & Sons of Adding-ham, Yorkshire, advertised identical models at 2s. each about 1900. *Bradford Museums*

featuring a tray for toys or made adjustable for height survive.[3] 'These machines' by which 'children readily learn to walk without danger of falling' were, according to Loudon, also 'frequently made of willow rods without castors'. This is confirmed by a letter written in 1707 by Lord George Hay, describing how his nephew Thomas 'runs up and down the room in a machine made of willows, but my lady the Countess takes care that he does not stress himself with walking too much'.[4] William Brear & Son, country chairmakers and turners of Addingham, Yorkshire, advertised 'walking stools' virtually identical to Loudon's model at 24 s. a dozen in their trade catalogue of *c.* 1900[5] (Plate 400). Larger, sturdier versions called 'walking horses' were sometimes made to help an adult 'to stand and move about who is too weak to be able to stand without such assistance'.[6]

Loudon concludes his paragraph with instructions and a diagram on how to weave a wicker commode chair which 'for cleanliness and decency deserves imitation in every country' — they were apparently unknown in his native Scotland. The seat was provided with a wooden cover 'so as to be quite flat for a child to sit upon when the vase is not is use'. There were two holes in the elbows to place a restraining bar or attach a small D-shaped table flap supported by a single front leg. Small elm or painted pine commode chairs of plank construction, with wings which closely resemble this pattern, are fairly common which suggests it was a successful design (Plate 401). Low stools, often called 'crickets', were frequently used by children; Loudon illustrates an improved example with a box frame and sliding seat 'for a child to put its playthings in'.[7]

The first piece of furniture used by an infant was either a cradle or a bassinet.[8] Both have a long ancestry. Bassinets, made of wicker (see Plate 241), or straw, were popular because they could easily be carried from room to room without disturbing a sleeping baby; a stand, perhaps on rockers, might be provided. Wooden cradles could either be of box form (often with a hinged hood) mounted on rockers or designed to swing between two uprights — rural joiners and their customers seem nearly always to have preferred the former type. Until about 1750, most were of framed panel construction executed in oak or elm, but later examples are made of painted pine boards with nailed or dovetailed corners. Provincial Price Books normally list them under 'deal work'. The *Bolton Supplement to the London Book of Cabinet Piece Prices* (1802) contains the following specification:

	£	s	d
For a Cradle 3 feet long, with an octagon head	0	8	0
Arched head, extra	0	1	0

Making ditto to slide	0	2	0
If ditto be hung with hinges	0	1	0
Canted sides	0	2	0
Scolloping top edges	0	1	3
Making a frame to rock on	0	1	6
Halving the arch	0	0	2
Each inch longer	0	0	2
A single one, extra	0	0	6
Polishing	0	0	3

A small cradle of this type, vividly decorated with fancy zig-zag graining in black on an orange-red ground, the interior painted blue, is inscribed underneath 'Lilla Eliza Milner 1864 / Gunthorpe' — a hamlet in the parish of Owston Ferry, Lincolnshire[9] (Plates 402 and 403). The 1861 census records that John Milner, a master wheelwright, lived at Gunthorpe with his wife Maria, but the birth of Lilla Eliza is not registered. Since 'lilla' is a dialect word meaning little, this cradle was presumably built and named by John Milner as present for one of his daughters' dolls.

Cribs or cots came into use when a child was about one year old, they were sometimes made with a removable side so that the cot could be fastened against the side of the mother's bed by hooks and eyes at night. Loudon stated that: 'Any joiner might make such cribs of deal or any other cheap wood; and they may be painted or stained';[10] however, it is likely that poor families managed without cots. Small children sometimes slept on bedding in an empty drawer.

Common chairs made for infants were of two kinds — low versions of adult models, often with a hole in the seat for a pot (see Plates 16 and 404), and traditional high chairs for elevating children to the height of a table so that they could sit and eat with their parents. Many ladder, spindle-back, Windsor and other regional child's chairs were made (Plate 405). *The Norwich Chair Makers' Price Book* (1801) describes six childrens' high chairs; all reflect local East Anglian patterns, could be fitted with a

401. Child's rocking-chair with a pierced seat, probably Victorian in date. *Bradford Museums*

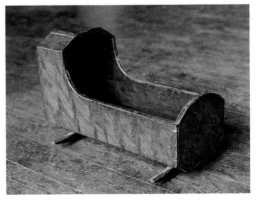

402. A painted pine cradle apparently made for a doll. *Gainsborough Old Hall*

403. Inscription beneath the cradle.

404. (*far left*) Baby's common chair. The chamfered posts allowed the chair to be tipped up for use as a drying-rack. *Bradford Museums*

405. (*left*) Child's Windsor high chair for use at table, the arms drilled for a restraining rod. Possibly by B. Gilling, Worksop, Nottinghamshire, 1840–50. *Bradford Museums*

406. (*right*) A child's deportment high chair to encourage correct posture when seated at table; elm painted apple-green, with well-splayed back legs. Probably Scottish, *c.* 1830–40. *Private collection*

407. (*far left*) Child's chair and table stool with bar and foot rest as described in *The Preston Book of Prices* (1802). *Tennants of Yorkshire*

restraining bar between the arms and had an adjustable footboard.[11] They are termed 'Table-Chairs' and were regularly made in either elm, ash, beech or walnut. Another popular type, well-described in *The Preston Cabinet and Chair-Makers Book of Prices* (1802), was a small armchair which could be bolted, by means of a thumb screw passing through a hole in the central stretcher, on to a flat-topped stand to create a high chair; and, when separated, the stand functioned as a convenient play table (Plate 407). The specification includes the stand, along with several other optional extras:

CHILD'S CHAIR

For do. with a foot-board to move,			
a turned pin to screw into the arms,			
plain banister or three plain splats;			
the top end of the feet turned to receive the arms,	0	8	0
Framing the stool for chair to stand on and fixing,	0	3	6
Polishing rails and loose seat for do	0	1	0
A table with a bead bent round do fixed to the arms,	0	0	9
A bottom for a pot	0	0	6

A rather more up-market child's chair, intended to promote good deportment, was prescribed by the eminent surgeon, Sir Astley Cooper (1768–1841).[12] They have narrow caned seats and tall straight backs to encourage a correct posture and were made in large numbers during the second quarter of the nineteenth century (Plate 406).

Mrs William Parkes's *Domestic Duties* (1825) contained sensible advice for young wives.[13] 'Nurseries', she declared, 'Should be airy and cheerful . . . and no more furniture in them than is absolutely necessary. In the day room in particular, there should be as little as possible to impede the active sports of the little inhabitants. Sharp cornered tables, projecting shelves and low fenders should never be admitted. The sleeping nursery too cannot be too plainly furnished. Beds and cribs without hangings, a low washing table, a few chairs, a wooden tub for the children to stand in when they are washed, one or two small wooden horses and a sufficiency of drawers and shelves are the chief articles of furniture which it requires'. Twenty years later Thomas Webster, in his *Encyclopaedia of Domestic Economy* (1844), illustrated a repertoire of nursery furniture[14] including a bassinet, cradle, a swing cot, a crib, a child's wash-stand, a milk warmer and various chairs including one made of wicker 'without legs, which some use to place very young children who cannot support themselves' (Plate 408). French peasant families were even more adept than English parents at creating a homely range of straw, wicker or wooden baby-cages, walkers, minders, carts and similar equipment to serve the needs of infants.[15]

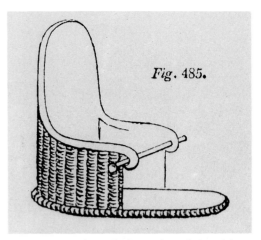

Fig. 485.

408. Design for a little wicker chair without legs 'which some use to place very small children in'. From T. Webster, *Encyclopaedia of Domestic Economy* (1844)

25 Cricket and Tennis

Cricket has been played in England for over four hundred years, and our national love of the game, whether it be a Test Match at Lords or a contest on the village green, is reflected in many paintings and prints.[1] Today most grounds have a pavilion containing changing-rooms, equipment stores, desks for the scorers and often a verandah with seats for spectators and players. Although a pavilion was built by the MCC in 1787, other teams at this time made do with tented accommodation and basic furniture. The only visible furniture, in a print showing a game between the Earls of Winchelsea and Darnley at Lords in 1793, is a plank form on which the two scorers are seated.[2] When the Lords Jubilee Match was played in 1837 the scorers were still in the open, but had chairs and a table, while other framed tables held refreshments and spectators were provided with either slab-end or stick-leg forms positioned in front of the pavilion and around the boundary[3] (Plate 411).

Several scenes of the period show scorers seated at tripod tables to master uneven ground (Plate 409); players and spectators taking refreshments spread on tables sat either beneath trees or in marquees, and a scattering of common chairs. The MCC owns a painted plank form on trestle legs lettered in white 'Seat used at Lords 1814'. Seating of this pattern lasted until 1864 when replaced by benches with back rails. The Long Room at Lords, which dates from 1889, still contains three dozen contemporary high bentwood armchairs with foot rests supplied by SBC & Co. Ltd of London, plus several purpose-made square oak stands for resting score cards. Just as cricket fields on landed estates made use of furniture from the great house, so local teams sometimes used tables and chairs from the village pub to supplement fixed seating around the green. During late Victorian times folding canvas chairs, wicker seats, slatted cast-iron benches and other types of proprietary garden or park furniture made their appearance, but at smaller grounds old school benches and redundant chapel pews were (and still are) pressed into service.

The Wimbledon Lawn Tennis Museum houses the original furniture from the Gentlemen's Dressing Room at the Worple Road courts, home of the All England Tennis and Croquet Club from 1869 to 1921.[4] The centre of the room is occupied by a ponderous double-sided pine bench having a solid back and shelves under the seats. A two-tier range of croquet lockers stands against one wall, each with its own hat and coat pegs; there are also three blue and white china wash basins set into a marble surround, while a mirror, and umbrella stand and a clock complete the ensemble. Old trade catalogues advertising tennis equipment sometimes illustrate items of furniture.[5] One issued by F.H. Ayers in 1890 includes a 'lawn tennis bat stand', available in walnut or mahogany; it is of circular design having a central turned stem supporting a bracket with slots to take raquet handles and a round tray base for balls (Plate 410). Billiard cue stands may have provided the inspiration. The same catalogue features 'Hope's patent lawn tennis scoring chair' consisting of a well-braced step-ladder with a platform top and seat back; models with a metal arm to hold the score sheet were also available. These umpires' seats gave greater height and stability than the earlier makeshift expedient of perching a chair on a table.

BAT STANDS.

The Circular Lawn Tennis Racket Stand is intended to be placed in the Hall, on the Lawn, or for showing Rackets for sale, and are very strong & ornamental.

410. Bat Stand, from the trade catalogue of F.H. Ayres (1890). *Wimbledon Lawn Tennis Museum*

409. (*Opposite*) The Sussex Scorer, William Davies of Brighton, lithograph, 1842. *Marylebone Cricket Club*

411. *Cricket at Newark on Trent* by J.D. Curtis, dated 1823, showing spectator forms, refreshment marquee with trestle-table and scorer seated at a tripod table. *Marylebone Cricket Club*

This survey suggests that the basic requirements of sports pavilions and playing fields have altered little over the years: seats, lockers and washing facilities in changing-rooms; racks for storing equipment; amenities for the scorer; seating for spectators and tables for serving refreshments.

26 Ducking Stools

Ducking stools have an ancient ancestry as instruments of justice. For instance in 1313, a jury, summoned to settle a dispute between the Crown and the Prior of Plympton over the exercise of certain privileges, confirmed the latter's right to a ducking stool and pillory.[1] By the mid-seventeenth century these rights were vested in Plymouth Corporation who, in 1656–7, enacted that fisherwomen who traded unlawfully should be set in the ducking stool and haled up and down three times.[2] Two wrought-iron ducking stools from Plymouth are, in fact, known: one, now in the City Museum, is elaborately styled with scroll-work and could well be of seventeenth-century date (Plate 414); another plainer example, designed more like a low-back Windsor chair supporting a canopied framework, with a large hook at the top, is apparently later, but was destroyed during the last war[3] (Plate 413).

The antiquary William Andrews published a well-documented and illustrated chapter on ducking stools in *Old-Time Punishments* (1890), to which curious readers are immediately referred. In many places ducking stools were permanent fixtures traditionally in the form of a post standing by a pond or river with a chair fixed to a long beam which was worked up and down like a see-saw (Plate 415); elsewhere a similar apparatus, set on wheels, was kept in some convenient buildings such as the Town Hall, until needed. Many surviving specimens are of oak or occasionally pine, with an arched wrought-iron superstructure headed by a suspension ring so that the chair could be hung from the beam end. A typical example made for Ipswich Corporation is said to date from 1579, but the blocked column supports, scrolled terminals and dovetail joints, uniting the lattice seat to the rails, suggest it was built at least a century later (Plate 412). A strikingly similar ducking chair, advertised by Edgar Smith, antiques dealer[4] from Southwold, also in Suffolk, is now at Hall i' the Wood, Bolton, while a third (now lacking the iron canopy), preserved in Scarborough Museum, was attached to a projecting pole or crane located on the old East Pier in the harbour at a spot known as 'Douker's Hole'. The Scarborough stool, although partly rebuilt, is of undoubted antiquity and was last used in 1795 to duck a Mrs Gamble. The one at King's Lynn Museum is of mid-eighteenth-century ladder-back design[5] (Plate 417).

Documentary evidence is surprisingly plentiful in town records. At Southam, Warwickshire, a man was sent to Daventry in 1718 to make a drawing of the ducking stool at that place; subsequent payments refer to making, painting, fixing iron-work to it and finally deepening the village pond.[6] The accounts of the township of Skipton record new ducking stools being made in 1734, 1743 and 1768,[7] while there are, nationwide, many similar charges for constructing or mending these 'engines' for punishing bitter-tongued women or public nuisances — although documentation becomes increasingly rare after about 1760.

Some remarkably interesting details about ducking stools are to be found in the Town Session Books of Cambridge and other local sources.[8] On 4 February

412. The Ipswich ducking stool probably dates from the late seventeenth century. The seat was suspended over the water from a high beam which was worked up and down to plunge the victim. *Ipswich Borough Museums and Galleries*

253

416. Engraving of the famous ducking stool preserved at the Priory Church, Leominster, Herefordshire. It was also known as a cucking-stoole, timbrill or gumstole and was last used in 1809. From F. Andrews, *Old-Time Punishments* (1890)

1745–6, the Court ordered the Chief Constable to pay Alderman Pretlove (a carpenter by trade) £1. 6s. for a ducking chair at the Great Bridge. Twenty years later, at the Town Sessions held on 18 July 1765, Mary Malden was indicted as a common scold and the Court, in anticipation of a conviction, ordered 'that a Ducking Chair be made and put up at the Great Bridge at the expense of the Town of Cambridge, and that the same be suffered to hang there at all times until this Court shall otherwise order'. Charles Day, joiner, was subsequently paid £1. 15s. 6d. for the frame and Samuel Booth, Smith, £3. 2s. 3d. 'for Iron Work for the Ducking chair'. A contemporary chronicler provides first-hand information about these particular chairs which were splendidly ornamented in a popular folk idiom akin to fairground art:

> Mr Cole mentions that when he was a boy and lived with his grandmother in the great corner house at the bridge foot, next to Magdalene College, he saw a woman ducked for scolding. The chair hung by a pulley fastened to a beam about the middle of the bridge (then of timber), in which the woman was confined and let down under the water three times and then taken out. This ducking stool he says was constantly hanging in its place, and on the back panel were engraved devils laying hold of scolds, etc. Some time after a new chair was erected in the place of the old one, having the same devices carved on it and well painted and ornamented. This was taken away when the bridge was rebuilt of stone about 1754. In October 1776 Mr Cole saw at the Town Hall a third ducking stool of plain oak with an iron bar before it to confine the person in the seat.

The Sandwich ducking stool was embellished with figures of men and women scolding and inscribed across the top rail: 'of members ye tonge is worst or best, / an yll tonge oft doeth breede unrest'.[9]

The most famous and impressive ducking machine is at the Priory Church, Leominster. This is in the form of a very long beam with a seat at one end in which the culprit was strapped; it is mounted on a wheeled platform and was pushed to the

413. (*Opposite, above, left*) Wrought-iron ducking stool from Plymouth, probably eighteenth century, destroyed in 1941. From F. Andrews, *Old-Time Punishments* (1890)

414. (*Opposite, above, right*) Plymouth ducking stool, wrought-iron, probably late seventeen century. Used at the Barbican where it was lowered into the waters of Sutton Pool from a crane. Preserved at Plymouth Museum. From F. Andrews, *Old-Time Punishments* (1890)

415. (*Opposite, below*) Ducking stool at Broadwater, Sussex, as it appeared in 1766. The see-saw beam, which was normally kept padlocked to the stump, could be moved horizontally so as to bring the seat to the edge of the pond. From F. Andrews, *Old-Time Punishments* (1890)

edge of the water where, by raising the other end, the victim was plunged into the pond (Plate 416). The Leominster ducking stool was engraved in the *Illustrated London News* for 27 March 1858, and a handbill of about the same date displayed in the Priory states: 'The latest recorded use of this instrument in England was at Leominster in 1809 when a woman Jenny Pipes . . . was ducked in one of the adjacent streams. The Ancient and Universal Punishment for common scolds and for Butchers, Bakers, Brewers . . . and all who gave short measure or vended adulterated articles of food'. Ducking stools, like the village stocks, fell into disuse long before they were officially abolished in 1853.

417. The ducking stool at King's Lynn, Norfolk, where in 1754 Hannah Clarke was ducked for scolding. *Norfolk Museums Service*

Appendix One　Bibliography of Provincial Price Books

The following bibliography of provincial Books of Prices is arranged alphabetically by town. Owing to the ephemeral nature of these publications, especially during periods of rapid inflation, this checklist is unlikely to be definitive. Indeed, since compiling a bibliography which appeared in *Furniture History* XVIII (1982), pp. 18–20, a further six previously unrecorded editions, supplements or new titles have come to light. In view of their rarity, an effort has been made to give the location of at least one copy of each item cited. Details of modern studies are given a special section of the Select Bibliography.

PROVINCIAL BOOKS OF PRICES 1791–1890

BELFAST

The Belfast Cabinet-Makers' Book of Prices (1822). With various tables, 122 pp. 5 engr. pls (Modern Records Centre University of Warwick: MSS/78/TC/Bel/1/1, tp. missing). There may have been another edition in 1836.

BIRMINGHAM

A Supplement to the London Cabinet Makers' Price Book of 1797 as agreed in Birmingham, 1 January 1803. 16 pp. Printed by M. Swinney (1803). (Birmingham Reference Library).
Articles of Agreement made between the members of the Society of Cabinet-Makers who have agreed to meet at the sign of the Green Man, in Moor Street, Birmingham. 9 pp. Printed by T. Wood (1808). (Birmingham Reference Library).

BOLTON

Bolton Supplement to the London Book of Cabinet Piece Prices. Printed by J. Gardner (Bolton, 1802). 16 pp. (Private Collection).

EDINBURGH

The Edinburgh Book of Prices for manufacturing cabinet-work. Second Edition. Enlarged and improved. by the Masters and Journeymen. Printed by Alex Smellie (Edinburgh, 1805), xvi, 128 pp. 3 engr. pls (Victoria and Albert Museum, National Library of Scotland, Edinburgh).
The Edinburgh Book of Prices for manufacturing cabinet-work. Second Edition. Enlarged and improved. Printed by J. Pillans & Sons, Lawnmarket (Edinburgh, 1811), 294 pp. 7 engr. pls (Edinburgh University Library).
The Edinburgh Book of Prices for manufacturing cabinet-work. With various tables as mutually agreed upon by the Masters and Journeymen. Printed by J. Pillans & Sons (Edinburgh, 1821). 128 pp. with List of Deductions as agreed in 1817 (Shoreditch Library).
The Edinburgh Chair-Makers' Book of Prices for Workmanship. Printed by James Auchie (Edinburgh, 1825). (Glasgow University Library, Special Collections).
Supplement to the Cabinet-Makers' Book of Prices (Edinburgh, 1825). 44 pp. 1 engr. pl. (Private Collection).
The Edinburgh Book of Prices for manufacturing cabinet-work. With various tables as mutually agreed upon by the Masters and Journeymen. Printed by J. Glass (Edinburgh, 1826). (Winterthur Library; Metropolitan Museum of Art, New York).
The Edinburgh Chair-Makers' Book of Prices. Printed by Schenck & M'Farlane for the Edinburgh Cabinet and Chair Makers' Society (Edinburgh, 1870). 56 pp. 14 engr. pls (Shoreditch Library).
The Edinburgh Cabinetmakers' Book of Prices. Printed by Schenck & M'Farlane for the Edinburgh Cabinet and Chair Makers' Society (Edinburgh, 1870). 18 engr. pls (Private Collection).

GLASGOW

The Glasgow Book of Prices for manufacturing cabinet-work. With various tables. Printed by James Hedderwick & Co (1809). 48 pp. 2 engr. pls. The preface, dated 1806, suggests that an earlier, as yet untraced, edition was published. (Mitchell Library, Glasgow).

The Glasgow Book of Prices for manufacturing cabinet-work. With various tables. Printed by James Curll (1825). 48 pp. 2 engr. pls. Apart from the tp. a reprint of 1806/09. (Glasgow University Library, Special Collections).

List of Prices as agreed to by the Operative Cabinet & Chair Makers of Glasgow Nos 1 & 2 Branches of the United Operative Association of Scotland. Printed by A. Hunter (Glasgow, 1890). 31 pp. (Glasgow Reference Library).

LEEDS

The Leeds Cabinet and Chair-Makers Book of Prices. Instituted 29 March 1791. Printed by Thomas Gill (Leeds, 1791). 121 pp. (Leeds Reference Library).

Orders and Articles Mutually and Severally Agreed upon by the Journeymen Cabinet and Chair-Makers of Leeds (1792). 4 + 95 pp. (Leeds Reference Library).

The Chair Makers Book of Prices. Printed by T. Inchbold (Leeds, 1827). 83 pp. 10 pls (Leeds Reference Library).

LIVERPOOL

Supplement to the Cabinet and Chair Prices settled between the Masters and Journeymen Cabinet Makers in Liverpool, 15 March 1805 (Liverpool, 1805). 30 pp. illus. (Liverpool Reference Library).

The Carpenters' and Joiners' Price Book . . . containing the prices of wood and work . . . with new and useful tables, by . . . members of the Master Joiners' Committee (Liverpool 1811). (Winterthur Library).

MANCHESTER

The Cabinet-Makers' Manchester Book of Prices (1810).

Supplement to the Cabinet-Makers' Manchester Book of Prices (1825).

NORWICH

The Cabinet and Chair Makers' Norwich Book of Prices; containing the newest cabinet and chairwork ever yet published. The second edition with additions. Revised and corrected by a Committee of Journeymen Cabinet and Chair Makers. Printed by J. Payne for the Company of Cabinet and Chair Makers (Norwich, 1801). In two parts with emblematic frontispiece. (Norwich Reference Library; Winterthur Library.)

NOTTINGHAM

The Nottingham Cabinet and Chair Makers Book of Prices . . . as agreed by the Masters of the town of Nottingham 9 May 1791 (Nottingham, 1791). 12 pp. (Preston R.O.).

The Nottingham Cabinet and Chair Makers Book of Prices. Began 7 September 1795. Printed by C. Sutton (Nottingham, 1802). 32 pp. (Preston, R.O.).

The Prices of Cabinet-Work agreed by the Master Cabinet Makers of Nottingham (1805).

PRESTON

The Preston Cabinet-Makers and Chair-Makers Book of Prices. Began the 19th Day of August, 1799. Printed at Newby's Office (Preston). 32 pp. (Preston R.O.).

The Preston Cabinet and Chair-Makers Book of Prices. Agreed upon July, 1802. Printed by W. Addison (Preston, 1802). 140 pp. 2 pls (Preston R.O.).

WHITEHAVEN

The Prices agreed to between the Masters and Journeymen Cabinet Makers, in Whitehaven, 17 October 1810. Printed by T. Wilson (Whitehaven, 1810). 12 pp. (Carlisle Reference Library).

WYCOMBE

Chairmakers' Trade Union, Wycombe. List of Prices, July, 1872. Printed by Butler, Wycombe. 8 pp. (Wycombe Chair Museum).

Appendix Two   The *Bolton Supplement to the London Book of Cabinet Piece Prices* (1802)

The only recorded copy of the *Bolton Supplement to the London Book of Cabinet Piece Prices* (1802), descended in the Brumfitt family of cabinet makers, Skipton, Yorkshire. The flimsy sixteen-page publication represents an attempt by journeymen and masters in this Lancashire cotton town to improve labour relations by agreeing standard piece-work rates for making certain routine articles of furniture in common production. The title page names four leading masters who had endorsed the tables of labour costs: Thomas Seddon/Chas Brearley/Evan Marsden/George Grime. Evidently, the comprehensive specifications and piece-work rates contained in the current edition of *The Cabinet-Makers' London Book of Prices* provided a satisfactory basis for negotiating locally the costs of making a large number of items. However, there existed a demand in Bolton (and elsewhere) for certain types of furniture not described in the London book — hence the need for a local supplement. The schedules therefore help to define the regional character of ordinary domestic furniture and tell us something of value about how the provincial trade was organized.

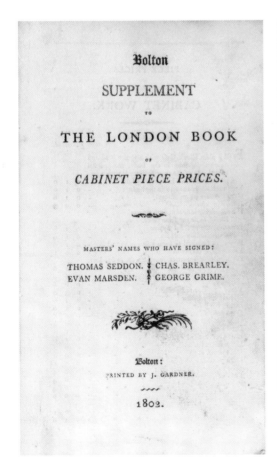

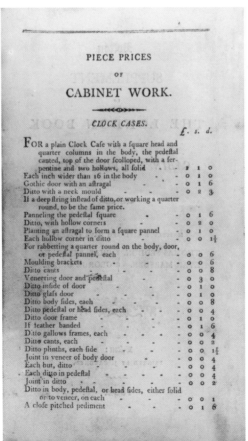

	£	s.	d.
An open pitched pediment	0	2	3
If ditto be returned, raking extra	0	0	9
A scrolled pediment	0	3	0
Veneering ditto board	0	0	4
Each nitch on a common door top or quirk	0	0	2
Hollow in head sides	0	1	0
Frize and astragal in body	0	1	0
Slipping door stiles or body sides to receive columns, each	0	0	1
Fluting quarter columns	0	1	0
Ditto head pillars each	0	0	6
Ditto back ditto, each	0	0	6
Gothic pillars in the head	0	2	0
Extra work or plinths of ditto, to be the same as other plinths			
Reeded pillars on one side, with four reeds	0	1	0
Ditto on two sides	0	2	0
Square pillars plain and solid, same as turned ditto			
Tapering ditto, each side	0	0	0½
For extra work on ditto, see square columns			
Veneering frieze in the head in front	0	0	3
Ditto sides	0	0	3
A band in head instead of an architrave, same price			
Each string in ditto	0	0	3
Dental or band in impost or cornice	0	1	0
Moulding glass door	0	1	4
Banding and stringing a pedestal square	0	1	6
Ditto, if hollow corners	0	2	6
Ditto cants, each	0	0	8
Ditto plinths, each side	0	0	6
Ditto body door	0	3	0
Ditto gothic ditto	0	4	0
Ditto frieze in body or head in front	0	1	0
If continued along the top and bottom edge of the ends, extra	0	0	6
Banding and stringing glass door	0	1	0
For grooving in strings to form a band, to be the half price of banding and stringing			
Polishing	0	0	9

For all banding above-mentioned to have a single string; for extra strings see London book.

	£	s.	d.
For an arch head Clock Case, with pillars in the head and quarter columns in the body, pedestal canted, top of the door scolloped the same as the square head, with a solid board for scrolls, all plain	1	12	0

	£	s.	d.
Each inch wider than 16 in the body	0	1	0
Fast pannel under the door veneered	0	2	0
If the plinths project and a small moulding on the top square of the surbase	0	2	0
A moulding on the front and sides between the door and fast pannel broke over the plinths	0	1	6
Moulding glass door	0	2	0
Banding and stringing fast pannel under door	0	0	8
Ditto glass door	0	1	10
If the arch be banded instead of an architrave	0	0	6
Each string in ditto	0	0	6
Key Stone	0	0	3
Cutting out three friezes for glass	0	1	0
Moulded dome or gothic ditto	0	2	0
Veneering head friezes, each	0	0	4
Grooving a string in ditto to form a band, each	0	0	9
Banding and stringing each ditto	0	1	6
Ditto scrolls	0	2	0
A battlement above the scrolls	0	0	9
Each plain pedestal capped	0	0	9
Veneering each side of the box	0	0	3
Polishing	0	0	9

For all other extras refer to square head Clock Case.

COLUMNS, &c.

	£	s.	d.
For plain quarter columns	0	3	6
Fluting ditto	0	1	0
Reeded columns, with four reeds on each side, the same price as Gothic ditto			
Each extra reed	0	0	1½
Whole columns, fluted extra from plain quarter do.	0	5	0
Reeding ditto, extra	0	1	0
Veneering brakes to receive ditto	0	1	0
Square columns, solid	0	3	6
Veneering ditto, each side	0	0	3
Ditto in two lengths, each length	0	0	2
Braking ditto in two, each brake	0	0	1
For cants, or Gothic columns, see London Book			
Solid plinths to cants	0	0	6
Glewing up Gothic, reeded, or square columns, each pair	0	0	6
For all other extras, see London Book			

CORNER CUPBOARDS.

	£	s.	d.
For a straight front cupboard, with framed doors, and one flat pannel in each, 3 feet 3 inches to the top of the cornice, all plain and solid	0	11	0

	£	s.	d.
Each inch higher	0	0	2
Each extra pannel	0	1	0
Each shelf more than three	0	0	7
Veneering cants	0	0	6
Ditto hanging stiles	0	0	3
A drawer in ditto	0	1	6
Each extra ditto	0	1	0
Veneering each ditto	0	0	2
Frieze and astragal	0	1	6
Dental or band in cornice	0	1	0
A single one to be extra	0	0	6
Polishing	0	0	6
For all other extras, see London Book.			

	£	s.	d.
A round front Corner Cupboard, three feet three inches to the top of the cornice	0	12	0
Each inch higher	0	0	2
Veneering doors	0	2	6
Ditto stiles	0	0	9
Frieze and astragal	0	1	9
Dental or band in cornice	0	1	3
Each Shelf more than three	0	0	7
A drawer in ditto	0	2	0
Each extra ditto	0	1	0
Veneering each ditto	0	0	3
A single one extra	0	0	6
Polishing	0	0	6
For ditto with framed doors, one pannel in each door, extra from start price	0	5	0
Each extra pannel	0	1	6
The mouldings for either of these Cupboards to be lengthway			
For all other extras, see London Book			

	£	s.	d.
For a Buffet, with two pannels in each upper door one in each lower ditto, seven feet to top of cornice, plain and solid	1	10	0
Each inch higher	0	0	3
Pilasters inside	0	2	0
Three drawers in ditto	0	3	0
Each extra ditto	0	1	0
Each extra pannel	0	1	0
Frieze and astragal	0	1	6
Veneering upper cants	0	1	6
Ditto lower ditto	0	1	0
Ditto upper hanging stiles	0	0	9
Ditto lower ditto	0	0	6

	£	s.	d.
Dental or band in cornice	0	1	6
Moulding brackets	0	0	8
Polishing	0	1	0
For all other extras, see London Book			

	£	s.	d.
For a Dresser, with four drawers and four sham ditto, 5 feet 6 inches long and 3 feet 6 inches high, with quarter columns, all plain and solid	2	1	0
Each inch more or less in length or height	0	0	6
Each extra sham	0	0	9
Each sham made into a real drawer	0	2	0
Veneering drawer fronts, each	0	0	6
Ditto long shams, each	0	0	6
Ditto short ditto, each	0	0	4
Ditto front framing long way	0	2	0
Ditto each end ditto	0	1	0
Ditto each pannel	0	1	0
Frieze and astragal in front	0	2	0
Ditto on the ends	0	1	0
A framed top	0	2	6
Moulding brackets	0	1	2
Scolloping back board or fixing ends to a plain one	0	0	6
Polishing	0	1	0
For all other extras, see London Book			
For a Dresser with two drawers and four sham ditto, 5 feet 2 inches long and 3 feet high, with quarter columns, all plain and solid	1	12	0
Veneering front frame lengthway	0	2	3

For all other extras, refer to the other Dresser.

BEDSTEADS.

	£	s.	d.
For a field bedstead, with screws and castors, and square roof sloped each way, 6 feet 4 inches by 4 feet 8 inches, or under, all of Dantzic oak	0	6	0
Circular or ogee roof, extra	0	1	6
Making each side or foot board	0	0	10
If ditto be mortised in, each, extra	0	0	6
Mortising in the head board	0	0	6
Base laths, each	0	0	6
Nailing in bottom	0	0	6
Over size either way, per inch	0	0	1
Colouring and polishing	0	1	0
English, American Oak, Maple, &c. extra	0	1	0

	£	s.	d.
Bedstead with long posts, tester lath, screws and castors, 6 feet 4 inches by 4 feet 8 inches, or under, all of Dantzic oak	0	7	0

£. s. d.

	£	s	d
Tapering each poſt below the mortiſe			4
Plinthing each poſt	0	0	8
Ditto head poſts, each ſide			4
Tapering poſts with hollow and ſquare, each poſt	0	1	4
Sinking each poſt to receive the caſtor	0	0	3
Aſtragal or band round each poſt	0	0	6
Each looſe pannel to cover the bed ſcrew, with a ſmall moulding or a white wood edge round ditto	0	1	0
Veneering each pannel	0	0	1
Fluting feet poſts, each poſt with twelve flutes	0	5	0
Each extra flute	0	0	2½
Reeding feet poſts, each poſt with twelve reeds	0	7	0
Each extra reed	0	0	3½
Faſt caps to either of theſe poſts, each poſt extra	0	1	0
Each finiſh to a bed ſide or end, with an extra ſcrew	0	0	8
Lath bottom			4
Canting each corner of a poſt above ſide	0	0	1
Round top end of ditto	0	0	1
Over ſize either way, each inch	0	0	1
Nailing in the bottom	0	0	6
Colouring and poliſhing	0	1	0
If Engliſh or American oak, maple, &c. extra	0	1	0

	£	s	d
For a Bedſtead with ſhort poſts, 6 feet 4 inches by 4 feet 8 inches, or under, all of Dantzic oak or deal, rabetted for bottom	0	4	6
Each bed ſcrew	0	0	2
Boring for cords	0	0	8
Slotting to ſtand againſt rabbetting for bottom			
A ſhelf on top of the head board	0	0	8
A back board to ditto	0	0	8
For all other extras, ſee Field or Long-poſt Bedſteads			
All Cornices to Bedſteads to be paid for according to time.			

SOFAS.

	£	s	d
For a ſquare Sofa, 6 feet long, or under, with ſix plain Marlborough legs and no lower rails	0	14	6
Commode or ſweep front rail	0	1	0
Each extra leg	0	0	6
Each inch longer	0	0	2
Tapering legs, each ſide	0	0	0½
Lower rails and ſtretcher	0	2	0
Looſe back	0	4	0
Each upright more than one	0	0	3
If the arms be ſquare from the back, and finiſh with two hollows down to the front foot, to be the ſame as common Sofa.			

£. s. d.

	£	s	d
If the arms finiſh with one hollow, and dove-tail'd into turn ſtumps, to be the ſame price.			
Rabbetting the front and end rails, for web, &c.	0	0	3
Nailing in bottom	0	0	6
Veneering the front rail, when ſtraight	0	0	6
Ditto the end rails	0	0	6
Ditto a ſweep front rail	0	0	10
Ditto a commode	0	1	0
If any of theſe rails be veneered croſsway, each joint, extra	0	0	1
Poliſhed ſeat rails	0	1	0
Poliſhing feet, &c.	0	0	6
A round corner Sofa, foot in centre, no lower rails, extra from a common Sofa with lower rails	0	4	0
Cloſe bracing each corner	0	0	2
Dowelling tenons, each dowel	0	0	0½
Sawing out ſeat rails, when ſtraight	0	0	6
Ditto ſweep front rail, extra	0	0	6
Ditto commode	0	0	4
Ditto round corners	0	0	6
Ditto feet and moulding ditto, ſee Chairs.			

CABRIOLE SOFA.

	£	s	d
For a plain Cabriole Sofa, 6 feet long and under, with ſix plain Marlborough legs	1	0	0
Mahogany ſtumps made plain	0	2	6
Ditto and arms moulded	0	2	0
Each extra leg	0	0	6
Each inch longer	0	0	2
Sawing out half moons	0	0	6
Ditto ſeat rails, ſee round corner Sofa.			
For ſweep or commode rails, and ſawing out ditto, ſee common Sofa.			
For ſawing out feet, tapering and moulding ditto, ſee Chairs.			
Poliſhing	0	0	3

SOFA STOOL.

	£	s	d
For a Sofa Stool, ſtuffed over the rail, 2 feet 6 inches long, with ſcrolled heads and plain Marlborough legs	0	5	6
Lower rails and ſtretcher	0	1	0
Each inch longer	0	0	1½
Poliſhed ſeat rails	0	0	6
Sawing out rails	0	0	3

£. s. d.

	£	s	d
Sawing legs, each	0	0	0½
Tapering and moulding, ſee Chairs.			
Veneering rails	0	0	10
Poliſhing, &c.	0	0	2
A ſingle one, extra	0	1	0

WINDOW STOOL.

	£	s	d
For a Window Stool, 2 ft. long, ſtuffed over the rail	0	2	6
Lower rails and ſtretcher	0	1	0
Each inch longer	0	0	1½
Poliſhed ſeat rails	0	0	6
Looſe ſeat for ditto	0	1	0
Commode or ſweep front rail	0	0	6
Ditto, if poliſhed	0	0	8
Looſe ſeat for ditto	0	1	4
For other extras, ſee Sofa Stool.			

SQUABS.

	£	s	d
A Squab, with four plain Marlborough legs, to be reckoned from a Sofa Stool, only deduct for ſcroll at one end	0	2	0
Each extra foot	0	0	6

COUCH CHAIRS.

	£	s	d
For a plain Couch Chair, 6 feet long and under, with 4 ſquare pannels and plain Marlbro' legs	0	13	0
Each inch longer	0	0	2
Raiſing each pannel	0	0	4
Each extra pannel	0	1	0
A top rail with hollow corners, each corner	0	0	6
Ditto with ogee or three hollows, each	0	0	6
Raiſing each pannel to top rail, with hollow corners	0	0	7
Ditto to ogee or three hollows	0	0	10
Dog legs, each	0	1	3
Nailing in bottom	0	0	6
If a rail to frame the pannels into above the ſeat rail, extra	0	1	6
Tapering, ſawing out and moulding feet, ſee Chairs			
For banding, ſee London Book.			
Sawing out ſeat rails	0	0	6
If a moulding in front under the capping	0	0	6
Poliſhing	0	0	9

B

£. s. d.

CHILD'S CHAIR.

	£	s	d
For a Child's Chair with a cover, plain	0	4	0
Rabbetting the ſides for the back and front, and beaded	0	0	6
Ditto for a hollow back	0	0	9
Hollow back	0	0	6
A ſquare table with a rim round	0	0	6
A ſweep or octagon front, extra	0	0	2
Dove-tailing a piece in the ſides to hold the table	0	0	3
Scollopping the top edge of the back	0	0	2
A ſingle one, extra	0	0	6
Joints in ſides, each	0	0	1
Ditto in back, front, or cover	0	0	0½
Poliſhing	0	0	3

CHAIRS.

	£	s	d
For a plain Chair ſtuffed over the rail, lower rails and ſtretcher	0	3	10
Each hole in the banniſter	0	0	1
Ditto top rail	0	0	2
Scraping and greaſing each hole	0	0	0½
Ditto in top rail	0	0	0½
Each ſweeped rail ſtuffed over	0	0	3
Veneering each ditto	0	0	3
Banding top edge, long or croſs way, refer to table of banding.			
Rounding top end of the feet to anſwer the turning	0	0	1½
Rabbetting rails for ſtuffing	0	0	1½
Cleaning up each ſweep'd rail, when not moulded on the top edge	0	0	1
Capping the top edge with a ſolid to form a moulding, each rail	0	0	3
Veneering back rail	0	0	1½
Ditto or quarter ſtuff on the top edge	0	0	1½
Beading ditto	0	0	1
Straight poliſhed rails for a looſe ſeat	0	0	6
Looſe ſeat for ditto	0	0	6
A commode or ſweep front rail, extra	0	0	6
Sweep ſide rails, extra from ſtraight poliſhed rails	0	1	0
A looſe ſeat for a ſweep front	0	0	7
Ditto for ſweep ſide rails	0	0	8
A round cornered ſeat ſtuffed over the rail, extra from ſweep rails	0	0	9
Dowelling the tenons, each dowel	0	0	0½
Hollow back	0	0	6
Sawing out top rail, each inch more than 2 in depth	0	0	1

£ s. d.

Slipping the backs up, a deep top rail behind in a dove-tail groove, extra - - - 0 0 4
If dove-tailed and tenonned - - - 0 0 6
Each nitch in a top rail - - - 0 0 1½
Each square or scroll in ditto - - - 0 0 1½
Scratch beading a plain back outside - - 0 0 3
Ditto inside - - - 0 0 3
Ditto, top rail or back with nitches, each ditto, extra 0 0 0½
Moulding back and top rail - - - 0 1 0
Ditto when a stay rail and moulded from the seat - 0 1 6
Ditto for a vase or urn pattern from the seat - 0 1 10
Each crooked joint in a balluster - - 0 0 9
A straight stay rail - - - 0 0 6
Scratch beading ditto, each side - - 0 0 1
A sweep'd stay rail - - - 0 0 8
Scratch beading ditto, each side - - 0 0 2
Notching the backs, and shouldering the stay rail in ditto - - - 0 0 2
If separate pieces glewed on, up and down way, same price.
Each plain upright splat more than three - - 0 0 3
Moulding each ditto - - - 0 0 2
Sawing out each splat hollow - - - 0 0 1
One upright splat plain scollopped, same as a *bannester* 0 0 6
Each extra ditto, more than one - - -
Each square nitch or scroll on the edge of splat or *bannester* - - - 0 0 0½
Two plain splats crossing each other, extra - 0 1 0
Two ogee ditto crossing each other - - 0 2 0
Scratch beading the straight, each edge - - 0 0 0½
Ditto each plain scollopped ditto - - 0 0 2
Ditto each nitch or scroll in ditto - - 0 0 0½
Fitting a splat with a crooked joint, each joint - 0 0 3
Each plain tie between the splats - - 0 0 1
Each ditto for drapery - - - 0 0 3
If ditto be framed into the splats, extra - 0 0 3
Tapering back feet - - - 0 0 1
Ditto each front foot, each side - - 0 0 0½
Moulding or terming ditto, refer to tables of moulding and terming cellect feet.
Sawing out each chair back - - - 0 0 1
Ditto each front foot - - - 0 0 0½
Ditto each sweeped rail - - - 0 0 0½
Ditto commode - - - 0 0 1½
Canting corners of back feet below the framing, each foot - - - 0 0 2
If no lower rails to a chair, deduct - - 0 0 6

£ s. d.

Arm Chair over-size, extra - - - 0 0 8
Plain arms and stumps - - - 0 2 9
Moulding ditto through - - - 0 1 8
Ditto three inches on each - - - 0 0 9
If the moulding be stopped at each end, to be the same price as moulding through.
If the stumps be moulded through and three inches on the arm - - - 0 1 3
Fixing the stumps on the top end of the feet, and working each side of the foot to answer ditto, each side - - - 0 0 1½
Hollow arms from top rail joint with turn'd stumps 0 3 9
If separate pieces be fitted to make out the sweeps 0 0 5
Moulding hollow arms - - - 0 1 6
Plain ogee or hollow stumps to ditto - - 0 1 0
Moulding ditto - - - 0 0 9
Polishing back, lower rails and feet - - 0 0 3

CROSS SPLAT BACK CHAIRS.

For a cross splat back Chair, with three plain splats and top rail, stuffed over the rail - - 0 5 6
Scollopping each edge of splat with a plain scollop 0 0 1
Ditto top rail, each edge - - - 0 0 2
Mitering the top rail - - - 0 0 6
For all other extras, see common Chair.

For a square stuffed back Chair, plain feet, stuffed over the rail - - - 0 3 0
An easy Chair, with lower rails and stretcher - 0 10 0
Saddle tree wings - - - 0 1 6
Hollow back - - - 0 1 0
Close stool in ditto - - - 0 4 0
Polishing - - - 0 0 2
For all other extras, see common Chair.

SMOKING CHAIR.

For a smoking Chair, with two plain *bannester* and loose seat - - - 0 6 6
Each pedestal in ditto - - - 0 0 4
Cross stretcher or framing lower rails - - 0 0 6
Close stool in ditto - - - 0 4 0
For all other extras, see common Chair.

CHILD'S CHAIR.

For a Child's Chair with a foot-board to move, a turned pin to go into the arm, a plain *bannester* 0 8 0

£ s. d.

Cutting ditto in two parts and fixing a half inch top to the lower part to answer for a foot-board - 0 2 6
Framing the lower part separate, to be extra - 0 1 6
Making plain stumps - - - 0 1 0
A table, with a bead bent round ditto, fixed to the arms - - - 0 0 9
A single one to be extra - - - 0 1 0
For work on arms and other extras, see common Chairs

CHILD'S CRIB.

For a Child's Crib, 3 feet 6 inches long, 1 foot 8 inches wide, rabbetted for ticken, the inside corners of the feet champered, the front to slide, or hung with hinges - - 0 8 0
Working a sash on the 3 outside corners of the foot 0 0 3
Returned ditto round the top end, each foot extra 0 0 2
Working a sash on the upper corner of the sides and ends, and mitering ditto in the feet - - 0 1 6
Veneering each side and top edge - - 0 0 6
Ditto each end - - - 0 0 4
A lath bottom - - - 0 1 4
A loose frame for ticken - - - 0 1 0
Fixing an upright in the slided back and working a sash on ditto - - - 0 1 0
If the slide be dove-tailed grooved, extra - 0 1 0
Fixing four posts with sweep or ogee roof - - 0 2 2
Each inch over-size either way - - - 0 0 2
Polishing - - - 0 0 3

CRADLES.

For a Cradle 3 feet long, with an octagon head 0 8 0
Arched head, extra - - - 0 1 0
Making ditto to slide - - - 0 2 0
If ditto be hung with hinges - - - 0 1 0
Canted sides - - - 0 2 0
Scollopping top edges - - - 0 1 3
Making a frame to rock on - - - 0 1 6
Halving the arch - - - 0 0 2
Each inch longer - - - 0 0 2
A single one, extra - - - 0 0 6
Polishing - - - 0 0 3

VENETIAN BLINDS.

For Venetian Blinds to meet in the middle, with 35 shades in each frame, or under - - 0 10 6
Each extra shade - - - 0 0 0½
Hanging stiles or extra, refer to London Book.

£ s. d.

FAST WASH BOARD.

For a fast Wash Board to a bason stand, plain sweep from the back down to the front, when two together, each - - - 0 1 3
If only one - - - 0 1 6
Each shelf in the corner - - - 0 0 4
If grooved in, extra - - - 0 0 1

NIGHT TABLE.

For a Night Table, with two tops, hung with hinges, hollow stumps, without pannels in the sides, plain and solid, 1 foot 8 inches long and 1 foot 6 inches wide - - 0 14 0
Each inch over-size, either way - - 0 0 3
Veneering front - - - 0 0 6
Pannels in sides with quarter worked round ditto 0 2 3
Round front to ditto veneered - - 0 2 0
Commode front ditto - - - 0 3 0
Clamping a lower flap - - - 0 0 6
Veneering ditto on top side - - - 0 0 9
Working an astragal on the edge of the upper flap 0 0 9
Ditto lower ditto - - - 0 0 4
A single one to be extra - - - 0 0 6
Polishing - - - 0 0 6
For all other extras, see London Book.

WORK TABLE.

For a Work Table, with ovalo corners, plain and solid, tapered legs - - - 0 8 0
Veneering the corners, each - - - 0 0 5
Ditto the straight rails, each - - - 0 0 3
A drawer in ditto - - - 0 2 3
If quarter round corners, deduct, each brake - 0 0 1
For all other extras, see London Book.

ROUND DRINKING TABLE.

For a round Drinking Table, with a triangle frame, plain feet, 2 feet 3 inches diameter - - 0 4 0
Each inch over size - - - 0 0 2
Ditto, when a compass rail - - - 0 0 3
Lower rails - - - 0 0 6
A shelf on ditto - - - 0 1 0
A compass rail, 3 inches deep - - 0 4 0
Each inch deeper - - - 0 0 3
Veneering ditto - - - 0 1 9
Ditto straight rails - - - 0 0 9
Ditto lower rails, when a shelf - - 0 0 6

	£.	s.	d.
Each extra leg	- o	o	8
Sawing out legs, each	- o	o	o¼
Tapering ditto, each side	- o	o	o¼
Extra work on legs, see Tables of ditto.			
Ditto on top, see Pillar and Claw Table.			
A single one, extra	- o	o	6
Polishing	- o	o	4

WRITING DRAWER.

	£.	s.	d.
For a writing drawer, 3 feet 6 inches long, with 6 loose covers and 2 fast ditto, with a slider lip'd for cloth	- 1	4	o
Each private drawer	- o	1	o
Veneering each cover	- o	o	1½
Each ditto, hung with hinges	- o	o	3
An elevating flap to write on	- o	3	6
Lining ditto with cloth	- o	o	6
If the flap be hung fair at the front, extra	- o	1	o
Making each hollow piece, the front to turn in to slide	- o	o	4
Each loose box in ditto	- o	o	4
Each inch longer	- o	o	2
For a round top to a cellaret	- o	3	6
Cove top to ditto	- o	3	o
A projecting bade over the cove	- o	o	6

CHEESE WAGGON.

	£.	s.	d.
For a cheese waggon, with half rollers and a partition to move	- o	7	o
If less than three together, each extra	- o	o	6
Gluing up bottom in two thicknesses	- o	1	o
Polishing	- o	o	2
Moulding common brackets, each side	- o	o	2
Letting in shades, all under 3 inches	- o	o	3
From 3 to 5 inches	- o	o	4
All above 5 inches	- o	o	6
If English or American oak, maple, &c. for drawer bottoms, each long drawer, extra	- o	o	3
Each short ditto	- o	o	2
If drawer sides of ditto, each drawer	- o	o	2

Sawing up cornice angle-way, slips for front edges, beads, &c. jacking down slabs, carrying home work, &c. to be paid for according to time.

DAY WORK.

The hours of working by the day to be from six o'clock in the morning till six o'clock in the evening; to be allowed half an hour at breakfast, and one hour at dinner.

TIME OF CANDLE-LIGHT

To begin on the 12th of October, and to end on the 12th of February. Time of candle-light in the morning to be six weeks before Christmas, and then to leave off.

Evan Marsden.
Charles Brearley.
George Grime.
Thomas Seddon.

Gardner, Printer, Bolton.

Appendix Three The Wycombe Chairmakers' *List of Prices* (1872)

The 'Wycombe' section of the chair trade produced a wide range of cheap chairs graded common, regular or best. Workers were paid very low rates and in 1872 the newly formed Wycombe Chairmakers' Trade Union compiled an eight-page list of piece-work rates in an effort to secure fair and uniform rates for their members. Chairmakers employed by up-market firms on better class work enjoyed far higher earnings. Most of the manufacturers refused to accept the price-list as submitted and a strike followed which was eventually settled by negotiation. The printed schedule is divided into eight parts, each describing standard components or workshop practices relating to different branches of the trade. Significantly only one of these processes involved the use of machinery. The detailed specifications and terminology provide a rich source for present-day furniture historians. A possibly unique copy of the piece price-list issued in July 1872 survives at the Wycombe Chair Museum (L.427/107 B. 684); its existence was first recorded by L.J. Mayes, *The History of Chairmaking in High Wycombe* (1960). Some entries have been altered in manuscript and the section on clothes-horses extended.

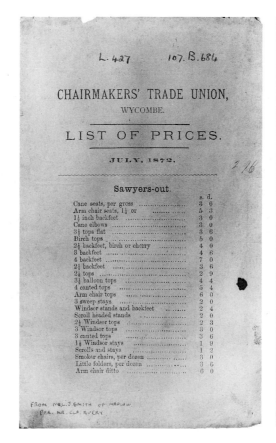

L. 427 107. B.684

CHAIRMAKERS' TRADE UNION,
WYCOMBE.

LIST OF PRICES.

JULY, 1872.

Sawyers-out.

	s.	d.
Cane seats, per gross	3	6
Arm chair seats, 1½ or	5	3
1½ inch backfeet	3	0
Cane elbows	3	0
3½ tops flat	3	6
Birch tops	5	0
2½ backfeet, birch or cherry	4	0
3 backfeet	4	6
4 backfeet	7	0
2½ backfeet	3	6
2½ tops	2	9
3½ balloon tops	4	4
4 canted tops	5	4
Arm chair tops	6	0
3 sweep stays	2	0
Windsor stands and backfeet	2	4
Scroll headed stands	2	0
2½ Windsor tops	2	3
3 Windsor tops	3	0
3 canted tops	3	6
1½ Windsor stays	1	9
Scrolls and stays	1	2
Smoker chairs, per dozen	3	0
Little folders, per dozen	3	6
Arm chair ditto	6	0

FROM MR. J. SMITH OF MARLOW
PER MR. C.P. AVERY

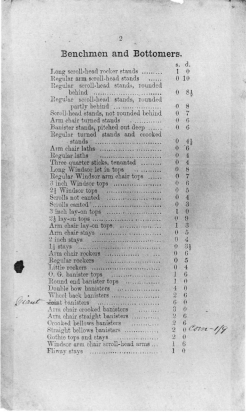

2

Benchmen and Bottomers.

	s.	d.
Long scroll-head rocker stands	1	0
Regular arm scroll-head stands	0	10
Regular scroll-head stands, rounded behind	0	8½
Regular scroll-head stands, rounded partly behind	0	8
Scroll-head stands, not rounded behind	0	7
Arm chair turned stands	0	6
Banister stands, pitched out deep	0	6
Regular turned stands and crooked stands	0	4½
Arm chair laths	0	6
Regular laths	0	4
Three quarter sticks, tenanted	0	4
Long Windsor let in tops	0	8
Regular Windsor arm chair tops	0	7
3 inch Windsor tops	0	6
2½ Windsor tops	0	5
Scrolls not canted	0	4
Scrolls canted	0	3
3 inch lay-on tops	1	0
2½ lay-on tops	0	9
Arm chair lay-on tops	1	3
Arm chair stays	0	5
2 inch stays	0	4
1½ stays	0	3½
Arm chair rockers	0	6
Regular rockers	0	5
Little rockers	0	4
O. G. banister tops	1	6
Round end banister tops	1	0
Double bow banisters	4	0
Wheel back banisters	2	6
Joint banisters	6	0
Arm chair crooked banisters	3	0
Arm chair straight banisters	2	6
Crooked bellows banisters	2	6
Straight bellows banisters	2	0
Gothic tops and stays	2	0
Windsor arm chair scroll-head arms	1	6
Fliway stays	1	0

Best arched tops 2/4

	s.	d.
Arched tops, carved at the ends	1	6
1¼ plain stays, per gross	2	9
Shop chair and table chair backfeet	0	6
1½ and arm chair backfeet	0	7
1½ rocker backfeet, pitched out	0	8
Roman backfeet rounded	1	0
Self backfeet	0	10
Self backfeet, rounded all down	1	6
Doffin backfeet	0	8
Thumb backfeet, rounded	0	8
Swan neck arm	0	10
Swan neck arm, rounded underneath	1	0
Table chair arms	0	10
Ditto, rounded underneath	1	0
Footboards	0	4
Best ditto	0	6
French tops	1	0
Mouldings, per gross	0	6
Self tops	1	0
Ditto stays	0	6
Little banister tops	1	6
Carved tops and stays	2	0
Carved chair with banister	4	6
Rush seats	0	4
Regular bottoms	1	3
Arm chair and smoker bottoms	1	6

De over 20 inches 2-0

Turners.

	s.	d.
Common backfeet, per dozen	0	4
Rocker backfeet	0	8
Regular arm backfeet	0	6
Regular stands	0	4
Best stands	0	10
Common scrolls	0	8
Arm chair scrolls	0	10
Sofa legs, over 3 inches square, per leg	0	4
Ditto, 3 inches and under, 1d. per inch	0	1
Smoke, per chair, out of beech	1	0
Smokers, not out of beech	1	6
Best stuffing forefeet and fronts, per doz.	1	6
Sweep back ditto		
Sweep back ditto, dry stuff	1	3

Plain backfeet & stands 5½

Double Cloths Horse complete 1/3 without rails 1/-
Common do complete — 1/- without rails 9d
Single horse complete — 8 without rails 6d

4

	s.	d.
Big rocker ditto	1	6
Roman feet and stretchers	0	8
Doffin feet and fronts	0	7
Arm chair feet and fronts	2	0
Table chair feet and fronts	2	0
Shop chair feet and fronts	1	6
Ladder back feet and fronts	1	6
Small feet	0	8
Best balloon feet and fronts	1	6
Arm chair legs	1	0
Stumps	0	6
Arm chair stretchers	0	5
Double stretchers	0	8
Birch and cherry regular legs	0	10
Scotch Roman chairs and bottom	1	4
Berger chair	2	0
Small ditto	1	4
Table chair sticks, per dozen	0	6
Double clothes-horse, each	1	4
Folding chair, back feet and buttons, per chair	0	9
Double spindles, per dozen	0	
Rush or Windsor spindles, per dozen	0	
Elbows, ditto	0	4
Ashley Cooper spindles and drops, ditto	1	0
Ashley Cooper back feet	1	0
Fore feet and fronts, not out of beech	2	0
Ladder back buttons, per gross	3	0
Common rush feet and fronts, ditto	1	0
Giant chair, each	1	0
Roman back feet, ditto	0	6
Sewing chair fore feet and fronts, per chair	0	4

Seat Makers.

	s.	d.
Common seats, table, and shopchairs per dozen	2	3
Sweep back seats	2	4
Compass side seats	2	6
Ladies' nursers—1 in. stuff	2	6
Ladies' nursers—over 1 in. stuff	3	0
Ladder backs, rounded one side	3	0

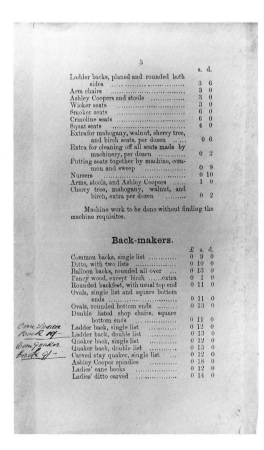

5

	s.	d.
Ladder backs, planed and rounded both sides	3	6
Arm chairs	3	0
Ashley Coopers and stools	3	0
Wicker seats	3	0
Smoker seats	6	0
Crinoline seats	6	0
Squat seats	4	0
Extra for mahogany, walnut, cherry tree, and birch seats, per dozen	0	6
Extra for cleaning off all seats made by machinery, per dozen	0	2
Putting seats together by machine, common and sweep	0	9
Nursers	0	10
Arms, stools, and Ashley Coopers	1	0
Cherry tree, mahogany, walnut, and birch, extra per dozen	0	2

Machine work to be done without finding the machine requisites.

Back-makers.

	£	s.	d.
Common backs, single list	0	9	0
Ditto, with two lists	0	10	0
Balloon backs, rounded all over	0	13	0
Fancy wood, except birch .....extra	0	1	0
Rounded backfeet, with usual top end	0	11	0
Ovals, single list and square bottom ends	0	11	0
Ovals, rounded bottom ends	0	13	0
Double listed shop chairs, square bottom ends	0	11	0
Ladder back, single list	0	12	0
Ladder back, double list	0	13	0
Quaker back, single list	0	12	0
Quaker back, double list	0	13	0
Carved stay quaker, single list	0	12	0
Ashley Cooper spindles	0	18	0
Ladies' cane backs	0	12	0
Ladies' ditto carved	0	14	0

6

	£	s.	d.
Best carved stay cane back table chair	0	13	0
Double cees	0	18	0
Crown oval backs	1	0	0
Prince of Wales' stay	0	11	0
Peake backs	0	10	0
4 scroll backs	0	10	0
Bible stay gothics	0	15	0
Gothic back, round	0	13	0
Ditto, square	0	11	0
Rabbiting cane backs ......per dozen	0	1	0
Ditto arms ....per dozen	0	1	6
Manchester backs	0	18	0

Windsor Framers.

	s.	d.
Stick backs, scrolls, and plain stays	5	6
Stick backs, driven in stands	5	0
Banister, single	6	0
Banister, with two	6	0
All sticks	6	6
Wheel backs	8	0
Spindle gothics	7	0
Lath backs	7	0
Plain stay, spindle	6	6
Arm chair—stay, stick, or scroll	1	0
" all stick	1	4
" wheel back	1	6
" wheel back, double bow		
" all stick, double bow		
All chairs, except arms, with double stretchers or back stretchers, 6d. extra		
Arm chair—lath arm, splice common	1	4
" arch gothic and banister	1	6
" lath arm, scroll elbow	1	10
" best ditto	2	2
" banister and laths	3	0
" banister turned stands	2	6
Table chairs	0	8
Best screwed	0	10
Two-stay nursers	0	9

	s.	d.
Sticks and single stay	0	8
Lath back nursers	0	10
Ladder backs	1	10
Cane smokers	0	9
Wood smokers	0	10
Child's, without arms	0	5½
,, with arms	0	6
Rockers, with arms	0	7
Stools	0	3
Putting rockers to arm chairs ...extra	0	2

Cane-seat Framers.

	s.	d.
Common and sweep back chairs	2	2
Common chairs, double back lists	2	5
Elliptic and sweep back rush	2	6
Common rush and 40 rush	3	0
Rush Romans	3	6
Cherry, birch, and walnut	2	6
Mahogany, nailed	3	0
Big rockers, dowled 10s., if mortised ...	11	0
Regular arm chairs	7	0
Arm chair, library, screwed	7	0
Small library, no arms, screwed	4	0
Woman's rockers dowled 4s., if mortised	4	6
Woman's nursers, no rockers	3	0
Boy's rockers, dowled 4s. 6d., if mortised	5	0
Best boy's rockers	6	0
Boy's arms, no rockers	4	0
Boy's trap seat rockers	6	0
Common table chairs	5	0
Ditto, list elbows	5	6
Best table chairs, right and left elbows	6	0
Box table chairs	6	0
Ashley Cooper	4	6
Shop chair	3	0
Common stools	2	2
Camp stools with handles	3	6
Single towel rails 2s. 6d., double	3	6
Duchess, screwed	4	0
Cane seat chairs, two banisters	3	6

Camp Stools no handles 3 - 0

	s.	d.
Ditto, wide banister	4	0
Regular banister chair	3	0

Where the screwing is not mentioned 6d. per dozen will be charged, or one farthing per hole; the same with pegged chairs.

Odd work will be regulated according to the price settled on cherry, birch, walnut, &c.

Polishers.

	s.	d.
Common cane seat chairs, per dozen	2	0
Sweep back, polished to the seats, ditto	2	6
Scroll, plain, regular Windsor, stickback	2	7
Common table chairs	2	6
Nursers	2	6

All other chairs equalised in proportion.

BUTLER, PRINTER, WYCOMBE.

Glossary

This glossary has been compiled to avoid heavy annotation of unfamiliar diction, archaic words and technical terms. Many specialist or dialect words, which are defined where they occur in the text, are omitted from the following list which also excludes trade terms found in Appendix Two and Appendix Three.

ADZE – a cutting tool with a blade set at right angles to the handle, used for removing heavy waste, shaping or trimming the surface of timber.

ANGEL HALF-TESTER – a bed in which the half-tester is supported by ceiling stays.

ARK – a meal chest constructed of boards wedged together, with a canted top.

ASTRAGAL – a small moulding or bead.

AWL – a sharp spike used for making holes.

BAMBOO RING TURNING – ornamental turning, simulating the ring joints on a bamboo stem.

BASS – a local name applied to rush chair seats.

BED SCREWS – the bolts holding together the posts and rails of a bedstead.

BIGGIN – a habitation, building, house, cottage.

BILLET – a short length of wood, roughly trimmed, ready for turning.

BILLHOOK – a short-handled axe with a long blade used by many woodland workers.

BLACKHOUSE – a single-storey straw-thatched building with a central hearth and walls of double thickness; the family lived at one end and their cattle at the other. Once common in West Scotland.

BOARDED KIST – a chest made up from six planks rather than being of framed panel construction.

BODGERS – a name given to the men who turned chair legs and stretchers in the Buckinghamshire beechwoods.

BOOT JACK – a device for aiding the removal of riding boots.

BORING LATHE – a small treadle lathe with a chuck and bit for boring holes.

BOTHY – a building in which unmarried labourers lodge together.

BROSE – a dish made by pouring boiling water on oatmeal.

BUFFET – a built-in corner cupboard or shelved recess, alternatively a low stool.

CAPPIE – a small drinking vessel.

CAT – a fireside plate-stand of tripod pattern.

CAUL – a piece of flat or curved wood used for holding down a veneer while the glue sets.

CHAFF BED – a mattress stuffed with the husks of corn separated by threshing.

CHAMBER HORSE – an exercising chair. The deep leather seat has a spring concertina movement allowing the occupant to simulate the motions of horse riding.

CHAMFER – a flat bevel made by cutting off a square corner.

CHAUMER – a room on a farm where unmarried labourers sleep.

CHIFFONIER BED – a folding bedstead concealed in a carcase that outwardly resembles a chiffonier or sideboard.

CLAMP STOOL – a stool with a jaw for holding work fast.

CLASS BOX – small locker or box used in Sunday Schools for keeping books or work.

COUCH CHAIR – a North Country term for a panel-back settle.

CRANK – a revolving disc to which a regulated pressure can be applied which criminals sentenced to hard labour were required to turn.

CRATCH – a wooden frame.

CREEL – a framework strung with cords suspended from the kitchen ceiling and used for storing soft oatcakes.

CRIB BED – a standing bed or cot with low sides once common in institutions.

CRICKET – a low wood-bottomed stool often used by children.

CRINOLINE STRETCHER – modern name for the bowed front stretcher of a Windsor chair.

CROGLOFFT – a low loft open to the roof at one end of a single room dwelling, reached by a ladder.

CRUCKS – a pair of large curved timbers inclined inwards from the outer walls of a building and meeting at the apex to support the ridge beam.

DAVENPORT – a small slope-top writing-desk with drawers below.

DEAL – fir or pine, also used to describe sawn softwood boards.

DESS BED – dialect word used in the North East for a fold-away bed.

DOG LEG – local term for a cabriole leg (Lancashire).

DONKEY – alternative name for a horse.

DUTCH MATTING – imported finely woven grass matting.

ESPALIER – a lattice framework on which fruit trees are trained.

FANCY CHAIR – contemporary term for lightly constructed decorative chairs with a painted finish (c. 1790–1850).

FELLOE – a segment forming the rim of a wooden wheel.

FIRE WINDOW – a small window lighting the hearth.

FIRKIN – a small cask.

FLEAK/FLAKE – a frame or rack hung from the ceiling and used for storing provisions.

FRENCH BED – a couch bed with head and footboards, the curtain draped over a pole projecting from the wall.

FROE – a tool with a wedge-shaped blade used for splitting timber.

FUMED OAK – oak given a rich dark colour by the vapours of liquid ammonia.

GILE VAT – a coopered vessel used in brewing for the wort to ferment.

GO-GIN – a type of baby walker following a circular track.

HALF-TESTER – a short tester or canopy bracketed forward from the headboard of a bed.

HARDEN – a very coarse cloth made from hemp or flax.

HASTER – a shelved screen lined with tin used for keeping dishes hot in front of a kitchen fire.

HECK – a short internal wall carrying one side of a firehood, usually with an entrance beside it.

HELM – stalks of straw.

HORSE – various work-holding devices are known as horses.

HOVEL – an open-sided shed or outhouse used as a shelter.

HULK – a prison ship moored offshore.

HURDLES – portable frames made from cleft poles or wattle used for temporary fences.

HURLEY BED – a low bed on castors kept under the built-in bed in Scottish tenements and wheeled out at night for the children to sleep in.

HUTCH – a storage chest, sometimes with cupboard doors.

INGLE-NOOK – the area under a large chimney or firehood.

JAPANNING – a term for simulated oriental lacquer, also used to describe painted finishes.

JONC – green rushes.

KERSEY – coarse woollen cloth of twill weave.

KIPE – basket or fish trap.

KNACK REEL – a wheel used in winding yarn.

KNEADING TROUGH – a splay-sided chest on legs with a board cover, the interior partitioned for keeping flour and making dough.

LAST BLOCK – a wooden model or mould.

LIP-WORK – the craft of making articles from coiled rolls of straw.

LOPER – a sliding rail that pulls out to support a flap.

MARLBOROUGH LEG – a straight, usually tapered, leg of square section.

MASH VAT COOLER – an oval tub used to cool the wort in brewing.

MELODION – a portable wind instrument with a keyboard and bellows.

MESLIN – mixed grain for breadmaking, especially rye with wheat.

MOREEN – a worsted cloth generally given a waved or stamped finish.

NAVE – the central hub or stock of a wooden wheel.

NONSUCH CHEST – a Germanic chest with intarsia decoration representing buildings (c. 1580–1620).

OAKUM – loose fibre obtained by untwisting and picking old rope.

OGEE (O.G.) – a continuous double curve profile.

OSIER WITHY – a willow wand.

OUT-RELIEF – payments made under the Poor Laws to pauper families living at home.

OUTSHUT – a projection or extension to a building under a lean-to roof.

PEGGY STICK – a long-handled dolly for plunging, pounding and working the dirt out of clothes in a wash-tub.

PRESS – a low drum-shaped stool or hassock made of rushes.

PIGGIN – a coopered vessel used for drinking and as a dipper.

PIRN – a weaver's bobbin.

POLE LATHE – a traditional lathe with reciprocating rotary action; the cord drive passes from the end of a springy sapling, round the work-piece to a foot treadle. Used by chair bodgers and bowl turners.

POLLARD – a tree cut back to produce a thick growth of young branches, forming twisted grain in the trunk.

PRESS BED – a folding bedstead built into a cabinet outwardly resembling a clothes press or cupboard.

PRESS DRILL – a hand-operated drill on which pressure is applied by means of a weighted beam or screw mechanism.

PUTCHEON – a wicker eel trap.

RABBET – a groove cut to receive a corresponding projection on another piece of wood forming a joint.

RAGGED SCHOOL – a free school for children of the poorest class.

RANDED – basketry term for a rod worked singly.

RECKON – an iron bar or hook for suspending pots over the fire.

ROOKERIES – a cluster of tenements densely populated by people of the lowest class.

ROUND – a short stick usually with tapered ends, such as the rung of a ladder or turned chair leg.

SADDLE TREE – the cheeks on a winged easy chair.

SCOTCH/SCOTS CARPET – an inexpensive flat reversible two-ply carpet without a pile.

SCRIM – a kind of thin canvas used for lining in upholstery.

SCUMBLE – a thin coat of paint in which soft lines are produced by rubbing over the surface.

SEED LIP – a container for seed corn used in open cast sowing.

SHAVING HORSE/BRAKE/MARE – a low bench on which the workman sits astride; the billet to be shaped, usually with a drawknife, is held fast in a pedal-operated jaw.

SHINGLE – a wooden roof tile.

SHOTTLE – small box with a hinged lid fitted inside a kist (Scottish).

SKEELS – broad coopered vessels.

SKEP – a domed beehive made of coiled straw rolls.

SLUBBING CREEL – a frame to hold bobbins of half-spun wool.

SNAP TABLE – a tripod table with a tip-up top.

SPEER – a fixed screen to exclude draughts from a doorway.

SPENCE – a pantry cupboard.

SPOKE SHAVE – a wing-shaped tool with a central cutting blade used for cleaning up circular work.

SPRIG – a thin strip of wood nailed to the seat edge of rush chairs.

SQUAB – a North Country term for a single-headed couch with an upholstered seat, alternatively a loose seat cushion.

STEERAGE – that part of a ship allotted to passengers who travel at the cheapest rate.

STRAINING BENCH – Windsor chair bows were steamed and bent into shape by straining them between pegs.

STRETCHER – a bar or rod used as a tie or brace between the legs of a chair.

STUMP BED – a low bed without any superstructure.

SUFFOLK CHAIR – a generic term for a type of East Anglian wood-bottomed chair that spread to other parts of the country during the early nineteenth century.

SUGAN – twisted straw rope.

SWILES – large wooden buckets.

TEMPLATE/TEMPLET – a flat piece of wood cut to the size or profile of the finished article and used as a pattern during manufacture.

THATCHING SPAR – lengths of split hazel used to hold roof thatch down.

TICKEN – strong cotton cloth with a twill weave with coloured yarn-dyed stripes on a white ground.

TRENCHER – a square or circular wooden platter.

TRUCKLE/TRUNDLE BED – a low bed on wheels for servants or children, often stowed beneath a standing bed.

TUSK TENON – a through-tenon, the protruding end pierced and secured with a wedge.

TWIGGEN CHAIR – a wicker chair.

VALANCE – a border of drapery hangings around the canopy of a bed.

VARDO – travelling people's name for a gypsy caravan.

WANDED – made of willow wands.

WATTLE – stakes interlaced with pliant twigs to make fences, walls, etc.

WINTER HEDGE/DYKE – a North Country term for a clothes-horse.

WISKER – a padded-leather knitting belt (Scottish).

WITHY – a flexible willow twig.

Notes

INTRODUCTION

1. Articles have mostly appeared in antique-collecting magazines. An exception is the series of exhibitions held at Temple Newsam, Leeds, between 1972 and 1982, and Bill Cotton's publications on regional chairs.
2. As long ago as March 1968, *Antiques* devoted an issue to articles by ten leading authorities on their interpretation of the term 'country furniture'.
3. R. Holme, *The Academy of Armory* (I.H. Jeayes, ed.), (London, for the Roxburghe Club, 1905), bk 3, p. 15.
4. J.M. Richards, *The Functional Tradition in Early Industrial Buildings* (1958), makes this point.
5. A. Wells-Cole, *Oak Furniture from Lancashire and the Lake District* (exh. cat.), Temple Newsam, Leeds, 1973 (17). A settle at Lotherton Hall is elaborately carved with degenerate traditional ornament and the date '1756'. C. Gilbert, *Furniture at Temple Newsam House and Lotherton Hall* (Leeds, 1978), vol. 2, p. 271.
6. The vernacular tradition which we are considering emerged about 1740 when stereotyped 'Jacobean'-style carving was virtually extinct.
7. The trade label of Richard Blakeborough, clockmaker and ironmonger of Otley, Yorkshire (*fl.* 1827–37) listed 'Stringings and Shells, for enlaying' amongst his varied wares. They were also stocked by Christopher Gabriel, toolmaker, in 1793. See W.L. Goodman, 'Christopher Gabriel his Book', *Furniture History*, XVII (1981), pp. 23–41.
8. The fullest study is D.A. Fales, *American Painted Furniture 1660–1800* (New York, 1972), but see also J. Kirk's three-part article 'The Tradition of English Painted Furniture', *Antiques*, May 1980; October 1980; January 1981; and B. Cotton, 'Painted Furniture A Vernacular Tradition', *Antique Dealer and Collector's Guide*, October 1987, pp. 43–6.
9. R. Southern, *The Georgian Playhouse* (London, 1948), pl. 25.

1 CRAFTS AND TIMBERS

1. The books from which I have derived most benefit whilst researching this chapter are: T. Sheraton, *The Cabinet Dictionary* (London, 1803); J.C. Loudon, *Arboretum et Fruticetum Britannicum* (London, 1838); W. Bullock, *Timbers for Woodwork* (nd London, *c.* 1910); H.L. Edlin, *Woodland Crafts in Britain* (London, 1949), Blackie & Son, *The Cabinet-Maker's Assistant* (London, 1853), and R.A. Salaman, *Dictionary of Tools* (London, 1975).
2. I. Sparkes, *The English Country Chair* (Bourne End, 1973), pp. 24–35, provides a full account of bodging. There are two well-illustrated articles by W.M. Webb on forestry and chairmaking in Buckinghamshire in *The Country Home*, October 1910 and April 1911.
3. I. Sparkes, *The Windsor Chair* (Bourne End, 1975), p. 112.
4. Loudon, *Arboretum* (1838), III, p. 2023.
5. J. Stevens and J. Arthur, 'Inventories of Household Effects', *Annual Bulletin Société Jersaise* (1972), p. 376.
6. Uxbridge Public Library, Middlesex.
7. B.D. Cotton, 'Shadford, Shirley and the Caistor Workshop', *Regional Furniture*, II (1988), p. 48.
8. Edlin, *Woodland Crafts* (1949), p. 23.
9. B.D. Cotton, 'A North Country Chair Making Tradition', *Furniture History*, XVII (1981), pp. 42–50.
10. Yorkshire Archaeological Society: DD54.
11. Yorkshire Archaeological Society: Farnley Papers (unlisted).
12. Blackie & Son, *Cabinet-Maker's Assistant* (1853), p. 16.
13. N. Moore, 'A Chester Cabinet Maker's Specification Book', *Regional Furniture*, I (1987), pp. 71–8.
14. J.C. Loudon, *Encyclopaedia of Cottage, Farm, and Villa Architecture and Furniture* (London, 1833), p. 294.
15. Sheraton, *The Cabinet Dictionary* (1803), p. 193.
16. Westminster City Libraries: Gillow Records 344/97A, p. 1391.
17. Loudon, *Arboretum* (1838), III, p. 1699.
18. C. Gilbert, 'An Early Price List from York', *Furniture History*, XXI (1985), pp. 227–8.
19. Winterthur Library, Delaware: Shelf Mark 76 × 9.
20. Worksop Public Library, Nottinghamshire: local collections.
21. W. Plomer (ed.), *Kilvert's Diary* (London, 1977), p. 18.

2 COUNTRY JOINERS

1. W. Rose, *The Village Carpenter* (Cambridge, 1937; republished 1973).
2. J. Stabler, 'Two Labelled Comb-Back Windsors', *Antique Collecting*, April 1977, discusses John Pitt and Richard Hewett (*fl. c.* 1750–70) who both combined these trades; others include Abraham Meade, High Wycombe; John Whitworth, Gamston and John Hubbard, Grantham.
3. A copy of the latter is at Temple Newsam House, Leeds; the earlier catalogue and a full set of account books, 1867–1940, are still owned by the family.
4. J. & R. Prior, Windsor chairmakers of Uxbridge, also supplied poles, stakes and pea-sticks in 1820, while in 1825 John Todd of Caistor invoiced chairs and hay rakes to a customer (p. 117 & p. 9).
5. Winterthur Library, Delaware: the Joseph Downs Collection of Manuscripts, Shelf Mark 76 × 9.
6. Similar points are made by Philip Zea in his contribution to B. Jobe and M. Kaye, *New England Furniture: The Colonial Era* (Boston, 1984), pp. 47–72.

7. Lincoln RO: Gretford – PAR.23.
8. Borthwick Institute, York: M.Y. 1–8 (most of the quotations are from M.Y.1).
9. Goodchild Loan Collection, Wakefield, Yorkshire, MD Libraries.
10. C. Gilbert, 'A Signed and Dated Common Elm Chair', *Furniture History*, XII (1976), p. 97.
11. The Trustees of Admiral Long's School, Burnt Yates, manuscripts (unlisted).
12. C. Gilbert, *Town and Country Furniture* (exh. cat.), Temple Newsam House, Leeds, 1972 (9), and frontispiece.
13. K.M. Walton, 'A Fitted Cupboard from Somerset', *Furniture History*, XII (1976), pp. 97–8.
14. Otley Museum: O/WE/ab/1.
15. C. Gilbert, *Common Furniture* (exh. cat.), Temple Newsam House, Leeds, 1972 (60).
16. Property of Miss V. Tomlinson.
17. I am grateful to the late Stanley Brumfitt for lending me the ledgers which are now owned by his daughter Sylvia Schindler.
18. Goodchild Loan Collection, Wakefield, Yorkshire, MD Libraries. For a definition of 'spell', see M.C.F. Morris, *Yorkshire Reminiscences* (Oxford, 1922), p. 297.
19. Yorkshire Archaeological Society: MD 397. The volume includes diminutive sketches of chiffonier beds.
20. J. Boram, 'Owen Fitzpatrick, a Birkenhead Cabinet Maker', *Regional Furniture*, III (1989), pp. 68–83.
21. Catalogues by the following firms were purchased from the family for Temple Newsam House: C. & R. Light, Henry Wood and George Large & Son.
22. There is a late Regency couch bearing Brumfitt's trade label.
23. M.L. Ryder, 'A Note on Sheep-Shearing Stools', *Folk Life*, 4 (1966), pp. 15–21.

3 PRICE BOOKS

1. The American scholar Charles Móntgomery was amongst the first to realize their significance in *American Furniture The Federal Period in the Henry Francis du Pont Winterthur Museum* (New York, 1966). P. Kirkham and C. Gilbert contributed introductory essays to a reprint of *The Cabinet-Makers' London Book of Prices*, published as *Furniture History*, XVIII (1982).
2. S. Stuart, 'Prices for Workmen in Lancaster – the Earliest Surviving Cabinet-Makers' Price List', *Regional Furniture*, II (1988), pp. 19–22.
3. C. Gilbert, 'An Early Cabinet and Chair Work Price List From York', *Furniture History*, XXI (1985), pp. 227–8.
4. A bibliography of British price books was published by C. Gilbert in *Furniture History*, XVIII (1982), pp. 15–20.
5. Owned by the author.

6. S. Stuart, 'Influences on the Design of 18th-Century North Lancashire Clock Cases', *Regional Furniture*, I (1987), pp. 50–60.

7. The *Leeds* book is exceptional in containing a section headed 'Spindle Chairs' with the bare statement 'Turn'd spindle chairs to be made by the day' (p. 90). There is also an ambiguous reference in the *Preston* book, p. 73.

8. There is a unique copy in Carlisle Public Library, Cumbria.

9. Confirmation is provided by a drawing and cost analysis dated 1787 in the Gillow Estimate Sketch Books (Westminster City Libraries: Gillow Records 344/94, p. 162).

10. *The Leeds Cabinet and Chair-Makers Book of Prices* (1827), p. vii, states 'Patterns and Calls to be provided for the workman, or paid for according to time'. Evidently templates were customarily supplied by the masters. A caul was a piece of wood used for holding down a veneer or other material while the glue sets.

11. D. Jones, 'Scottish Books of Prices', *Regional Furniture*, III (1989). P. Kane's essay on American price books in *The Work of Many Hands: Card Tables in Federal America 1790–1820* (exh. cat.), Yale University Art Gallery, 1982, demonstrates how they illuminate colonial styles.

12. G. Cotton, 'The Norwich Chair Makers' Price Book of 1801', *Regional Furniture*, II (1988), pp. 68–92.

4 FARMHOUSES AND COTTAGES

1. Notably the catalogues of three exhibitions held at Temple Newsam House, Leeds, covering Yorkshire (1971), Lancashire and the Lake District (1973), Gloucestershire and Somerset (1976).

2. J.S. Moore, *The Goods and Chattels of our Forefathers*, 1976 (Gloucestershire); R. Machin (ed.), *Probate Inventories and Manorial Excepts of Chetnole, Leigh and Yetminster*, 1976 (Dorset); B. Trinder and J. Cox, *Yeoman and Colliers in Telford* (Chichester, 1980) (Shropshire); P. Brears (ed.), *Yorkshire Probate Inventories* (Yorkshire Archaeological Society, Leeds: 1972); K.S. Bartlett (ed.), *The Will of Horbury, 1658–1757*, 1980 (Wakefield, Yorkshire).

3. Leeds RO: RD/AP1/136/112.

4. Over 1,000 survey reports by the Yorkshire and Cleveland Vernacular Buildings Study Group have been deposited in the Yorkshire Archaeological Society Library. R. Fieldhouse and B. Jennings, *A History of Richmond and Swaledale* (Chichester, 1978), contains a section on local buildings.

5. Leeds RO: RD/AP1/137/102.

6. Leeds RO: RD/AP1/143/67.

7. Leeds RO: RD/AP1/144/80.

8. Leeds RO: RD/AP1/143/15.

9. Thomas Webster's *Encyclopaedia of Domestic Economy* (London, 1844), p. 842 and fig. 706.

10. R. Hird, *Annals of Bedale* (Lesley Lewis, ed.) (North Yorkshire County Record Office, Northallerton: 1975), vol. 3, v.809–10.

11. Leeds RO: RD/AP1/141/60.

12. Leeds RO: RD/AP1/143/118.

13. Leeds RO: RD/AP1/145/82.

14. Leeds RO: RD/AP1/144/64.

15. Leeds RO: RD/AP1/138/57.

16. Leeds RO: RD/AP1/141/43.

17. Leeds RO: RD/AP1/139/62. For an interesting illustrated account of dairies and cheese rooms, see P.M. Slocombe, *Wiltshire Farmhouses and Cottages* (1988).

18. Hird, *Annals of Bedale* (1975), vol. 2, v.48.

19. Leeds RO: RD/AP1/141/43.

20. This theory, first advanced by W.G. Hoskins 'The Rebuilding of Rural England', *Past and Present*, 4 (1953), was amplified by M.W. Barley, *The English Farmhouse and Cottage* (London, 1961) (a study from which I have learned much).

21. I am grateful to Peter Brears for drawing this privately owned collection to my attention.

22. William Marshall, *The Rural Economy of Yorkshire* (London, 1788), pp. 318–9.

23. J.C. Atkinson, *Forty Years in a Moorland Parish* (London, 1891), p. 210; also *A Glossary of the Cleveland Dialect* (London, 1868), pp. 71–2.

24. Hird, *Annals of Bedale* (1975), vol. 4, p. 578.

25. B. Franks, 'Salt Boxes of the North York Moors', *The Dalesman*, December 1970, pp. 775–8; see also RCHM, *Houses of the North York Moors* (HMSO, London: 1987), pp. 218–9.

26. R. Brunskill, *Vernacular Architecture of the Lake Counties* (London, 1974), pp. 129–32.

27. M. Nattrass, 'Witch Posts and Early Dwellings in Cleveland', *Yorkshire Archaeological Journal*, 39 (1958), pp. 136–45; see also RCHM, *Houses of the North York Moors* (HMSO, London: 1987), p. 218, and P. Brears, *North Country Folk Art* (Edinburgh, 1989), pp. 26–31 (all known witch posts are of oak).

28. The four excerpts are quoted from the Supplement to Chadwick's 1842 report of the same title, pp. 38–41.

29. These were perhaps open-framed shelves fixed to the wall, like a 'hanging' corner cupboard.

30. C. Holdenby, *Folk of the Furrow* (London, 1913), especially pp. 39–40.

31. Poor Law Commissioners' *Report on the Employment of Women and Children in Agriculture* (1843), pp. 19–20.

32. Atkinson, *Forty Years in a Moorland Parish* (1891), pp. 20–21.

33. J.C. Loudon, *Encyclopaedia of Cottage, Farm, and Villa Architecture and Furniture* (London, 1833), pp. 631–2.

34. *Local Reports on the Sanitary Conditions of the Labouring Population of England* (1842), p. 419.

35. W. Howitt, *The Rural Life of England* (London, 1838), vol. 2, p. 168.

36. W. Cobbett, *Rural Rides* (G.D.H. and M. Cole, eds) (London, 1930), vol. 1, pp. 276–8.

37. Atkinson, *Forty Years in a Moorland Parish* (1891), p. 14.

38. Gertrude Jekyll, *Old West Surrey* (London, 1904), p. 44.

39. *Report of the Select Committee on Agriculture* (1833), p. 112.

40. S.O. Addy, *The Evolution of the English House* (rev. ed., London, 1933), pp. 75–9.

41. See footnote 44, p. 241; see also P. Brears, *Traditional Food in Yorkshire* (Edinburgh, 1987), p. 28.

42. M.C.F. Morris, *Yorkshire Reminiscences* (Oxford, 1922), p. 314.

43. *Report on the Employment of Women and Children in Agriculture* (1843), p. 110.

44. Published in *Transactions of the Devonshire Association*, pt. I (1920), pp. 158–91; pt. II (1922), pp. 224–66.

45. W. Plomer (ed.), *Kilvert's Diary* (London, 1938), p. 89. In other parts of the country, stools were called 'buffets' or 'tuffets'.

46. R. Leech, *Early Industrial Housing: The Trinity Area of Frome* (HMSO, London: 1981), p. 16, pl.20.

47. J. Ayres, *The Home in Britain* (London, 1981), p. 71, fig. 66.

48. All the quoted passages regarding dressers are from Loudon, *Encyclopaedia* (1833), pp. 294–8.

49. Loudon, *Encyclopaedia* (1833), p. 298.

50. Loudon, *Encyclopaedia* (1833), pp. 305–6.

51. This and the following quotations are from pp. 316–8.

52. The passages quoted are from the Penguin edition of Flora Thompson, *Lark Rise to Candleford* (introduction by H.J. Massingham; 1973), pp. 19, 77, 98, 170.

53. *Town and Country Furniture*, 1972, and *Common Furniture*, 1982, both held at Temple Newsam, Leeds; *Cottage and Farmhouse Furniture in East Anglia*, 1987, Norfolk Museum of Rural Life.

54. G. Olive, 'West Country Settles', *Furniture History*, XVII (1981), pp. 20–22, and G. Olive, 'Dressers in the West Country', *Regional Furniture*, III (1989), pp. 40–51. Also B. Cotton, 'In Search of the English Dresser', *Antique Dealer and Collector's Guide*, February 1986, pp. 33–5.

55. D. Jones, 'Scotch Chests', *Regional Furniture*, II (1988), pp. 38–47.

5 URBAN WORKING-CLASS HOMES

1. E. Gauldie, *Cruel Habitations, A History of Working Class Housing* (1974), p. 99.

2. I. Bird, *Notes on Old Edinburgh* (Edinburgh, 1869), quoted in D. Rubinstein, *Victorian Homes* (Newton Abbot, 1974), pp. 121–3.

3. R. Baker, *The State and Condition of the Town of Leeds* (extracted from the Poor Commissioners' Reports) (1842), p. 18.

4. J. Burnett, *A Social History of Housing* (Newton Abbot, 1978), p. 59.

5. P.E. Razzell and R.W. Wainwright (eds), *The Victorian Working Class* (selections from letters to the *Morning Chronicle*) (London, 1973), p. 167.

6. A.B. Reach, *The Yorkshire Textile Districts in 1849* (reprinted Helmshore, 1974), p. 5 and p. 47.

7. J. Simon, *Public Health Reports* (E. Seaton, ed.) (London, 1887), vol. 1, p. 55.

8. A. Mearns, *The Bitter Cry of Outcast London* (London, 1883), pp. 4–7.

9. P. Quennell (ed.), *Mayhew's London* (1951), pp. 296–7.

10. P. Gaskell, *The Manufacturing Population of England* (London, 1833), p. 133.

11. Burnett, *A Social History of Housing* (1978), p. 74.

12. Baker, *The State and Condition of the Town of Leeds* (1842), pp. 11–12.

13. *Ibid.*, p. 17. The Irish regarded animals as part of their household.

14. Quoted by I. Pinchbeck, *Women Workers of the Industrial Revolution* (London, 1930), p. 181.

15. This account is largely derived from F. Wordsall, *The Tenement* (London, 1979), pp. 45–7.

16. S. Bamford, *Walks in South Lancashire* (Blackley, 1844), pp. 275–6. There is another good description of beds in a weaver's loom chamber in A. Wrigley, *O'er the Hills and Far Away* (Staleybridge, 1931).

17. Quoted by Burnett, *A Social History of Housing* (1978), p. 56.

18. Wakefield MD Libraries, John Goodchild Loan Collection, Ossett cum Gawthorpe Poor MSS. They are quoted in full by P. Brears, *Traditional Food in Yorkshire* (Edinburgh, 1987), pp. 197–9.

19. Quoted by Razzell and Wainwright, *The Victorian Working Class* (1973), pp. 226–7.

20. Report of E. Chadwick to the Poor Law Commissioners, *Sanitary Conditions of the Labouring Population of England*, 'Minutes of Evidence', (1842), p. 421.

21. Quoted by Brears, *Traditional Food in Yorkshire* (1987), p. 19.

22. *Ibid.*, pp. 204–5.

23. Recollections of life in a miner's back-to-back house about 1900 were published by F. Atkinson, 'Yorkshire Miners' Cottages', *Folk Life*, 3 (1965), pp. 92–6.

24. Quoted by Razzell and Wainwright, *The Victorian Working Class* (1973), p. 167.

25. *Ibid.*, p. 167.

26. *Ibid.*, p. 168.
27. *Ibid.*, p. 207–8.
28. A. Wrigley, *Songs of a Moorland Parish* (Saddleworth, 1912), pp. 94–7. Peter Brears, *Traditional Food in Yorkshire* (1987), p. 7, has recreated this interior pictorially, and quotes in Appendix One a dozen records of how textile workers' houses were furnished where the old domestic system of spinning and weaving survived.
29. Quoted by Razzell and Wainwright, *The Victorian Working Class* (1973), p. 198.
30. E. Chadwick, *Sanitary Report* (1842), pp. 358–67.
31. P. Quennell (ed.), *Mayhew's London* (1951), pp. 150–55.
32. There is a copy of this report in Westminster City Library, Buckingham Palace Road: the quotations which follow are all lifted from it.
33. A number of these Aid Societies are mentioned by F. Huggett, *Life Below Stairs: Domestic Servants in England from Victorian Times* (London, 1977), pp. 128–9.

6 BACK-STAIRS FURNITURE

1. C. Gilbert, *Back-stairs Furniture* (exh. cat.), Temple Newsam, Leeds, 1977; the only available serious study includes a bibliography of the subject.
2. M. Harrison, *The Kitchen in History* (Reading, 1972), contains some very instructive illustrations. For early kitchens, see C. Davidson, 'Historic Kitchen Restoration, the Example of Ham House I & II', *Petits Propos Culinare*, 12 & 15.
3. H. Clifford Smith, 'Two Hundred Years of the Mansion House London, and Some of It, Furniture', *Connoisseur*, 130 (1952), p. 185, pl. xi.
4. Westminster City Libraries; Gillow Records 344/94, p. 38.
5. L.O.J. Boynton, 'Sir Richard Worsley's Furniture at Appuldurcombe Park', *Furniture History*, I (1965), p. 57.
6. Leeds RO, Harewood MS: 306.
7. Leeds RO, Harewood MS (drawings folder).
8. Mrs William Parkes, *Domestic Duties* (London, 1825), p. 186.
9. L.O.J. Boynton, 'Sir Richard Worsley's Furniture at Appuldurcombe Park', *Furniture History*, I (1965), p. 55.
10. Worcester Historical Society, *Miscellany*, I (1960), p. 77.
11. L. Willoughby, 'Penshurst Place', *Connoisseur*, 15 (1906), p. 212, repr.
12. Leeds RO, Harewood MS: 306.
13. *Leeds Arts Calendar*, 99–100 (1987), p. 44.
14. M. Tomlin, 'The 1782 Inventory of Osterley Park', *Furniture History*, XXII (1986), p. 124.
15. Leeds RO, Harewood MS: 491, p. 74.
16. J. Geddes, 'The Prince of Wales at The Grange, Northington', *Furniture History*, XXII (1986), p. 192.
17. Yorkshire Archaeological Society: DD5, Box 12, item 4.
18. Westminster City Libraries: Gillow Records 344/95, p. 731.
19. Any reader seeking more information about the management or equipment of laundries is referred to Thomas Webster's *Encyclopaedia of Domestic Economy* (London, 1844), bk XIII.
20. Mrs W. Parkes, *Domestic Duties* (1825), p. 204.
21. Kept at the house.
22. P. Horn, *Rise and Fall of the Victorian Servant* (Dublin, 1975), and A. Hartcup, *Below Stairs in the Great Country Houses* (1980), are two of many relevant modern studies.
23. Reprinted in J. Low, 'Newby Hall: Two Late Eighteenth Century Inventories', *Furniture History*, XII (1986).

24. C.G. Gilbert, *The Life and Work of Thomas Chippendale* (1978), pp. 183–93.
25. The original bill, reprinted in L.O.J. Boynton, 'High Victorian Furniture: the Example of Marsh and Jones of Leeds', *Furniture History*, III (1967), pp. 54–91, is now at Temple Newsam House, Leeds.
26. Trade catalogue in the Pratt Collection at Temple Newsam House, Leeds.

7 ALEHOUSES, INNS AND TAVERNS

1. M. Gorham and H.M.G. Dunnett, *Inside the Pub* (London, 1950), provides a good general survey of the subject.
2. This inventory is privately owned.
3. Leeds RO: RD/AP1/137/2.
4. J.C. Loudon, *Encyclopaedia of Cottage, Farm, and Villa Architecture and Furniture* (London, 1833), pp. 686–7.
5. F. Thompson, *Lark Rise to Candelford* (H.J. Massingham, ed.) (Penguin Books, 1973), pp. 64–5.
6. Mezzotint, published by W. Ward, London, 1797.
7. B. Cotton illustrated a branded example in *RFS Newsletter*, 3 (1986), made for Simonds Brewery, Reading.
8. G. Olive, 'This Length from London', *RFS Occasional Publication* (1985), pp. 6–7, illustrates two built-in screen-type settles at pubs in Somerset and Wiltshire.
9. Loudon, *Encyclopaedia* (1833), p. 706.
10. Two versions are reproduced by Gorham and Dunnett, *Inside the Pub* (1950), pl. 46, and J. Grego, *Rowlandson the Caricaturist* (1880), vol. 2, p. 266.
11. Pages 675–726 headed 'Country Inns and Public Houses'.
12. See also M. Girouard, *Victorian Pubs* (London, 1975), and R. Elwall, *Bricks and Beer* (London, 1983).
13. V & A Library: Press Mark 86 RR 40.
14. Otley Museum: O/SR/vb/2.
15. J. Boram, 'Owen Fitzpatrick, a Birkenhead Cabinet Maker', *Regional Furniture*, III (1989), pl. 12, illustrates a measured drawing of *c.* 1880 for bar seats.
16. V. Chinnery, *Oak Furniture: The British Tradition* (1979), p.80, illustrates an early nineteenth-century elm shove h'penny table from a pub at Marnhull, Dorset.
17. The Fleece, a village alehouse at Bretforton, near Evesham, now owned by The National Trust, retains well-preserved traditionally furnished interiors.
18. R.B. Wood-Jones, *Traditional Domestic Architecture of the Banbury Region* (Manchester, 1963), makes this point when discussing plans of The Dolphin Inn, Wigginton, Oxfordshire (pp. 186–9).
19. B. Trinder and J. Cox, *Yeomen and Colliers in Telford* (Chichester, 1980) (collection of probate inventories 1660–1750), nos 146 and 147(1708); 159(1716); 171(1725).
20. Leeds RO: RD/AP1/145/28.
21. Lincoln RO: LIND DEP 40/52 BRA 328.
22. LEEDS RO: RD/AP1/138/1.
23. Loudon, *Encyclopaedia* (1833), pp. 675–726.
24. British Library: ADD 15544/161 and 15537/27.
25. G.S. Sorin and E.K. Donald, *Gadsby's Tavern Museum: Historic Furnishing Plan* (Alexandria, Virginia: 1980).
26. A.P. Oppé, *Thomas Rowlandson* (London, 1923), pl. 6; R. Wark, *Drawings by Thomas Rowlandson in the Huntington Collection* (San Marino, 1975), pl. 153.
27. *Mémoires et Observations Faites par un Voyageur en Angleterre* (1719), p. 39. (I am indebted to Lindsay Stainton for this reference).

8 REGIONAL CHAIRMAKING TRADITIONS

1. A rather desultory start was made in *Town and Country Furniture* (exh. cat.); Temple Newsam House, Leeds, 1972; a valuable contribution was Tom Crispin's 'English Windsor Chairs: A Study of Known Makers and Regional Centres', *Furniture History*, XVI (1978), pp. 38–48. Bill Cotton's first important article 'Vernacular Design: The Spindle Back Chair and its North Country Origin' appeared in *Working Wood*, Spring 1979, pp. 41–9.
2. Dr Cotton outlined his research methods in 'Regional Furniture Studies in the Late 18th and 19th Century Traditions', *Regional Furniture*, I (1987), pp. 1–18.
3. *British Parliamentary Papers: Population*, vol. 5 (Irish University Press, 1970).
4. B. Cotton, *The Chair in the North West* (exh. cat.), Towneley Hall, Burnley, 1987.
5. Westminster City Libraries: Gillow Records 344/98, p. 1620.
6. N.J. Banks, 'Lancashire Chairmakers', *Lancashire Life*, November 1980, pp. 54–5.
7. Cotton, *The Chair in the North West*, 1987, p. 20.
8. J.T. Graham, 'The Macclesfield Chair', *Antique Finder*, October 1976, pp. 4–5. G. Beard and C. Gilbert, *Dictionary of English Furniture Makers 1660–1840* (Leeds, 1986), p. 537.
9. Cotton, *The Chair in the North West*, 1987, pp. 22–4.
10. J. Hill, 'Rush Seating of Ladderbacks and Spindlebacks', *Woodworker*, September 1980, pp. 582–4.
11. Westminster City Libraries: Gillow Records 344/98, p. 1490 and 344/99A, p. 1804.
12. There is a set of four in ash at the Judges' Lodgings, Lancaster; one at Temple Newsam preserves some green paint.
13. Cotton, *The Chair in the North West*, 1987, pp. 9–10, fig. 2.
14. B. Cotton, 'The North Country Chair Making Tradition: Design, Context and the Mark Chippindale Deposition', *Furniture History*, XVII (1981), pp. 42–50.
15. B. Cotton, 'Country Chairs and their Makers', *Antique Dealer and Collector's Guide*, May 1983, pp. 45–9 and 'Shropshire Chairmakers', *Country Quest*, May 1983, pp. 31–4.
16. Information communicated to the author by Tom Beardsley of Clun.
17. C. Gilbert, 'Windsor Chairs from Rockley', *Antique Finder*, February 1974, pp. 18–19.
18. B. Biggs, *Rockley Methodist Chapel 1875–1975* (centenary souvenier booklet). I am grateful to Mr Biggs for communicating additional information.
19. B. Cotton, *The Chair in the North East Midlands* (exh. cat.), Museum of Lincolnshire Life, 1987, makes this point in the section on Rockley, pp. 41–2 and 51–6.
20. I am grateful to the owner, Roy Wells, for providing a photocopy in 1982.
21. C. Gilbert, *Common Furniture* (exh. cat.), Temple Newsam House, Leeds, 1982 (51).
22. C. Gilbert, *Common Furniture* (exh. cat.), Temple Newsam House, Leeds, 1982 (52 and 53).
23. Dr Cotton disagrees with this interpretation of the evidence.
24. Cotton, *The Chair in the North East Midlands* (exh. cat.), 1987, pp. 43–9, has marshalled available evidence about the Worksop trade.
25. Nottinghamshire Archives Office: Gabbitass PRNW, Retford, 1840.
26. C. Gilbert, 'Two Worksop Windsors', *Connoisseur*, February 1975, p. 157.
27. Dr Cotton tells me Gillings sometimes used a label illustrating four chairs.

28. *RFS Newsletter*, 1 (1985) and 9 (1989) contains notes on these remarkable chairs.

29. There is a unique copy held by Worksop Public Library, along with an important collection of press cuttings, photographs, transcribed oral history and ephemera relating to the local chair industry.

30. Obituary in *Worksop Guardian*, 1948 (cuttings book); see also M. Jackson, 'The Last of the Worksop Chairmakers', *Nottingham Countryside*, December 1973.

31. Gilbert, *Common Furniture* (exh. cat.), 1982 (22).

32. May I at once refer anyone requiring further information to Dr Cotton's magnificently detailed exhibition catalogue, *The Chair in the North East Midlands*, 1987, pp. 11–34.

33. See Dr Cotton's catalogue, pp. 35–40.

34. Lincoln RO: Dixon 19/12/7, first noted by C. Gilbert, *Common Furniture*, 1982 (28) and the subject of an important illustrated article by B. Cotton, 'Shadford, Shirley and the Caistor Workshop', *Regional Furniture*, II (1988), pp. 48–67.

35. The subject of two books: L.J. Mayes, *The History of Chairmaking in High Wycombe* (London, 1960), and I. Sparkes, *The English Country Chair* (Bourne End, 1973).

36. Wycombe Chair Museum: L 74931.

37. Wycombe Chair Museum: L 427.

38. In the possession of the firm. An earlier instance of the practice of buying in, is a High Wycombe-type Windsor chair of *c.* 1810 in Dr Cotton's collection bearing the stamp of an upmarket cabinet maker 'ADAMS 22 MINORIES LONDON'.

39. T. Sheraton, *The Cabinet Dictionary* (London, 1803), p. 145.

40. G. Herbert, *Shoemaker's Window* (rev. ed., Chichester, 1971).

41. B. Cotton, 'Windsor Chair Making: an Oxfordshire Tradition', *Oxfordshire Life*, Winter 1983.

42. Owned by Hillingdon Borough Libraries (Uxbridge).

43. Owned by Hillingdon Borough Libraries (Uxbridge).

44. G.W. Beard and C.G. Gilbert, *Dictionary of English Furniture Makers, 1660–1840* (Leeds, 1986), p. 718.

45. P. Agius, 'English Chair Makers Listed in Trade Directories', *Furniture History*, XII (1976), pls 1 and 2.

46. J. Stabler, 'Two Labelled Comb-Back Windsor Chairs', *Antique Collecting*, April 1977, pp. 12–14, and T. Crispin, 'Richard Hewett's Windsor Chair', *Antique Collecting*, January 1975, pp. 12–13.

47. The following articles deal with the early history and social usage of the Windsor chair: S. Jervis, 'The First Century of the English Windsor Chair 1720–1820', *Antiques*, February 1979, pp. 22–5. N. Goyne Evans, 'A History and Background of English Windsor Furniture', *Furniture History*, XV (1979), pp. 24–53. M. Haworth-Booth, 'The Dating of 18th Century Windsor Chairs', *Antique Dealer and Collector's Guide*, January 1973, pp. 63–8.

48. T. Crispin, '10th December 1838', *Antique Collecting*, November 1990, pp. 10–11.

49. B. Cotton, *Cottage and Farmhouse Furniture in East Anglia* (exh. cat.), Norfolk Rural Life Museum, 1987, pp. 44–5.

50. B. Cotton, *Windsor Chairs in the South West* (exh. cat.), Area Museum Council for the South West, 1989.

51. B. Cotton, 'Spinning Wheels', *RFS Newsletter*, 4 (Autumn, 1986).

52. F.C. Morgan, 'Philip Clissett, a Bosbury Chairmaker', *Woolhope Club Transactions* (1946), vol. 1, no. 9, pp. 16–18 and p. 251.

53. M. Comino, *Gimson and the Barnsleys* (London, 1980), pp. 43–4.

54. A large set of 'improved' chairs were ordered for

the Art Workers' Guild where they remain.

55. A copy of the 1900 catalogue is owned by the firm, the later edition is at Temple Newsam House, Leeds.

56. E. Bains's *Directory of the County of York* (Leeds, 1822), vol. 1, records John Inman of Otley eight miles lower down Wharfedale as a Windsor chairmaker. Little is known about the scattered Yorkshire workshops. There were two Windsor makers at Kirby Moorside in 1848 and makers in the south of the county (Banks of Selby) copied Nottinghamshire designs.

57. Information communicated to the author by Job Brear (1880–1982).

58. Owned by the firm, a page was reproduced by C. Gilbert, *Town and Country Furniture* (exh. cat.), 1972 (51).

59. Leeds RO: Harewood MS 491, p. 74.

60. C. Gilbert, 'A Signed and Dated Common Elm Chair', *Furniture History*, XII (1976), p. 97 and pl. 39.

61. This chair and one of the corner chairs dated 1820 are illustrated in *Common Furniture* (exh. cat.), 1982 (42 and 63).

62. Nostell and Aske Hall; Chippendale may, of course, have bought them in.

63. Yorkshire Archaeological Society: MD/272.

64. An important study of the volume linking specifications to extant chairs was contributed by G. Cotton to *Regional Furniture*, II (1988), pp. 68–92.

65. Otley Museum: O/SR/vb/2.

66. Cheshire RO: DAR/J/15, fol. 78.

67. I.F. Grant, *Highland Folk Ways* (London, 1961), pp. 167–97, provides a general account of houses and furnishings.

68. R. Ross Noble, 'The Chairs of Sutherland and Caithness: a Northern Tradition in Highland Chair-Making?', *Regional Furniture*, I (1987), pp. 33–40.

69. R. Ross Noble, *Regional Furniture*, I (1987), pl. 1.

70. C. Gilbert, *Common Furniture* (exh. cat.), Temple Newsam House, Leeds, 1982, nos 70–72.

71. Typical models were illustrated by A. Fenton, *The Northern Isles* (Edinburgh, 1978), p. 166.

72. N. Loughnan, *Irish Country Furniture* (1984), pl. 11.

73. A. Davies, 'Welsh Regional Furniture', *RFS Occasional Publication* (1985), pp. 1–2.

74. Loughnan, *Irish Country Furniture* (1984), pl. 10.

75. B. Cotton, 'Irish Vernacular Furniture', *Regional Furniture*, III (1989), pls 26 and 27.

76. R. Ross Noble, *Regional Furniture*, I (1987), pl. 9.

9 REGIONAL BEDS

1. A. Fenton, *Scottish Country Life* (Edinburgh, 1976), pp. 124–136.

2. T. Pennant, *A Tour in Scotland and Voyage to the Hebrides 1772* (London, 1790), 1, p.246.

3. J. Walton, 'Charcoal Burners' Huts', *Gwerin*, II (1958), pp. 58–67, and H.S. Cooper, 'The Sod Hut – an Archaic Survival', *Trans of the Cumberland and Westmorland Antiquarian and Archaeological Society*, 1, new series (1901), pp. 140–43.

4. HM Commission of Enquiry, pp. 270–80.

5. Quoted by C. Sinclair, *The Thatched Houses of the Old Highlands* (Edinburgh, 1953), p. 38.

6. A. Fenton, *The Northern Isles: Orkney and Shetland* (Edinburgh, 1978), pp. 191–4.

7. F.L.W. Thomas, 'On the Primitive Dwellings and Hypogea of the Outer Hebrides', *Proceedings of the Society of Antiquaries of Scotland*, VII (1870), pp. 153–60.

8. Quoted by E.C. Curwen, 'The Hebrides: A Cultural Backwater', *Antiquity*, XII (1938), p. 271.

9. A. Fenton, *The Island Blackhouse* (HMSO, Edinburgh: 1978).

10. Quoted by Fenton, *Northern Isles* (1978), p. 193.

11. H. Brooksby, 'Bed-outshuts in the Gower', *Vernacular Architecture*, VII (1976), pp. 21–33.

12. Quoted by L. Twiston-Davies and H.J. Lloyd-Johnes, *Welsh Furniture* (Cardiff, 1950), p. 9.

13. I. Peate, *Tradition and Folk Life: A Welsh View* (London, 1972), pp. 35–6.

14. *Rural Housing in Ulster in the Mid 19th Century*, Ulster Folk Museum (information pack) sheet A3.

15. *Rural Housing in Ulster in the Mid 19th Century*, Ulster Folk Museum (information pack) sheet A2.

16. The foregoing account is indebted to F. Carragher, 'Settle Beds in the Ulster Folk Museum', *Ulster Folklife*, 31 (1985), pp. 36–40; also H. Pain, *The Heritage of Upper Canada Furniture* (Toronto, 1978), pp. 159–62.

17. The information which follows is based on J.H. Lenfestey, 'The Guernsey Green Bed', *Channel Islands Review* (1971), pp. 69–91. Examples are preserved at the Saumarez Park Folk Museum.

18. E. Brontë, *Wuthering Heights* (Macdonald, London: 1955), p. 19.

19. A. Wells-Cole, 'A Painted Bed dated 1724', *Regional Furniture*, I (1987), pp. 27–32.

20. RCHM, *Westmorland* (HMSO, London: 1936), p. 234, pl. 59.

21. RCHM, *Westmorland* (HMSO, London: 1936), p. 228, pl. 59.

22. Leeds RO: RD/AP1/127/170. Photographs and plans of the farmhouse were published by F. Atkinson in *Beamish Report*, I (1978), pp. 60–63.

23. Quoted by M. Barley, *The English Farmhouse and Cottage* (London, 1961), p. 238.

24. See p. 195.

25. These are discussed by M. Hartley and J. Ingilby, *Life on the Moorlands of North East Yorkshire* (1972), pp. 11–12.

26. J. Walton, 'The Built-in Bed Tradition in North Yorkshire', *Gwerin*, III (1961), pp. 114–25. See also RCHM, *Houses of the North York Moors* (1987), pp. 92–7.

27. J.C. Atkinson, *Forty Years in a Moorland Parish* (1891), p. 19.

28. Atkinson, *Forty Years in a Moorland Parish* (London, 1891), pp. 20–21.

29. *First Report of the Commissioners on the Employment of Children, Young Persons and Women in Agriculture* (1868), pp. 262–3.

30. J.C. Loudon, *Encyclopaedia of Cottage, Farm, and Villa Architecture and Furniture* (London, 1833), pp. 332–3.

31. *Illustrated London News*, 29 January 1859, p. 116.

32. W. Ashley Bartlam, 'Box Beds on the Island of Stroma', *Scottish Vernacular Buildings Working Group Newsletter*, 6 (1980), pp. 6–10.

33. C. Gilbert, *The Life and Work of Thomas Chippendale* (London, 1978), pp. 240–42, pl. 62. There is also an elegant example at Grimston Garth, Yorkshire.

34. Westminster City Libraries: Gillow Records, 344/94, p. 310.

35. Westminster City Libraries: Gillow Records 344/94, p. 288.

36. K.S. Bartlet (ed.), *The Will of Horbury* (Wakefield, 1980), 2, pp. 6 and 89.

37. Leeds RO: RD/AP1/136/28.

38. Heal & Co., *Heal's Catalogues 1853–1934* (Newton Abbot, 1972), pp. 36–7.

39. D. Jones, 'The Press Bed in Scotland', *Aspects of Scottish Decorative Art in the Twentieth Century* (Scottish Society for Art History Yearbook) (Glasgow, 1988), pp. 28–35.

40. Loudon, *Encyclopaedia* (1833), p. 329.

41. F. Atkinson, 'North Country Cottage Beds', *Beamish Report*, I (1978), pp. 64–8.

42. Yorkshire Archaeological Society: MD 397.

43. K.S. Bartlet (ed.), *The Will of Horbury* (Wakefield, 1980), pp. 29 and 74.

44. L. Twiston-Davies and H.J. Lloyd-Johnes, *Welsh Furniture* (1950), p. 10 and pl. 6.

10 Straw and Wicker Furniture

1. J.C. Loudon, *Encyclopaedia of Cottage, Farm, and Villa Architecture and Furniture* (London, 1833), pp. 346–7.
2. J. Geraint Jenkins, 'A Cardiganshire Lip-worker', *Folk Life*, 3 (1965), pp. 88–9.
3. D. Hartley, *Made in England* (London, 1939), pp. 72–7.
4. Loudon, *Encyclopaedia* (1833), pp. 315–6.
5. John Aubrey, *Brief Lives* (O.L. Dick, ed.) (London, 1949), p. 233.
6. P. Agius, 'Late Sixteenth and Seventeenth Century Furniture in Oxford', *Furniture History*, VII (1971), p. 78.
7. J.S. Moore (ed.), *The Goods and Chattels of our Forefathers* (Chichester, 1976), pp. 244, 246.
8. C. Davidson, *The World of Mary Ellen Best* (London, 1985), fig. 36; also E. Cartwright-Hignett, *Lili at Aynhoe* (London, 1989), p. 34.
9. Webster, like Loudon, illustrates a simple beehive chair, p. 248.
10. W.T. Dennison, 'Manufacture of Straw Articles in Orkney', *Orcadian Papers* (1905), pp. 32–42; also A. Fenton, *The Northern Isles: Orkney and Shetland* (Edinburgh, 1978), pp. 149–50, 261, 270–72.
11. An excellent general account of willow crafts and basketry is given by H.L. Edlin, *Woodland Crafts in Britain* (London, 1949), pp. 100–14. D. Hartley, *Made in England* (London, 1939), pp. 88–100 is also useful.
12. R. Holme, *The Academy of Armory* (I.H. Jeayes, ed.) (London, for the Roxburghe Club), vol. 2, ch. 14. Holme's manuscript is dated 1649.
13. Dorset RO: Banks Papers, no. 246 (information from Gabriel Olive).
14. P.K. Thornton, *Seventeenth Century Interior Decoration in England, France and Holland* (Yale, 1978), p. 208, pls 197, 198, 320.
15. P. Agius, 'Late Sixteenth and Seventeenth Century Furniture in Oxford', *Furniture History*, VII (1971), p. 78.
16. It has been suggested that a circular wicker fire-screen at Hardwick Hall may relate to entries in an inventory of 1601.
17. William Howitt, *The Rural Life of England* (London, 1838), p. 168.
18. J. Pigot & Co., *New Commercial Directory* (London, 1822–4).
19. F.W. Steer (ed.), *Farm and Cottage Inventories of Mid-Essex, 1635–1749* (Chelmsford, 1950).
20. Leeds RO: Richmondshire wills.
21. B. Trinder and J. Cox, *Yeomen and Colliers in Telford* (Chichester, 1980), and J.S. Moore (ed.), *The Goods and Chattels of our Forefathers* (Chichester, 1976).
22. Luke Millar, 'An Alehouse Inventory of 1765', *Regional Furniture*, II (1988), p. 37.
23. S. Jervis, *Printed Furniture Designs Before 1650* (Leeds, 1974), pl. 159, illustrates an engraving by Hans Vredeman de Vries showing a canopied wicker chair beside a bed.
24. M. Praz, *Conversation Pieces* (London, 1971), pl. 35.
25. Loudon, *Encyclopaedia* (1833), p. 351.
26. Copy in the Pratt Collection at Temple Newsam House, Leeds (No. 91).
27. Bedford RO: CRO X 171/274. I am grateful to Anne Buck for drawing my attention to this price-list and to the heirs of T.W. Bagshawe, F.S.A., for permission to quote from it.
28. Bedford RO: CRO X 171/275.
29. The Pratt Collection, listed in C.G. Gilbert, *Furni-* ture at Temple Newsam House and Lotherton Hall (Leeds, 1978), vol. 2, p. 507.

11 Schools

1. M. Seaborne, *The English School 1370–1870* (London, 1971), p. 123. I would like to pay tribute to this very lucid history.
2. C. Gilbert, *School Furniture* (exh. cat.), Temple Newsam House, Leeds, 1978 (1), ill. This publication illustrates an anthology of mainly Victorian furniture, plus designs from trade catalogues.
3. Seaborne, *The English School* (1971), pls 54 and 64.
4. *Ibid.*, pl. 79.
5. There is an example in the Museum of Eton Life at Eton College.
6. These quotations are from an amusingly disparaging account of Dame Schools in G.T.C. Bartley, *Schools for the People: History, Development and Present Working of Each Description of English School for the Industrial and Poorer Classes* (1871), pp. 400–407.
7. Borthwick Institute, York: Wills, Stillington Peculiar, 1766.
8. R.M. Healey, 'Artist Among the Lacemakers', *Country Life*, 19 August 1982, p. 510, pl. 1.
9. T.W. Laqueur, *Religion and Respectability Sunday Schools and Working Class Culture 1780–1850* (Yale, 1986), provides an excellent account of the Sunday School Movement. I am also indebted to Mrs Louanne Collins and Andy Skelhorn of the Macclesfield Sunday School Heritage Centre for their helpful interest.
10. The following archive references are: John Goodchild MS. Collection, Wakefield and Chester RO: Macclesfield SS, Cash Accounts SP 2/16/1. Trade catalogues illustrating Sunday School furniture are to be found at Beamish Museum: G. Hammer & Co. (London) *Catalogue of Church Furniture, Mission Room Fittings etc*, 9th ed. nd (c. 1900), pp. 48–9 and p. 75, and the Bennett Furnishing Co. (London & Glasgow) *Catalogue of Church and Hall Furniture* (1901), pp. 45–8.
11. Joseph Lancaster expounded his theories in two books: *The British System of Education* (London, 1810), and *Hints and Directions for Building, Fitting-up and Arranging School Rooms on the British System of Education* (London, 1811). The British and Foreign School Society's *Manual of the System of Primary Instruction*, 1816, also contains an illustrated text of great value.
12. J.C. Loudon, *Encyclopaedia of Cottage, Farm, and Villa Architecture and Furniture* (London, 1833), pp. 728–31.
13. Seaborne, *The English School* (1971), pl. 125.
14. D. Stow, *The Training System* (Glasgow, 1836), and S. Wilderspin, *The Infant System* (London, 1832), both contain informative illustrated texts. Plates from these books showing gallery lessons in progress are reproduced by Seaborne, *The English School* (1971), pl. 124 and C. Martin, *A Short History of English Schools 1790–1965* (Hove, 1979).
15. Loudon, *Encyclopaedia* (1833), pp. 728–39 and 758–62.
16. P. Horn, *Education in Rural England* (Dublin, 1978), p. 122.
17. There are six late Victorian catalogues issued by this firm at Temple Newsam House, Leeds.
18. E.J. Arnold catalogues are at the Museum of Education, Leeds University.
19. C. Gilbert, *School Furniture* (exh. cat.), Temple Newsam House, Leeds, 1978 (2); the items mentioned below are also illustrated in this publication.
20. *Ibid.*, (4).

12 Workhouses

1. One of the best outline histories is by Norman Longmate, *The Workhouse* (London, 1974). A directive listing appropriate furniture for sick wards is published by M.E. Rose, *The English Poor Law 1780–1930* (Newton Abbot, 1971), pp. 176–7.
2. *Cambridge Antiquarian Society Communications*, XV (1911), pp. 71–142.
3. North Yorkshire RO: PR/ARK 6.1.
4. M.C. Wadhams, 'Development of Buildings in Witham from 1500 to 1800', *Post-Medieval Archaeology*, 6 (1972), pp. 14–16.
5. Gloucester RO: P76 ov 8/1.
6. Hereford & Worcester RO: W31. The sketches are for furniture in the Boardroom and chapel. (I wish to thank A.M. Wherry for this reference.)
7. Norfolk RO: MS 20281, 126 x 2 (I am grateful to Dr Anne Digby for this reference).
8. R. Palliser, 'Workhouse Education in County Durham 1834–1870', *British Journal of Educational Studies*, XVI, no.3 (1968), pp. 279–91.
9. Bedford RO: No. P 30/18/19. (I am grateful to Patricia Bell for her comments).
10. Yorkshire Archaeological Society, MS 439 (Day Book 1788–92).
11. Bedford RO: P.U. A.M.1. Inventory sources are fairly abundant. Gabriel Olive has kindly drawn my attention to a fine schedule of furniture belonging to the Downton workhouse which was purchased in 1836 by the Guardians of the newly formed Alderbury (Salisbury) Union. Their minute book also refers to commissioning iron double bedsteads and spinning-frames. (Wiltshire RO: H1. 110/1, 2 and 4 January and 18 April 1836).
12. Longmate, *The Workhouse* (1974), fig. 12.
13. *Ibid.*, fig. 9.
14. *Ibid.*, fig. 8.
15. *Ibid.*, fig. 18.
16. Harold Walker, *This Little Town of Otley* (Ilkley, 1974), pp. 70–77.
17. Gabriel Olive published in *Regional Furniture*, I (1987), p. 86, an annotated drawing for a wrought-iron bedstead in a cost book of Woodfin & Co., ironfounders of Trowbridge (Wiltshire RO: 1119/3). It was evidently designed for the Melksham Union workhouse at Semington (now St George's Hospital), built in 1838 for 300 paupers.
18. J.C. Loudon, *An Encyclopaedia of Cottage, Farm, and Villa Architecture and Furniture* (London, 1833), pp. 331–2.
19. This account of workhouse furniture (now revised) first appeared in *Regional Furniture*, I (1987), pp. 61–70.

13 Houses of Correction, Bridewells and Prisons

1. I am indebted to S. and B. Webb's *English Prisons Under Local Government* (London, 1922) and M. Ignatieff, *A Just Measure of Pain: the Penitentiary in the Industrial Revolution, 1750–1850* (New York, 1978), for valuable background information.
2. North Yorkshire Record Office, *Annual Report* (1968), pp. 17–19.
3. All relevant documents are in the NYRO filed under QAG.
4. The building is now a museum.
5. I am grateful to Ann-Rachael Harwood for details of Littledean.
6. Other illustrations of cells are reproduced by John Bender, *Imagining the Penitentiary* (Chicago, 1987), figs 5 and 27.
7. Line engraving, published 31 August 1787; there is a copy at Colonial Williamsburg — 1959–83, 10.

8. A. Pugin and T. Rowlandson, *Microcosm of London* (London, 1808).
9. Report on Marshalsea Prison to the House of Commons, 14 May 1729. Reproduced by R.S. Plees 'Some Old Prison Broadsides', *Connoisseur*, 43 (1915), p. 90.
10. In 1911 the London Museum dismantled the walls of two old cells at Wellclose Square Prison and also collected a plain oak mid-eighteenth-century table covered in graffiti said to be original to the prison (Acc. No. A6151).
11. There are several early Victorian prints at Lancaster Museum showing day rooms in the Castle called 'The Pigeons', 'The Chancery', 'The Quakers', etc., where debtors clearly enjoyed a very civilized existence waited on by servants, reading newspapers around a comfortable fireside and enjoying upholstered couches, tablecloths, even a piano.
12. H. Mayhew and J. Binny, *The Criminal Prisons of London* (London, 1862), p. 180.
13. *Ibid.*, opp. p. 178.
14. *Ibid.*, pp. 192 and 293.
15. *Ibid.*, p. 132.
16. *Report on the Construction . . . of Pentonville Prison* (1844), pls 8 and 12 (reprinted Irish University Press).
17. Mayhew and Binny, *The Criminal Prisons of London* (1862), opp. p. 108.
18. *Ibid.*, opp. pp. 362 and 356.
19. *Ibid.*, opp. pp. 376 and 388.
20. *Ibid.*, opp. p. 367.
21. *Ibid.*, p. 210 and opp. p. 214.
22. *Ibid.*, opp. p. 223.

14 LUNATIC ASYLUMS AND HOSPITALS

1. Kathleen Jones, *A History of the Mental Health Services* (London, 1972), contains much useful background information.
2. Borthwick Institute, York: Retreat MS H/1 26 February 1794.
3. Quoted by J.D. Thompson and G. Goldin, *The Hospital: a Social and Architectural History* (Yale, 1975), p. 71.
4. Retreat MS H/1 (Letters 1794).
5. Retreat MS H/1 (Vouchers).
6. Oxford Area Health Authority Archives: Radcliffe Asylum Papers (I am grateful to the archivist Mrs B. Parry Jones for drawing this document to my attention).
7. Gloucester RO: H022 40/1.
8. Patricia Allderidge, archivist of the Bethlem Royal Hospital was outstandingly helpful in sharing her knowledge and supplying photocopies of documents.
9. The only extant furniture traceable in the 1816 inventory is a set of twelve hall chairs.
10. Minutes of Evidence at Bethlem given by George Waller, p. 36ff.
11. Charity Commissioners' Report (City of London, 1837), p. 518.
12. Holloway Sanatorium for the less prosperous middle classes was unbelievably baronial and extravagant.
13. There is a photocopy of this important document at Lancaster Museum, the whereabouts of the original is unknown. I am grateful to Ros Allwood for drawing it to my attention.
14. F. Oppert, *Hospitals, Infirmaries and Dispensaries, their Construction, Interior Arrangement and Management* (London, 1867), pp. 21–3.

15 ALMSHOUSES

1. The standard works are S. Heath, *Old English Houses of Alms* (London, 1910), and W.H. Godfrey, *The English Almshouse* (London, 1955).
2. Leeds RO: Richmondshire wills.
3. C. Gilbert, *Furniture at Temple Newsam House and Lotherton Hall* (Leeds, 1978), vol. 2, pp. 414–5.
4. Morden College archives (I am grateful to Irene Dyer for photocopies).
5. Eileen Gooder, *Temple Balsall: a Short History* (Temple Balsall, 1980).
6. M.W. Farr, Warwickshire County Archivist and Richard de Peyer kindly supplied extracts from the papers. The Manor Courts and Governors' meetings were held at the Old Hall, Temple Balsall.
7. N. Burton, *The Geffrye Almshouses* (London, 1979), pp. 38–9.
8. The same issue illustrates a soup kitchen in the East End of London. M. Harrison, *The Kitchen in History* (Reading, 1972), pl. 43, reproduces an engraving of a kitchen run by the Society of Friends during the Irish Famine of 1847.
9. P. Searby, *Weavers and Outworkers in Victorian Times* (London, 1980), p. 60.

16 MEETING HOUSES AND CHAPELS

1. W. Pearson Thistlethwaite, *Yorkshire Quarterly Meeting 1665–1966* (Harrogate, 1979), p. 97.
2. Two valuable general studies are: RCHM, *An Inventory of Non-Conformist Chapels and Meeting-Houses in Central England* (1986), and H. Lidbetter, *The Friends Meeting House* (York, 1961).
3. J. and R. Mortimer (eds), *Leeds Friends Minute Book 1692–1712* (Yorkshire Archaelogical Society, Leeds: 1980), p. 112.
4. The Friends Library in London contains an excellent collection of photographs based on the Lidbetter albums, recording Meeting Houses throughout the country.
5. D.M. Butler, *Quaker Meeting Houses of the Lake Counties* (London, 1978), p. 150.
6. *Ibid.*, p. 112.
7. *Ibid.*, p. 128.
8. W. Beck and F.T. Ball, *The London Friends Meetings* (London, 1869), p. 264.
9. Cumbria RO (Kendal): WDFC/F1 Building Committee minutes (March 1816–October 1817) – a splendidly detailed source.
10. Meeting House strong room packets 2.C.1 and 2.C.VI.
11. An interesting small collection of benches and other furniture has been brought together by Roger Warner at the Burford Meeting House.
12. K. Lindley, *Chapels and Meeting Houses* (London, 1969). I acknowledge with gratitude my debt to this survey for the historical framework for this section.
13. RCHM, *Non-Conformist Chapels and Meeting-Houses in Central England* (HMSO, London: 1986), illustrates many fine period interiors.
14. I am indebted to G.W. Dolbey, *The Architectural Expression of Methodism* (London, 1964).
15. A.R. Ronald Bielby, *Churches and Chapels of Kirklees* (Huddersfield, 1978), pls 70 and 71.
16. L. Twiston Davies and J. Lloyd Johnes, *Welsh Furniture* (Cardiff, 1950), pl. 35; a preaching-desk, used by John Wesley in 1749, is also illustrated, pl. 89.

17 FACTORIES AND WORKSHOPS

1. There is a typical example at the Ryedale Folk Museum, Hutton-le-Hole, North Yorkshire.
2. R.A. Salaman, *Dictionary of Tools* (London, 1975), illustrates many models.
3. C. Tomlinson (ed.), *Cyclopaedia of Useful Arts* (London and New York: 1854), p. 109, repr. There is a basket-maker's seat and lap board at St Albans Museum.
4. *Ibid.*, p. 643, repr.
5. The tilt shop at Abbeydale Industrial Hamlet, Sheffield, contains a typical suspended seat.
6. Tomlinson, *Cyclopaedia of Useful Arts* (1854), p. 767, repr.
7. Models are preserved in Industrial Museums at Leeds, Halifax and Macclesfield.
8. *The Process of Making China . . . Descriptive of the Works of the Royal China Manufactory, Worcester,* printed for J. Wallis (Worcester, 1810).
9. R.W. Binns and E.P. Evans, *A Guide Through the Worcester Royal Porcelain Works* (Worcester, 1881).
10. Owned by the Dyson Perrins Museum Trust.
11. Many Museums feature reconstructed workshops and the following are especially noteworthy: Castle Museum, York (confectioner's shop); Abbey House museum, Leeds, and the Black Country Museum (nail shops); Ironbridge and Beamish (printer's and chemist's shops); Gressenhall, Norfolk (saddler's); St Albans, the Salaman Collection of trade tools.
12. *The Book of English Trades and Library of the Useful Arts,* printed for Sir Richard Phillips & Co., London (various editions from *c.* 1800 onwards); the new enlarged edition (1823), has been used.
13. P. Searby, *Weavers and Outworkers in Victorian Times* (London, 1980) and H. Mayhew, *London Labour and the London Poor* (London, 1861), contain vivid descriptions of outworkers and domestic trades.
14. There is a fine loom chamber and weaver's house at the Colne Valley Museum, Golcar, Yorkshire.
15. Otley Museum, Yorkshire: O/WE/ab/1.
16. Goodchild Collection, Wakefield, Yorkshire (private archive).

18 OFFICES AND SHOPS

1. P. Kirkham, 'Samuel Norman: a study of an Eighteenth Century Craftsman', *Burlington Magazine*, August 1969, p. 513.
2. H. Hayward and P. Kirkham, *William and John Linnell* (London, 1980), p. 170.
3. Copy at Temple Newsam (auctioneer T. Stringer, 18–21 June 1832).
4. *Illustrated London News*, 29 December 1855, p. 776, depicts the interior of the Bank of London, Threadneedle Street, where all the clerks are shown standing at their desks.
5. C. Hibbert, *Social History of Victorian Britain* (London, 1975), p. 27, reproduces a page from the *Illustrated London News*, 1883, showing the switchroom in a telephone exchange staffed by women seated on high chairs.
6. G. Anderson, *Victorian Clerks* (Manchester, 1976), charts the rapid expansion of offices during the Victorian period.
7. T. Ingram, 'Some Furniture of a Merchant Banking House', *Furniture History*, X (1974), pp. 80–81, figs 33–41.
8. *Wooton Patent Desks* (exh. cat.), Indiana State Museum and Oakland Museum, 1983.
9. Copy at Temple Newsam, Leeds (Pratt Collection, No. 212).
10. *Ibid.*, Nos 213–14.
11. *Ibid.*, No. 226.
12. Quoted by H. Hayward (ed.), *World Furniture* (London, 1965), p. 86.
13. M.W. Barley, *The English Farmhouse and Cottage* (London, 1961), p. 252.
14. *Ibid.*, p. 280.
15. B. Trinder and J. Cox, *Yeomen and Colliers in Telford* (Chichester, 1980), pp. 302–8.
16. F.W. Steer, *Farm and Cottage Inventories of Mid-Essex 1635–1749* (Chelmsford, 1950), pp. 212–13.
17. Trinder and Cox, *Yeomen and Colliers in Telford* (1980), pp. 20–34.

18. Steer, *Farm and Cottage Inventories* (1950), p. 258.
19. In the possession of Mrs Schindler, daughter of the late Stanley Brumfitt.
20. Otley Museum; O/WE/ab/1.
21. Otley Museum: O/D/UB/2.
22. *Illustrated London News*, 14 November 1885, p. 507.
23. All the illustrations discussed are reproduced either by J.E. Hodgson, 'Romance and Humour of the Auction Room', *Connoisseur*, 103 (1939), pp. 329–34 or W. Roberts, *Memorials of Christie's* (London, 1897), 2 vols.

19 Railway Premises

1. W.R. Mitchell, *Men of the Settle–Carlisle* (Clapham, Yorkshire: 1985), pp. 49–50.
2. A. Vaughn, *Pictorial Record of Great Western Architecture* (Oxford, 1977), p. 480.
3. J. Boram, 'Owen Fitzpatrick, a Birkenhead Cabinet Maker', *Regional Furniture*, III (1989), pp. 68–83.
4. R. Anderson and G. Fox, *Pictorial Record of LMS Architecture* (Oxford, 1981), fig. 70.
5. Quoted by R. Christiansen and R.W. Miller, *The North Staffordshire Railway* (Newton Abbot, 1971), p. 177.

20 Army Barracks

1. Quoted by R.E. Scouller, 'Quarters and Barracks', *RUSI Journal*, February 1953, p. 92.
2. Iain MacIvor, 'Fort George I & II', *Country Life*, 12 and 19 August 1976, pp. 410–13, 478–81.
3. J.A. Houlding, *Fit for Service: The Training of the British Army 1715–1795* (Oxford, 1980), pp. 40–41.
4. *Army Regulations* (1788), pp. 140–47 (NAM, Press Mark 355.6).
5. J. Williamson, *A Treatise on Military Finance*, (London, 1796), pp. 62–3.
6. *Records of the Royal Military Academy, Woolwich* (Woolwich, 1851), pl. 2.
7. There is a reconstructed Army schoolroom at Berwick Barracks.
8. George Godwin, *Town Swamps and Social Bridges* (London, 1859), pp. 80–81.
9. *The Navy and Army*, 18 August 1906, p. 189 (illus.); Boris Mollo, *The British Army from Old Photographs* (London, 1975), pls 52 and 53.
10. Two useful studies are J. Phillips, 'Travelling and Campaigning Furniture' *Antique Collecting*, June 1984, pp. 7–11, and P. Johnson, 'Camp Comforts', *Art and Antiques*, 8 February 1975, pp. 18–23.
11. A number of items are illustrated by J.B. Saunders, 'Camp Furniture of the Victorian Officer', *NAM Annual Report*, 1981, pp. 50–56.
12. Quoted by T. Rosoman, 'Military Furniture', *RFS Occasional Publication* (Spring 1985), p. 13.
13. NAM, Press Mark: 355.66.

21 Bothies, Chaumers and Campaign Furniture

1. Folio of press cuttings (undates, source unknown) *c.* 1900, pp. 75–8 in Forfar Public Library. I am grateful to Ian Neil for supplying photocopies of the five articles.
2. Quoted by A. Fenton, *Farm Servant Life in the 17th–19th Centuries* (Scottish Country Life Museum Trust, Edinburgh, 1975), p. 3. The Scottish Country Life Archive maintained by the National Museums of Scotland contains a wealth of information about bothies and bothy life.
3. Quoted by I. Carter, *Farmlife in North East Scotland 1840–1914* (Edinburgh, 1979), p. 121.
4. D.K. Cameron, *The Ballad and the Plough* (London, 1978), p. 79.
5. Quoted by Carter, *Farmlife* (1979), p. 123.
6. M.B. Bochel, *Dear Gremista: the Story of Nairn Fisher Girls at the Gutting* (Nairn Fishertown Museum, 1979), pp. 16–18. The Nairn Fishertown Museum contains a collection of kists and old photographs.
7. Private letter to the author 25 September 1980.
8. North Yorkshire and Cleveland Vernacular Buildings Study Group, Report No. 916, 1983.
9. Appx. pt. II (Lead Mines in Durham, Northumberland and Cumberland), pp. 740–42. Much additional evidence is recorded. See also Chadwick's *Report on the Sanitary Conditions of the Labouring Population of England* (1842), pp. 109–11.
10. *Epitome of Evidence*, pp. 192–5.
11. J. Lindsay, *History of the North Wales Slate Industry* (Newton Abbot, 1974), pp. 232–3.

22 Ships

1. Two useful publications are B. Greenhill and A. Gifford, *Travelling by Sea in the Nineteenth Century* (London, 1972), and J. Munday, 'Captains and Cabins', *Connoisseur*, February 1979, pp. 90–97.
2. Quoted by Munday, *Ibid.*, p. 93.
3. An engraving titled 'Emigration Vessel — Between Decks', in *Illustrated London News*, 10 May 1851, p. 387, records the conditions.
4. A small mahogany secretaire with lifting handles at the Captain Cook Museum, Whitby, belonged to the botanist George Forster who sailed on the *Resolution* in 1772.
5. A print by R. Seymour, *After Cabin – Captain's Drawing Room*, after a sketch in James Hore's *Journal of a Landsman From Portsmouth to Lisbon* (London, 1832), shows a circular pedestal table and a chest of drawers anchored by such stays. Reproduced Munday, *Connoisseur* (1979), p. 94.
6. Munday, *Connoisseur* (1979), p. 93, fig. 6; Greenhill and Gifford, *Travelling by Sea* (1972), pl. 24.
7. Hanging cots and tables are recorded in Greenhill and Gifford, *Travelling by Sea* (1972), pls 5 and 16.
8. J. Boram, 'Owen Fitzpatrick, a Birkenhead Cabinet Maker', *Regional Furniture*, III (1989), pp. 68–83.
9. National Maritime Museum, reproduced Munday, *Connoisseur* (1979), p. 95.
10. *Ibid.*, quoted p. 93.
11. An interesting anthology of these carved blocks is illustrated as end-papers to C.W. Ashley, *The Ashley Book of Knots* (London, 1947).
12. NMM No. MS (63).
13. The NMM Collection includes several sailmakers' horses and a dispensary-rack.

23 Caravans, Narrowboats and Living-Vans

1. C.H. Ward-Jackson and D.E. Harvey, *The English Gypsy Caravan* (Newton Abbot, 1972), is well researched and illustrated and includes sectional drawings and plans showing the arrangement of furniture, pp. 152–67. H. Hugill, 'Caravanning in Comfort', *The Country House*, April 1910, pp. 26–30, describes furnishing a weekend caravan.
2. T. Chaplin, *A Short History of the Narrow Boat* (Upper Halliford, 1979), provides a good introduction to the subject which also receives detailed treatment in T. Lewery, 'Soap 'oles, Bed 'oles and Bugs', *Waterways World*, October 1989, pp. 51–6.
3. R.J. Wilson, *Life Afloat* (Rothwell, Northamptonshire: 1976), p. 29, contains line drawings of a typical cabin interior.
4. A.J. Lewery, *Narrow Boat Painting* (Newton Abbot, 1974), discusses traditional treatments.
5. The Leeds Industrial Museum owns a copy.

24 Children's Furniture

1. E. Gelles, *Nursery Furniture* (London, 1982), is typical of the genre.
2. J.C. Loudon, *Encyclopaedia of Cottage, Farm, and Villa Architecture and Furniture* (London, 1833), pp. 350–51.
3. T.W. Bagshawe, 'Baby Cages', *Apollo*, December 1937, pp. 325–7.
4. Quoted in S. Bourne, *Children's Furniture* (exh. cat.), Towneley Hall, Burnley, 1977, p. 15.
5. Copy at Temple Newsam House, Leeds.
6. One is illustrated in T. Webster, *Encyclopaedia of Domestic Economy* (London, 1844), p. 282.
7. Loudon, *Encyclopaedia* (1833), p. 315.
8. *Ibid.*, pp. 335–6 and 1086.
9. At Gainsborough Old Hall, Lincolnshire.
10. Loudon, *Encyclopaedia* (1833), p. 335.
11. G. Cotton, 'Common Chairs from the Norwich Chair Makers' Price Book of 1801', *Regional Furniture*, II (1988), pp. 90–92.
12. An example is illustrated and discussed by Loudon, *Encyclopaedia* (1833), p. 1087.
13. Page 204.
14. Pages 286 and 287.
15. Nicole de Reyniès, *Le Mobilier Domestique* (Paris, 1987), vol. 1, pp. 268–80.

25 Cricket and Tennis

1. The Cricket Memorial Museum at Lords contains an outstanding pictorial collection and library. I am grateful to Stephen Green, the curator, for assistance.
2. A. Bury, 'Rare Cricket Prints and Paintings', *Antique Collector*, April 1955, p. 68, repr.
3. I. Rosenwater, *A Portfolio of Cricket Prints* (London, 1962), no. 1.
4. I am indebted to Valerie Warren, assistant curator, for her helpful interest.
5. The Lawn Tennis Museum has built up a small collection.

26 Ducking Stools

1. L. Jewitt, *A History of Plymouth* (London, 1873), pp. 37–8.
2. R.N. Worth, *History of Plymouth* (rev. ed. Plymouth, 1890), p. 346.
3. W. Andrews, *Old-Time Punishments* (Hull, 1890), pp. 29–30 illustrates both.
4. *Connoisseur*, September 1905 (trade advertisement).
5. Andrews, *Old-Time Punishments* (1890), p. 28, illus.
6. *Ibid.*, *Old-Time Punishments* (1890), pp. 11–12.
7. *Ibid.*, *Old-Time Punishments* (1890), pp. 21–2.
8. C.H. Cooper, *Annals of Cambridge*, IV (Cambridge, 1852), pp. 255 and 340.
9. Andrews, *Old-Time Punishments* (1890), p. 10, illus.

Select Bibliography

It is not feasible to record here every publication that has yielded information of value for such a wide-ranging survey. This list is intended to provide a background to the various chapters and covers the main printed sources on which my study is based. References to manuscript material are given in the Chapter Notes which also cite many books and articles not included in this Select Bibliography.

JOURNALS

Folk Life
Furniture History
Illustrated London News
Regional Furniture
Vernacular Architecture

PARLIAMENTARY REPORTS (Reprinted by Irish University Press)

Reports of the Charity Commissioners (HMSO, various dates).
Report on the Administration and Practical Operation of the Poor Laws (1834).
Handloom Weavers' Report (1840).
Population of Great Britain: Occupation Abstract — 1841 and 1851 Census Returns.
Report on the Sanitary Conditions of the Labouring Population of England (1842).
First Report of the Commission for Inquiring into the Employment of Children in Mines and Manufactures (1842).
Report on the Employment of Women and Children in Agriculture (1843).
Report on the Construction of Pentonville Prison (1844).
Reports of the Statistical Society (1848).
Kinnaird Report on the Condition of Mines (1862–4).
First Report on the Employment of Children, Young Persons and Women in Agriculture (1867–8).
Second Report (1868–9).
The Conditions of the Crofters and Cottars in the Highlands and Islands of Scotland (1884).

GENERAL BOOKS

Beard, G.W. and Gilbert, C.G., *Dictionary of English Furniture Makers, 1660–1840* (Furniture History Society, Leeds: 1986).
Brears, P., *Yorkshire Probate Inventories 1542–1689* (Yorkshire Archaeological Society, Leeds: 1973).
Chinnery, V., *Oak Furniture: the British Tradition* (Woodbridge, 1979).
Davidson, C., *A Woman's Work is Never Done* (London, 1982).
Gilbert, C.G., *Town and Country Furniture* (exh. cat.), Temple Newsam, Leeds, 1972.
Gilbert, C.G., *Common Furniture* (exh. cat.), Temple Newsam, Leeds, 1982.
Hall, R. de Zouche (ed.), *A Bibliography of Vernacular Architecture* (Newton Abbot, 1972).
Hayden, A., *Chats on Cottage and Farmhouse Furniture* (London, 1912).
Loudon, J.C., *Encyclopaedia of Cottage, Farm, and Villa Architecture and Furniture* (London, 1833).
Moore, J.S., *The Goods and Chattels of Our Forefathers* (Chichester, 1976).
Pyne, W.H., *Microcosm; or Picturesque Views of Rural Occupations* (W. Miller, London: 1808) (Dover Reprint, 1977).
Rowlandson, T. and Pugin, A.C., *Microcosm of London* (R. Akermann, London: 1808–10).
Sheraton, T., *The Cabinet Dictionary* (London, 1803).
Steer, W.F., *Farm and Cottage Inventories of Mid-Essex* (Chelmsford, 1950).
Trinder, B. and Cox, J., *Yeomen and Colliers in Telford* (Chichester, 1980).

TRADITIONAL CRAFTS, NATIVE TIMBERS AND COUNTRY JOINERS

Blackie & Son, *The Cabinet-Maker's Assistant* (London, 1853).
Bullock, W., *Timbers for Woodwork*, nd (London, *c.* 1910).

Edlin, H.L., *Woodland Crafts in Britain* (London, 1949).
Loudon, J.C., *Arboretum et Fruticetum Britannicum* (London, 1838).
Rose, W., *The Village Carpenter* (Cambridge, 1937).
Salaman, R.A., *Dictionary of Tools* (London, 1975).
Sparkes, I.G., *Woodland Craftsmen* (Princes Risborough, 1977).
Woods, K.S., *Rural Crafts of England* (London, 1949).

PROVINCIAL PRICE BOOKS (Listed in Appendix One, see pp. 257–8)

Cotton, G., 'The Norwich Chair Makers' Price Book of 1801', *Regional Furniture*, II (1988), pp. 68–92.
Gilbert, C.G., 'London and Provincial Books of Prices: Comment and Bibliography', *Furniture History*, XVIII (1982), pp. 11–20.
Gilbert, C.G., 'An Early Cabinet and Chair Work Price List from York', *Furniture History*, XXI (1985), pp. 227–8.
Gilbert, C.G., 'A Labelled Whitehaven Cabinet', *Regional Furniture*, III (1989), pp. 84–7.
Hutchinson, C., 'The Leeds Cabinet and Chair-Makers Book of Prices', *Furniture History*, X (1974), pp. 71–4.
Jones, D., 'Scottish Cabinet Makers' Price Books 1805–1825', *Regional Furniture*, III (1989), pp. 27–39.
Jones, D., 'An Early Cabinet Makers' Club in Belfast and their Book of Prices', *Regional Furniture*, IV (1990), pp. 100–12.
Kane, P.E., 'Design Books and Price Books for American Federal Period Card Tables' in Hewitt, B., *The Work of Many Hands* (exh. cat.), Yale University Art Gallery, 1982.
Montgomery, C., *American Furniture: the Federal Period* (New York, 1966).
Moore, N., 'A Chester Cabinet Maker's Specification Book', *Regional Furniture*, I (1987), pp. 71–8.
Stuart, S., 'Prices for Workmen in Lancaster: the Earliest Surviving Cabinet-Makers' Price List', *Regional Furniture*, II (1988), pp. 19–22.
Weil, M., 'A Cabinetmaker's Price Book', *Winterthur Portfolio*, 13 (1979), pp. 175–92.

FARMHOUSE AND COTTAGE FURNITURE

Addy, S.O., *The Evolution of the English House* (London, 1898: rev. ed. 1933).
Atkinson, J.C., *Forty Years in a Moorland Parish* (London, 1891).
Ayres, J., *The Home in Britain* (London, 1981).
Barley, M.W., *The English Farmhouse and Cottage* (London, 1961).
Brunskill, R.W., *Vernacular Architecture of the Lake Counties* (London, 1974).
Cobbett, W., *Rural Rides* (London, 1830).
Cotton, B., *Cottage and Farmhouse Furniture of East Anglia* (exh. cat.), Norfolk Museum of Rural Life, 1987.
Crispin, T., 'English Dressers', *Antique Finder*, May 1973, pp. 40–43.
Hird, Robert, *Annals of Bedale* (L. Lewis, ed.) (North Yorkshire County Record Office Publication, 1975).
Holdenby, C., *Folk of the Furrow* (London, 1913).
Hoskins, W.G., 'The Rebuilding of Rural England', *Past and Present*, 4 (1953), pp. 44–89.
Jekyll, G., *Old West Surrey* (London, 1904).
Kilvert, F., *Diary 1870–1879* (W. Plomer, ed.) (London, 1938).
Laycock, C.H., 'The Devon Farmhouse, its Interior Arrangements and Domestic Economy', *Transactions of the Devonshire Association*, pt I (1920), pp. 158–91, pt II (1922), pp. 224–66.
Olive, G., 'Dressers in the West Country', *Regional Furniture*, III (1989), pp. 40–51.
Olive, G., 'West Country Settles', *Furniture History*, XVII (1981), pp. 20–22.
RCHM, *Houses of the North York Moors* (HMSO, London: 1987).
Slocombe, P.M., *Wiltshire Farmhouses and Cottages 1500–1800* (Wiltshire Buildings Record, Devizes: 1988).
Thompson, F., *Lark Rise to Candleford* (Oxford, 1945).

URBAN WORKING-CLASS HOMES

Atkinson, F., 'Yorkshire Miners' Cottages', *Folk Life*, 3 (1965), pp. 92–6.
Baker, R., *The State and Condition of the Town of Leeds* (HMSO, London: 1842).
Bamford, S., *Walks in South Lancashire* (Blackley, 1844).
Beames, T., *The Rookeries of London* (London, 1850).
Brears, P., *Traditional Food in Yorkshire* (Edinburgh, 1987).
Burnett, J., *A Social History of Housing 1815–1870* (Newton Abbot, 1978).
Gaskell, P., *The Manufacturing Population of England* (London, 1833).
Gauldie, E., *Cruel Habitations, A History of Working Class Housing* (London, 1974).
Mayhew, H., *London Labour and the London Poor* (London, 1861–2).
Mearns, A., *The Bitter Cry of Outcast London* (London, 1883).
National Philanthropic Association, 5th Report, *Santory Progress* (London, 1850).
Pinchbeck, I., *Women Workers of the Industrial Revolution* (London, 1930).
Razzell, P.E. and Wainwright, R.W. (eds), *The Victorian Working Class* (selection of letters to the

Morning Chronicle 1849–51) (London, 1973).

Rubinstein, D., *Victorian Homes* (Newton Abbot, 1974).

Wordsall, F., *The Tenement* (London, 1979).

BACK-STAIRS FURNITURE

Beeton, Mrs I., *Book of Household Management* (London, 1861).

Gilbert, C.G., *Back-Stairs Furniture* (exh. cat.), Temple Newsam, Leeds, 1977.

Girouard, M., *The Victorian Country House* (Oxford, 1971).

Glass, H., *The Servant's Directory* (London, 1760).

Harrison, M., *The Kitchen in History* (Reading, 1972).

Hartcup, A., *Below Stairs in the Great Country Houses* (London, 1980).

Horn, P., *Rise and Fall of the Victorian Servant* (Dublin, 1975).

Kerr, R., *The Gentleman's House* (London, 1864).

Marshall, D., *The English Domestic Servant in History* (Historical Association, London: 1949).

Parkes, Mrs W., *Domestic Duties* (London, 1825).

Webster, T., *Encyclopaedia of Domestic Economy* (London, 1844).

ALEHOUSES, INNS AND TAVERNS

Elwall, R., *Bricks and Beer, English Pub Architecture 1830–1939* (British Architectural Library, London: 1983).

Girouard, M., *Victorian Pubs* (London, 1975).

Gorham, M. and Dunnett, H.M.G., *Inside the Pub* (London, 1950).

Lillywhite, B., *London Coffee Houses* (London, 1963).

Sorin, G.S. and Donald, E.K., *Gadsby's Tavern Museum: Historic Furnishing Plan* (Alexandria, Virginia, 1980).

Whitbread & Co., *Inn Crafts and Furnishings* (London, 1950).

REGIONAL CHAIRMAKING TRADITIONS

Agius, P., 'English Chair Makers Listed in Trade Directories', *Furniture History*, XII (1976), pp. 1–16.

Cotton, B., 'Vernacular Design: the Spindle-Back Chair and its North Country Origin', *Working Wood*, Spring 1979, pp. 41–9.

Cotton, B., 'The North Country Chair Making Tradition: Design, Context and the Mark Chippindale Deposition', *Furniture History*, XVII (1981), pp. 42–50.

Cotton, B., 'Country Chairs and their Makers', *Antique Dealer and Collector's Guide*, May 1983, pp. 45–9.

Cotton, B., 'Windsor Chair Making an Oxfordshire Tradition', *Oxfordshire Life*, Winter 1983.

Cotton, B., *The Chair in the North East Midlands* (exh. cat.), Museum of Lincolnshire Life, 1987.

Cotton, B., *The Chair in the North West* (exh. cat.), Towneley Hall, Burnley, 1987.

Cotton, B., 'Shadford, Shirley and the Caistor Workshop', *Regional Furniture*, II (1988), pp. 48–67.

Cotton, B., *Windsor Chairs in the South West* (exh. cat.), Area Museum Council for the South West, 1989.

Crispin, T., 'Richard Hewett's Windsor Chair', *Antique Collecting*, January 1975, pp. 12–13.

Crispin, T., 'English Windsor Chairs: A Study of Known Makers and Regional Centres', *Furniture History*, XVI (1978), pp. 38–48.

Crispin, T., '10 December 1838', *Antique Collecting*, November 1980, pp. 10–11.

Gilbert, C.G., 'Windsor Chairs from Rockley', *Antique Finder*, February 1974, pp. 18–19.

Gilbert, C.G., 'Two Worksop Windsors', *Connoisseur*, February 1975, p. 157.

Goyne Evans, N., 'A History and Background of English Windsor Furniture', *Furniture History*, XV (1979), pp. 24–53.

Graham, J.T., 'The Macclesfield Chair', *Antique Finder*, October 1976, pp. 4–5.

Haworth-Booth, M., 'The Dating of 18th Century Windsor Chairs', *Antique Dealer and Collector's Guide*, January 1973, pp. 63–8.

Jervis, S., 'The First Century of the English Windsor Chair 1720–1820', *Antiques*, February 1979, pp. 22–5.

Mayes, L.J., *The History of Chairmaking in High Wycombe* (London, 1960).

Noble, R., 'The Chairs of Sutherland and Caithness: a Northern Tradition in Highland Chair-Making', *Regional Furniture*, I (1987), pp. 33–40.

Olive, G., 'Windsor Chairs from Devon', *Furniture History*, XII (1976), pp. 95–7.

Sparkes, I.G., *The English Country Chair* (Bourne End, 1973).

Sparkes, I.G., *The Windsor Chair* (Bourne End, 1975).

Sparkes, I.G., 'A Checklist of Books and Articles on Rural Chairs, the Windsor Chair and Chairmaking', *Furniture History*, XII (1976), pp. 86–9.

Stabler, J., 'An Early Pair of Wheelback Windsor Chairs', *Furniture History*, IX (1973), pp. 119–22.

Stabler, J., 'A New Look at the Bow-Back Windsor', *Connoisseur*, December 1974, pp. 238–45.

Stabler, J., 'Two Labelled Comb-Back Windsor Chairs', *Antique Collecting*, April 1977, pp. 12–14.

Regional Beds

Atkinson, F., 'North Country Cottage Beds', *Beamish Report*, I (1978), pp. 64–8.
Bartlam, W.A., 'Box Beds on the Island of Stroma', *Scottish Vernacular Buildings Working Group Newsletter*, 6 (1980), pp. 6–10.
Brooksby, H., 'Bed-outshuts in the Gower', *Vernacular Architecture*, VII (1976), pp. 21–33.
Buchanan, R.H., 'Box Beds and Bannocks', *Review of Scottish Culture*, I (1984), pp. 65–9.
Carragher, F., 'Settle Beds in the Ulster Folk Museum', *Ulster Folklife*, 31 (1985), pp. 36–40.
Jones, D., 'The Press Bed in Scotland', *Scottish Society for Art History Yearbook* (Glasgow, 1988), pp. 28–35.
Lenfestey, J.H., 'The Guernsey Green Bed', *Channel Islands Review* (1971), pp. 69–91.
Walton, J., 'The Built-in Bed Tradition in North Yorkshire', *Gwerin*, III (1981), pp. 114–25.

Straw and Wicker Furniture

Dennison, W.T., 'Manufacture of Straw Articles in Orkney', *Orcadian Papers* (1905), pp. 32–42.
Hartley, D., *Made in England* (London, 1939).
Jenkins, J.G., 'A Cardiganshire Lip-worker', *Folk Life*, 3 (1965), pp. 88–9.

Schools

Bartley, G.T.C., *Schools for the People: History, Development and Present Working of Each Description of English School for the Industrial and Poorer Classes* (1871).
British and Foreign School Society, *Manual of the System of Primary Instruction* (London, 1816).
Gilbert, C.G., *School Furniture* (exh. cat.), Temple Newsam, Leeds, 1978.
Horn, P., *Education in Rural England 1800–1914* (Dublin, 1978).
Lancaster, J., *The British System of Education* (London, 1810).
Lancaster, J., *Hints and Directions for Building, Fitting-up and Arranging School Rooms on the British System of Education* (London, 1811).
Laqueur, T.W., *Religion and Respectability* (Yale, 1976).
Seaborne, M., *The English School 1370–1870* (London, 1971).
Stow, D., *The Training System* (Glasgow, 1836).
Wilderspin, S., *The Infant System* (London, 1832).

Workhouses and Prisons

Bender, J., *Imagining the Penitentiary* (Chicago, 1987).
Eden, Sir F., *The State of the Poor* (London, 1797).
Gilbert, C.G., 'Workhouse Furniture', *Regional Furniture*, I (1987), pp. 61–70.
Ignatieff, M., *A Just Measure of Pain; the Penitentiary in the Industrial Revolution, 1750–1850* (New York, 1978).
Longmate, N., *The Workhouse* (London, 1974).
Mayhew, H. and Binny, J., *The Criminal Prisons of London and Scenes from Prison Life* (London, 1862).
Palliser, R., 'Workhouse Education in County Durham', *British Journal of Education*, XVI, 3 (1968), pp. 279–91.
Rose, M.E., *The English Poor Law 1780–1930* (Newton Abbot, 1971).
Webb, S. and B., *English Prisons Under Local Government* (London, 1922).

Asylums, Hospitals and Almshouses

Godfrey, W.H., *The English Almshouse* (London, 1955).
Heath, S., *Old English Houses of Alms* (London, 1910).
Jones, K., *A History of the Mental Health Services* (London, 1972).
Oppert, F., *Hospitals, Infirmaries and Dispensaries, their Construction, Interior Arrangement and Management* (London, 1867).
Thompson, J.D. and Goldin, G., *The Hospital: a Social and Architectural History* (Yale University Press, Newhaven and London; 1975).

Meeting Houses and Chapels

Alexander, W., *Observations on the Construction and Fitting up of Meeting Houses* (York, 1820).
Bielby, A.R., *Churches and Chapels of Kirklees* (Kirklees Libraries Service, Huddersfield: 1978).
Butler, D.M., *Quaker Meeting Houses of the Lake Counties* (Friends Historical Society, London: 1978).
Dolbey, G.W., *The Architectural Expression of Methodism* (London, 1964).
Lidbetter, H., *The Friends Meeting House* (York, 1961).
Lindley, K., *Chapels and Meeting Houses* (London, 1969).
RCHM, *Non-Conformist Chapels and Meeting Houses in Central England* (HMSO, London: 1986).

FACTORIES, OFFICES, SHOPS AND RAILWAY PREMISES

Anderson, G., *Victorian Clerks* (Manchester, 1976).
Anderson, R. and Fox, G., *Pictorial Record of LMS Architecture* (Oxford, 1981).
The Book of English Trades (various editions: printed for Sir Richard Phillips & Co, London, *c.* 1802–30).
Heal, A., *London Tradesmen's Cards of the XVIII Century* (London, 1925).
Knobel, L., *Office Furniture* (London, 1987).
Searby, P., *Weavers and Outworkers in Victorian Times* (London, 1980).
Simmons, J., *The Railways of Britain* (rev. ed., London, 1986).
Tomlinson, C. (ed.), *Cyclopaedia of Useful Arts* (London and New York, 1852–4).
Vaughn, A., *Pictorial Record of Great Western Architecture* (Oxford, 1977).
Whitehouse, P., *Railway Relics and Regalia* (1976).
Wooton Patent Desks (exh. cat.), Indiana State Museum and Oakland Museum, 1983.

BARRACKS, BOTHIES AND MINE SHOPS

Army Regulations
Bochel, M., *Dear Gremista: the Story of the Nairn Fisher Girls at the Gutting* (Nairn Fishertown Museum, 1979).
Cameron, D.K., *The Ballad and the Plough* (London, 1978).
Carter, I., *Farmlife in North East Scotland 1840–1914* (Edinburgh, 1979).
Godwin, G., *Town Swamps and Social Bridges* (London, 1859).
Johnson, P., 'Camp Comforts', *Art and Antiques*, 8 February 1975, pp. 18–23.
Lindsay, J., *History of the North Wales Slate Industry* (Newton Abbot, 1974).
Mollo, B., *The British Army from Old Photographs* (London, 1975).
Phillips, J., *Travelling and Campaigning Furniture* (exh. cat.), Hitchin, 1984.
Raistrick, A. and Jennings, B., *A History of Lead Mining in the Pennines* (London, 1965).
Rosoman, T., 'Military Furniture', RFS occasional publication (1985), pp. 12–15.
Saunders, J.B., 'Camp Furniture of the Victorian Officer', *NAM Annual Report*, 1981.
Scouller, R.E., 'Quarters and Barracks', *RUSI Journal*, February 1953, pp. 91–4.
Williamson, J., *A Treatise on Military Finance* (London, 1796).

SHIPS, CARAVANS AND NARROWBOATS

Chaplin, T., *A Short History of the Narrow Boat* (Upper Halliford, 1979).
Greenhill, B. and Gifford, A., *Travelling by Sea in the Nineteenth Century* (London, 1972).
Lewery, A.J., *Narrow Boat Painting* (Newton Abbot, 1974).
Munday, J., 'Captains and Cabins', *Connoisseur*, February 1979, pp. 90–97.
Ward-Jackson, C.H. and Harvey, D.E., *The English Gypsy Caravan* (Newton Abbot, 1972).
Wilson, R.J., *Life Afloat* (Rothwell, Northamptonshire: 1976).

CHILDREN'S FURNITURE

Bagshawe, T.W., 'Baby Cages', *Apollo*, December 1937, pp. 325–7.
Bourne, S., *Children's Furniture* (exh. cat.), Towneley Hall, Burnley, 1977.
Child, G., 'Children's Chairs', *Antique Collecting*, February 1972, pp. 22–6.
Gelles, E., *Nursery Furniture* (London, 1982).

IRELAND, SCOTLAND, WALES AND THE CHANNEL ISLANDS

Cotton, B., 'Irish Vernacular Furniture', *Regional Furniture*, III (1989), pp. 1–26.
Davies, A., 'Welsh Regional Furniture', RFS occasional publication (1985), pp. 1–5.
Fenton, A., *Scottish Country Life* (Edinburgh, 1976).
Fenton, A., *The Northern Isles: Orkney and Shetland* (Edinburgh, 1978).
Fenton, A., *The Island Blackhouse* (HMSO, Edinburgh: 1978).
Guernsey Society, *The Guernsey Farmhouse* (The Guernsey Society, St Peter Port: 1963).
Gwerin
Irish Country Furniture Society, Newsletters and occasional publications.
Jones, D., 'Scotch Chests', *Regional Furniture*, II (1988), pp. 38–47.
Loughnan, N., *Irish Country Furniture* (Dublin, 1984).
Peate, I., *Tradition and Folk Life; A Welsh View* (London, 1972).
Review of Scottish Culture
Rural Housing in Ulster in the Mid-19th Century (Ulster Folk Museum, nd).
Sinclair, C., *The Thatched Houses of the Old Highlands* (Edinburgh, 1953).
Stevens, J. and Arthur, J., 'Inventories of Household Effects', *Société Jersaise Annual Bulletin* (1972), pp. 361–78.
Twiston-Davies, L. and Lloyd-Johnes, H.J., *Welsh Furniture* (Cardiff, 1950).
Ulster Folklife

Special Issue 'Symposium on American Country Furniture', *Antiques*, March 1968.

Baraitser, M. and Obholzer, A., *Cape Country Furniture* (rev. ed., Cape Town, 1978).

Csillery, K.K., *Hungarian Village Furniture* (Budapest, 1972).

Denoke, B., *Bauernmöbel* (Munich, 1979).

Erixon, S., *Möbler Och Meminredning I Svenska Bygder* (Stockholm, 1926).

Fales, D.A., *American Painted Furniture 1660–1880* (New York, 1972).

Hummel, C.F., *With Hammer in Hand; the Dominy Craftsmen* (University Press of Virginia, Charlottesville, for the Henry Francis Du Pont Wintherthur Museum, 1968).

Jobe, B. and Kaye, M., *New England Furniture: the Colonial Era* (Boston, 1984).

Kirk, J.T., *American Furniture and the British Tradition to 1830* (New York, 1982).

List, C., *Alte Bauernschränke* (Munich, 1981).

Melchor, J.R. *et al.*, *Eastern Shore, Virginia Raised Panel Furniture* (exh. cat.), Chrysler Museum, Virginia, 1982.

Morse, J.D. (ed.), *Country Cabinet Work and Simple City Furniture*, Winterthur Conference Report, 1969.

Pain, H., *The Heritage of Upper Canada Furniture* (Toronto, 1978).

Palardy, J., *The Early Furniture of French Canada* (Toronto, 1965).

Parsons, C.S., *The Dunlaps and their Furniture* (exh. cat.), Currier Art Gallery, New Hampshire, 1970.

Peddle, W.W., *The Traditional Furniture of Outport Newfoundland* (St John's, 1983).

Reynies, N. de, *Le Mobilier Domestique, Vocabulair Typologique*, I (Paris, 1987).

Ritz, G.M., *Alte Gechnizte Bauernmöbel* (Munich, 1974).

Ritz, J.M. and Ritz, G.M., *Alte Bemalte Bauernmöbel* (Munich, 1972).

Tardieu-Dumont, S., *Le Mobilier Regional Français Normandie* (Paris, 1980).

Trent, R., *Hearts and Crowns: Folk Chairs of the Connecticut Coast 1720–1840* (exh. cat.), New Haven Historical Society, 1977.

Ward, G.W.R. (ed.), *New Perspectives on American Furniture* (W.W. Norton, New York, for the Henry Francis Du Pont Winterthur Museum, 1988).

Index